A FAITHFUL HEART

Women's Diaries and Letters of the South
Carol Bleser, Series Editor

A Woman Doctor's Civil War: Esther Hill Hawks' Diary
Edited by Gerald Schwartz

A Rebel Came Home: The Diary and Letters of Floride Clemson, 1863–1866
Edited by Ernest McPherson Lander, Jr., and Charles M. McGee, Jr.

The Shattered Dream: The Day Book of Margaret Sloan, 1900–1902
Edited by Harold Woodell

The Letters of a Victorian Madwoman
Edited by John S. Hughes

A Confederate Nurse: The Diary of Ada W. Bacot, 1860–1863
Edited by Jean V. Berlin

A Plantation Mistress on the Eve of the Civil War:
The Diary of Keziah Goodwyn Hopkins Brevard, 1860–1861
Edited by John Hammond Moore

Lucy Breckinridge of Grove Hill: The Journal of a Virginia Girl, 1862–1864
Edited by Mary D. Robertson

George Washington's Beautiful Nelly:
The Letters of Eleanor Parke Curtis Lewis to Elizabeth Bordley Gibson, 1794–1851
Edited by Patricia Brady

A Confederate Lady Comes of Age: The Journal of Pauline DeCaradeuc Heyward, 1863–1888
Edited by Mary D. Robertson

A Northern Woman in the Plantation South: Letters of Tryphena Blanche Holder Fox, 1856–1876
Edited by Wilma King

Best Companions: Letters of Eliza Middleton Fisher and Her Mother, Mary Hering Middleton,
from Charleston, Philadelphia, and Newport, 1839–1846
Edited by Eliza Cope Harrison

Stateside Soldier: Life in the Women's Army Corps, 1944–1945
Aileen Kilgore Henderson

From the Pen of a She-Rebel: The Civil War Diary of Emilie Riley McKinley
Edited by Gordon A. Cotton

Between North and South: The Letters of Emily Wharton Sinkler, 1842–1865
Edited by Anne Sinkler Whaley LeClercq

A Southern Woman of Letters: The Correspondence of Augusta Jane Evans Wilson
Edited by Rebecca Grant Sexton

Southern Women at Vassar: The Poppenheim Family Letters, 1882–1916
Edited by Joan Marie Johnson

Live Your Own Life: The Family Papers of Mary Bayard Clarke, 1854–1886
Edited by Terrell Armistead Crow and Mary Moulton Barden

The Roman Years of a South Carolina Artist: Caroline Carson's Letters Home, 1872–1892
Edited with an Introduction by William H. Pease and Jane H. Pease

Walking by Faith: The Diary of Angelina Grimké, 1828–1835
Edited by Charles Wilbanks

Country Women Cope with Hard Times: A Collection of Oral Histories
Edited by Melissa Walker

Echoes from a Distant Frontier:
The Family Correspondence of the Brown-Anderson-Aldrich Family in Frontier Florida, 1835–1855
Edited by James M. Denham and Keith L. Huneycutt

A Faithful Heart: The Journals of Emmala Reed, 1865 and 1866
Edited by Robert. T. Oliver

A FAITHFUL HEART

THE JOURNALS OF EMMALA REED, 1865 AND 1866

EDITED BY ROBERT T. OLIVER

University of South Carolina Press

Published in Columbia, South Carolina, by the
University of South Carolina Press

Manufactured in the United States of America

08 07 06 05 04 5 4 3 2 1

Library of Congress Cataloging-in-Publication Data

Reed, Emmala, 1839–1893.
A faithful heart : the journals of Emmala Reed, 1865 and 1866 / edited by Robert T. Oliver.
p. cm. — (Women's diaries and letters of the South)
Includes bibliographical references and index.
ISBN 1-57003-545-8 (alk. paper)
1. Reed, Emmala, 1839–1893—Diaries. 2. Women—South Carolina—Anderson—Diaries. 3. Reconstruction—South Carolina. 4. Anderson (S.C.)—Biography. 5. Anderson (S.C.)—Social life and customs—19th century. 6. Anderson (S.C.)—Social conditions—19th century. 7. South Carolina—History—Civil War, 1861–1865—Social aspects. 8. United States—History—Civil War, 1861–1865—Social aspects. I. Oliver, Robert T., 1952– II. Title. III. Series.
F279.A5R44 2004
975.7'03—dc22 2004004536

For my family:
my parents, Robert Lacy and Lillian H. Oliver,
and my sister, Deborah Jane Prevatte

CONTENTS

ILLUSTRATIONS

SERIES EDITOR'S PREFACE

A Faithful Heart: The Journals of Emmala Reed, 1865 and 1866 is the twenty-second volume in what had been the Women's Diaries and Letters of the Nineteenth-Century South series. Now redefined and renamed Women's Diaries and Letters of the South, the series enables us to include some remarkably fine works from the twentieth century. This series includes a number of never-before-published diaries, some collections of unpublished correspondence, and a few reprints of published diaries—a potpourri of nineteenth-century and, now, twentieth-century Southern women's writings.

The series enables women to speak for themselves, providing readers with a rarely opened window into Southern society before, during, and after the American Civil War and into the twentieth century. The significance of these letters and journals lies not only in the personal revelations and the writing talent of these women authors but also in the range and versatility of the documents' contents. Taken together, these publications will tell us much about the heyday and the fall of the Cotton Kingdom, the mature years of the "peculiar institution," the war years, the adjustment of the South to a new social order following the defeat of the Confederacy, and the New South of the twentieth century. Through these writings, the reader will also be presented with firsthand accounts of everyday life and social events, courtships and marriages, family life and travels, religion and education, and the life-and-death matters that made up the ordinary and extraordinary world of the American South.

Carol Bleser

ACKNOWLEDGMENTS

I will always be grateful to Dr. Carol Bleser and Dr. Edward Bleser, not only for teaching me this craft, but for their guidance, their friendship, and their unfailing confidence in this project and in me. Professor Roy Talbert of Coastal Carolina University has been a mentor, colleague, and friend throughout my academic career. Unwavering support and assistance always came from Donna Roper, Jo McConnell, Hurley Badders, and the Pendleton District Historical, Recreational, and Tourism Commission, as well as from Martha Jeffries of the Pendleton District Commission. This project could not have succeeded without the help of myriad other librarians, researchers, clerks, and genealogists from libraries, courthouses, historical societies, and homes across Georgia and South Carolina.

I would like to extend my sincere thanks to the editors and staff on the University of South Carolina Press, and especially Alexander Moore and Scott Evan Burgess. I deeply appreciate the staff at Clemson University's Robert Muldrow Cooper Library and its Strom Thurmond Institute as well as the staff of the South Caroliniana Library at the University of South Carolina. The South Carolina Historical Society Archives provided a wealth of invaluable resources. The Johnson Memorial Library at Anderson College allowed me to reproduce a remarkable collection of Reed family photographs. A special thanks goes to the staff at the Kimbel Library, Coastal Carolina University, Conway, South Carolina, and of course I will always be grateful for the support of my colleagues and the staff at Coastal Carolina University, particularly Stephanie Freeman, administrative assistant extraordinaire and a good friend.

Many others have contributed simply by helping me out when I needed it, freeing me to pursue this project. I wish to extend my gratitude to the Echolses, the Talberts, Terry Johnston, Mike McArdle, Dave Amberg, and Georgia Leonard. Finally I must thank my family, including my mother, Lillian, for her eternal patience, my sister, Deb, a true Renaissance woman, my brother-in-law, Steve Prevatte, and my nephew, Robert Lacy Prevatte.

PREFACE

The Pendleton District Historical, Recreational, and Tourism Commission was home to three journals penned by Emmala Butler Thompson Reed. These journals, now in the possession of the Anderson County Museum, were written by a young woman from Anderson, South Carolina, and span the years 1865 and 1866. I first saw them in 1995 while searching out an "original document" for a graduate seminar on editing at Clemson University. I met historian and archivist Donna Roper at the Old Hunter Store in Pendleton, South Carolina, who told me how the journals had been contributed to the Pendleton Commission after the donor purchased them at a garage sale and later wanted to see them preserved properly.

Miss Roper provided anecdotes and background concerning Emmala and the Reed family and concerning Anderson Court House, a prosperous little town in South Carolina's western hill country. She showed me an initial transcription of the "1865 Journal" (Part I of this work), then offered the two remaining journals for my thesis. That offer I readily accepted. Donna assisted me in a long and tedious transcription process involving all three journals, placing the Pendleton Society archives and her extensive personal knowledge of the topic at my disposal. Eventually I edited all three journals, and Miss Roper's input and assistance proved invaluable to the creation of this work.

Emmala Reed's three journals chronicle her life in Anderson from the age of twenty-five through twenty-seven. The journal written in 1865 covered March 27 through June 26, 1865 and portrayed life in Anderson, South Carolina, as the Civil War ended. With paper and money both in short supply, Emmala was forced to write across an old school workbook in a crosshatch style. As she said, "having filled up every blank book that I could with my silly journalizing I will have to resort to crossing some of the old ones – for I feel that I can scarcely live without giving some such expression to my feelings." Emmala's penmanship, best characterized as a minuscule scrawl made worse by the necessity of crosshatching, added considerable difficulty to the transcription process.

Many Southern women abruptly stopped writing in their journals and diaries when the war ended, but Emmala wrote on, a part of her nightly routine and she rarely wavered. Determined to maintain a constant record of her life, Emmala wrote for personal pleasure and inadvertently left behind an excellent portrayal of postwar life in Anderson. On April 11, 1865, she wrote, "Our whole country turned topsy-turvy. The revolution reached a dreadful crisis. No money, no stores – no ammunition – guns – no salt – or anything. It cannot last much longer surely!" In 1865, as the Confederacy crumbled, civilian refugees and treasury employees had swelled the population of upstate Anderson. The burning of Columbia in February 1865 and the subsequent evacuation, coupled with the fall of Charleston, drove a new stream of refugees west, away from the destruction. The destitute received shelter all over the South Carolina upcountry, but Emmala Reed's family already had their hands full with family and friends and those lowcountry refugees who had found a safe haven in Anderson earlier in the war. Many of the refugees, especially the women, would stay on in Anderson long after the war ended and so became active members of the little town's social life.[1]

Throughout the war Emmala patiently waited and pined for Robert Broyles, a cousin she obviously adored, and a surgeon still with his unit in Virginia. On March 1, 1865, she recorded, "What is the fate of my Robere? I long to know when shall I? May God preserve & bless him forever." Hearing of a great battle in North Carolina, she wrote, "Perhaps Robert's manly form & noble heart lies among the wounded or dead." His safe return on April 28 brought her only more heartache, because from that day forward Robert intentionally avoided Emmala, leaving her baffled and confused. Already a mature belle by the spring of 1865, she found her prospects for personal fulfillment through marriage were unraveling amid the backdrop of military defeat.

The month of May 1865 brought the long anticipated invasion of Anderson by Union troops, as forward units of Union cavalry swept into town just as the townfolk prepared to gather for a May Day celebration. The festival was a curious thing to undertake with federal raiders already only thirty miles away in Greenville the day before, yet, as Emmala observed, "no one seemed to care or believe it." Anderson had no real strategic value aside from the new treasury press and a commissary depot where the dwindling rations of cornmeal were meted out to the veterans as they passed through on their way home. The journal entry for May 1, 1865, reads, "Rumours" of their approach came all day. . . . And for a moment I did not dream, it was the foe, but then it came – "the Yankees, the Yankees!" The mounted raiders were gone by May 4, and she wrote, "Very dusty streets seem polluted still by Yankee steps & breath." Emmala's life soon settled back into a familiar pattern of socializing with family, friends and refugees, teaching music and letters to her siblings, reading, sewing, knitting, and entertaining. Fortunately for later readers, every evening she wrote her impressions of life in Anderson after the war, leaving behind an insightful record of a small Southern town and its population during the

1. Mary Elizabeth Massey, *Refugee Life in the Confederacy* (Baton Rouge: Louisiana State University Press, 1964), 40.

less-studied period of Presidential Reconstruction, that short span of time between the South's surrender and the beginnings of Radical Reconstruction.

Her 1866 journal opened on New Year's Day of 1866, six months after the previous journal ended on June 26, 1865. By January 1866, Anderson, South Carolina, had seen a garrison of federal troops and the first postwar election. In the opening months of 1866 James L. Orr, the newly elected governor of South Carolina and a close friend of Emmala's father, conferred with advisors and organized his cabinet at his home, Arlington, outside Anderson. A month earlier, in December 1865, the United States Congress had refused to allow the representatives of the former Confederate states to assume their legislative seats in Congress and prevented their return to the Union. Governor Orr worked tirelessly to restore South Carolina to the fold by establishing a functional state government amid a highly charged political environment.

In January 1866 Emmala Reed's family, like most other local families of the former planter class, had little cash, one old horse, an almost empty larder, and many mouths to feed. Emmala wrote, "Yet whilst feeling that 'tis all very bad, I must acknowledge it might be worse and others are not so fortunate, so I will be content and hope for the best." The journal reveals that by March of 1866, the courts were back in session, the social scene had returned to somewhat normal, and the Reeds had opened a new dry goods store. There was reason to hope that the transition from war to peace might be uneventful. Emmala Reed's third journal contains a collection of random journal entries, various lists, tallies, synopses of literature, and short notations on subjects ranging from Reconstruction to church business.

These journals commenced as the military conflict ended and consequently depict life in Anderson during a period of unprecedented adjustment. For Emmala, the end of the war simply marked the start of a personal struggle to maintain her pride in the face of great hardship. Her journals provide a rare glimpse into life in western South Carolina after the Confederacy surrendered in the spring of 1865 and before Radical Reconstruction commenced in March 1867, the period historians Francis Simkins and Robert Woody in *South Carolina during Reconstruction* characterized as "Provisional Reconstruction."[2]

2. Francis Butler Simkins and Robert H. Woody, *South Carolina during Reconstruction* (rept. Gloucester, Mass.: Peter Smith, 1966), 29–63. After the Union victory in April, 1865, South Carolina drafted a new state constitution. The state legislature felt they had acted in accordance with the stipulations of "Presidential Reconstruction" and should be readmitted to the union. However, the 1865 Constitution contained the "Black Codes," which attempted to re-indenture the newly freed slaves. Northern political sentiment slowly turned away from reconciliation and toward reproach. Eventually the Radicals won the issue; federal troops occupied the state, and South Carolina would remain outside the union until 1877.

During this tumultuous time the Reed family resided at Echo Hall, one of Anderson's finest homes. Emmala's father, Judge Jacob Pinckney Reed, had worked at a variety of occupations, including merchant, lawyer, editor, planter, and judge. Teresa Hammond Reed, Emmala's mother, raised nine children, coordinated household and garden business, and contributed to both church and community affairs. Before the war the Reeds owned more than twenty slaves, many of whom worked in and around Echo Hall. The lives of the Reed children were apparently quite comfortable within their milieu, though rigorous study and musical practices were always maintained.

A wide array of published sources, both specific and general, provide context for the period. Historians such as Carol Bleser and Lesley Gordon, Catherine Clinton, George C. Rable, Gaines M. Foster, Anne Scott, Mary Elizabeth Massey, Drew Gilpin Faust, and Elizabeth Fox-Genovese have interpreted the Southern mindset through extensive use of firsthand accounts gleaned from the journals and diaries of contemporary Southern witnesses. These works, often largely based on a collection or collections of original manuscripts, letters, or diaries, are a useful resource that expand our knowledge through firsthand accounts of Southern women in the mid–nineteenth century.[3]

3. Carol K. Bleser and Lesley J. Gordon, *Intimate Strategies of the Civil War* (New York: Oxford University Press, 2001); Catherine Clinton, *The Plantation Mistress* (New York: Pantheon Books, 1982); George C. Rable, *Civil Wars: Women and the Crisis of Southern Nationalism* (Urbana: University of Illinois Press, 1989); Gaines M. Foster, *Ghosts of the Confederacy: Defeat, the Lost Cause, and the Emergency of the New South* (New York: Oxford University Press, 1987); Anne Firor Scott, *The Southern Lady: From Pedestal to Politics 1830–1930* (Chicago: University of Chicago Press, 1970); Mary Elizabeth Massey, *Women in the Civil War* (Lincoln: University of Nebraska Press, 1966); Drew Gilpin Faust, *Mothers of Invention: Women of the Slaveholding South in the American Civil War* (Chapel Hill: University of North Carolina Press, 1996); Elizabeth Fox-Genovese, *Within the Plantation Household: Black and White Women of the Old South* (Chapel Hill: University of North Carolina Press, 1988). See also Catherine Clinton, "In Search of Southern Women's History: The Current State of Academic Publishing," *Georgia Historical Quarterly* 76 (summer 1992), 420–27.

A sample of contemporary letters and diaries might include C. Vann Woodward, ed., *Mary Chesnut's Civil War* (New Haven: Yale University Press, 1981), Bell Irvin Wiley, ed., *A Southern Woman's Story: Life in Confederate Richmond* by Phoebe Yates Pember (rept. New York: Ballantine, 1974), Mary D. Robertson, ed., *A Confederate Lady Comes of Age: The Journal of Pauline DeCaradeuc Heyward* (Columbia: University of South Carolina Press, 1992), Mary D. Robertson, ed., *Lucy Breckinridge of Grove Hill: The Journal of a Virginia Girl, 1862–1864* (Columbia: University of South Carolina Press, 1994), and Carol Bleser, ed., *Tokens of Affection: The Letters of a Planter's Daughter in the Old South* (Athens: University of Georgia Press, 1996).

Emmala was not the only unmarried woman in upstate South Carolina to keep a record of her life during these turbulent years of war and Reconstruction. Grace Elmore, Floride Clemson, and Emma LeConte, all unmarried women living with their parents, also recorded their experiences in South Carolina.[4] Elmore and LeConte endured the war years in Columbia, while Clemson resided in nearby Pendleton during the federal raids in May 1865. As the conflict ended, Anderson, secluded in the South Carolina upcountry, provided Emmala Reed a unique position from which to observe the sociopolitical effects of the war's conclusion and early Reconstruction.

The journals of Emmala Reed are significant because she presents a much more detailed account of the crisis of change in the early years of Reconstruction than those of many of her fellow chroniclers who stopped writing at the war's end. And though Anderson was a small town in the northwestern hills of upstate South Carolina, a steady procession of historically noteworthy people and events are described in her journals and add importance to the contents. Emmala relied on the largesse of a resourceful and loving father to provide for her and her siblings and to give her the leisure to keep these most interesting journals.

Indeed, these journals possess a faint scent of magnolia: the indignation of rejection by a suitor, the triumph of love, and a wide assortment of potential romantic fictionalizations. Yet their true significance lies in the scope of information gained through her descriptions of people, events, food, and literature as Emmala gave life and depth to her words. Such works as this have always been valuable resources for the social historian, and the journals of Emmala Thompson Reed are no exception. They provide the reader with a wealth of information about everyday life in a small town and an opportunity to gain insight into the early postwar life of a Southern woman whose whole world had been circumscribed by a series of historical changes beyond her control.

4. Marli F. Weiner, *Heritage of Woe: The Civil War Diary of Grace Brown Elmore, 1861–1868* (Athens: University of Georgia Press, 1997); Charles M. McGee, Jr., and Ernest McPherson Lander, Jr., *A Rebel Came Home: The Diary of Floride Clemson, 1863–1866* (rpt. 1961, Columbia: University of South Carolina Press, 1989); Earl S. Miers, *When the World Ended: The Diary of Emma LeConte* (Lincoln: University of Nebraska Press, 1957).

EDITORIAL POLICIES

Emmala Reed wrote easily, expressing her most intimate thoughts and impressions with unusual candor, imparting to the reader a unique sense of familiarity with a woman who lived more than a century ago. To make this work accessible, all three journals were transcribed from holograph originals. Emmala's handwriting was, at times, difficult to decipher, and I was lucky to have Donna Roper's generous assistance in a long and tedious transcription process.

The form of this work has undergone as few changes as possible, to preserve the integrity and flavor of the original text. I have created paragraph and sentence breaks to facilitate reading the long, almost continuous journal entries. Emmala rarely complied with the rules of composition, form, or punctuation. Her use of dashes and "&c"s are redundant, but they relate her rapid-fire manner in a way conventional punctuation does not manage, and they have been retained here. Likewise, punctuation has not been supplied where it was missing in the text, except infrequently for clarification. Unorthodox usage, particularly in the case of the word "don't" for "doesn't," has been retained. Emmala was a generous underliner of words for emphasis and effect. All her underlined words are faithfully reproduced, though I could discern no pattern of significance. She also tended to be casual in matters of orthography ("surprize," "leasure," "marraige," for example) and was sometimes inclined to British spellings (such as "rumour" and "connexion"); such choices have been left unremarked except where clarification is necessary.

People mentioned in the journal are identified using contemporary and present-day sources; variant spellings of their names are glossed. In annotations, numbers in parentheses denote the age of persons at the time of journal entries in which they are mentioned.

GENEALOGY

The Reed Family

Jacob Pinckney Reed
(July 31, 1814–Aug. 19, 1880)
married April 3, 1835

Teresa Hammond
(Feb. 12, 1819–April 24, 1887)

- **Emmala Thompson Butler Reed** (June 11, 1839–January 27, 1893)
  married November 28, 1867 to George William Miller (1837–92)
  - —Lee Reed (died at age 5)
  - —William Yarbrough "Will" (b. 1870)
  - —George (b. 1872)
  - —Caroline "Caro" [twin] (b. 1873)
  - —May [twin] (b. 1873)
  - —James Reed (b. 1880)
- **Julia Susan** (December 17, 1842–January 13, 1883)
  married January 12, 1860 to John Peter Brown (1838–70)
  - —Frederick
  - —Sumter
  - —Catherine H. "Carrie"
  - —Paul
  - —Daisy
  - —Anna
  - —Mary
- **Clifton "Clif" Augustus** (July 5, 1845–November 10, 1924)
  married October 1864 to Francis E. "Fannie" Kingsley (1845–1902)
  - —Helen
- **Eleanor "Nell" Caroline** (October 23, 1847–December 31, 1909)
  married December 1867 to William C. Davis (widowed)
  married James Albert "J. A." Brock
  - —One child
- **Mary "Mamie" Eliza** (April 15, 1850–February 1, 1932)
  married May 22, 1872 to Benjamin Franklin "B. Frank" Mauldin (1850–1921)
  - —Elise
  - —Eilleen
  - —Benjamin Franklin, Jr.

Sara "Cora" Cornelia (1835–April 14, 1929)
married December 22, 1875 to William Seibels Ligon (1853–87)
—Lucy "Lucie" Eoline (1857–?)
married November 8, 1882 to Henry Arthur Ligon (1856–?)
—Four children

Jacob Pinckney "J. P.," Jr. (1862–188?)

Teresa "Pet" Hammond (1864–1939)
married Charlton Hines Strickland (1861–98)
—Lily
—Two other children

INTRODUCTION

The town of Anderson is the seat of government for present-day Anderson County, South Carolina. Once, Anderson County was the southern half of a vast district known as "Old Pendleton," which included present-day Oconee and Pickens Counties. The village of Pendleton, located roughly at the center of Pendleton District, served the entire area as a hub for commerce and justice. In 1826 the state created Anderson and Pickens Districts. The new Anderson District required a centrally located seat of government, hence the creation of Anderson Court House in February 1827.[1]

The place-name honored General Robert Anderson, a Revolutionary War commander at the battles of Ninety-Six and Cowpens. General Anderson laid out the village of Andersonville in 1801 ten miles west of the courthouse, at the headwaters of the Savannah River, near the junction of the Tugaloo and Seneca Rivers. The railroad did not reach Anderson Court House until 1854, so the Andersonville quays, ferries, and barges continued to connect the western hillcountry town with northwestern Georgia, the South Carolina Railroad at Hamburg, and the seaport at Savannah. The remote western region of the state offered an opportunity for upward social mobility unattainable among the ancestral lowcountry gentry.[2]

Jacob Pinckney Reed, the diarist's father and a leading citizen of Anderson, was born July 31, 1814, at Calhoun, a crossroads trading post near present day Belton, South Carolina. The illegitimate son of Sallie Reed White, he acquired a good

1. Louise Ayer Vandiver, *Traditions and History of Anderson County* (Atlanta, Ga.: Ruralist Press, 1928), 1–17. Vandiver's history suffers from many mistakes, misspellings, and misidentifications, and though it may hardly be considered a fully reliable source, it does contain a wealth of useful and accurate information. Moreover, Vandiver wrote the history while living in New York City and received much of the information via correspondence with friends back in Anderson, South Carolina.

2. Anderson Court House was not incorporated until 1833 and did not become simply "Anderson" until 1883. The city of Anderson, South Carolina, has a circa 2004 population of approximately 27,000. Pendleton village, established in 1790, was named for Virginia-born Judge Henry Pendleton (Vandiver, *Traditions,* passim). Oconee County, long considered a distinct territory, was not designated a county until 1868 (David L. Carlton, *Mill and Town in South Carolina, 1880–1920* [Baton Rouge: Louisiana State University Press, 1982], 14–16).

education despite his disadvantageous birth and limited opportunities. Young and personable Jacob Reed entered the mercantile trade as a clerk in Hamburg, South Carolina, a once vital market town and railhead near the Savannah River and Augusta, Georgia. Crops and cattle came to Hamburg from northeastern Georgia and western South Carolina because they shared a natural barrier, the Southern Appalachian highlands to the north.[3]

Emmala's mother, Teresa Caroline Hammond, was the oldest daughter of Captain William and Francis Acker Hammond of Carnesville, Georgia, and Anderson District, South Carolina. Teresa was the daughter of a wealthy planter, building contractor, attorney, and judge. Emmala writes nothing of her parents' initial meeting, of their disparate backgrounds, or of how long they courted. They married when Teresa was sixteen years old, in a civil ceremony conducted by a magistrate at the Carnesville courthouse—the same courthouse where the bride's father practiced law and presided over the district bench. The marriage was a big step up the ladder of success for Jacob Reed.[4]

The young couple moved first to J. P.'s childhood home, Calhoun, South Carolina, where they established a successful mercantile business. Emmala Butler Thompson Reed was born there on June 11, 1839, the third child and the first to survive infancy. Teresa Reed, only twenty years old when Emmala was born, gave birth every few years for three decades. Nine children (seven girls and two boys) survived to adulthood: Emmala, Susan, Clifton "Clif" Augustus, Eleanor "Nell" Caroline, Mary "Mamie" Eliza, Sara "Cora" Cornelia, Lucy Eoline, Jacob Pinckney, Jr., and Teresa "Pet" Hammond Reed. The last two children were born during the Civil War. Emmala's journals seldom mentioned her mother, but in an Anderson County history published in 1929, author Louise Vandiver described Teresa Reed as "a tiny, quiet, elegant lady in the full sense of that word as used by Carolinians of two generations past, one of the people that everybody loved."[5]

J. P. Reed, an extraordinarily ambitious man, having wed a Georgia belle, built a successful business then entered politics. Elected to the South Carolina state legislature in 1838, he founded a newspaper, the *Highland Sentinel*, in 1840. In

3. Elise Mauldin Paget, "Ancestry on the Maternal Side of Mary Francis Mattison, Anderson, South Carolina—Prepared for Her by (Aunt) Elise Mauldin Paget, In Honor of Her Graduation from High School." This undated manuscript is in the possession of Mary Francis Mattison Spearman of Clemson, South Carolina, and divided into family sections, with no page numbers. The information cited was gleaned from material made available to me at the Pendleton Society Archives and from Ulysses R. Brooks, *South Carolina Bench and Bar* (Columbia, S.C.: The State Company, 1908), 208.

4. J. E. Hayes, comp., *Abstract of Marriage Licenses, Franklin County, 1827–35* (Atlanta: Georgia Department of Archives, 1939), 10.

5. Paget, "Ancestry"; Vandiver, *Traditions,* 273.

February 1840 he moved with his family to the village of Anderson Court House, about twelve miles west of Calhoun, in order to study law with Judge Joseph N. Whitner. In November 1842 Reed entered into a law partnership that lasted three years, with Benjamin F. Perry, a prominent attorney from Greenville, South Carolina. Then he entered into a legal firm with another prominent Unionist, James L. Orr of Anderson. The partnership of Reed and Orr rapidly achieved success, and the two young men formed a lifelong personal and professional association.[6]

Like Reed, Orr and Perry had emerged from humble beginnings in western South Carolina to become significant figures in state and national politics. The three men shared a uniquely Southern contradiction: although they were slaveholders, absentee planters, and Democrats, they espoused a Unionist political philosophy. This was a decidedly minority opinion in the Palmetto State before the war. All three edited their own newspapers, practiced law as attorneys, presided as judges, and held public office. In 1849 they participated in organizing the Greenville and Columbia Railroad; Perry represented Greenville interests, while Reed and Orr spoke for Anderson. All three men served on the railroad's board of directors.[7]

These men were bound in their own intellectual "sacred circle." They collectively campaigned against secession from the Union when South Carolina considered the question, both before and after the Compromise of 1850, but by 1860 they put aside their many reservations, casting their lot with South Carolina for secession and lending their support to the Confederacy. All three men signed the South Carolina Ordinance of Secession in December of 1860 and later played significant roles in the post war politics of South Carolina. Prewar Unionist sentiment and associations brought postwar political rewards and wary glances from less fortunate townsfolk.[8]

6. Brooks, *Bench and Bar,* 208–9; *Anderson Intelligencer,* August 26, 1880. The family of Judge Joseph Newton Whitner are mentioned throughout the journals. Whitner signed the South Carolina Ordinance of Secession in 1860 when he was sixty-one years old. He was apparently an avid teacher who instructed dozens of attorneys, including J. L. Orr and J. P. Reed.

7. Lillian A. Kibler, *Benjamin F. Perry: South Carolina Unionist* (Durham, N.C.: Duke University Press, 1946), 213–16, 222–25; Roger P. Leemhuis, *James L. Orr and the Sectional Conflict* (Washington, D.C.: University Press of America, 1979), 16–17.

8. Benjamin Perry (1805–1886) served in the South Carolina House of Representatives (1836–42) and the South Carolina Senate (1844–48) (1849–60). He was called upon to serve as a Confederate commissioner in 1862, Confederate district attorney in 1863, and district judge in 1864. Perry was appointed provisional governor of South Carolina in 1865, but when elected U.S. senator in 1866, he was denied his seat by the Radical Republicans

When the Reeds first moved to Anderson in 1840, they lived in a small home near the courthouse square. Eventually, the steadily growing and prosperous family moved into Echo Hall, a spacious home on South Main Street with ornately landscaped grounds and a wide central piazza. Reed's political career never reached the lofty positions achieved by his associates Orr and Perry. He may have opted to pursue a less public course because his illegitimate birth was a potentially provocative campaign issue and could have easily brought anguish to his family.

J. P. Reed started his public service with a term in the South Carolina House of Representatives from 1838 to 1840 and served again from 1848 to 1850. He also served many terms as the intendant (mayor) of Anderson. In 1850 the legislature elected him solicitor of the Western Circuit, a position he retained until after the Civil War. It was not until 1874 that Reed was elected judge of the First Circuit (Charleston), where he presided until 1877.[9]

One of Judge Reed's most significant contributions to his community was the founding of Johnson Female Seminary, constructed in 1848 and located within sight of his home on South Main Street. Emmala graduated from the school in 1855 at the age of sixteen. The school served the Anderson community and its environs, and coincidentally helped keep the Reed girls living at home in Echo Hall.[10]

In the years before the Civil War the Reed children lived a very comfortable existence in the small town of Anderson. Back then Echo Hall bustled with parents, children, student boarders, extended family members, and slaves. J. P. Reed's law practice prospered, and while he rode the court circuit at length, his wife, Teresa, managed the large and vibrant household. The children attended the local

---

(*National Cyclopedia of American Biography*, vol. 12 [New York: James T. White & Company, 1904], 174–76. See also Leemhuis, *James L. Orr*, 1–15, and *South Carolina Biographical Dictionary* [New York: Somerset Publishers, 1994], 240–42.)

James L. Orr (1822–73) served in the South Carolina House from 1840 until 1848. He then served in the U.S. House of Representatives (1849–59), and became Speaker of the U.S. House of Representatives in 1857 (resigned 1859). He signed the South Carolina Ordinance of Secession in December 1860 and immediately organized a mounted regiment, "Orr's Rifles," then served in Confederate States Senate (1860–65). Orr was elected governor of South Carolina in 1866 and ended his career as an ambassador to the Russian court in St. Petersburg (Jon L. Wakelyn, *Biographical Dictionary of the Confederacy* [Westport, Conn.: Greenwood Press, 1977], 334–35.

9. Brooks, *Bench and Bar*, 209. The Western Circuit included Abbeville, Anderson, Pickens, Greenville, Spartanburg, and Laurens Districts, or northwestern South Carolina.

10. Vandiver, *Traditions*, 116–18. The building and grounds of the former Johnson Female Seminary served as an infirmary and barracks for the First Maine Garrison, which occupied Anderson in late 1865.

schools, the stables contained fancy carriages and fine horses, and the parlors were often filled with music and conversation.

Anderson was a vital market town, a seat of government, and the social center for a large part of western South Carolina. Rail travel and transport eventually provided direct contact with the markets and amenities of Charleston, the cradle of South Carolina society. The Reeds wanted for little as they raised their large family in the tranquil town, surrounded by a large circle of friends composed mainly of merchants, educators, doctors, and attorneys. However, the advent and aftermath of war created inexorable changes for Emmala, the Reeds, and the town of Anderson.

When the war came in 1861, the townsfolk of Anderson Court House rigorously fulfilled their obligation to the Confederate war effort, sending troops, donating provisions, and also making room for the many refugees fleeing from the embattled cities of Columbia and Charleston. Very late in the war, the town's relative isolation also prompted President Jefferson Davis to move the Confederate treasury presses to Anderson when the fall of Columbia was imminent. When General Lee surrendered at Appomattox Court House on April 9, 1865, Anderson was filled with Confederate civil servants and affluent refugee families from the midlands and lowcountry of South Carolina, many of whom had arrived early in the war.

The war years were a time of exuberant pride in the South and among its people, offset by the loss of loved ones to battle and disease. Shortages of everything from horses and cloth goods to food and money meant doing without many frivolous items, including guitar strings, corset stays, candy, sheet music, writing paper, all once so common in the Reed home. Yet despite the need to "make do with less" throughout the war years, the Reeds apparently never went hungry. As the war ended in the spring of 1865, Judge Reed, capitalizing on his honest reputation, borrowed enough money to stock a dry goods store and plant a new crop. The Reed family entered the postwar years remarkably unscathed from an economic standpoint.

Emmala's journals generally focused on her siblings, who merit a closer review here. When the war broke out, Emmala's brother Clifton was attending a local military academy. In February 1863, seventeen-year-old Clifton joined Company A, Rutledge Mounted Rifleman. In May 1864, at the Battle of Hawe's Shop, Virginia, he was wounded in both hands. His right hand was amputated, and the badly damaged left hand remained a lifelong handicap. While recuperating from his injuries Clifton married an orphaned cousin from Georgia, Francis E. "Fannie" Kingsley, and the couple had an infant daughter, Helen. Emmala described Clif as "so young and dependent on my father – who has no good education or profession or means with one arm lost in the service of his country – a fair – loving wife who has been sick for a month and looks as if she might never be quite well – with her sweet – chubby – good little Helen – none of them knowing what the future can have in store for them."[11]

Julia, Emmala's younger sister, married promising young attorney John Peter Brown in January 1860 when she was seventeen years old. The psychological effects of the war, coupled with the humiliation of defeat, created untold stress on many young families. Many a promising future would remain unfulfilled and unfortunately the Browns were no exception. The Browns had five children in six years and lived in the old Reed home on Main Street near the Columbia and Greenville Railroad depot. Emmala, in April 1866, worried in her journal for her sister and spared no disparaging remarks in reference to her brother-in-law because of his habitual public drunkenness and failure to earn a living for his family. Emmala lamented, "Julia here a moment but in such distress – John Peter – a drunken brute lying in the streets at this hour an everlasting disgrace to us all – and she has <u>no wood</u> – nothing to eat – nothing to <u>live</u> on & no hope for the future but bears up bravely – my poor sister! May heaven save them!"

Eleanor, called "Nell" in Emmala's journals, was eighteen years old in 1865, and men of all ages found her attractive—a situation twenty-five-year-old Emmala found both understandable and difficult. "<u>Nell</u>," she wrote, "with her beauty & <u>tricky</u> ways – always affects the <u>conquest</u> in despite of my <u>superior accomplishments</u> &c&c but I am getting too old alas!" Emmala and Eleanor were constant companions, so Nell was mentioned in the journals far more often than the other younger siblings. With so many teenagers in the house, Echo Hall was the scene of numerous gatherings, opportunities for the young Reed ladies to court and to flirt.[12]

Emmala, tall and dark-haired, desired to marry and start a family of her own, but not just because it was the fashion ("The mania seems prevalent everywhere!" she observed.) The Civil War changed the marriage conventions of the Old South society. Many young couples had married impetuously at the beginning of the war or during the conflict, though at the same time the war prevented many other couples from marrying until war's end. The high mortality rates of the Civil War destroyed many a young woman's hope for love and marriage as years of warfare decimated a generation of future husbands. Emmala Reed, already in her

11. Vandiver, *Traditions,* 234; Yates Snowden, *History of South Carolina* (Chicago: Lewis Publishing Company, 1920), 3:152–53; Reed, *Journals,* chap. 1, Jan. 1, 1866.

12. Reed, *Journals,* chap. 2, Feb. 3, 1866.

mid-twenties, still yearned for romance, but by antebellum standards Emmala could expect a future of barren spinsterhood.[13]

In early 1866, with the war almost a year in the past, Emmala remained at home with six younger siblings. She displayed considerable talent in music and letters, but she worried over her lack of interest in domestic skills. Having recently been jilted by her childhood sweetheart, Emmala carefully weighed the benefits of marriage with the comforts of home, and she feared the implications of both. She considered the possibilities of new lifestyles, yet she found no alternative but to persevere with traditional social routines and obligations and to wait and see what the future might hold.

Her journals lament the loss of her beau, Robert Broyles. The Broyles and Reed families were uniquely enmeshed by proximity and kinship. Anderson physician Dr. Ozey Robert Broyles and his wife, Sarah Ann Taliaferro Broyles, who lived next door to the Reeds, had ten children. Dr. Broyles's brother, Aaron, was J. P. Reed's father, making the men great-uncle and nephew, and their children first cousins once removed.

Emmala and cousin Robert were childhood playmates, lifelong neighbors, and wartime correspondents. She wrote, "Ah Robert! one year ago we had far different feelings I fancy – when you were a soldier in Va. and wrote so constantly and warmly – now we are estranged for ever more and he has acted a shameful part." She had expected a loving reunion, but without a word of explanation Robert completely shunned her upon his return from Virginia in May 1865. Though the two were only a few years apart in age, their prospects for the future were quite different. He could finish his medical studies, marry a younger woman, and start life anew. She, on the other hand, faced the prospect of remaining unwed and living at Echo Hall, as one by one her younger sisters married and left home. As late as April 1866, Robert had yet to speak more than a polite greeting to the woman he had once held so dear.[14]

13. Reed, *Journals*, chap. 3, Mar. 7, 1866. Jane Turner Censer, *North Carolina Planters and Their Children, 1800–1860* (Baton Rouge: Louisiana State University Press, 1984), offers statistical evidence that only 10.3 percent of twenty-six-year-old Southern planter-class women could expect to marry (91). Catherine Clinton's survey, which included a sampling of the whole South, concluded that 4.3 percent of twenty-six-year-old women would marry for the first time (*Plantation Mistress*, 105–6, 233).

14. Dr. Oze Robert Broyles, Jr. (1837–94), known in Emmala's journals by "R.," "R. B.," "Robert," or "Robere," attended medical school at New York City College, but the Civil War interrupted his career plans. No Oze Robert Broyles was found in any regimental rolls, but a Private Robert E. Broyles is listed on the "Roll of Company G, Second Regiment of Rifles, Confederate States Provisional Army," commanded by Captain Peter K. Norris. The roll states

On January 1, 1866, Emmala started a new journal and ushered in "a new season of joys and sorrows – hopes and fears." The words expressed the concerns of most southerners that their way of life hung precariously between a bittersweet past and an indefinite future. During the war Emmala had served as secretary for the Anderson Soldiers Aid Society, a benevolent organization dedicated primarily to the production of clothing for the troops. The responsibilities of her position provided Emmala with much useful industry and abundant social interaction. When the war ended she sought to maintain social contact with the women of Anderson by visiting neighbors. She also collected for various relief funds, reorganized church activities, and coordinated programs of popular entertainment. The entire Reed family shared a strong sense of civic responsibility and felt obligated to participate in Anderson's social life. These activities continued throughout the war years and accelerated in the winter of 1866 after family friend James L. Orr became governor.

The following pages portray a time and place when the Confederacy ceased to exist, yet the distinctiveness of Southern culture persevered. Emmala viewed the future with equal measures of fear and expectation. She feared punishment at the hands of the enemy, while she remained optimistic for her own fate and that of her entire community. Emmala's journals, though a deeply personal record of events, depict a poignant blend of apprehension and hope shared by all Southerners during those extraordinary times.

---

that Private Broyles "surrendered at Appomattox." U.S. Bureau of the Census, *Eighth Census of the United States, 1860 Census,* Population Schedule, Anderson District, 158; U.S. Bureau of the Census, *Ninth Census of the United States, 1870 Census,* Anderson County, 694; Vandiver, *Traditions,* 151; M. L. Boyd, *The Broyles, Laffitte, and Boyd Relatives and Ancestors* (Savannah, Ga.: Einar Storm Trosdal, 1959), 3, 21, 55; Reed, *Journals,* chap. 1, Jan. 7, 1866.

Part I

March–June 1865

ONE

MARCH

March 1865 Anderson home S. Carolina. The war is in the fourth year of progression – having filled up every book with my silly journalizing that I could find – I will have to resort to crossing some of the old ones – for I feel that I can scarcely live without giving some such expression to my feelings.[1] There is bloodshed, famine and suffering ahead in the land – our state almost destroyed and humiliated. Sherman's army of thieves & villains passed safely through – but in North Carolina they are about to meet with a just retaliation we hope for Johnston and Beauregard have surrounded Sherman's army & defeated it on the 19th & 20th and we hope will finally destroy them – as much a deserved punishment upon them! Tis a dark and gloomy day for our cause & country – much demoralization & desertion &c but we hope the tide has turned now and victory will attend our struggle for liberty henceforth, but how many thousands more must fall or suffer and we can scarcely learn their fate – no mail or letters scarcely. Dreadful![2]

Sheridan's forces were destroying everything in East Va. and trying to cut the only remaining railroad to Richmond & force its fall, but we hear that Longstreet's corps have met & defeated them – hope tis true & all may end there for the best, but many loved ones may have fallen. What is the fate of my Robere? I long to know but when shall I? May God preserve & bless him forever![3]

1. In March 1865, Emmala Butler Thompson Reed (b. June 11, 1839, d. Jan. 27, 1893) was twenty-five years old and lived at Echo Hall, her family home in Anderson, South Carolina. She was a graduate of Johnson Female University, well read, articulate, and an accomplished vocalist and musician (*1860 Census,* Anderson District, 156; Vandiver, *Traditions,* 112, 271). Vandiver misspells the name as "Emilia" Reed, a mistake repeated several times by subsequent researchers.

2. The diarist refers to the Battle of Bentonville, North Carolina, March 18–21, 1865. General Joseph Johnston, outnumbered three to one, attempted to impede the progress of Union forces under General William T. Sherman. Johnston hoped to help Robert E. Lee's Army of Northern Virginia escape Petersburg, eventually uniting the two forces for a withdrawal in force to the southwest. The desperate measure failed, and Johnston's command was either captured or dispersed. In command of part of Johnston's army, General Pierre G. T. Beauregard was recuperating from an illness. He managed to join Johnston's command in time to participate in the battle. Robert E. Denney, *The Civil War Years: A Day-by-Day Chronicle of the Life of a Nation* (New York: Sterling, 1992), 548–49; Walter Edgar, *South Carolina: A History* (Columbia: University of South Carolina Press, 1998), 371–74.

3. General Philip Sheridan and his mounted marauders were indeed destroying the Shenandoah Valley, in a wave of destruction that moved inexorably east toward Lee's besieged

We are blessed with peace, safety & content here so far in our quiet little village and if we were a better people all would be well, but there is vice & sin everywhere! We are blest with plenty & comforts & friends health & all things here in my home with the beautiful Spring coming on, the orchards full of white & pink blossoms, the gardens teeming with flowers & all nature redolent with new life & beauty, so may our spirits all be revived![4]

(Auntie Vie Hammond is here with us today.) Tom Osburne & Andrew Moreland happened here together again as two years ago with Eleanor. One suffered in prison ever since. The last brought his wife here. A sweet little thing, devoted to him & he to "Carrie" (Chisholm). I hope, but he retains too much of his former feeling for Eleanor! She has been blest with love & devotion – will soon find the one true heart I hope – so pretty & sensible &c. But Andrew talked too much & significantly to her today! Carrie & I sang with pleasure meanwhile![5]

---

army, inside of Petersburg, Virginia. Defenseless, Richmond was in fact about to fall, with Lee and Longstreet's Corps nearby at Petersburg (Denny, *Civil War Years,* 551).

4. The "our" Emmala refers to are her family, the Reeds. Her father, Jacob Pinckney Reed, was a tall, large-framed man with dark, wavy hair. Judge Reed usually sported a top hat and gold-handled walking stick. He was a mainstay of the Anderson District Court House and the community surrounding it, contributing to the area's economic, social, and political life (*1860 Census,* Anderson District, 156; Vandiver, *Traditions,* 20, 26, 27, 47, 90, 109, 111, 133, 223, 256, 262, 271–72, 305; Stephan Meats and Edwin T. Arnold, ed., *The Writings of Benjamin F. Perry* [Spartanburg, S.C.: The Reprint Company, 1980], 511; Brooks, *Bench and Bar,* 208–12; *Anderson Intelligencer,* August 26, 1880; Clement A. Evans, ed. *Confederate Military History: A Library of Confederate States History, in Seventeen Volumes,* vol. 6, *South Carolina,* [Atlanta, Ga.: Confederate Publishing Company, 1899], 810).

Theresa Caroline Hammond Reed (Feb. 2, 1819–Apr. 24, 1887), Emmala's mother, was rarely mentioned in the journals, though her father appears on page after page (*1860 Census,* Anderson District, 156; Vandiver, *Traditions,* 273; Brooks, *Bench and Bar,* 208).

5. Vie Hammond may have been a great aunt to Emmala by marriage. Often Emmala's companion and apparently a dear friend, Vie was a welcome fixture at Echo Hall. Vandiver states that a "Vic" Hammond taught at Professor Ligon's school in the 1870s, and a membership roll of the Baptist Church reports a "Mrs. V. E. Hammond" as a member (Vandiver, *Traditions,* 118; Hurley E. Badders and Donna Roper, *The 1897 Anderson County Courthouse Time Capsule: Linking the Past to the Future* [Pendleton, S.C.: Pendleton Historical and Recreational Commission, 1991], 35).

Thomas James Osborne (Emmala spelled the name "Osberne" or "Osburne"; the 1860 census-taker spelled it "Osborn"; all others use "Osborne") was the son of farmers Thomas A. and Jane. He was nineteen years old in 1865. His siblings included Emma, Andrew, and Elizabeth. A Thomas J. Osburne appears on the roll of Company D, Orr's Rifles, or the First South Carolina Rifles, but there are no details of his capture in 1863 or his release in 1865 (*1860 Census,* Anderson District, 258; Evans, *Confederate Military History,* 366).

In aft. Fannie & I went out to pay some visits – found three elegant Ladies at Mrs. Benson's – Mrs. Whitehead, Carter & Borland. All so charming, chatty & dressy &c. Went on to the Harrisons' cozy little home. Bettie & Julia, two pretty lovely girls, so social & plain &c. We talked social & parted with kisses for the first time. I stopped in to see Lida Pickrell at the hotel whom I have not seen in a long time. A fine girl – so smart & conversable but peculiar, talked up that dear, good man Theodore Smith. She Likes him much, but he is no <u>good</u> for any means I fear.[6]

Home late – a quiet evg all together, but I was gladdened by another letter from my ever <u>faithful</u> Robere. Yet twas a letter older than the two last I rec'd for they

---

Andrew Moreland, a Charleston refugee, was with a small entourage of family, including his wife, Carrie Chisholm, and his mother and young sisters Ellen and "B. P." The entire family stayed with cousins Edward and Carrie Hall Moreland of Anderson. An A. M. appears on the rolls of the First Infantry (Charleston) Battalion, Company E (*1860 Census,* Charleston, 222; Evans, *Confederate Military History,* 386).

6. Fannie, or Francis E. Kingsley Reed (1845–1902), one of Emmala's constant companions, was the wife of Emmala's brother Clifton or C. A. Reed. Fannie, a cousin from Claytonville, Georgia, had recently married C. A. in October of 1864, while he was recuperating from wounds suffered in battle (Snowden, *History of South Carolina,* 152; Vandiver, *Traditions,* 148).

Mrs. Catherine Sloan Benson was forty-two years old and a boarding-house keeper in March of 1865. The rush of lowcountry refugees must have created a windfall for homes with finer accommodations, like that of Mrs. Benson (Vandiver, *Traditions,* 203; *1860 Census,* Anderson District, 260).

Mrs. Stephen Whitehead of Augusta, Georgia, was the sister of a renowned contemporary landscape artist, Thomas Addison Richards (1820–1900). The Richardses emigrated from England in 1831. See Reed, *Journals,* Appendix F. Paul Lagasse, ed., *Columbia Encyclopedia,* 6th ed (New York: Columbia University Press, 2000), 1802.

Mrs. Carter and Mrs. Borland were lowcountry refugees.

Mary "Julia" (age 18) and Elizabeth "Bettie" (19) Harrison were two daughters of attorney J. W. Harrison of Anderson (*1860 Census,* Anderson District, 258).

Lida Pickrell was most likely another refugee, but from the upcountry. She was the daughter of J. L. Pickrell, a jeweler who moved to Greenville, South Carolina, in 1851. The family, or just Lida, may have been staying in the relative safety of Anderson as the danger of Yankee raiders intensified. Lida married a gentleman from New Orleans (E. Milby Burton, *South Carolina Silversmiths, 1690–1860,* 3d ed. [Charleston, S.C.: Charleston Museum, 1991], 243); see Reed, *Journals.*

Theodore Smith, or "Theo," a friend of Emmala's with similar tastes in culture and entertainment, was ending a long recuperative period. Though he appears throughout the journals, the precise cause of his illness remains vague. Four years after this time a Theodore Smith registered with the census as a government employee who lived in Charleston (*1870 Census,* Charleston, 257).

were numbered 1, 2 & 3 as he spoke of. All breathing new devotion to me, an unveiling of the long mystery, for his feelings can no longer be repressed, even though he thinks me unkind &c as he gets no letters from me, but writes on so kindly that I shall bless him forever! But when can we exchange letters again? Hope he has my letters & I can soon get replies, but this last is very clear about keeping momentoes &c if we never meet again, as if he expected some sad fate and I fear he may have met it in some late battle or be destined to it.

May a merciful Providence save & protect him safe back to me one day that our future may be better & happier, yet may all end for the best. He wrote that he had an honest conscience in his restraint so long but we must now know all of each &c. Wants my type [photograph] & would send his if he could &c. Wish I had it! Can't send my own – none suitable. Late & cold, but I must write a little more to the notes & flowers I've prepared for him & can't get off (too late) & I must dream of him tonight.

Tues. March 28th. Mild cloudy day. Sewing, finished a nice new calico dress. My last I guess. (10c per yd) George Brown here for dinner – queer as ever. Took a letter for me to R, but I fear it will never reach him. Didn't talk like going to the front, too cheerful. Hope so & may get back safely. Brought me some pretty fancy goods.[7]

In the aft. I went to Mr. Brown's. Sang some to sweet piano, & he & I walked later. My good friend – to R too. I stopped at Tupper's – sweet Kate & all in distress about her brothers, wounded & exposed to dangers. Their father left in Charleston with the Yanks &c. I gave what sympathy I could. In evg letter from Tom Carter – a brave & funny fellow[8]

7. George Brown was a son of Daniel Brown.

8. Daniel Brown (1799–1876) of Charleston became a successful merchant in Anderson, South Carolina. Brown's store once stood on the northwest corner of the Anderson Court House Square. Daniel Brown's home, Sunnyside, stood on McDuffie Street. Brown built the town's first hotel, the Waverly House, and was instrumental in the development of Johnson Female University. Brown's first wife, Rhoda Acker (1804–39), died prematurely, and he remarried Eleanor St. Clair Waller Nardin (1813–79). A prime factor in the development of Grace Episcopal Church, Eleanor raised eight children, including William Holbert, George, John, Ben, Samuel, Elijah W., Theresa, and Nancy Elisa (Vandiver, *Traditions,* 15, 16, 24, 57; *1860 Census,* Anderson District, 157; Virginia Wood Alexander, Colleen M. Elliot, and Bettie Willie, *Pendleton District and Anderson County, S.C., Wills, Estates, Inventories, Tax Returns, and Census Records* [Easley, S.C.: Southern Historical Press, 1980], 189; Vandiver Report, Item #6, 1846, Housed at the Pendleton Commission Archives, Pendleton, S.C. "The Vandiver Report" is a typescript housed at the Pendleton Commission Archives. A copy of a letter sent from P. S. Vandiver, a local Anderson banker, to W. A. Cleveland, an insurance agent, dated May 23, 1849. It is a unique statement regarding the strengths and weaknesses of many

<u>Weds. March 29th</u>. A dreamy day – misty – peach trees & gardens glowing with beautiful bloom – sunny &c, but Wm. Walters came in & disturbed my equanimity. Wanted me to go in the country with him to Mrs. Skelton's. I felt it would be funny to go alone with him. Too dull &c not decided yet. Aunt Anna here – had letters & gone home. My many excuses rather provoked Mr. Walters I guess for he didn't return to me. I couldn't decide whether to go or not. I was much worried but releived when he had gone. Not vexed I hope, yet he was kind in calling for me & I may have no other opportunity of going there. But my want of decision is a great trial to me and a serious fault leads me into many unforeseen difficulties & I can't have more, it seems, or discretion. Busy all evg.[9]

---

local (Anderson) businessmen. Varina D. Brown, *A Colonel at Gettysburg and Spotsylvania* [Columbia: The State Company, 1931), 4).

Theresa Clementine (later Clement) Brown (1828–99) is not listed in the 1860 census but was mentioned in her father's will, dated July 2, 1879. Theresa Brown found a touch of immortality when she wrote a combination recipe and domestic instruction book titled *Theresa C. Brown's Modern Domestic Cookery, 1871, Being a Collection of Receipts Suitable for All Classes of Housewives Together with Many Valuable Household Hints* (Charleston, S.C.: Edward Perry, 1871; rept. Pendleton, S.C.: Pendleton District Historical and Recreational Commission, 1985).

The Tuppers were Allen, Cordelia, Dick, Fred, Kate, and Ted. According to the 1860 census, every Tupper in South Carolina lived in Charleston County, though none of the aforementioned names could be found. The family is possibly related to the Hon. James Tupper of Charleston, an attorney who addressed the Johnson Female University commencement of August 1, 1854. There is also evidence suggesting these Tuppers were from coastal Georgia (*Le Bas Bleu,* newspaper of Johnson Female University, vol. 1, no. 5 (Aug. 1854), 2; *1860 Census,* Charleston, 373). In *South Carolina Women in the Confederacy,* a Miss K. A. Tupper appears on a list of members for the Ladies Auxiliary Christian Association of Charleston, which met at the King Street YMCA (United Daughters of the Confederacy, South Carolina Division [Columbia, S.C.: The State Company, 1907]).

Tom Carter was a resourceful, dependable overseer/foreman of the Hammond property. In the closing months of the war Carter was captured in Virginia, but he escaped and made his way to Anderson. Vandiver mentions a Thomas Carter of Belton, an exceptionally clever man, known for inventing a popular two-room fireplace, heater, and cookstove. The 1870 census registered a Wm. T. and Nancy Carter, both from Georgia, as living in Anderson County's Fork Township; in the spring of 1870, she was a housewife and he a house carpenter (Vandiver, *Traditions,* 300; *1870 Census,* Anderson County, 516); see Reed, *Journals,* Appendix F.

9. The Rev. William F. Walters, a Baptist clergyman, also taught at the Johnson Female University (Vandiver, *Traditions,* 113).

"J. O." (John) and Eliza C. Skelton raised a foster child named Willie. John was most likely a descendant of stagecoachman John Skelton, an early upcountry settler. J. O. Skelton was a corporal in the Fourth Regiment, S.C. Volunteer Infantry, Company I. After the war,

Thurs. March 30th. We lazily dreamed away the early morn for the rain was pouring down, then the clouds dispersed but the wind blew high all day. The high carnival of the windy season was very disagreeable, yet the flowers smiled out freshly. I sent some to Kate Tupper with inquiries for their family. Their fears relieved on one wounded. No news today – busy sewing & reading. Finished "The Midnight Sun" by Mrs. Fredericka Bremer that queer Swedish writer. Very pleasant but not a wonderful book – simple. Tales of the splendid Midsummer in the Norland – of simple industry & tastes of the people. All interesting, no hero or heroine scarcely.[10]

Clif & Fannie walked home with Vie to Grandpa's, 7 miles. Blustery night, all quiet reading &c, this old annal amused us – rediculous! So are all.[11]

Friday March 31st. Delightful day. Made a soldiers shirt in the morning, at noon was suprized by the coming of Fannie Smith to pay me a long promised visit. Dressed in deep elegant mourning, her tall, beautiful form, so queenlike. Such fine

---

Eliza was instrumental in reorganizing the Anderson County Fair (Vandiver, *Traditions,* 244, 257; Richard W. Simpson, *History of Old Pendleton District* [Covington, Tenn.: Bradford Publishing Company, 1978], 43; *1860 Census,* Anderson District, 282).

Aunt Anna, Uncle June, and Cousin Willie Jones spent a fair amount of time in the Anderson area during the postwar years. The identity of the Joneses and the exact nature of the familial relationship to Emmala has yet to be determined.

10. Fredrika Bremer (1810–65), a Swedish novelist, wrote contemporary accounts of upper-middle-class life in Sweden. Bremer wrote and lectured on commentary social issues in the various locations she visited, including the American South. The particular title Emmala notes cannot be located (Laurie Lanzan Harris, ed., *Nineteenth-Century Literature Criticism,* vol. 2 [Detroit, Mich.: Gale, 1986], 13–14).

11. Clifton Augustus Reed (b. July 5, 1845, d. Nov. 10, 1924) married Francis "Fannie" E. Kingsley (1845–1902). C. A. Reed used his father's credit and contacts to enter the mercantile trade in Anderson. Brother Clif proved a very successful and independent merchant. C. A. merchandised in dry goods, music and instruments (especially pianos), and the manufacture of carriages. By 1870 the family of C. A. Reed had their own town home, surrounded by servants and employees with large families. The large, white-columned home on the north side of the junction of North Main Street and the Greenville Road had a tame deer in the yard. Helen (June 29, 1865–Nov. 3, 1953) was the couple's only child (Vandiver, *Traditions,* 185–86, 234, 240, 264, 272; John Conway Garlington, *Men of the Time, Sketches of Living Notables: A Biographical Encyclopedia of Contemporaneous South Carolina Leaders* [Spartanburg, S.C.: Garlington Publishing, 1902], 358–59; *1860 Census,* Anderson District, 156; *1870 Census,* Anderson County, 465; Kate Crowther, "Anderson's Boys Who Wore the Gray," United Daughters of the Confederacy, South Carolina Division, *Recollections and Reminiscences, 1861–1865 through World War I,* vol. 5 [1994], 529–32; Evans, *Confederate Military History,* 810–11).

dark eyes & brownish golden hair & very fair and graceful ways and gentle voice. So smart, no wonder she has been so beloved by noble Harry, who is gone forever. She has lamented & loved him truly I think.[12]

Says she can never love so again, but she is beginning to get over it, with her gay nature rather subdued but often excited to mirth and sarcasm often too, but she is much changed for the better from the wicked, scornful girl she has been. She will yet be blest and happy I hope. Is much petted by all the Millers. Comes now to see her friends, she is a warm friend of mine too. Hope it may remain so.[13]

We sat chatting &c all evg. Mrs. Carter and Miss Gibbes called on us. Nice ladies; the last told us her peculiar fancy for pet snakes, little green grass snakes which she twines in her hair, so strange! Fannie & I walked round to Hattie Brissey's – nice girl, but cool to me. I think they had a children's party there – a houseful.[14]

At night Theodore came to see his lovely niece & I. They seemed quite congenial & fond of each other, but Eleanor carried on too much nonsense with him. [H]e talked to me very pleasantly, enjoyed my songs as usual.[15]

12. Fannie (or Fanny) Smith was an acquaintance of Emmala's and a cousin of Theodore Smith. One source suggests that she was most probably the daughter of Charleston merchants Joshua and Elizabeth Smith who refugeed in Pendleton, South Carolina, during the war years, but Emmala's journals clearly name Charleston banker William B. Smith as Fannie's father; "Miss Fannie," a central character in *Far, Far, from Home,* was a mysterious woman with a vague interest in Tally Simpson and his cousin, Harry Miller (Guy R. Everson and Edward W. Simpson, Jr., *Far, Far from Home: The Wartime Letters of Dick and Tally Simpson, Third South Carolina Volunteers* [New York: Oxford University Press, 1984], 281, 297–98).

13. Caroline Virginia Taliaferro Miller (1811–77), daughter of Zachariah and Hannah Taliaferro (1759–1831), had four siblings: Sarah Anne (1803–88) married Dr. O. R. Broyles (1798–1875); Lucy Hannah (1805–73) married Colonel David S. Taylor (1805–67); Mary Margaret (1808–96) married Major Richard F. Simpson (1798–1882); and Caroline married Dr. Henry C. Miller (1820–99).

The Millers' home, Valambrosa, stood close to the contemporary town of Central, South Carolina, on Eighteen Mile Creek (Simpson, *Old Pendleton,* 132–33; *Houses of Old Pendleton,* 10, # 81, information collected by Henrietta Seabrook and Mrs. H. P. Sitton, typed from copy owned by Gaillard Hunter, Clemson, S.C., 1962; Everson and Simpson, *Far, Far from Home,* 216). The wartime letters of Caroline Miller to nephew Tally Simpson appear in Everson and Simpson's *Far, Far from Home.*

14. There is not enough information to identify either Mrs. Carter or Miss Gibbes, aside from the fact that they were both refugees from Charleston.

15. Eleanor "Nell" Reed (1847–1909) was apparently a very popular young lady and often Emmala's competition for available beaux. The two women were constant companions, and there are more references in Emmala's journals to "Nell" than to any other single person except possibly Judge Reed (*1860 Census,* Anderson District, 156; Vandiver, *Traditions,* 272; Silas E. Lucas, *Early Anderson County, S.C., Newspapers, Marriages, Obituaries, 1841–1881* (Easley, S.C.: Southern Historical Press, 1978), 72.

TWO

APRIL

Sat. April 1st. A bright pleasant day. Many little fool's tricks going on as usual. Jim Hoyt had tried the game, advertizing "Barnum's Wooly Horse" as having turned up here for exhibition & many children were taken in I guess. Fannie & I had a sweet social time together talking & reading Thackery's [*sic*] last book "Philip" (She & Theodore admire his works most of all others – pets of theirs).[1]

I was sewing &c, but spent the aft. on a sad errand. We were greatly shocked by learning that Mrs. Andrew Moreland had died here suddenly with convulsions. In two days, after our seeing her so well & happy here Monday! It awakened great sympathy & surprize. Andrew used to visit Eleanor years ago, married Carrie Chisholm, a nice girl, about six months ago. They have run from houses in Charleston, Savannah, Columbia &c; she was there during all the week of horror when the Yankees were there, & has been starving there ever since. Undergoing many trials & anxiety about her husband. Then he came for her & brought her

1. James Alfred Hoyt was born October 11, 1837 at Waynesboro, Virginia. His father, J. Perkins Hoyt, was a jeweler from New Hampshire who moved south for his health and soon married Virginian Jane Johnson. Hoyt apprenticed with newspapers in Laurensville and Anderson, then in 1860, at twenty-three years old, he became editor of the *Anderson Gazette.* Within a year he started his own paper, the *Anderson Intelligencer.*

Hoyt commanded a regiment, the "Palmetto Sharpshooters," and after the war formed a Home Police Force and a Survivor's Association. Colonel Hoyt recounted his unit's wartime exploits in a "historical sketch" titled *The Palmetto Riflemen,* published in 1885 and reproduced in Badders and Roper, *Time Capsule.*

James Hoyt married Rebecca "Becky" Webb at Echo Hall on January 20, 1866, and she soon became Anderson's first female journalist. The Hoyts went on to publish the *Baptist Courier* and the *Greenville Mountaineer,* among other newspapers. Hoyt was an ardent Democrat until an unsuccessful gubernatorial bid as a Prohibition Party candidate in 1900 (Garlington, *Men of the Time,* 212–14; Vandiver, *Traditions,* 29, 82, 84, 194, 239, 249, 252, 257, 258, 312; *1860 Census,* Anderson District, 156; Alexander S. Salley, *South Carolina Troops in Confederate Service,* vol. 2 [Columbia, S.C.: The State Company, 1914], 571, 573; UDC, *South Carolina Women in the Confederacy,* 185, 187).

William Makepeace Thackeray (1811–63) wrote *The Adventures of Philip on His Way through the World in 1861–1862* (Ian Scott-Kilvert, *British Writers,* vol. 5 [New York: Charles Scribner's Sons, 1982], 45–46).

here to rest & safety with his brother Edward's family where she was happy to be, but the rough ride over broken roads & fatigue in her delicate situation caused her death they say.[2]

They came here Sunday; Monday morn he brought her to see Lida Pickrell & us whom he begged to be her good friends. We were all delighted with her. She was a sweet little thing, smart & chatty & interesting, pretty & social. Played & sang well but her voice was weakened by circumstances which they both regretted so. She enjoyed my music. She talked so fondly of her husband. He seemed proud & fond of her, kind & thoughtful – yet foolish in his continued admiration for Eleanor, which he expressed too freely & she there. Showed his feeling too plainly & said "you don't know what may yet happen" in teasing Eleanor. She said the same thing, "I may drop off & leave him to you &c"

What a just retribution this seems! But what a shock it will be to him. He left her here on Tues. to return to his Com'd – not to meet again for months or years perhaps. Left her so well & happy & fond and now they'll meet no more for she is cold & dead, away from all she loved is happy forever we hope. Was taken with violent convulsions alone in her room Thursday. She died next morn. A time of fearful watching & responsibility to the brother & sister.

I went to see them that aft. & take flowers to deck the bier. A beautiful cross & wreath of white flowers & arbor vitae, nicely made by Joe McCully. There she lay in her coffin, but her face so unnatural, badly misshapen, no loved ones near. Almost strangers, but very kind. Oh the fate of frail mortality! Edward & Carrie Moreland were sitting there alone with the dead, seemed desolate, glad to see me.[3]

Carrie was sad & weak, threw herself in my lap & wept. I remember when she & I used to correspond years ago as Carrie Hall – a bright sweet woman. Sat talking of the sad calamity & came by the Bap. ch. – where we were to sing, but 'twas failure; then went to the Pres. church to attend the funeral – services read by Mr. Keith. Few there. I had to raise the hymn, no one else did and there they left the fair young bride of a few months to rest.[4]

2. Carrie Chisholm Moreland, wife of Andrew M. Moreland, died at the home of Edward M. and Carrie Hall Moreland. Edward served with Eighth Battalion Reserves, Company A, known as Stalling's Battalion, married an Anderson county woman, and moved to town before the war ended (*1860 Census,* Charleston, 222; Evans, *Confederate Military History,* 345).

3. Anna Josephine McCulley was the daughter of merchant Stephan McCulley and his wife, Elmira. "Joe" soon wed attorney W. W. Humphreys (*1860 Census,* 260; Vandiver, *Traditions,* 90, 93, 182, 268). See Reed, *Journals,* Appendix F.

4. The Rev. Paul Trapier Keith and his family came to Anderson from Charleston as wartime refugees. While in Anderson, Reverend Keith preached at Grace Episcopal Church and after the war returned to St. Michael's Church in Charleston. The 1860 Census reports

Alexander walked home with Eleanor again – strange! I found Theodore here with Fannie. Seemed to be having a cozy chat – pleased to see me, they went to walk.

I met them in the garden, then he came in & spent the evg – very pleasant. The young moon & stars were soft & lovely, the evg delightful. We sat in the piazza awhile. I sang to the guitar many sweet love ballads and he sat near & hummed along very nicely. Slipped in some spicy words or delicate flattery now & then – repeated much sweet poetry. Said "How is it we've happened on such a holy hour & scene." A rare relief to him, so soul-weary generally, couldn't bear to leave the spot for tea – begged me to return afterwards and so we sat a long time singing and talking pleasantly of many things.

Repeated the "Prisoner of Chillun" as his own dark embodiment of feeling. This life is weary blank & waste to him. He feels he has no object in living, is useless to himself & others & can't be otherwise with his health & temperment &c he thinks. "Is no marrying man" – though he cordially thinks more of me than any other. He was appreciative & fascinated that night, yet not presuming. Only hoped when he had to leave me last I would permit him to kiss my hand. That he would write to me & I must answer, though he hates writing. I was the only bird, as to the prisoner of Chillon, that could cheer him, but so short lived.[5]

He couldn't spend all his time so, seemed entranced with the stem of a Scotch Jonquil I gave him – one from Dr. Broyles' yard, reminded me of R – he prized the gift of fragrance more. We came in & talked to Fannie awhile – she teazed us about "such a queer couple" – so unlike – always quarrelling yet making up – wondered how &c? He laughed (& thought it all very spicy) – but said I wouldn't make up &c. Laughed over "Philip" awhile. Lou's Lily White which we spilt amongst us & touched each others faces with it in joke, yet he treats me most respectfully. Hope he will ever retain the highest regard & he deserves mine as a friend.[6]

---

the Keith family living in Charleston's Ward 4. Rev. P. T. (58) and wife Anna had eleven children: Madeline (29), Susan (27), Willis (21), McA. and Anna (twins, age 20), Maria (18), Eleanor (16), Maggie (14), Ann (13), Mary (11), Paul (9). Ella later married Emmala's sweetheart, Oze Robert Broyles, Jr. (Albert Sidney Thomas, *A Historical Account of the Protestant Episcopal Church in South Carolina, 1820–1957* [Columbia, S.C.: R. L. Bryan Company, 1957], 46, 265; *1860 Census,* Charleston, 358).

5. Emmala refers to a stanza in the 1818 poem "The Prisoner of Chillon," by George Gordon, Lord Byron, in which a bird briefly lands on a high portal and gives the prisoner a fleeting moment of joy.

6. Dr. Ozey (or Oze) Robert Broyles (1798–1875) and Sarah Anne Taliaferro (1803–88) moved to Anderson Court House from Ashtabula, a plantation outside of Pendleton, South Carolina. Dr. Broyles practiced medicine and was an agriculturalist of considerable renown.

Sunday April 2nd. Pleasant day – all lazy – went to S.S., a good many new scholars, practicing singing hymns. Heard a large class of children. Mr. Murray gave us a very good sermon, drawing a comparison as Gen. Lee had offered pardon to all deserters who would plea back to their allegiance &c, so God offers pardon to all wanderers who will come back to him & so carried it out.[7]

Grandma (Hammond) & Aunt Anna here to dinner, had heard Mr. Jones preach. Lucy & Vie had walked up – too bad. Fan & I had a sweet time after dinner in parlor, looking over books, types &c, talking of H & R. She went to Epis.ch. & home with Hattie B. for the night. I went to a prayer meeting late & weak. Alexander failed to walk with me as he seemed to wish – glad.

In evg Mr. Frank McMillan came in for the night. Brother of Sue & all in Barnwell. Fine looking, clever man, travelling on Gov't business. Told us much news of the state of the country where Sherman's vile army passed. Great destruction, but people better off than expected. Horses & other stock gone to cripple the country. His father had lost much, not all, but what trials they've passed through since I was there last year![8]

Ozey Broyles was the son of Major Aaron Broyles and Frances "Fannie" Broyles. Aaron Broyles's sister, Sallie Broyles White, was the mother of Jacob Pinckney Reed. This made Oze Broyles and J. P. Reed great-uncle and nephew, so Emmala and Robert Broyles were first cousins once removed. The 1860 census reports that the family of O. R. and Sarah lived in the village of Anderson. Robert, Emmala's sweetheart, was a twenty-two-year-old medical student in 1860 (*1860 Census,* Anderson District, 158; Vandiver, *Traditions,* 132; Simpson, *Old Pendleton,* 133–35, 173; Everson and Simpson, *Far, Far from Home*). The story of the Simpsons and the Broyleses are inexorably intertwined by marriage and friendship (Boyd, *The Broyles Ancestors,* 1–60). Variously spelled "Oze" and "Ozey," the name is probably French in origin, but the meaning is obscure.

7. John Scott Murray (44) was minister of Anderson's Baptist congregation, also serving as president and classics instructor at the Johnson Female University. His wife, Claudia, also came to Anderson to teach at the university. After the school closed in 1861 Claudia Murray continued to teach in her home, known for many years as the Old Murray Place, at the junction of North Main and Greenville Streets, where a lavish flower garden surrounded the home. In 1866 the young Reed girls attended Mrs. Murray's school. In 1889 Mrs. Murray was a cofounder of the Anderson Women's Christian Temperance Union. According to the 1860 census, the Murrays had three children, Edwards (age 12), Fanny (10), and John Scott (8), and had assets totaling $16,000 (*1860 Census,* Anderson District, 156; Vandiver, *Traditions,* 112, 119; Frank A. Dickson, *Journeys into the Past: The Anderson Region's Heritage* [Anderson, S.C.: Anderson County Heritage Committee, 1975], 169).

8. The McMillans were the children of Henry and Sophrona McMillan of Forest Home plantation in Bamberg, South Carolina. Dr. Francis Marion "Barnie" McMillan (1837–66) served as a surgeon in the western theater for the duration of the war, only to die in 1866 from an unnamed disease contracted during the war. William Franklin "Frank" McMillan signed

Sue back at home. We can't write or hear. Barnie had acted bravely & with charity & escaped safely. Many negroes were faithful to owners. Some of them claimed & saved much of their property at home. Thank heaven so many were faithful & grateful. Gilmore Simms, the writer, had lost everything, his books & all – sad. We sat talking of many things till late. The negro choir holding forth splendidly outside – shames the whites.[9]

Monday April 3rd A delicious day – rearranging the parlor. I wrote letters to send out by males. Milton Brown called at noon to say goodbye as he was off to Va. and took some notes for me to Peter & R. Where can I get answers as to what is now their fate, as we hear rumors of a battle there. I sent small boquets to each to cheer them. Mr. McMillan was here to dinner & sat chatting with me long after "I gave him a letter to send to Sue."[10]

---

bank notes and bonds for the Confederate Bank; he died in Charleston, South Carolina, of yellow fever shortly after the war ended. Susan H. McMillan married Dr. Thomas Bailey, D.D., a renowned Baptist minister and church administrator (Carnice J. Groves, *Jennings-McMillan-Faulling-Whaley-Bluer and Other Early Families of South Carolina* [Daytona Beach, Fla.: Daytona Beach Community College, 1977], 71, 99, 102, 103, 181, 182; *Bamberg Herald,* Sept. 1, 1977; verified via correspondence with McMillan family historian Sybile McMillan Pierce of Sumter, S.C. on August 15, 2003).

Between February 5 and 10, 1865, General Sherman's cavalry destroyed the county and the village of Barnwell, South Carolina.

9. William Gilmore Simms (1806–70) was a poet laureate of South Carolina whose work included poetry, novels, biographies, and history. His homes and worldly possessions were lost twice, once in a Barnwell plantation and again in the bombardment of Charleston (David C. Roller, ed., *The Encyclopedia of Southern History* [Baton Rouge: Louisiana State University Press, 1979], 1106).

10. Milton Brown was Joel Milton Brown, son of Helena Brown of Townville, South Carolina, who had eight children, including Mary S., Joseph Newton, Samuel Franklin, Emmaline Elizabeth, John Peter (Emmala's brother-in-law), twins Mary Lucinda and Susan, Daniel Edward, Joel Milton, and William Sanford Brown.

Joel Milton Brown served in Company E, Third South Carolina Cavalry. He married Emma Virginia Farmer, and they were buried in the cemetery of the Townville Baptist Church (Janet B. Hewett, ed., *South Carolina Confederate Soldiers, 1861–1865,* vol. 1, *Name Roster* [Wilmington, N.C.: Broadfoot, 1998], 58; R. M. Smith, *The Book of the Dead: An Alphabetical Arrangement of the Dead Buried in the Cemeteries of Anderson County.* A bound typescript, privately published in 1966 and housed at the Pendleton Commission Archives, 45.

University of Virginia graduate John Peter Brown (1838–79) of Townville married Emmala's sister Julia Susan Reed (b. Dec. 17, 1842, d. Jan. 13, 1883) on the evening of January 12, 1860. Julia was educated at the Johnson Female University. She was exceptionally dear to Emmala, who never stopped worrying over the welfare of her younger sister. In September 1861, attorney J. P. Brown became Second Lieutenant John Peter Brown of the Palmetto

He was fine looking, agreeable, intelligent, practical, "moral gentleman" of the world – smoothe, soft voice & pleasing. Would have been rather dangerous. Widower and the scamp rather joked on the subject. Seemed to fancy me much, loved music, talked of his brothers to me &c &c. At last he was off to Pendleton to get his horses. Will go to Greenville again to see Dr. Barney, the Medical Dept. Will settle in Newberry. He may visit his family below there. He is a genial man, such as one likes to meet sometimes.

In aft. Fannie came home from a prolonged visit to Hattie B. in a gala mood for joking & abusing people &c. We walked together late to the Benson's to see her friends (Mrs. Carter & Miss Clancy). Theodore on his way to see us joined us a matter of course & went in. Was in a romantic mood since my guitar songs he said. Spoke of my looking "particularly bright" &c & many nice little things.[11]

We found the ladies very agreeable, but Miss Clancy rather teazing him about me and neglecting her. He professed to regard us both &c, was not so pleasant. Walked home late & in "excusing" various things. He said "Thank heaven Miss Emmily there is one person who needs no excuse" the jewel of Anderson &c. He & F agreed – pleasant!

We found Miss Mary Waller here to see Fan. Urged Theo to come in. He thought we would tire of him, too great a breach of etiquette or would awaken more gossip &c So he wouldn't come, much as he desired it I'm sure. When Miss

---

Riflemen, Company B. Two of his brothers, Samuel and Daniel, died in the war, while older brother Colonel Joseph Newton Brown eventually commanded a brigade. The 1860 census, conducted on June 2, records that Julia S. (age 17) and J. Peter (22) Brown possessed $3400.00 in assets. The 1870 census records the Browns living in Anderson County's Fork Township, with children Frederick (9), Sumter (8), Catherine H. (Carrie) (7), Paul (5), Daisy (4), Anna (3), and Mary (7 mos.) (Brent H. Holcomb, comp., *Marriage and Death Notices from the Up-country of South Carolina, as taken from Greenville newspapers, 1826–1863* [Greenville, S.C.: SCMAR, 1983], 231; *1860 Census,* Anderson District, 156; *1870 Census,* Anderson County, 573). The nomenclature Anderson District was changed to Anderson County in accordance with a mandate stipulated by the South Carolina State Constitution of 1868 (Smith, *Book of the Dead,* 319; Vandiver, *Traditions,* 139, 271; Ron Field, *South Carolina's Volunteers of the Civil War: Fourth South Carolina Volunteers (Sloan's)* [Lower Swell, Gloucestershire, U.K.: Design Folio, 1992], 12; Brown, *A Colonel at Gettysburg,* 8, 162).

11. In the 1860 census, Greenville registry, Francis Brissey (age 33) and Arlena Brissey (29) each gave their occupation as seamstress; both had young children at the time of the survey, one of whom could have been the Hattie mentioned in the journal entry (*1860 Census,* 409, 417).

Miss Clancy hailed from a large family who were all residing in Charleston at the time of the 1860 census, all in Charleston's Ward 6 (*1860 Census,* 438).

Mary asked him to come & spend an evg. there soon, he said "When are you going Miss E!" as usual and she was quite provoked.[12]

We had a quiet evg. Fan played & sang well on piano, we joined in some duetts. She grew excited over the question of her father's gold being taxed so heavily (25 per cent would sweep one fourth) and quite raved about the injustice. An imbecile congress who have no gold – making such laws – wished they were all in Europe &c. She spoke eloquently and her queenly form in sable robes, a graceful train, rosy face & dark flashing eyes as she caressed sweet little white robed baby sister.

It was quite a picture! I argued some about patriotism &c but we all laughed at her! She is a smart, funny girl; makes apt & ludicrous comparisons of people & things. Hope she may yet be loved & happy for she would grow sad & calm again & talk of her "darling Harry" to whose loss she cannot be reconciled. As rebellious, we slept sweetly together after all.

Mr. Brown & Kate Gadsden came around to see her too & take Miss Mary home. Kate thinking the refugees were so hardly treated. Nothing left, homes & property & money all gone. How can they buy things from the extorted farmers at such prices. Corn $20 per bushel – wood $80 a load – and may rise. It is dreadful hard & cheap living but that is degrading I think. [T]he Gadsdens are a cool – practical lot. Mr. Brown more generous than we imagined of his sordidness.[13]

A General Peck came to town this evg so aloof he could scarcely talk, but it came out. There was bąttle in Virginia (nothing from Sherman & Johns[t]on save the disorganized army just united under the old leader had fallen back to discipline &c) and I hope all may yet be well, but what's the fate of our loved ones there? A sweet moonlit evg.[14]

12. Mary and Carrie Waller came to Anderson in 1837. Their father, identified only as Mr. Waller, came to establish an Episcopal congregation, and died on June 7, 1844. His daughters Mary, Carrie, Rosa (Mrs. Elijah Webb), and Eleanor St. Clair Nardin (Mrs. Daniel Brown) carried on and helped found Grace Episcopal Church in 1860. Mary, Rosa, and Carrie all taught at Johnson Female University (Vandiver, *Traditions,* 57–58; *1860 Census,* Anderson District, 157; *Centennial Program and History of Grace Church, Anderson, S.C.,* 22, pamphlet located at Anderson County Library).

13. Mr. Brown's exact identity is uncertain.

Catherine "Kate" Gadsden, a refugee from Charleston, along with her sister Anna and a rather large family group, all moved to Anderson for the war (*1860 Census,* Charleston, 404).

14. General William Rainey Peck (1818–71) of Tennessee enlisted as a private in the Ninth Louisiana Infantry in 1861 and by February 1865 was a brigadier general. General Peck never received so much as a flesh wound during four years in the field, remarkable considering he stood about six foot six and often placed himself in harm's way. He was paroled at Vicksburg, Mississippi, on June 6, 1865 (Ezra J. Warner, *Generals in Gray: Lives of the Confederate Commanders* [Baton Rouge: Louisiana State University Press, 1959], 231).

By April 3, 1865, both Richmond and Petersburg, Virginia, were occupied by Union troops.

Tues. April 4th. Brilliant spring morning! Fan & I ran round the garden among the early flowers. [H]yacinths & narcissus all just fading, thrift blooming in brilliant beauty. White & green tipped hair bells, purple verbena, blue periwinkles &c Yellow crocus or old fashioned rose, pink almond and the white flowering fragrant delicate lilac was most admired after peach & plum & other blooms were passing away. The white cherry & rosy apple blossoms appear amid new green leaves and every shrub & tree is beginning to unfold a new life of verdure that gladdens the eye & heart – whilst the green fields of grain & grass are refreshing to the soul!

Mrs. Carter called to bring a bundle for Fan to take – was very elegant & agreeable – a real smart woman of society. Spoke of the huge, splendid Gen. Peck now in town on his way to his Louisiana home – wish I could meet him! A crowd of Bleckleys & Webbs &c came by & took Eleanor with them to Grandpa's for the day – brought Vie back.[15]

15. Sylvester (1832–92) and Elizabeth Hammond (1837–1914) Bleckley ran England, Bleckley and Company, a mercantile established in 1853. In 1860 the couple had two young children, Josephine and Mary; eventually there were five, all girls. Sylvester Bleckley, whom Emmala called "Bleck," was born in Clayton, Georgia. Sylvester had seven relatively successful siblings, including elder brother Logan E. Bleckley, chief justice of the Georgia Supreme Court. Elizabeth (a first cousin of Emmala's mother, Theresa) was born at Rosewood plantation, built by her father, Col. Benjamin "Frank" Hammond. She attended Johnson Female University, graduating in 1853. She wed Sylvester Bleckley in September of 1856, at twenty-three years of age, and the marriage appears to have been quite happy. Sylvester Bleckley served Anderson as a school commissioner, director of the National Bank of Anderson (1873–91), and a member of the town council. He ran the Confederate commissary depot in Anderson and remained one of Anderson's most prominent merchants in the years following the war (*1860 Census*, Anderson District, 158; Andrew Jackson Ritchie, *Sketches of Rabun County History* [Clayton, Ga.: Private publication, 1948; rept. 1959, 49–50, 53, 60, 61]; Vandiver, *Traditions*, 235, 273–74; Dickson, *Journeys*, 138; *Cyclopedia of Eminent and Representative Men of the Carolinas*, vol. 1 [1892; Easley, S.C.: Southern Historical Press, 1972], 625; Brown, *A Colonel at Gettysburg*, 150; Carlton, *Mill and Town*, 29–30). Carlton makes particular note of the entrepreneurial spirit of Anderson's merchants and businessmen. In Anderson, a man could often work his way up from clerk to owner, without necessarily having the benefit of kinship.

Elijah and Rosa Waller Webb had five children in 1860, Louisa (Lou), Rebecca (Becky), Rosa, Charles, and Warren. Mr. Webb, known as "Jeff," served as Anderson county clerk of court for many years. Rosa Webb taught at Johnson Female University. The Webb women were involved with the Soldiers Aid Society, which supplied soldiers with cloths and comestibles during the Civil War. Rosa was a president of the society and Becky served as secretary. Becky later married James A. Hoyt (UDC, *South Carolina Women in the Confederacy*, 50; Dickson, *Journeys*, 137; Vandiver, *Traditions*, 82; Thomas D. Clark, ed. and comp., *South Carolina: The Grand Tour, 1780–1865;* Micajah Adolphus Clark, "Visiting South Carolina Style" [Columbia: University of South Carolina Press, 1973], 284–306).

Fan & I sang & read & sewed &c until we hurried to the depot at noon without dinner for her to take the cars for Williamston, as Hattie Gibbes was going there – then to Newberry & Columbia. We had a race down there in the sun – found a disagreeable crowd as usual. Hattie Gibbes there, but we couldn't be very cordial she had been fibbing to each of us &c but W. B. Smith glad to see & to walk up with me, he said. A fine looking, genial man, when he chooses.[16]

Music lessons &c in evg. Soft moolight night. We were invited to the Bleckleys at night as we were this time last year when R, Jim Townsend &c were there. We hoped to meet the Humphreys &c but they didn't come. Clif & Fan, Eleanor & I walked up there, found only Liz & Bleck, quite merry. Sallie Cresswell – nice girl rather blue I think. Vie & Becky Webb – Billie Hammond in love with her – Dud Webb little thing & cousin Lou Wilkes. No beaux could be started. All sang & romped around merrily, had a nice eggnog. Bleck partial to me. Home rather late.[17]

16. Williamston, South Carolina, founded on the land owned by West Allen Williams, was once a health resort renowned for its mineral springs. Dr. Samuel Lander founded a Methodist school named Williamston Female College there in 1871. The school, later moved to Greenwood, S.C., was renamed Lander College (Walter Edgar, *Works Progress Administration Guide to the Palmetto State* [Columbia: University of South Carolina Press, 1941], 352.

Newberry, South Carolina, seventy miles east of Anderson, was on the Greenville and Columbia Railroad line. Newberry was established in 1789; it is thought the name honors Revolutionary War Captain John Newberry, an officer in General Sumter's command.

The Newberry Court House was built in 1850; the railroad meetings took place there because it was home to the law and railroad offices of Judge John Belton O'Neall, the original director of the Columbia and Greenville Railroad. Newberry College, with its beautiful quad and bell tower, was established in 1856 (Edgar, *WPA Guide,* 378). For an excellent perspective on the Newberry area during this same period see James E. Kibler, *Our Father's Fields: A Southern Story* (Columbia: University of South Carolina Press, 1998), chapters 12 and 13. Columbia, capital city of South Carolina, had a population of 8,000 in 1860, but the devastation caused by Union troops depleted the city of people and structures by the spring of 1865.

Hattie Gibbes cannot be identified.

17. James Townsend, of Bennettsville, South Carolina, was a captain with the South Carolina Second Infantry, Company F (Evans, *Confederate Military History,* 488; *1860 Census,* Marlboro County, 153).

Sarah "Sallie" Cresswell (1844–1919), daughter of attorney John Hunter Creswell, later married George Reese Cherry and lived in the Pendleton area (Vandiver, *Traditions,* 29, 122; Smith, *Book of the Dead,* 93).

William Wirt or "W. W." Humphreys (1836–1913) served with the Palmetto Riflemen. He rose from first lieutenant to major and gained notice for remarkable bravado and skill as a

Weds. April 5th. Hazy morn – pleasant. We're all going on a raid to cousin Frank Hammond's today. Liz Bleckley & Sallie Cresswell went first. Clifton & Fannie – Billy H & Becky Webb in buggies. Dudley Webb driving Vie & I in a little carriage which we feared would break down, but all very merry & comfortable. Pleasant ride watching the budding forests first tinges of green & red maples, white dogwood & plum & other shrubs. Blue violets, wild yellow strawberries dotting the ground.

Reached the solid old homestead – six miles at H. Cousin Mary so fat & good natured, Cousin Frank, little, scrawny, but so dry & clever. All laughing at each others jokes. Sat chatting nonsense all day, knittings &c, discussed Florida much. Cousin Frank just got back from his plantation through the country. Brought much sugar to sell at $15 or 20 per lb. Spoke of the oranges, lemons & bannanna[s] & every pleasant thing in abundance there, bright flowers &c.[18]

We longed to all be there, but it is now being raided by the vile foe I guess. We had some sugar cakes, blackberry wine & sugared molasses for lunch. I fear the

---

skirmisher. After the war, attorney Humphreys married Anna Josephine McCulley, who raised their many children. He served as a commissioner in equity, a judge in probate, Anderson city alderman, and president of Anderson's Patrick Military Institute. Kate Crowther, in her essay "Anderson's Boys Who Wore the Gray," writes that Anderson's Confederate Monument actually depicts the image of Major Humphreys (Vandiver, *Traditions,* 30, 82, 120, 223, 232, 246, 312; Smith, *Book of the Dead,* 196; Salley, *South Carolina Troops,* 572; *1860 Census,* Anderson District, 159; James A. Hoyt, *The Palmetto Riflemen,* from *Time Capsule,* 54; Crowther, "Anderson's Boys Who Wore the Gray," 531).

Billie or William A. Hammond was the oldest child of William F. and Mary Hammond. He was twenty-six years old in 1865. His siblings included Benjamin F., Catherine, and Oscar. W. A. Hammond served with various units and ended the war with the Fourth S. C. Infantry, Company B (*1860 Census,* Anderson District, 162; Hewett, *Confederate Soldiers,* 204).

Dudley Webb lived on a farm eight miles north of Anderson. "Dud" was a son of Elijah and Rosa Webb. His siblings included Lou (Mrs. Samuel) Wilkes, Becky, and Rosa (Mrs. Charles) Sinclair. Dudley married the former Helen Wilson and had two children, Thomas Jefferson and Elizabeth Caroline. He worked four "hands" on his productive little farm (*1860 Census,* Anderson District, 257; Clark, *Grand Tour,* 292–94).

18. This "Old" Hammond homestead was about six or seven miles south of Anderson Court House. Frank and Mary Hammond evidently moved south to Florida. The 1860 census shows a Francis and Mary Hammond living in Hamburg, South Carolina, located in Edgefield County. Sugar was a rare commodity in the upcountry of 1865. Walter Edgar noted that in Columbia, South Carolina, sugar was virtually unobtainable, even before Sherman captured the city (Edgar, *South Carolina,* 368).

boys went off to imbibe rather often – disgusting! A nice dinner – turkey a rarity now, mussels tasted like oysters – pies &c – coffee made of okra that was splendid. We girls strolled around after dinner – lay under the large old pine tree talking. Sallie Cresswell & I walked to the brook & gathered moss, white daisies &c. She is smart, nice & quiet.

Starting home rather late, had a merry ride, but Dud was spinning some very silly yarn for us, indeed I felt very little congeniality with all. Cousin Lou Wilkes here tonight, rather blue & disappointed about so many others &c – shocking. She & some of them here went to Mr. Webbs for the evg. I felt tired & indifferent. Mamie had her first document – a sentimental April fool – wonder who from. I have no letters now. Lonely tonight. Cloudy but pleasant. Poor Josie & Ben long since in their graves forgotten today. Cousin Lou Wilkes came & slept with Eleanor.[19]

Thurs. April 6th. A delicious day of sunbeams & shadows & sweat fresh odurs. Cousin Lou & I concluded we ought to visit the Skelton's so Pa let us have the buggy and go out to spend the day. We drove early by Mr. Webbs. Vie & Becky there & Mrs. Webb scolded me for leaving the society. I was loathe to leave it but went and after a pleasant ride of four miles reached the cozy little cottage home of the good couple John & Eliza Skelton and their pet foster son "Willie." Mr. Walters coming into town talked rather carelessly about coming back and being in business &c, but I am sure he hurried, as he was back by noon.

We found Bettie Gaines, the young widow. Sallie Whitmire's cousin, whom I used to know in Greenville. With her little boy for the day. A nice looking, quiet little woman, living so alone here. Lou was so gay & chatty. Quite a different type of widow. We all sat knitting & talking pleasantly. Had a nice dinner, squirrel pie &c, fine pudding & sauce. Still blessed with many comforts here. Mr. Walters came, looked quite handsome. He is well, but has no voice, only whispers. Too sad that he should be thus deprived of his usefulness &c. Seems very cheerful, has rather an abrupt, impudent way, but means nothing with such good friends. He & Lou full of confidences & jokes. He evidently regards me lightly, but not seriously.[20]

19. "Mamie" refers to Emmala's sister, Mary Eliza Reed, who was fifteen years old in 1865 (*1860 Census,* Anderson District, 156, 180; Vandiver, *Traditions,* 46, 223, 272).

20. Eliza A. "Bettie" Gaines was the thirty-seven-year-old widow of Thomas H. Gaines of Williamston. The couple had five children in 1860, all girls (*1860 Census,* Anderson District, 179).

We went out & gathered flowers to arrange the vases. He cut strips of cedar, red woodbine, cherry blossoms, green snowball, hyacinths and the "Wisteria," a large bush or vine covered with rich clusters of the rich purple blooms, so fragrant & graceful. A purple world of bloom & fragrance covered with the first butterflies & insects of pretty cases. Lovely contrasts which we both enjoyed & admired. After much nonsense we departed. He loaned me a volume of "Spurgeon's Sermons." We had a delightful ride home.[21]

Vie was with us at night, all in a social mood. Fan & Clif were petting a young snake they had found – or rather, we were all rather horrified at it! I sang a number of sweet old songs to suit the tastes of Eleanor & all – sentimental ballads & duetts with her & dreamed some in the soft moonlight – for my heart was full of love and gratitude this lovely night – for the wealth of devotion I have received from my Robere at length!

We had news of battles in N. C. & Va. and of the evacuation of Richmond. Can it be true & why is it? What is the fate of my loved ones! Great attacks on Mobile – raids all around – our whole country endangered now – 'though Lincoln &c are talking of peace. On their own terms, I guess, but surely we will hold out bravely to the end, do our duty & be successful! God grant it, but what sad startling times for us! What trying times for human hearts – when all the nearest ties have been severed, forever perhaps![22]

After a silence of several weeks Peter wrote us cleverly & R sent me his revelations in 14 close pages that employed the evgs reading in a happy way – yet Vie would see too much – being much interested in him she pretends & all. 'Though

21. Charles Haddon Spurgeon (1834–92) was a renowned preacher of the late 19th century. A Baptist minister at twenty years old, Spurgeon pioneered modern evangelism, mission work, and church participation in a wide variety of benevolent efforts. Between 1855 and 1917, some 2,500 of his sermons were published in a sixty-three-volume collection (*Columbia Encyclopedia,* 2025).

22. The fighting in North Carolina ended as Sherman's forces moved relentlessly north. Richmond, Virginia, capital of the Confederate States of America, fell to Union forces on April 3, 1865. President Jefferson Davis and his entourage, including fifty naval cadets, left the city late the night before and were trying to make their escape via the Gulf of Mexico. On April 6, 1865 the final battle between the Army of the Potomac and the Army of Northern Virginia took place at Saylor's Creek, Virginia (Burke Davis, *The Long Surrender* [New York: Random House, 1985], 25, 31–4, 52, 65, 73).

Mobile, Alabama, was a city under siege by Union forces that had stormed the bay's defenses —Spanish Fort and Fort Alexis—on April 8, 1865, leaving Mobile defenseless to attack by Union forces.

he objects so much to my sharing his letters – I cannot resist such entreaties & her interest in him. He touches on every point on which we are mutually (he & I) interested – gave noble views of all – was the devoted, honourable man I should have ever trusted. He fully revealed his long & deep devotion and future hopes & fears, but there was much left unsaid on account of obstacles. Though he admitted no one else to such a solemn decision, yet doubtful which would make our happiness.

He is wise too in these uncertain times – tells me many feelings and prospects. All appreciated "that his family didn't dare speak against me, but only gave wild advice that he paused to heed," yet we would live in hopes of the better future. New fancies filled my mind this evg, but I can't write all. Would that he could be here awhile that we might realize all, but all may end for the best. Fierce battles may be raging there now – God protect & save him! I must pray for him as requested – lone & lonely – must dream of him – my Robere.

Friday April 7th. A mild – wet day – when each leaf and plant seemed visibly to grow, or have grown since yest., though the Spring begun later. Pa says 'tis as advanced now as he has ever known it (a sudden resurrection of nature!) He said that "when the Spanish oak leaves are nearly grown by the 10th of April – it is uncommonly early." There are more fruit blossoms this year than ever seen – wonder if there will be much fruit? Surely – as we have been so long deprived. Misfortunes of every kind attend us now, but we will be made hopeful yet.

The children did not go to school. I had to give lessons to them, but wasted the day – gave in to sweet but idle dreams. Looked over all my fifty volumes of old journals – the silly items of events & feelings in my unimportant life which I have scribbled & kept & wrote things that may bring me to harm – hope not. Their perusal someday may prove interesting if I ever find the time – or there is a congenial heart to sympathize & enjoy – as Robert's would be![23]

I read over his long – precious letter & studied its noble sentiments and avowals & delicate feelings & requests &c. Thought of the long happy past of our love, full of sunbeams & shadows alternating: wondered as to our future destiny! He had asked me to tell him from my journal when our romance began. I find in 1850 – 1 & 2 – our families were very intimate. I stayed there much – loved them all – sad, merry old days. Bobbie was always there or here, but not much favored then

23. Only a few of the fifty journals Emmala refers to have ever surfaced. They have apparently been lost or destroyed in the past 138 years. Two journals, dated 1860 and 1861, are in the possession of a great-grandson in North Carolina. The contents of these journals remain unknown at the time of this publication.

it seems – yet I've no doubt we felt the greatest interest in each other then. I remember the first time we ever met unless as babies when they lived in Pendleton. He rode down here on horseback to our back gate to see Pa on business, I suppose. I remember standing there talking to the clever lad – wonder if he does![24]

In 1853 & 4 we were all very intimate. So many schoolgirls here, he & Mollie devoted, I must have been a little jealous, but think he cared much for me even then. We met often & he wondered just when his happy moments would come. In 51 we chatted in our piazza one night, pointed out Lyra to each other as a star of interest – ran when we saw Mr. Baker coming. All along in the coming years there's much of each other & our meetings & interest, but he was absent much I guess.

In 57 & 8 begun to be more demonstrative on returning from Va. University – attended me to parties – church &c. Serenaded me with violin – asked for my likeness once – which Will Munro had at a celebration of Washington's birthday at the hotel. Feb. 22nd/59. We had a fine time – he came home with me – some soft words &c – which incident he mentions. Says "he has loved & worshipped me since childhood, but didn't mean to reveal so much now" &c.

In the winter of 59 & 60 he began to reveal much. We spent delicious evgs together – in love & quarrels – neither asking or granting much. He was afraid all that time, knowing the serious opposition. "Common family" & no wealth – estranged our families much, to my regret, for the happy old days all over, much as I used to love Maggie & all.

He says there are serious obstacles to overcome – but death to withdraw now after going so far! The night before Lucie & I went to Charleston together – April, 1860 – Waller & he with us, a delicious night of love. He asked me for my likeness – gave me his heart in return – he begs me now for mine. I wish we had exchanged – would that I had his – for I may never now. Opportunities lost & he may be wounded or killed or lost to me forever!

We met again with love & fond adieux when he was off to New York in June/60 to attend medical lectures – estranged awhile – devoted again on his return. Off to the wars with kind partings &c – March 1862 – where he has been ever since, three long years. Home once – one year ago – a short unsatisfactory time – not fondly remembered. He still hesitated from full declarations knowing the uncertainties of our future. A noble principle amid the opposition. He feared he might be forced to act dishonorably were our agreement made. He has written me all this time – not very agreeable or candid letters for a long time – until this winter.

24. The young Robert Broyles had to ride about fifteen miles from Ashtabula Plantation, the Broyles residence outside of Pendleton, to Anderson Court House.

Since communication has been obstructed he has regretted the lost golden opportunities. Been crazy to hear from me and written every chance by hand. Many long, sweet letters – full of devotion – "fervently thine &c." But this last is full of his long hidden feelings – repressed for our own good – because of the advice of old folks with good intentions – though he will decide such things himself.

Yet spoke of his devoted – precious mother – fondly & fears this might kill her. She is proud & opposed & advises him. His greatest love lies between she & I – a hard case – poor boy – what is right? Should I proudly resign all claims? I cannot. Have they a right to sever congenial hearts that fate seems to draw together thus? No time or change or circumstances altered us. No promises either asked or given – strange! He speaks of our overcoming the opposition & if providence directs he hopes to win the heart & hand of the noblest woman living. His souls congenial companion. Could not bear to wed or care more for another love, full of jealousy. I may have had suitors more eloquent & better off – none more devoted.

His heart is so sensitive – he is scarcely to be called unaccountable being in his depressions. Phrenologists tell him he may go crazy – God forbid – yet 'twould be possible were he disappointed & being thus worried about it all. He is miserable, Peter says he speaks of my music charming his soul away. How more blessed than Croesus the man I love &c. I must be free to speak – call him Robert if I prefer, yet he calls me nothing. If we are to bear this may it all grow better – for 'tis joy to get such letters.[25]

Spoke of earning his living in Tenn. or California. I don't relish such places, but could manage all right perhaps. He wants to be a Christian – tries but can't – will still try. May be indeed and if not on earth may we meet in better worlds above! Wish he could come now to see me & talk freely, but hope it may yet end right – if my Robert & I are destined for each other or for whom or what fate? Not sad I hope! God bless him forever!

In the aft Clifton and poor Andrew Moreland had come up – too sad – to his wife's grave. Brought a pirated sheet announcing that Richmond was evacuated! And there was a shadow fell on all our hearts! Yet people do not realize these horrors of war & disaster as they once did – natural but strange. It seems that we are fast turning to total disgrace & destruction and what will be the end? Our proud capital, so long defended, for which so many lives have been sacrificed, given up thus. It is terrible sweet triumph for the vandal foe. Were all our cities & ports fallen fast and now what have we to depend on – can we succeed?

But there were four days fighting between Grant's & Lee's armies, we driven out of Richmond in such haste – not much saved – awful! But who of our loved ones

25. A reference to Croesus, King of Lydia in 540 B.C.E., and his legendary wealth.

may have fallen! Perhaps my Robert's manly form & noble heart lies among the wounded or dead and we cannot hear. Too sad to think so – heaven help him! Would that I could hear all particulars soon or that I could him again & know all!

Sat Quietly talking & singing sad old songs. I must dream of R & write to him. Mamie & Cora gone to musical meeting again at Wilhites – Vie here. Sad night.

Sat. April 8th. A cool – bright morning. A radiant, lovely day. The fresh green earth & sunny sky so calm & lovely, but I spent it all in dreaming of the sad fate of Richmond & our soldiers – in reading my precious letter from Robert and replying to it kindly I thought, though he always thinks otherwise! But will it even reach him now?

The children all walked to the river for flowers &c. In aft I went out to the Bap. ch. as promised with some servants to have it well swept & dusted as 'tis so dirty there & no one to attend to it regularly. Always dirty – too bad – our churches sadly neglected these days. Some girls there running about & Betty Clark helped shake carpets &c. Lula Sloan decorated her father's grave with flowers &c, but our graveyard needs attention sadly.[26]

I came home late – or rather stopped awhile to chat with Jane Fant where some girls would have me play & sing some; they had a letter from their brother at Richmond & I hoped to know particulars of the fighting there and the fate of my friends! But feared I would not hear again soon, but thank heaven – I did![27]

As I came home – met Theodore who joined me with delight having just come from our garden gathering flowers to inhale. He walked immediately back & sat down by me on the luxuriant bed of thrift blossoms – the myriad of sweet pink blooms which we crushed to death. We sat there to admire the garden – the fading twilight & lovely moonlight & all – for awhile, but he kept staying & talking nonsense which I should have indulged perhaps – until we missed out suppers & sat for several hours in a perfect Paradise he said. Thinking that was the best we could make of life – a blessed hour – for him, such as he does not otherwise enjoy!

I had my guitar and sang many sweet ballads which he loved, but not for the sentiment. He joined in singing now & then – very well. Repeated much poetry to me as usual from Byron, Shelly &c. Exquisite & pointed – some of it. He told

26. Margaret "Betty" J. Clark (Clarke), wife of Anderson merchant J. B. Clarke, had twin sons, John H. and William and five other children at the time of the 1860 census (Vandiver, *Traditions,* 29; *1860 Census,* Anderson District, 156).

Tallulah Sloan (age 15) was the daughter of Mary L. Sloan (33) and sister to Curran (13), Thomas (12), and Luella (8) (*1860 Census,* Anderson District, 157).

27. Jane Fant was the daughter of widow Esther Fant, proprietor of Fant's Boarding House. Jane was the oldest of seven children, including brothers Woodard, Preston, and Joseph. Jane Fant wed Marshall Clinkscales on July 17, 1867 (*1860 Census,* Anderson District, 157); see Reed, *Journals,* Appendix F.

funny jokes & flattered in a pleasing way – because he seemed sincere and I know he does value me more than others. Said "you are so pretty tonight – your hand so small & lovely – you look like fine pictures of Catherine 2nd of Russia. You are my queen, my star, my opiate, my adorable – you know you are."

Disconnected sentences nicely intended yet he expects & asks nothing to my delight – has no intentions but to be edified &c. Does he believe me capable of a single absorbing passion? Too genial & general.

When I spoke of my letter of 14 pages &c he wondered & said "such a letter could only have been written by a man for a woman!," but I joked it off – however true. He hoped R was killed – or "my soldier friend" as he said, & I should write him all the letters. Cruel! Pray not – yet whilst I sat there in music & nonsense tonight my own best love may have been wounded or dying for liberty & loved ones on the bloody battle fields of Richmond – for they say his family has such a presentiment. God Forbid! I didn't know then there was a letter from him to me in the house or should not have idly dallied there with a false one, who could never fill my heart or prize a true woman &c!

In asking "Why he didn't come to teach me Italian" – he said sincerely – "Miss E you would teach me more serious language that would be death to me and you would be no scholar I fear!" Which might be true too & so 'tis well not to attempt to learn it together. He begged me to sing Wilt thou be gone & add love! – but I would not. And so after all nonsense he departed. He serves to while away many rare pleasant hours by his refined intellect & tastes &c but does not satisfy the heart as my R would do by his presence.

I went in to get a little scolding from Ma for staying out. Read news in the Augusta paper of the evacuation of Richmond and Pres't Davis proclamation from Danville, Va. – bidding us struggle & hope on that all is not lost. But there were several days of hard fighting & many thousands killed & wounded. Who were they – we all long to know! Dreadful! After all the long and glorious defense – Lee's army thus humiliated! How do they feel – where are they now? Heaven help them & give us future success! But truly our affairs are at a low ebb, many despairing. I will hope on – hope ever. What costly sacrifices we are offering for liberty! Hope Peter & Robert safe.[28]

28. Emmala refers to President Davis's last proclamation, read at Danville, Virginia, April 5, 1865. It started with an explanation for the evacuation of Richmond, but does indeed end stridently: ". . . meet the foe with fresh defiance, and with unconquered and unconquerable hearts" (E. A. Pollard, *Echoes from the South: Comprising the Most Important Speeches, Proclamations, and Public Acts Emanating from the South during the Late War.* [1866; rept. Westport, Conn.: Negro Universities Press, 1970], 203–5; Allen Tate, *Jefferson Davis, His Rise and Fall: A Biographical Narrative* [1929; rept. New York, J. S. Sanders & Company, 1998], 274–75); also see William E. Dodd, *Jefferson Davis* (1907; rpt. Lincoln: University of Nebraska Press, 1997).

To my joy I found another long, dear letter from him, but alas! I had given him cause for sadness & reproach – had worried his sensitive heart – until he is almost crazy as he fears he may be! My poor darling – such scenes & so far away & thinking only of such trials &c – sad! My two letters he rec'd – rather cold & reproachful. He was grieved & cut – didn't know how to reply when all obstacles should be removed from between us – or was it Providence trying to thus sever & prevent a [illegible] of our hearts? He couldn't think so – such congenial natures must be united, not stronger ties &c. Will it ever be now?

He joked about when he would have to come to wed someday – joked about others – but meant me the darling. How strange – all this is not of us, but comes so natural! He was grieved at my tone & begged me to be more unsuspicious & confident & kind &c and I never meant otherwise.

Wrote of the terrible thunder of artillery he heard – their time coming to suffer. Safe so far – 31st of March at night – thank heaven! And me sick from last night – mighty changes have taken place – fighting & retreating & what now and is he safe? I pray my Father that he may be spared to me – my "heart's true congenial companion" he said and bring him safe back to me some day – if well for us – or grant him relief & happiness eternal & a better letter from me to him &c.

He asked would I sign my text Melodia – Emmala – or Miss Reed. He preferred the second – "May I?" Yes indeed – I long to have him call me "Emmala" as a right – which he claims in some things after our years of intimacy, but then he bid me adieu – can it be for the last time? Oh no – I must see & hear from him again – my noble hearted, devoted lover! Must dream of him tonight & pray for us both & the future. But I cannot dream of him it seems.[29]

Sunday April 9th A cool – cloudy day. All went to S. S. to practice singing for the celebration today. A good many people there – some strangers come here with this State Treasury Dept – which I fear may attract the Yankees – & there is rumours of a raid by Kirk from Ash[e]ville N. C. by Greenville. I trembled but hope they've been repulsed.[30]

29. Robert knew that Emmala used the pen name "Melodia" to write anonymous columns in local newspapers (the author has yet to locate an actual article written by the mysterious Melodia). Victorian propriety often postponed familiarities like the use of first names, but such formality between cousins and lovers appears rather unusual.

30. Sunday, April 9, 1865, was the day that General Robert E. Lee surrendered the Army of Northern Virginia at Appomattox Court House. Emmala was mistaken with her allusion to the "State" Treasury Department. In fact the Confederate States Treasury Note Bureau was about to set up a printing press in Johnson University's central hall, making Anderson one of the last locations for such operations in the Confederacy. The Anderson treasury operation required the services of Charlestonian W. N. Leitch to run the mint presses. Other personnel

We had near 60 S.S. scholars – boys & girls – & a dozen teachers perhaps. Mr. Hall there as Superintendent – sings very well, but worthless otherwise. All blame him for not going to the wars – loiters at home. Mr. Murray delivered a very sensible address on the importance & pleasure of attending Sabbath school & training up children in this way – to worship & know God & sing his praise – & the fearful results of Sabbath breaking. Here are the best schools now – so many orphans &c in the land. Hope some good effect may be produced.[31]

We all sang with a glad spirit. Many sweet hymns – near a dozen – which the congregation enjoyed. In the light – calls to S. School – Oh do not be discouraged, Rest for the weary – sweetly singing – Days & weeks &c – all sweet. I led a second & directed all. The girls & boys answered in "Say brothers or sisters will you meet us?" Reminded me of Augusta S.S. & Greenville. Wish ours was more flourishing & we all were useful & good.

I read one of Spurgeon's sermons on my return – on "the Faithful friend" – would that I could hear such sermons or Mr. Kramers preaching in Augusta. The whole gloomy aft. I was thinking of the fate of country & loved ones – rereading Robert's two last long, precious letters of confession and replying to the last freely, but when & how will he ever receive them? When shall we meet & what's our future? Heaven direct! I must read now – Vie gone home.

Eleanor attracting too many beaux at the Method. Epis. church &c. Thinks of nothing else & poor Andrew Moreland is here – but they must not meet &c Would that R was with me – all my own – as we [are] free in heart. Will it be well?

Monday April 10th A real dark rainy day – not variable, a dreamy day too for I could do nothing but dream of my beloved. Read paper first, giving the speech of Mr. Long in the Yankee Congress in Feb. showing the weakness & folly of the North. Their strength failing their war debt left for posterity – far greater than that accumulated in 800 years by all the wars of England with its much greater resources than could never be paid &c, of the moral degredation in the North &c. Will such people conquer us?

---

included twenty-two engravers and lithographers, all Scottish men and women, plus four young ladies from Virginia who signed the notes (Dickson, *Journeys,* 125–27).

Lt. Colonel George W. Kirk was in command of the Third North Carolina Mounted Infantry Regiment, "Kirk's Raiders," a band of partisan guerillas who terrorized the North Carolina mountain regions, but the journal entry refers, in fact, to the Eleventh Michigan Cavalry under the command of General Simeon B. Brown (Thomas Bland Keys, "The Federal Pillage of Anderson, South Carolina: Brown's Raid," *South Carolina Historical Magazine* 76 [April 1975]: 80–86).

31. Marion Hall was a refugee from Charleston who has not been further identified.

We hear today only rumours from the front of other battles & great slaughter to all. Oh they must be suffering on the bloodied dark fields of Va. where we fear our wounded can meet with no attentions. Richmond – Petersburg – Charlottesville &c all gone with their hospitals, medicines and appliances needed. What will become of them & who of my friends are there? I tremble to hear of the fate of my Robere. Heaven save and bless him.

I gave music lessons, knit &c – read the controversy between Sec. Siddon (of war) and the self-willed, presumptuous – sensible, Gov. Joe Brown of Ga. – who will have every thing his own way. Wanted to keep all the militia in Ga. – when ordered out by Pres. &c. Then I tried to spin some cotton on our nice new wheel for which we had to pay 150 lbs of flour. I succeeded very well. I like it – if forced to the necessity in some Western home "Tenn. or California" with the loved one! But will such ever be my fate?[32]

I read over all the package of his letters. Only 43 in three years absence, but there were many intervals & misunderstandings formerly. More letters rec'd from him since the New Years than ever before & more precious and will it continue so or all over – God forbid! I still have my long replies of encouragement &c written to send him, but will they ever be rec'd & enjoyed or what will be their fate – to bring happiness I hope!

At night there was to be an eclipse of the moon 'twas said and explained scientifically by Dr. Gibbes here from Charleston, but it was cloudy and couldn't be observed at all – 'though the glimpses revealed of the silvery orb 'neath floating vapours shew no such signs. After 1 I must watch a little longer.[33]

32. Confederate Secretary of War James Alexander Seddon (1815–80) of Virginia served in his cabinet post from November 1862 until he resigned in January 1865 (Burton J. Hendrick, *Statesmen of the Lost Cause: Jefferson Davis and His Cabinet* [New York: Literary Guild of America, 1939], 324–29).

Joseph Emerson Brown (1821–94) was born in Pickens District, South Carolina. He attended the "field schools" of Anderson District, where he met the three men he would later claim encouraged him to succeed in public life: "Dr. O. R. Broyles of Pendleton, the doctor's father Mayor Aaron Broyles of Calhoun and . . . Judge J. P. Reed." Brown graduated from Yale Law School in 1846 and was elected as Georgia's governor in 1856. Reelected three more times, Brown was in office throughout the war years. A staunch state-rights advocate, Brown conflicted with many of Jefferson Davis's policies till the end of the Confederacy, especially opposing handing over state militia to the Confederate Army (Joseph H. Parks, *Joseph E. Brown of Georgia* [Baton Rouge: Louisiana State University Press, 1977], 3).

33. Dr. Lewis R. Gibbes was a renowned scientist and president of Charleston's Elliott Society for Natural History (Walter J. Fraser, *Charleston! Charleston!: The History of a Southern City* [Columbia: University of South Carolina Press, 1989], 226).

A soft – mild oderous night the apple blossoms – lilacs &c perfume the garden – a sweet scene below and sweet music heard in the distance. How different & horrible the scenes presented in Virginia perhaps or elsewhere – of the wounded & dying and anguished. Pray God be merciful! If my Robert lies 'neath this pale moon dying would that like Irene in Macaria – I could rush my noble "Ansel Aubrey" to cheer and sustain through all, but this is impossible! Hope 'tis not true, yet may we meet ere long & both be blest! I must read & dream & pray &c tonight. Fannie Smith came to Reeve's & went home – strange. I heard the first whipporwill singing its mournful chant tonight – sweet.[34]

Tues. April 11th Pleasant day arranging vases. Gave music lessons to Ella Davidson who had heard that Pres't Davis was to be here today – much excited – all a mistake, of course. Great excitement about the Treasury Dept. coming here – crowds of ladies & men – who will crowd the houses and ruin the market &c. Our whole country turned topsy-turvy. The revolution reached a dreadful crisis. Our cities & forces all gone it seems. No money, no stores – no ammunition – guns – no salt – or anything. It cannot last much longer surely! How sudden & dreadful this crisis – what a fall for Carolina – Virginia & all. Devestated by the foe, negroes on an equality, Lee's grand army whipped & demoralized. We fear thousands killed & wounded & no hospital arrangements made for them I fear – or broken up – defeat everywhere – Providence against us, but we will still hope![35]

I read Gov. Brown's last message before the Ga. Leg. – extra session called to abuse the Pres't & bad management of affairs – for he has acted very independently and made many enemies lately.

Eleanor & I walked out to Col. Orr's to see Mr. Leitch's family, having known his daughter Mattie before; they have lost everything by fire in Charleston & Columbia & come here now to settle awhile. He is at the head of the Treasury Department in this State and it is being rumored here to the regret of all as it will

34. *Macaria, or Altars of Sacrifice* was written by Augusta Jane Evans (1835–1909) of Columbus, Georgia. The novel, published in 1863, was a strong wartime commentary on the potentially detrimental effects of emancipation, enflaming soldiers and citizens on both sides of the issue (Wakelyn, *Biographical Dictionary,* 180).

The Reeveses were Charleston refugees Matthew and Ellen J. Reeves. Matthew, a professor of music before the war, apparently moved his wife and six children to a safer location. It is likely they had family in the Anderson area (*1860 Census,* Charleston, 422; Vandiver, *Traditions,* 12, 192).

35. Ella Davidson was the daughter of Colonel James Wood Davidson, Thirteenth Regiment South Carolina Volunteers, a unit largely comprised of Anderson District men (American Genealogical Research Institute, *Davidson Family History* [Washington, D. C.: Heritage Press, 1978], 77–78).

attract Yankee raids we fear & be so hard to accommodate so many more people here with lodging &c too bad[36]

We found only Mrs. Orr at home. (Mattie at school in Greenville.) Mary Waller & Catherine Gadsden there sewing &c and Col. Orr just home from Richmond. The last Congress to be held there perhaps, but he was rather sick & depressed on account of our many disasters – though he is always blue. Never been sanguine of our success I believe & dispirited the people too much as one of our public men – yet cautious too.[37]

They urged me to remain to dinner which was very good & plain. Their friend Hon. W. H. Trescott of Charleston – now of Pendleton – former secretary of Legation to England &c&c came in abruptly. Greeted me with due obeisance &c and too much flattery. Wanted at once to drink my health in brandy – which I declined – he loves it far too well.[38]

36. W. Y. Leach, South Carolina's chief treasury officer, was in charge of the Confederate Treasury office in Anderson. The treasury workers joined the growing crowd of refugees from all over South Carolina and Georgia who gathered at Anderson Court House. In August 1865 U.S. President Andrew Johnson appointed a W. Y. Leitch surveyor of customs for the Port of Charleston Customs House, a job he held before the war (*Directory of Charleston, S.C. 1860: To Which Is Added a Business Directory, 1860,* vol. 1, *Charleston* [Savannah, Ga.: W. Eugene Fershaw, 1860], 91; Dickson, *Journeys,* 125; *Charleston Courier,* Aug. 31, 1865; Richard Cecil Todd, *Confederate Finance* [Athens, University of Georgia Press, 1955], 17, 88).

37. James Lawrence Orr (1822–73), perhaps Anderson's most significant son, lived in a large white mansion named Arlington that displayed wide porticos, frontal columns, and a golden cupola. Raised in Anderson District, Orr graduated from the University of Virginia in 1839 and published the *Anderson Gazette,* which he purchased from Judge Reed, who was also a partner in Orr's law firm.

Mary Jane Marshall Orr married J. L. in 1844 and gave birth to Eliza (1845, d. in childhood), Martha or "Mattie" (1847), James Lawrence, Jr. (1852), Samuel or "Sammie" (1855), Mary (1858), Amelia (1860), and Christopher (1862) (Leemhuis, *James L. Orr,* iv–v, 12, 13; *South Carolina Biographical Dictionary,* 240–42; Patricia L. Faust, *Historical Times Illustrated Encyclopedia of the Civil War* [New York: Harper & Row, 1986], 549; Wakelyn, *Biographical Dictionary,* 334–35; *1860 Census,* Anderson District, 159).

38. William Henry Trescot (1822–98) was a South Carolina native who studied law at Harvard and started a Charleston practice in 1843. Trescot, an accomplished historian, published three books on diplomacy and the early republic during the 1850s. Appointed acting secretary of state in June, 1860, he was an intermediary between the secessionists and President Buchanan. During the war Trescot served on the staff of General Roswell S. Ripley and in the diplomatic corps, but returned to Washington soon after the war to serve as a Southern spokesman to President Andrew Johnson. He died in Pendleton, South Carolina, on May 4, 1898. Trescot achieved a degree of immortality by writing the text for the Confederate Soldiers Monument on the statehouse grounds in Columbia (Edgar, *South Carolina,* 356; Vandiver, *Traditions,* 57, 262, 263; Vandiver also spells the name "Trescott").

After dinner in promenading the piazza we had a discussion about superiority of mere physical & sensual over intellectual & moral enjoyments. He argued for the former – I the last, but merely to draw me out, I thought, as he was so quick to seize all points, but I answered only from impulse – feeling every connection. He is a rude, worldly man – cares only for earthly pleasures, said I spoke as a true woman – her intentions were always wonderful & pure &c. Wish I could remember all his smart sayings & 'tis such intellectual discussions & society as I enjoy – wish I could be thrown with often – yet his influences, like most men of the world, would be injurious I fear.

I came in & sang & played for them. Col. Orr likes it – calls for my favorites. "Gentle Annie" "Willie _____" &c. Last rose of summer &c Seemed to enjoy all. Mr. Trescott pretended to like none of it – no taste or ear – "played too fast &c" – but pretended to be a critic. Loves the voice without the instrument. Says I play brilliantly, don't sing with enough feeling in which I thought I excelled. Says I am one of those cool – calm, placid blondes – amiable & pleasant but not ardent, can't feel deeply &c. Wonder if that is true? Probably I do not feel as much as others, but I thought I did.[39]

As I started home – without his having talked to Col. Orr any – who spoke of expecting to be hung by the Yankees &c, he offered to walk with me & came off abruptly – though Cool. and all laughed at him and he talked to me in such a way! Wonder if 'tis mere gallantry he uses to all – if he is trying to lead me on or test me, or he especially admires – or what – the old wretch with his wife & children! He was very respectful – save to criticize a lady's track he saw &c.

Urged me to sing for him in the woods – then he could judge freely of my powers – to sing "The Jay Bird" out on a hickory limb – as we heard one then & other nonsense, but I could not; his ideas of perfect enjoyment a rare dinner table & guests & conversation &c. I don't like such surroundings for mental enjoyments. He said he would follow me anywhere. Begged that I should not pay any visits but walk on with him &c, until I really wondered what he meant, for he urged it so, yet I am glad I finally resisted. Though 'tis pleasant to meet up with an intellectual man. Talked & appreciative & admired as he seemed at least drew me out & raised my self esteem, as I think I excited his &c, but 'twas all folly.

I went in the nice new cottage of the Leitch's, but he followed in only to get another drink I suppose – shocking. When I advised not, he said "You would not grant my request, so I won't grant yours" & that's the last I saw of him. Went off

39. "Gentle Annie," a popular song by Stephen Foster, was written in 1856. "'Tis the Last Rose of Summer" (1813) was written by Richard Millikin, with words by Thomas Moore (Roger Lax and Frederick Smith, *The Great Song Thesaurus* [New York: Oxford University Press, 1989], 240, 397).

to Pendleton without an adieu. Very well, but wonder when I'll meet the little man again and if he will behave strangely.

I came on by to see the Murrays. Found dear Mrs. M sick in bed & troubled about many things. I guess Fannie & Florence Earle there ready to take Angie & Jeffie Edwards home with them for the night, much worried about the bad news from Va. & all & horrible fate of her idolized brother Preston &c. I stopped in to see the Sloans awhile. was suprized to have Mrs. S teaze me about "my bright eyed soldier in Va. – hold on to him & don't take (Theodore)." Wonder where she heard it, but 'tis getting too common – talk of R & I.[40]

On my way home Theodore joined me, delighted & with a visable blush walked in & sat on the steps without a word and talked on very pleasantly. Much interested in all my affairs. Advizing our removal in case of a raid – now rumoured. We invited him to stay for the evening – with a light handed tea, which I left to he & Eleanor (she had a letter from Hal Mosely safe & true).[41]

Then I sang for Theo & he seemed charmed as usual. Couldn't bear to be disturbed by the coming of others. Had just recommended to me "Forget me not." The only sentiment he ever thus applied directly & all he said more sincere – when a very merry crowd entered on a raid as they say. Liz & Emily Bleckley, Lou Wilkes, Becky Webb, Sallie Cresswell & Kate Hammond. All rather awed by Theo's dignity

40. Elias (1823–97) and Harriet Earle had six children. Before the war Elias Earle, in partnership with his brother-in-law James Harrison (m. Sarah Earle), operated a dry goods mercantile in Andersonville, South Carolina, and another in the Anderson Court House square with Alexander Evins and John C. Griffin. Though portrayed as a "sickly man," Elias Earle was known to be one of Anderson's wealthiest citizens, with "near 100 slaves" and vast land holdings in 1849.

E. Preston was the only surviving son of Elias and Harriet when Wilton Robinson Earle died in the battle of First Manassas at twenty-three years of age. In the 1870s Preston became editor of the *Anderson Journal,* a weekly newspaper of the day. Of the three Earle daughters, Mary married Joe Berry Sloan, Florence married Dr. James H. Thornwell, and "Fannie" (Francis) never married (Simpson, *Old Pendleton,* 131; Vandiver, *Traditions,* 84, 151, 163, 167; *1860 Census,* Anderson District, 290; Vandiver Report, Item #3; Smith, *Book of the Dead,* 114–15).

Jeffersonia (22) and Agnes (20) Edwards were two of Claudia Murray's sisters. Other sisters included Angeline (25) and Eliza(beth) J. (31). All these women taught school as a vocation: Jeffie (1842–1919) and Agnes or "Angie" (1833–1912) taught at Mrs. Murray's home school after the war. Angeline and Elizabeth both taught at the Johnson Female University when Claudia Edwards Murray was the institution's principal. In 1854 Elizabeth Edwards joined the university staff as principal of the Academic Department (Vandiver, *Traditions,* 112, 119, 122; *1860 Census,* Anderson District, 155; *Le Bas Bleu,* vol. 1, no. 5 [Aug. 1854], 2; Smith, *Book of the Dead,* 115).

41. Hal Mosely was probably Henry T. Mosely of Twelve Mile Township in Pickens District (*1860 Census,* Pickens District, 125).

awhile: the Secret Word or proverbs – very good. Theo showed most aptness, acted his part finely. Billy, a clever posing chap soon off for the front. All left late & in the soft moonlight Theo hesitated to leave me, yet all the time I was thinking of my noble soldier's fate in Va. for we hear that great battles are still going on there. No particulars.[42]

Wed. April 12th A grand house cleaning day here – Mrs. Pinkind giving Eleanor lessons. Urged me to sing at her concert &c. I wrote letters to Julia &c, but can't get off my long reply to R & will he ever reach it or reply? I hope so.[43]

In aft went visiting – trying to pay up all I owe – so irksome! Walked to Sam Brown's. Scott as excitable as ever, but a nice person. Charlotte a nice girl. Elvira Belcher there too. We all discussed the news painfully. the death of their brother Dave Gaillard seems to shock them much. Can never be reconciled to the war of Pres't or soldiers.[44]

42. Louisa "Lou" C. Wilkes, was the thirty-six-year-old widow of attorney Samuel "S. M." Wilkes, the first Anderson man killed in the Civil War. The couple had one six-year-old child, named Willie. Captain Samuel M. Wilkes was adjutant of the South Carolina Fourth Infantry (*1860 Census,* Anderson District, 261; Hewett, *Confederate Soldiers,* 336).

Rebecca "Becky" Webb was a favorite of the Reed children and the adults. Becky, the only child of Elijah Webb's first wife, Rebecca Gaillard, was apparently raised by a stepmother, Rosa Waller Webb, who had three more children, Rosa, Charles, and Warren (*1860 Census,* Anderson District, 258; Simpson, *Old Pendleton,* 212–13; Vandiver, *Traditions,* 13, 14, 47, 113, 127, 257; Dickson, *Journeys,* 137; UDC, *South Carolina Women in the Confederacy,* 369–71). The last citation refers to a contribution to the publication titled "The Yankee Raid on Anderson" written by R. C. Hoyt (Mrs. Col. James Hoyt of Greenville, S. C.) (Lucas, *Early Anderson,* 55).

Sarah "Sallie" Cresswell (b. May 9, 1844; d. Dec. 17, 1919) wed George Reese Cherry; they are buried at the Presbyterian Old Stone Church (Smith, *Book of the Dead,* 93).

Catherine "Kate" Hammond was the daughter of William H. and Mary A. Hammond, very successful farmers. Fourteen-year-old Kate had four siblings, William, Benjamin, Jarond, and Oscar (*1860 Census,* Anderson District, 162).

43. Mrs. Pinkind, also known as Madam Girard (Gerrard), was a Polish countess exiled from her homeland. She was once an operatic vocalist of considerable merit who somehow lost her singing voice. Louise Vandiver wrote that Mrs. Pinkind was "the first woman to play the violin on stage in America." She went from New York to Charleston, where she married, then to Pendleton for a summer season; she eventually moved to Anderson. She had two children, both born in Charleston, Antoinette (Nettie) and Anthony or (Tony). Nettie later married Norton Hunter of Pendleton (Vandiver, *Traditions,* 23; Smith, *Book of the Dead,* 307; Simpson, *Old Pendleton,* 183).

44. Sam Brown (1815–85) was a successful merchant. He had two brothers, Scott and Daniel, also local merchants (Vandiver, *Traditions,* 26, 137, 270; *1860 Census,* Anderson District, 257; Smith, *Book of the Dead,* 47).

We disputed affairs rather. I went then to Mr. Hydes. Mrs. H & Eliza very pleasant & good & chatty. Her Sunday school scholars think her perfect & she is a model of a pious – devoted – modest – useful – studious – happy young lady. She walked with me as far as Georgia Brown's, the little widow who rec'd me with smiles & flattery as usual & many questions about R.[45]

Walked home late & tired. Sang some new music at night. I found Andrew Moreland here to call on both of us – he said – but with Eleanor more than pleased of course. Though his sweet little "darling" has been dead but for two weeks now and he talks of her very feelingly & may have loved & regretted her. Yet he is not heartbroken & anxious for another it seems already. Clings too much to his old love. Tells her of all his experiences. Asks sympathy, yet interested in her affairs as a brother. Only preparing for hereafter I fear. Yet he was very respectful &c Talked to me very properly with thanks for attentions to her "life not worth living now," but alas! How faithless we all are to the dead even the most loving & beloved, how "inhuman" R considers this. Would he be so? No, but I fear I would, my temperament is so variable &c I fear, but better prove our happiness.

At night Eleanor & I went over to see the Reeves – John & Mattie & Capt. Daniels, their boarder – Clerk of Court here. A wounded soldier, fearfully disabled. has suffered for three years with his leg. So lame & has yet to be amputated. Soon may kill him. He dreads it of course, but chatted very merrily. Was a graduate of the Citadel in Charleston. May be right smart, but the polish has worn off by rude associations in Texas &c. John & Mat very happy there I suppose.[46]

Elvira Brown Belcher was the widow of teacher Manning Belcher, a native of Massachusetts, who established the Old Field School near Tugaloo Creek in 1848. The 1860 census shows her son Edward residing with Daniel Brown (Elvira's father), but she is not listed (Vandiver, *Traditions,* 99, 100; *1860 Census,* Anderson District, 157).

Dave Gaillard died October 7, 1864, on the Darbytown Road in Northern Virginia (Randolph W. Kirkland, Jr., comp., *Broken Fortunes: South Carolina Soldiers, Sailors, and Citizens Who Died in the Service of Their Country and State in the War for Southern Independence, 1861–1865* [Charleston, S.C.: South Carolina Historical Society, 1995], 123).

45. Ann E. Hyde, wife of Charleston merchant Linnus Hyde, was a refugee who transported her large family to the relative safety of Anderson. She may have been kin to E. F. Hyde of Townville. Eliza was twenty-one years old in 1865 (*1860 Census,* Charleston, Ward 1, 196).

Georgia Ann Brown was the widow of Private John J. Brown of the Second South Carolina Rifles, who died in October of 1862 from wounds received at the Battle of Malvern Hill or Gaines Mill, Virginia. She raised three sons and lived on River Street, near Silverbrook, a park and cemetery on the outskirts of Anderson (Vandiver, *Traditions,* 270; Smith, *Book of the Dead,* 46; Kirkland, *Broken Fortunes,* 42).

46. Captain John W. Daniels (1833–1901) was a schoolteacher raised in Pendleton who "got up a company" of local men when the war started. Later Daniels was elected Captain,

Thurs. April 13th Pleasant day – quiet at home, worrying over children's old summer clothes &c. Angie Edwards & Jemima Nevitt called late. Angie has been teaching in the family of a relative of theirs in Fairfield – where the Yankees have been & burned their house &c. She almost met them carrying a pistol – related the heroism of Mrs. Crosby &c.[47]

At night I rec'd letters from Albert Blackman safe with Johnston's army in N.C. & Dr. Barney McMillan still at Prof. Judson's in Greenville – came there some weeks ago from prison at Camp Chase – a man full of hope on his way home is now a child in weakness, but he must be recovering. Hopes to go down soon. Begs me to write & cheer the invalid – as I shall certainly do. He was noble specimen of manhood – so large & strong & fine looking. So moral & good, a Brigade Surgeon in Johnston's army & now I wonder if he is broken down completely & not thirty yet. He was at the Medical College of N. Y. with my R. Sent me too a Yankee paper "Baltimore Clipper" – full of their boasts and exultation over our downfall, Alas! They are living as well as ever – we have nothing – why is this our destiny?[48]

Company L, Palmetto Sharp Shooters. The place and nature of his wounds are unknown, but he lived a long life regardless of their severity. He later married Julia D. Webb, an instructor at the Johnson Female University. Daniels served as a clerk of courts in Anderson and continued to teach in the town (Vandiver, *Traditions,* 14, 156; Smith, *Book of the Dead,* 28; Simpson, *Old Pendleton,* 19; Hewett, *Confederate Soldiers,* 120; Tom C. Wilkinson, *Early Anderson County, S.C., Newspapers, Marriages and Obituaries, 1842–1882,* 148).

47. Angeline Edwards was possibly from Georgia.

Jemima L. Nevitt (1832–1924) was possibly the wife of R. C. Nevitt, sergeant with the Palmetto Rifles and a member of the Baptist church. (Smith, *Book of the Dead,* 287; *1860 Census,* Anderson District, 186; Vandiver, *Traditions,* 224).

Fairfield County, South Carolina, organized in 1798, was located eighty miles east of Anderson. The county seat is Winnsboro (Writers' Program, South Carolina, *Palmetto Place Names* [1941; rept. Spartanburg, S.C.: The Reprint Company, 1975], 14, 15).

Emmaline Nevitt Crosby (age 35) was the wife of David A. Crosby (38), a local merchant. The couple had three daughters, Bettie M., Jemima L, and Ramah, who later wed John H. Clark (*1870 Census,* Anderson County, 434; Smith, *Book of the Dead,* 94).

48. Brigade Surgeon Albert Blackman was most likely on his way home after Johnston's Army surrendered in North Carolina.

Charles H. Judson was a professor of mathematics and president of Furman University, which was closed for the duration of the war. Judson, a Connecticut native, graduated from the University of Virginia and served as president of Furman until 1878. Judson and wife Emily, a native Virginian, resided in Greenville along with in-laws Charles and Ada Judson. The Charles H. Judson Female College of Greenville remained open throughout the war years

An Augusta paper gave us some news but not much. Lee's army & Grant's fighting at Danville & beyond – must be great losses – in taking Richmond. 'Tis said they lost 60,000 – we 15,000 & several officers – A.P. Hill & a son of Gen. Lee &c and how many of the noble brave – who knows! Dreadful sacrifice & all for nothing – yet we will not quite despair. Mobile & Montgomery still hold out – a sad state of affairs in Charleston – negro celebrations – all at schools &c – shocking![49]

Friday April 14 A cool – pleasant day – arranging house & flowers &c. Wanted to go to grand-pa's but our horse is lame and couldn't drive – too late to walk. Pa gone to Greenville – a R.R. meeting. Some applications to board ladies of the Treasury Dep't – don't feel inclined. When prepared to go we learned that one of the horses was lame – so we would have to walk or stay & we had to make up our minds to go today – yet too late to walk four miles by dinner & I dreaded it awfully. Mamie, Lucie & I started out to walk but found an empty carriage going that way of the Mansfields. So we got in & rode halfway, to our delight. Had rather a tiresome walk afterwards – pleasant – the green leaves coming out – few wild flowers scattered about – violets in abundance &c. We reached there late. All well, but Aunt Anna, who had been sick for sometime (not bad). Dr. Holland came down to see her – high prices talked.[50]

(Archie Vernon Huff, Jr., *Greenville: The History of the City and County in the South Carolina Piedmont* [Columbia: University of South Carolina Press, 1995], 124, 165, 201–2; *1860 Census,* Greenville District, 419).

49. The last days of the war were chaotic. Neglected telegraph lines operated sporadically and were unreliable, as were the railroads. Travelers arrived constantly with newspapers, rumors, and conflicting reports. Lt. General Ambrose Powell "A. P." Hill was in fact killed at the Petersburg siege lines on April 2. General Lee surrendered the Army of Northern Virginia at Appomattox Court House, Virginia, on April 9, and the Confederate defenders of Mobile, Alabama surrendered April 12. On that same day Union General James Wilson's cavalry entered Montgomery, Alabama, the first Confederate capital (Denny, *Civil War Years,* 552–57).

50. Judge Reed was on the board of directors for the Greenville and Columbia Railroad.

Physician W. T. Holland and his extended family were planters from the Fair Play area of the county. Jennette Holland, eleven years younger than her husband, had two sons (as of 1860), Samuel (9) and David (7). William Holland (twin of W. T. or born within same year) and his wife Evaline (five years his senior) had three children, Sarah, Robert, and Nancy)Vandiver, *Traditions,* 155, 258; *1860 Census,* Anderson District, 269).

Lucie "Lucy" Eoline Reed (b. 1857) grew up in Anderson and, like her sisters, received her education there (Vandiver, *Traditions,* 272).

Vie as ever. All had letters & papers much pleased. Aunt Liz writes she spent $10,000 for corn since Christmas – heavy! That Uncle Ned was now in the Dep't of Sec. Trenholm. Lucie & I enjoyed a talk about R. She admires him & urges me to marry him. We will be so happy & move away together. When will he ever come – no news of him from nowhere.[51]

Had a nice dinner and started home after four to walk, but Henry came for us in the wagon going to mill & took us up so we jogged along home very pleasantly. Tired – no news at night – sang some – an April shower. Must write & read & dream & pray. Rumours today of French recognition – peace – I pray so![52]

Sat. April 15th A dark – rainy day – every tree & shrub heavy with green – dew laden leaves. I tried to sew & teach the children &c, but but could not resist the inclination to read scraps of poetry & write letters to Dr. Barnie, my Robere & soldier friends.

A refugee lady came to try & get board here: Mrs. Pensifoy of Charleston. Niece of Dr. Barnie belonging to the Treasury Dp't – all forced here, but can find no lodging I fear. Our hearts have not suffered enough yet to make us – merciful! Pa refuses to take any – 'though we may yet be compelled. We have not yet endured our share of suffering & will it come upon us? Heaven protect![53]

At sunset the clouds dispersed and the evening was gloriously beautiful, with its dripping world of leaves & flowers. We gathered some to send to friends. I was at the gate when Dr. Broyles' servant passed with the mail & longing to know if there was anything from Robert, if he was alive – I asked to look at it – not thinking then how it might appear or be reported. I found nothing from him, but the girl

51. Elizabeth Rice (1799–1866) and Dr. Herbert (1797–1866) Hammond lived near Augusta, Georgia, then moved to Anderson District. The Reed family called Dr. Herbert "Uncle Ned." The Hammonds' children included Stacy, Julia, Lucie, and Josie (Smith, *Book of the Dead,* 166; *1860 Census,* Anderson District, 159).

C. S. A. Treasury Secretary George Alfred Trenholm (1807–76) was an extremely wealthy South Carolinian before the war. Trenholm had interests in shipping, hotels, plantations, banks, and railroads, including the Blue Ridge line. He wed Anna Helen Holms in 1828; they had thirteen children. He assumed the position of treasury secretary in July 1864, holding it until the end of the war. After a period of very liberal confinement Trenholm was released to rebuild his lost fortune. Dr. Hammond was apparently working for the treasury department (Wakelyn, *Biographical Dictionary,* 414; *Charleston Courier,* July 21, 1865).

52. Henry was a Reed family servant.

The long-anticipated diplomatic recognition by the French or the English never actually materialized, despite constant effort by Confederate diplomats, including William Trescot.

53. Most likely the journal refers to L. A. Pensifoy of Saluda, South Carolina. In 1860 all the Pensifoys in South Carolina resided in Edgefield County (*1860 Census,* Edgefield County, 166).

said knowingly "Miss Emmala I won't tell on you!" – which made me feel quite mean & I was afraid mischief would come of it – hope not, but I had no news of my Robert either. What can be his fate! Rumours that Lee's army is quite surrendered & may be destroyed – terrible! Quiet, sad night of suspense at home.

Sunday April 16th A splendid day! A glorious resurrection of nature on this Easter of our Lord's resurrection! So fresh & dewy & fragrant & musical, with leaves & flowers & bird voices! yet we were all lazy at home. Dr. Broyles came in before breakfast – full of life – saying "all nature was full of beauty and promise now and only man brings ruin & suffering on the world! That it is a wonderful springtime – we have only to throw in the seeds & they will spring up full of promise & fruit trees all laden as yet with bloom & genious."

He came to learn the news from Pa & both could only conclude that "Lee's army was surely cut off & ruined – starved anyway – and the whole affair wound up." I wondered what he thought of the probable fate of his sons there – for he knew nothing. I longed to ask him of my Robert, but did not dare – too hard. When we are nearest to each other! He spoke of the new Yankee State formed in the heart of our country – East Tenn. & West N. C. – to be presented to Lincoln under Brownlow – dreadful! And his plantation & property is there – his no longer I guess.[54]

I went to S. S. & taught a large [class] of little ones – sang &c; a large congregation at church. Mr. Murray longer & as dull to me as usual – too bad. I ought to appreciate my religious advantages & comforts more, when so many are deprived of all. Grandpa here to dinner – the dear old man.[55]

Add notes to R's letter – hope he may get it & I may hear soon. I dreamed of him & many things last night. Thought the Yankees dashed in one evg while we were at walk and we had nothing saved or prepared. Awfully frightened, but I waked up before we were harmed. I dreamed that I was walking. Almost met

54. William G. Brownlow was the recently elected governor of Tennessee. An anti-Confederacy newspaper editor, imprisoned and escaped, he went on a speaking tour to relate his experiences and viewpoints. Brownlow was a harsh Reconstructionist, disfranchising former Confederates and crushing the Ku Klux Klan with martial law enforced by federal troops. Brownlow had long espoused the creation of the pro-union state of "Frankland" in eastern Tennessee. The proposal never gained serious consideration from Congress.

The Broyleses had land and family in the Johnsonville, Tennessee, area, where Robert and many of his siblings eventually made their home.

55. William and Francis Acker Hammond, Emmala's maternal grandparents, came to Anderson from Carnesville, Georgia, where they maintained property and family business interests. Captain William Hammond was an attorney, judge, planter, architect, and builder. The Hammond place, about six miles south of town, was called Gravel Hill (Vandiver, *Traditions,* 159; Hemphill, *Men of Mark,* 1:39).

Robert who was walking with Harry Miller – George Brown & other of his cousins & they all played some trick on me. Scarcely spoke. He had not visited me & we were doubting each other as formerly. He placed a note for me at the gate & I heard him say "Traitress" – distinctly – and felt so badly! That all seemed natural, but 'twas a cruel greeting from my love – whom I ought to meet in joy.

This bright afternoon I have been helping Cora with a letter to Julia, & Mamie analyze a sermon. Read some from Spurgeon's &c. Now the bell rings for dinner. Few persons at church. A pity, when Mr. Murray was to begin his exposition of "Hebrews" for our benefit. Quite interesting too – showing he had studied it; went on to prove that 'twas written by Paul to the Jews in Greek – to show that we all have ministering spirits hovering around us &c. Wish I could remember all the points.

Lovely evening – read some sweet poems. After tea John Reeves & nice little wife & Capt. Daniels their afflicted boarder came & sat awhile chatting nonsense. He is an object of pity – suffers with his leg wound & may yet have it amputated & fears 'twill kill him – awful! He talked very silly about various things – laughed too much – a right good face. We sang some hymns, but they were not appreciated.

Monday April 17 A glorious day! Leaves & flowers & buds rejoicing. We arranged vases, a few bright pink roses to gladded music lessons & sewing. Made J. P. a small suit – spun a little & helped plant a few beans &c. John Peter came down at last to see us – on his way to camp as they were ordered to Tunnel Hill – to repel any raiders. Brought me a long letter from Julia who is interested in all we do & the news here &c, but can't come – lives off there, so lonely, with few friends, only her cares with negroes & children & reading to amuse her.[56]

Joe brought the buggy for Mamie or some of us to go back to pay a visit, but no one could until Ma concluded after much discussion – to go with our dear little baby sister & Louisa as nurse. All went in an open buggy in the sun – afraid to brake down. We all felt badly at seeing them go. We will miss her so much.

56. Jacob Pinckney Reed, Jr. (b. 1862) was Emmala's youngest brother. J. P., Jr., worked as a clerk in C. A.'s store, matriculated at the University of Virginia, and by the 1880s started to practice law in Atlanta, Georgia (Vandiver, *Traditions,* 272–3; *1870 Census,* Anderson County, 697).

John Peter Brown, still on active duty, was called upon to protect the mountain passes leading west from Dalton, Georgia. "Tunnel Hill" was a vital passage through the Southern Appalachian Mountains and the scene of a battle in May of 1864 (Mark Mayo Boatner, *The Civil War Dictionary* [New York: David Mckay Company, 1988], 556). The federal cavalry opted to avoid this approach and entered South Carolina via Caesar's Head, west of Greenville.

Hope they may get back safely. We all settled down very quietly to work – a pleasant day.[57]

Mrs. Whitehead called to see us – very sweet & pretty & so pleasant & intelligent & social – ought to see more of her. Then as I sat reading, Andrew Moreland came up to bid us good bye & take letters for us, but he was sick with intermittent fever. Looked so badly – thin & sad & sick – good fellow we were sorry for him. Yet he says he must go to the front. It may be the last we'll ever see of him. Hope not – he seems to have very fine feelings &c.

He & E were both disappointed at not having a few last words perhaps forever after all they have been, yet I feared 'twould be imprudent &c & I didn't leave them – I may regret it. Sorry for the poor man. He has no interest now – his "Carrie" gone – his mother & sisters in Charleston. Says "he don't care if he is killed" &c. I had written the obituary of his sweet little wife as requested – wonder what he will think of it? Pa didn't like his being here.

We spent a quiet evening at home – no news – can we never hear facts or anything from my R! God bless him! I sent him a letter by Andrew. Will he ever get it? I had one from Mrs. Lizzie Johnson asking me to come over to Greenville during the session of the Legislature – the last may ever meet here &c. I should like to be there awhile, but fear to undertake it.[58]

Tues. April 18th Pleasant morn. Stormy evg. A real April shower, some thunder – nature clothed in sunset radiance & beauty & fragrances! All busy arranging domestic affairs & sewing &c in morn. Eleanor with the Keys, Fan helping to arrange meals – I to sew & teach & arrange all the vases &c. Read all afternoon & after tea – all dull – no news-papers to read.[59]

Weds. April 19th A warm – bright, sunny day – feels like summer. I fear it will be an oppressive season. Everything in extremes now. I devoted morn to visiting. Could get the buggy awhile. Cora & J. P. my bright – pretty buddie, went with me just to good Mrs. Dave Anderson's – the widow who has been so unfortunate. Lost husband & eight children – most of them been ungrateful &c. One grown son blown to a shocking death at Charleston. The only grown son left – her comfort

57. Joe and Louisa were servants.

Theresa Hammond Reed (1864–1939) was a yet unnamed infant in early 1865.

58. Mrs. Lizzie Johnson cannot be identified.

Governor Andrew G. Magrath attempted to convene the state legislature in Greenville on April 25, 1865, but few attended the meeting. This failing, Magrath issued a series of statements designed to rally the flagging spirits of Carolinians at large. When the governor refused to stop this activity he was arrested and temporarily imprisoned in Georgia (Edgar, *South Carolina,* 378).

59. Eleanor was visiting the Keys family at Key's Springs, about two miles west of Echo Hall.

– Dave. Right pious &c, lost his health & has wasted away & died here after her long nursing & expense. She had but two little ones left. The elder, a foolish – bad boy – the girl married & worthless & mean to her &c. Lou Wilkes there doing all she could for them, his body at rest from much suffering. A horrible skeleton – she greiving – such is humanity![60]

I went on to the Silcox's – nearly all the wealth he had acquired by hard work swept away – in Charleston & Columbia. The good old man nearly forced down by sorrows. Lost a young son & his grown up soldier son & idol – Jimmie – last year. The younger, Manley, in service & came near being hanged to death by a robber lately. The grown daughter, poor Tilly has not been expected to live all this time – a great sufferer. She married Dave Willard, her early love. Together but a short while. He went off & was killed eight months ago – she had never left her room since – been ill with many complaints. Has a new baby, a month old. Pretty little black haired child – like Dave – Mattie Dupree. Even then, she had pains in every way – looks like a skeleton, but aroused from grief to love her child, George – a sweet, amiable little creature & a nice baby boy – Seymour.[61]

Mr. & Mrs Hugers escaped the Yankee visitation in Columbia with many blessings. I felt exempted from many ills as yet. I went over to John Webb's comfortable farm place – he & Mrs. Webb – pleasant Bessie, a nice girl. They have a daughter, Mrs. O – whose husband has been missing for months. Never leaves house &c Such people have true depth of feeling. I can scarcely conceive now. I came by the Bleckleys awhile – Emily to leave on cars today – for Ga. home. By Murrays – Mrs. M – better off for Greenville to try & improve herself. Then home – Aunt Cynthia here – went to plantation. Pa at work there planting all evg.[62]

60. Sara Cornelia "Cora" Reed (b. 1853, d. April 14, 1929) grew up and was educated in Anderson. Later in life Cora delighted many church and civic gatherings with her singing (Vandiver, *Traditions,* 28, 118, 272).

Matilda and David A. Anderson were farmers. "Dave" was sixty-two years old when he died. In 1860 the couple had five children: Robert, Mary, David Jr., Edward, and James. Matilda Anderson died in 1881 at age sixty-nine (*1860 Census,* Anderson District, 261; Vandiver, *Traditions,* 132; Smith, *Book of the Dead,* 9).

61. James Silcox served in a variety of Charleston units during the war, achieving the rank of lieutenant (*1860 Census,* Charleston, 427; Hewett, *Confederate Soldiers,* 441).

Mattie Dupree was the third child of Dave and Tilly Silcox Willard. George and Seymour were both born during the war. Simpson, however, notes a Miss Silcox marrying Charles David Gaillard (Simpson, *Old Pendleton,* 212).

62. The Hugers of Charleston were an old and venerated family from the Carolina lowcountry. Emmala probably refers to the family of General Benjamin Huger, who moved to their Pendleton home in 1865. Huger, born in 1805, graduated from West Point (class of 1825). He served as General Zachary Taylor's chief of ordnance during the Mexican War but proved lackluster when given a field combat command at the Battle of Seven Days. General Huger died in 1877 (Lander and McGee, *A Rebel Came Home,* 95; Warner, *Generals in Gray,* 143–44).

I was giving lessons & gathering flowers as usual. Jane Fant here awhile – wants to get in the Treasury Department that moved her – occupying an inconvenient building. Old desks & benches & three schools all turned out to find quarters elsewhere. Dick Tupper & Joe Hyde – Eleanor's little beaux here. She had invites – walked about in her gay candy coloured deleoure, with black flowers &c – much admired. She had a letter from Ben at last – in Ga. – faithful I hope & may come to see her – hope so. Pa tried to get her to show it, but she wouldn't – to any one – selfish – but happy. I can get none from R – never more I fear. Promenaded in the twilight & longed for him in vain. Shall we ever meet again? Reports that Lee's army is captured – awful – pray not true! Joe H very shy &c Sang scotch songs &c at night – now to scribble & read &c.[63]

Thursday April 20th A bright – warm day – summer at hand. Mrs. Brown called for me. We went to the society – found Mrs. Webb, but few others came – talked of the times &c. The Charleston ladies Mrs. Mannington, McPherson – Lowndes &c have resigned &c. We have cloth & garments on hand, but can't help the poor needy soldiers now, scarcely.[64]

I read all aft. – too absorbed to work. Anna Gadsden & two Miss Newtons – daughters of a commadore of that name now in the Treasury – came seeking a guard for a friend – nice girls, accomplished in music &c.[65]

Fannie & I went late to pay some necessary visits; found the Halls pleasant – Mrs. Wilkinson chatty & the ladies at the Perroneau's discussing the news. Hopeful until the confirmation of the worst was received. Then we were all so shocked and yet there is a painful apathy almost on us all, yet we can do nothing![66]

Wm. (E. W.) Webb, a bookkeeper married to Julia Webb, apparently lived in same place as brother Thomas J. (a railroad agent) and his wife, Elizabeth or Bessie Webb, a "mantuamaker" or dressmaker by profession. In 1860 the Webb siblings all lived in the home of their parents, retired physician Edmund Webb and his wife, Martha. All of the Webb children were Emmala's contemporaries. John Webb and his family were evidently refugees from Charleston (*1860 Census,* Anderson District, 257).

63. Possibly cousin "Ben" Hammond.

64. The local sewing society was a benevolent and productive group duplicated throughout the South and North. They acquired, or made, thread and cloth, and then created garments for the soldiers. The society was often the focal point of community activity in the war years. Local ladies, like Mrs. Brown and Mrs. Webb, volunteered their time as needed. Refugees from Charleston, like Mrs. Mannington McPherson and Mrs. Lowndes, helped out when they could.

65. The Newton family were bureaucratic refugees who accompanied the treasury presses being set up in the old Johnson Female University.

66. Mrs. Wilkinson was the wife of Captain J. W. Wilkinson, a Charleston attorney who served with the Seventeenth South Carolina Infantry, Company H (T. Michael Parrish and

Pa was reading loud to an anxious crowd in the streets – perfect silence reigned and then Mr. Crayton came to the window and read aloud to we ladies the extra sheet containing particulars of the surrender of Lee's proud army! How awfully humiliating & deplorable – and what is to be the result? What our fate – are we ruined – subjugated? It looks like there was no hope – but I can't help yet hoping something may yet save us! Johnston's army still remains I suppose – surely all brave spirits will rally around it & though they fall back – save us in some way – or peace may be made now – or Europe interfere &c. God save us in some way & make us a better people![67]

After desparate battles, I guess Lee's army was reduced to 10,000 effective men and of the Virginia & N. C. & other troops deserted we hear. Many were killed & wounded no doubt & will we ever learn their fate? The saddest part! But we were pushed back at A – C.H. Lee's army was surrounded by Grant's army of 200,000 men. Stoneman's &c and thus we were forced to yield our noble leader & gallant veterans, but with a noble spirit that was highly commended! Gen. Ulysses Grant

---

R. M. Willington, *Confederate Imprints: A Bibliography of Southern Publications from Secession to Surrender* [Austin, Tex.: Jenkins Publishing Company, 1984], 180; Hewett, *Confederate Soldiers,* 523).

Mamie and Margie Perroneau were two of the daughters of Henry P. Perroneau, who came to Anderson to teach at the Johnson Female College and stayed through the war and many years after (Vandiver, *Traditions,* 116).

67. Baylis Franklin Crayton (1820–1907) of Greenville, South Carolina, moved to the village of Anderson in 1838. Baylis F. clerked in a store belonging to his uncle, B. F. Mauldin, and married Martha Evelyn Benson in 1843. The Craytons owned a mercantile business, farmlands, and slaves. Captain Crayton served as the first quartermaster for Orr's Rifle Regiment. The Craytons raised three children: Samuel M., Kate, and Frank S.. Martha died in October, 1905; Baylis F. passed away in February, 1907. Both are buried at Anderson's Silverbrook Cemetery.

Kate B. Crayton (1847–1927) was nineteen years old when she married Dr. David Sloan Maxwell (1841–1904) in 1866. The elder Dr. Maxwell (1817–89) and wife Lucy G. (1823–96) were retired by this time. The good doctor served the Anderson County's Fork Township for many decades. Samuel married Sallie Nevitt on October 31, 1866, and Frank married Mary Broyles (Vandiver, *Traditions,* 152–55, 203–4; Smith, *Book of the Dead,* 248; *1860 Census,* Anderson District, 258; Vandiver Report, Item #2, 1849; Brown, *A Colonel at Gettysburg,* 315; N. Louise Bailey, Mary L. Morgan, and Carolyn R. Taylor, *Biographical Directory of the South Carolina Senate, 1776–1985,* [Columbia: University of South Carolina Press, 1986], 1:340–41; Lucas, *Early Anderson,* 53, 62).

went to Lee & his officers under an apple tree, but generously refused to accept the sword of the great man.[68]

There was no exultation in our defeat – but praise – for Lee is revered too by them – he was only overpowered by numbers! All were subdued & wept! Grant must have some nobility in him yet, hope it may prove so. 'Tis said Gen. Gary wept – the hard, stern, wicked man – tore off his stars, refused to surrender – broke through the lines & a few of them escaped to Johnston's army. Brave man![69]

20,000 of our men paroled. Lee & officers in Richmond pardoned. Lincoln there & they may make terms of peace. We know not what is left for us – must only wait & pray! Yet out hearts do not realize the worst here! Who of our loved ones may slumber in the bloody field – or in Yankee hospitals & when can we know their fate? And where is my Robere? Perhaps he has met some awful fate – & we never more may meet – & I may never know such love again! But he may be on his way home & we may meet & what then? Heaven direct!

New raids on Ga. – Columbus fallen – Montgomery &c. They may be here – heaven help us all! I must read & dream & pray! The schools all moving about – great revolution here.

Friday April 21st A delightful day at home – sewing all morn – made a pair of soldier's drawers. Aunt Cynthia here – amazed me – Mrs. Wilhite here too – Talked too much & freely – cynical &c. Dick Tupper with Eleanor nearly all today – silly one. Frazier Wilson of Clif's company with him – just from army of Va. & scenes of our losses, but both degraded by drinking – shocked me! Edmond Broyles came in awhile for that too I think & Whit Broyles here to tea, a genial face.[70]

68. Lee surrendered an army of 22,000, but the rate of desertion was staggering after the fall of Richmond. Appomattox Court House was the end of the line for the remnants of the Army of Northern Virginia. General George Stoneman's cavalry units were sweeping into western North Carolina and points south. (It was Lee who rode to meet Grant, and Grant did indeed refuse to accept Lee's sword in surrender, but the act took place in the parlor of Wilbur McLean's home, not beneath an apple tree.)

69. Brigadier General Martin W. Gary led a brigade of cavalry under the command of Major General Fitzhugh Lee. At 5 A.M. on the morning of Sunday, April 9, Fitzhugh Lee's cavalry managed to break out of the encirclement at Appomattox Court House. By early afternoon Robert E. Lee capitulated, taking all 22,000 troops to surrender. The number surrendering apparently included those who had been captured at Petersburg and Richmond. The exact whereabouts of General Gary's brigade at this time is uncertain. The story of General Gary rending his stars and bolting from the surrender sight is yet another embellished rumor. Gary was born in Cokesbury, South Carolina, and attended South Carolina College until expelled for inciting a student riot. He finished his schooling at Harvard in 1854 and joined the South Carolina bar in 1855 (Douglas, *Lee's Lieutenants,* 456).

70. Cora Lavinia Hilly (40) and Dr. Philip A. "P. A." Wilhite (1820–92) came from Carnesville, Georgia, and built a home on the corner of South McDuffie and East River Streets.

But I spent the whole afternoon & night until late absorbed in one of Bulwer's charming novels. "What will he do with it?" Such graphic power in the delineation of character & sings such harmony & unraveling difficult points such an insight into human hearts! It seemed to him & is to all of us a momentous question: "What will we do with any of the talents & gifts we possess – so as to use them aright" & may we so consider it?

Guy Darnell, the noble English lawyer & statesman had great pride to subdue – a noble heart – buried himself from the world after his first love seemed false – reappearing again in new grandeur of character – after finding truth & love in "the Caroline of old!" Guy of Montfort, Sophy & Lionel, two pure exquisite characters. Wolf, a rare, pure man. The woman in iron gray, with her devotion to the desperado – sublime! All of it fascinating, but I was too absorbed to notice home duties & guests.[71]

Then I was trying to forget this sad disaster to our armys – and the evils & dangers around – to wait thus in suspense ere hearing of Robere's fate! Thought he might come – as other soldiers were arriving, but not yet. May it be soon & all well! News of an armistice in Johnston's army. France recognizing the South, probable peace or renewed war. No Mail! Plenty of people here now – men enough to

---

The Wilhite children were Mary (age 17), Cora Hilly (11), Frank (9), and Joe (6). Joe grew up to be Dr. J. O. Wilhite, who served Anderson as his father and grandfather had done. Patriarch M. P. Wilhite taught a school for children but returned to Georgia and grew very old.

Dr. P. A. Wilhite had the distinction of discovering the anesthetic qualities of ether while serving an apprenticeship for Dr. Crawford W. Long of Athens, Georgia. The "discovery" came after the accidental overdosing of a servant at an "ether sniffing party." Dr. Long's precedent-setting ether-assisted surgery on James Venerable received accolades from the medical establishment and relegated Dr. Wilhite to a unique historical footnote. The association with Major W. W. Humphreys is unclear (Dickson, *Journeys,* 101–4; Vandiver, *Traditions,* 111, 208, 259, 268, 316; *1860 Census,* Anderson District, 158).

Frazier Wilson, veteran and wealthy Charlestonian refugee, has not been identified further.

Major A. R. "Whit" (or "Witt," as Emmala sometimes spells it) Broyles and Martha Brown had a plantation in the northwestern Fork section of Anderson District, beyond the Seneca River. They had three daughters: Clara, Mary, and Lula Broyles were cousins of the Reeds. Mary Broyles lived with the Reeds at Echo Hall in order to attend school with the Reed girls; she later married local merchant Frank Crayton. Lula married John Baker "on the Seneca River" on August 15, 1867, but little more is known of her life. Emmala repeatedly referred to the failures of someone named "Whit," who neglected to maintain an obscure confidence, but Captain Broyles was not the betrayer (Vandiver, *Traditions,* 151–52, 194); see Reed, *Journals,* Appendix F.

71. Baron Edward George Bulwer-Lytton (1803–73), an English statesman and novelist, specialized in historical fiction romances. *What Will He Do With It?* by Pisistratus Caxton was a novel published in 1858.

have won independence had they done their duty – but the neglect & greed & sin in the land brings our ruin!

Earth radiant with green leaves & flowers – exquisite roses. I made vases – sent boquets to Carrie Ravenel – and Julia as Pa took Buddy & went up there to bring Ma home. Left us all alone tonight, but we were safe – 'though Clif was rather free in his treats – I indignant, but read on & rested sweetly. Yet I can't dream of R – wonder why – and what are the true feeling of our hearts & our future?[72]

Sat. April 22nd Awakened with the radiant dawn of a perfect day in Spring & thank thee oh Lord for all thy mercies! The sunlit skies – & verdant, flowery, fragrant earth – the voice of birds & fowls & young hearts around! Preserve us and make us do our duty now & always! Was knitting, teaching S.S. lessons & practicing mostly. Becky Webb here in morn & some boys as usual to see Eleanor.

At noon Pa & Ma & children came from Julia's. She had spent a pleasant week there. Julia remembered our little wants thoughtfully in more than she could spare I fear. High wind & cold today – I fear frost may injure the fruit.

Many rumours today of news. A raid thought to be advancing here &c, then all hostilities stopped by an armistice, the French Gov't recognized & aided the South – already at our ports, our soldiers sent home by way of Charleston, but we get no news from loved ones yet! Papers at night telling of the particulars of the surrender of Lee's army and their brave daring previously – all honored by the foe – no exultation, but what will be the end? I had letters from Aunt Susan Noble & Sue McMillan. so crazy about her darling brother Barnie – sick in Greenville. How the Yankees despoiled them of them of all provisions. They were living hard & hoping for the best – a noble girl.[73]

72. Carolina "Carrie" Ravenel (age 20) was the daughter of wealthy Charleston merchants and bankers James and Augusta Ravenel. Her siblings included Marianne (14) and Augusta (10) (*1860 Census,* Charleston, 208). Carrie Ravenel was in Pendleton when the Yankee raiders arrived, and her account of the events are retold in Mary Stevenson's edition of *The Diary of Clarissa Adger Bowen* (Pendleton, S.C.: Foundation for Historic Restoration, 1973).

73. In 1860 Susan A. Noble lived in the town of Calhouns, Abbeville County, where J. P. Reed was raised. Susan was the daughter of Abbeville attorney Edward Noble and Martha Means Bratton Noble and granddaughter of Patrick Noble, a former governor of South Carolina (1838–40) (*1860 Census,* Abbeville District, 3; Simpson, *Old Pendleton,* 192; Stevenson, *Diary of Clarissa Adger Bowen,* 19; Lander and McGee, *A Rebel Came Home,* 80, 101).

Greenville, South Carolina, a town thirty miles east of Anderson, had a population of about 2,400 in 1860. The textile boom of the late nineteenth century served to enhance the importance of Greenville, already an important manufacturing center and transportation hub in 1865. Benjamin F. Perry maintained a law office near the Greenville Court House square. Many of Emmala's friends and acquaintances were from the Greenville area (Huff, *Greenville,* 48, 49, 421; James M. Richardson, *History of Greenville County, South Carolina: Narrative and Biographical* [1930; rpt. Spartanburg, S.C.: The Reprint Company, 1980], 17–21.

A Newberry paper sent me by Andrew Moreland contained the obituary of his wife. He urged I would write & he dared sign my name. I was vexed about it. Late & cold.

Sunday April 23rd A cold, clear day – but too windy for frost we hope. I didn't feel well, half frozen all day as we could get no fires. Went late to S.S. Heard children & sung, but was thinking sadly of our momentous conditions now & of Robere – his fate. Mr. Murray gave us a very good sermon on "Search the Scriptures."

Reading &c all evg – Lula Broyles came up here from Belton where she has been sick – a tall, fair, amiable, smart, lovely girl – I am much attracted to her. We were all so excited about the news – reported that Abe Lincoln was killed & Seward wounded by assassins in Washington & Andy Johnson to be inaugurated Pres. of U.S. and a general cessation of hostilities & terms of peace &c. How much is true & how it will all end, who can tell! But these are momentous – stirring times & we have reached a crisis. God deliver & help us!

But I heard that Robert was missing for several days before the surrender & might be killed or wounded &c. I felt so shocked – as I dwelt upon the idea of my only & faithful love meeting such a fate & never returning to me – whilst others will come back to their loved ones. I couldn't endure the thought. Prayed & wept & hope all may yet be well with us, for I can't believe all this. Read over his last dear letters – both unsatisfied, yet so much to explain – surely this is not all – 'though it may be best! I have ever feared that some such fate would be his – yet still hope for the best!

Hear that Dr. Jimmie Brown & Bob ____ were captured at Richmond. What will become of the last? Many other rumours. Negro choir singing here tonight. I had no heart to sing. Long for R. Eleanor seemed to be made happy by a letter & gift from Ben & hopes soon to see him – 'though flirting now with Dick Tupper – a nice little red headed youth. Andrew Moreland back here – sent out my letters, but will they ever be rec'd. George & Milton Brown have come back – didn't get on to the army nor letters to P & R I guess, but may I hear from them soon.[74]

Belton, South Carolina, ten miles south and east of Anderson, was the place where the railroad spur to Anderson met the trunk line of the Greenville and Columbia line. The town's name honored Judge John Belton O'Neall, railroad director, attorney, judge, and historian (Edgar, *WPA Guide,* 420).

74. Dr. James Nardin Brown was the son of Daniel Brown, a town founder and very successful farmer and merchant. In 1865 James Brown was a medical officer in Company B, South Carolina Fourth Infantry. Those taken prisoner at Richmond were not prisoners very long before the war ended, when they were paroled and released (*1860 Census,* Anderson District, 157; Hewett, *Confederate Soldiers,* 58).

Monday April 24th A splendid day- 'though a cold night & heavy frost – which we feared would injure everything – but we hope has not. So much frost expected! May fortune favour the bountiful gifts of nature at least. Pa was croaking, but little silly J.P. was exulting in the nice sunny day & tried to kill birds & butterflies all day. Pulled flowers as I ran in the piazza singing as usual – Watching the dewy leaves & flowers & rising mist from the hills & many shades of green. I saw a little tame rabbit run about in the yard, "lives here in clover" – free & happy I hope. When Pa & Clif would have shot it – I objected; a harmless happy life here I hope! I arranged flowers as usual – swept & knit.

Vie H. came & stayed all day. Lula Broyles a sweet lovely girl, hope to see more of her. George Brown came for her – got as far as Danville & returned – mailed my letter. Teazed me about R &c. They would go home for dinner – queer people. Ma had a sick spell in the morning – better.

Music lesson in evg – then went with Vie to Mr. Brown's – saw all folks, discussing news &c and Lucie looking very sweetly. We talked a little of R – fearing he might not come & she said I ought not to go to Ga. & I can't – but Mr. Brown came with the news & reported "that Jeff Davis says we may have an honorable peace in 30 days" – negotiating – that our soldiers are all coming home. Dr. B's sons both safe & on their way home! I couldn't help starting with delight & all noticed it laughed at my expense, but I'm sorry they understand. Lucie was glad with me & says "Kiss him for me" – dare I ever?

They went home. I came to the Tuppers & found Kate – sweet & chatty as ever, with a cold & Miss Sue Perroneau with her – an intelligent, elegant person. I would like to see more of them both, concluded we are all petrified with so much news. We can scarcely feel or realize all our late calamities & the great changes at hand. Even the fate of loved ones can scarcely stir us, but I am stirred. I am sure at news of R's coming & all the past & future for us & all.

I stopped to chat with Caro Ravenel on the steps at home. Been confined indoors for weeks with a sore foot. Such a sweet – smart girl, reading McCauley's England – fitting herself for hard work or boot blacking if reduced to the worst. She & Kate T call me "Emmala." Seem more social & congenial than any refugees I've met – hope to remain friends. They appreciate my flowers I send. Caro a great friend to Margie Calhoun & all the family of John C. the great.[75]

75. Thomas Babington Macaulay (1800–59) was an English historian, poet, and author. His *History of England from the Accession of James II* (5 vols., 1849–61), was acclaimed as a contemporary historical masterpiece.

Margaret "Margie" Calhoun is probably Margaret Maria Calhoun, daughter of Andrew Pickens Calhoun (1811–65) and his second wife Margaret Green (1816–91) (Ernest McPherson Lander, Jr., *The Calhoun Family and Thomas Green Clemson: The Decline of a Southern*

Home late and in the gathering twilight & breath of sweet flowers to haunt me with dreams of love & beauty – I thought only of his coming! How it will be – our greeting our feelings & fate – surely all will end for the best!

Tues. April 25th A glorious day – so bright & pleasant – the flowers so luxuriant. I made four boquets out on the lawn – one dainty, one of the most fragrant flowers to send Theodore whom I knew would appreciate it more than any other and he seemed delighted; gave the servant six dollars for taking it. In the aft sent me a charming note, so elegant and unique, such delicate flattery & sincerity too from him – for he has known & appreciated me for years as few others have. As he wrote "one who knew how to appreciate the gift & giver – the enchanting fragrance breathed of my own dear self, your dear ladyship – my notes &c will have to be their own reward. I have learnt from past experience – your affectionate & obedient servant &c"

Of course I prize such feelings from so cultivated & refined a person with such delicate feelings &c and his admiration is a source of pride, but I would not have him love – or seek more, for I could not be all to him. If he is not practical &c. He is not a man to marry, to entertain me much and hope always to retain his regard & the power to entertain him with music &c, for he is a loveless, joyless man who never cared for any other. Wish I could have corresponded with him – his letters could have been so rare, but I never may now I guess.

Fannie & I went in the buggy visiting – left a boquet with Mrs. Moreland. Went to Col. Orr's He has been very ill for weeks with fever & depression of the spirit I guess – in this crisis. Some gentlemen with him & I could not see him – Mrs. Orr asleep. Mattie talked to us pleasantly – just come from school in Greenville to see her father – very smart & dignified – but rather scornful towards lesser merit – likes me I think. Old Mrs. Webb there & Mrs. Cody.[76]

Patriarchy [Columbia: University of South Carolina Press, 1983], 8, 21, 27; Harriet Hefner Cook, *John C. Calhoun, the Man* [Columbia, S.C.: R. L. Bryan Company, 1965], 117.

John C. Calhoun (1782–1850) was born near Abbeville, South Carolina, attended Yale University, and read law in Connecticut. Calhoun's political career ran the gamut of public life, starting in the state legislature, then the U.S. House of Representatives and Senate. He served as James Monroe's secretary of war, Andrew Jackson's vice president, and secretary of state for John Tyler. He married Floride Bonneau (1792–1866), and they had ten children. The Calhoun homeplace, located in Pendleton District, was called Fort Hill, site of today's Clemson University (Lander, *The Calhoun Family,* passim).

76. Charlestonian S. C. Moreland, Andrew's mother, married Andrew, Sr., born in Ireland and twenty-five years her senior. The couple had three children at home in 1860: Andrew, Ellen, and B. P. (*1860 Census,* Charleston, 222).

Mrs. Cody could be Anna Cody of York County, but evidence is slight (*1860 Census,* York County, 369).

We went then to the Leitch's – Mattie & Mary L very sweet & pleasant – then home. We had met a crowd of soldiers coming from the cars. I thought Robert might be one – and I longed to see him, but he came not.

Pa went off to attend an Extra Session of the Legislature in Greenville. Miss Lizzie Johnson had begged me to go, but I declined. Some dangers of raids &c – 'though I might have had a fine time there, yet missed more here. But Robert was coming and my future might depend on it – I stayed. May it all end for the best!

At noon Clif told me of hundreds of hungry soldiers coming home – who want some soldier's rest here & find none – have to go on west. 'Tis a pity so I thought we ought to exert ourselves to feed them. Struck with a fit of usefulness I went from the dinner table in the hot sun to Mrs. Webb's, all just leaving table & got them interested in the object – so Mrs. W. & I went to the Commissary Dpt. under S.[77]

Thinking they could furnish the food – if we could have it prepared at a certain place and as there seems no other use for the stores now – it would be a good plan – but they had no such authority & could not yield, for the soldiers all draw their rations there & can get them cooked. We tried at the hospital – under Dr. Ravenel, but nothing could be done. Only the cooks (white & black) in a large – clean kitchen – said they would cook any rations that were brought to them & this is all we could affect. felt disappointed, but perhaps 'tis just as well – provisions are so scarce & soldiers so ungrateful & they are going home now. We had to give them clothes from out Society too. Poor, ragged, dirty – lousy fellows after their hard service.[78]

I came home & found Keys McCulley & Tom Osborne – two of Clif's old school friends. Clever boys – but all love to treat & drink too well. Keys fine looking – right smart & lively. I entertained them with music &c awhile – then they & Eleanor went to the depot to welcome the soldiers. I longed, but could not be seen there. Disappointed again – R did not come – will he never?[79]

77. Sylvester Bleckley was in charge of the C.S.A. commissary depot at Anderson.

78. Dr. Henry E. Ravenel of Seneca Place Plantation, Pendleton, died in 1863. Dr. Ravenel had many sons, several of whom could have been in Anderson during the war.

79. Peter Keys McCulley, also known as "P. K." or "Keys," was the son of Stephan and Elmira McCulley. Born June 22, 1845, Peter was a Citadel cadet when the Civil War commenced. He soon returned to Anderson to be appointed captain of the Second South Carolina Regiment of Rifles (Jenkins Brigade). This regiment was created due to the overflow of Anderson-area volunteers who answered the call from Colonel James L. Orr when he formed Orr's Rifles. P. K. became a cotton merchant (McCulley & Cathcart) and a banker. He wed his partner's sister, Margaret J. Cathcart, on November 12, 1867. The couple had four children (Vandiver, *Traditions,* 225, 239; Dickson, *Journeys,* 137, 183; *Cyclopedia of Eminent and Representative Men,* 626–27; Hewett, *Confederate Soldiers,* 317; Smith, *Book of the Dead,* 259).

Mattie Leitch & a gentleman friend of hers came to see me. She is a sweet fair girl, dressed so pretty – in brown & blue &c He was a tall, large man. Col. Childs of Columbia (or NC) man of family – cut off now – owned a Saluda Fact. destroyed. A man of wealth – buys jewels for toys – pets certain girls – Mattie one. Wants to adopt her – brings her gifts, a parasol &c. He seems a very generous soul for the genial gifts of life, though too much for the sensual – I guess drinks &c.[80]

He told me all the war news, just from Columbia – knows all plans and generals &c. Thinks we will soon have a favourable peace – Grant will permit and desired the death of Lincoln and Seward. The ultras who could never have let us go without being destroyed – property &c, but we may now get better terms. They won't submit to vile Andy Johnson.

He blames Jeff Davis for all our misfortunes – in his stubborn partialities and hates – his dislike for Joe Johnston & reversals &c have ruined us, he thinks. For "old Joe" is his special friend & admiration. He venerates Johnston & Lee as do all the Yankees & everybody. They have done their best & been overpowered – will not be insulted – as our army were all well treated by Grant's &c. Wonderful times – What is to come![81]

But he wanted to hear music. Made me sing Russel's fine old songs & listened to them with his soul in his eyes – "Appreciated them & me" as few have done. "Ship on fire" – Newfoundland dog – "Old Armchair &c" Could have heard much more. Wished we had met before &c. "I sang with so much feeling & ease" "Why was I left here all this time unmarried" Might he send me a lover. Mentioned Col. Gardner – Gen. Hoke &c. He will send one of nature's noblemen for me &c[82]

Then he wanted me to gather him flowers & he pulled a choice boquet of roses – to take with him to Greenville – would give to the most worthy man he saw – for me &c &c. Went away late with much nonsense, but he was an interesting –

80. Captain Frederick Lynn Childs of Saluda commanded an artillery company known as Child's Company (Hewett, *Confederate Soldiers,* 90).

81. The "overwhelmed by numbers explanation" for the Union victory evidently worked its way into the Southern mindset immediately following the war. See Foster, *Ghosts of the Confederacy,* 57–58.

82. "Ship on Fire" was a popular tune of the era, with both North and South, by H. Russell (Minnie Sears, ed., *The Complete Catalogue of Sheet Music and Musical Works: 1870* [New York: H. W. Wilson, 1926], 116).

"Newfoundland Dog" has not been identified.

"Old Armchair," a ballad composed by Henry Russell, was first published in 1840.

Colonel Gardner has not been identified.

Major General Robert Frederick Hoke, C.S.A., a married man with eight children, was already with his family in Lincolnton, North Carolina, where he officially surrendered in April 1865 (Wakelyn, *Biographical Dictionary,* 233–34).

appreciat[iv]e person – such as one likes to meet – such as I enjoy to talk to – or rather any rare people – few here. But all the twilight I dreampt of R's coming & how will he prize me &c. Can we please each other – is it right &c.

Billy Hammond here with Clif – all night – loves to drink too well, but a good, jolly, clever fellow – loves me as a cousin – amuses us with funny talk. He was regretting the death of our good young friend Bob Hunt & so long ago – not forgotten.[83]

Weds. April 26th Another radiant morn, but growing dry & dusty. The blue smoke rests on vast stretches of sunlit green & dewy flowers – as I sat in the piazza reading & singing & scribbling this. Clif & Billy H came out to chat nonsense – looked through telescope at the scene, shot off pistol &c. Then we gathered roses & I made Cora a pretty boquet for school & a dainty one for Bill to give his gentle love – Becky Webb. Heard Sissy's lesson &c, but I accomplished little good. Must go to Society now.

Several ladies there – talking of news – the state of Charleston. Anxious to go back to their homes. We cut out garments to make for the soldiers – shirts, drawers & socks – to give out to the needy who call for them every day. Sold some to a major. The streets were crowded with soldiers passing from the captured, disbanded armies – crowds of cavalrymen – deserters we fear. It seemed strange to see our streets so crowded with men after all who have been killed, & sad to welcome them back so quietly under these circumstances, yet few appreciate it. Brought drawers home to make. Sewing &c in evg.

Mary Morris called on me – we chatted very pleasantly. Then when the cars came in the lovely afternoon I sat & watched the soldiers pass looking so anxiously for my Robere – who came not. Will he never come? – "Will he ever be – my own?"[84]

83. William A. "Billy" Hammond, Emmala's cousin, was the son of William A. and Mary Hammond (*1860 Census,* Anderson District, 162).

Bob Hunt may be Robert Hunt of the White House section of Greenville District. A twenty-two-year-old farmer in 1860, he shared a farm with siblings William and Evaline. Private Hunt served with the Fourth South Carolina Volunteer Infantry, Company G. He died on August 24, 1861, in Germantown, Virginia (*1860 Census,* Greenville District, 511; Kirkland, *Broken Fortunes,* 254).

84. A household of women who lived at the head of Morris Street, the Morrises included mother Mary A. (45 years old in 1865), the widow of Edward P. Morris, Mary G. (23), Elizabeth P. (23), Julia (19), and a younger sister (17) whose name has been obscured by time. In later years Elizabeth taught a school at her home on Manning Street and became the organist at Grace Episcopal Church (Vandiver, *Traditions,* 57, 58, 114, 123, 305; *1860 Census,* Anderson District, 159).

Later – Theodore walked home with Eleanor from town & lingered around till he saw me – came in & chatted merrily, both of them teazing me about R – having come – which I almost believed, but evince nothing. He is anxious to learn how I receive it. He came in to hear me sing & flatter some – then spent the evg, but wouldn't go to tea. Enjoyed our flowers &c & my music – & me. Spoke of our being "such congenial friends."

We must write to each other when he is away – praised my style &c. He cares to visit no one but me. He laughs at love, or regrets for the loss in anyone else, but says "he could love the woman he chose" – forever &c. Wished he could spend every evening here, but 'twould not do. He feels there is another in the way & I'm glad. He is so silent &c. Had a pleasant evg with him for the last time soon perhaps. The faint young moon boded new love & joy I hope.

There were two soldiers came for tea & spent the evening pleasanty. Belonged to Morgan's (now Duke's Com'd). Disbanded in West Va. and now wandering about as if lost. Scarce know what to do – not anxious to go home under the circumstances. Mortified, rather go back to the front & help Johnston fight for liberty – or go on to Trans. Miss. D'pt. Hurrah for the patriots still left! Garvin – was son of eminent lawyer by that name in S.C. – now of Miss. but he has no kindred ties now spoke of it sadly & of a mother with reverence – seemed to be a true, good man – pious & brave & noble & gentle. Good looking – reminded me of dear cousin Milton Townsend. He discussed the state of affairs freely. How the loved John Morgan was so kind – lamented his death.[85]

Alex Morgan had left the Com'd & gone home to his family in Tenn. & where is my type [photograph], would that I had it. Jones of Alabama – we should judge to be rich & clever & brave – rather gay & jolly. Was a roommate of Bob Broyles – he said – at the Medical University of New York. Went to see him today – will wait to see him tomarrow. (may he come). Likes him &c, that seemed a lie to me. I want to hear them speak of each other &c. How happy R will be to get home with his family & friends & all again in this bright season. May he be safe & well & all I could wish![86]

85. General Basil Wilson Duke took command of the Second Kentucky Cavalry after the death of General John Tyler Morgan, Duke's brother-in-law. The last remnants of Duke's "brigade" were at that very moment accompanying Jefferson Davis through the South Carolina upcountry (Wakelyn, *Biographical Dictionary,* 174, 325).

The name "Garvin" is quite common in Anderson District; in fact, a northern section of the district, near the village of Pendleton, was once named Garvin Township.

86. Alex Morgan of Tennessee and Medical Officer Jones of Huntsville, Alabama, has not been identified further.

I sang war songs and a variety for the soldiers & Theo. Frazier Wilson was here calling too – a stupid kind of fellow. All seemed to appreciate music & left late. Must rest & dream now.

Thursday April 27th Delightful day – gathered roses &c. Mary Keith of Pickens & niece Ella Allan called here – plain, but nice girls – sad – for departed ones – orphans & homeless, but high minded. Refined & clever &c, enjoyed my songs. Thinks herself shut out of the world in Pickens. Sewing &c in evg – did up some laces. Liz Bleckley here & then Maria Keith called late – very pretty & pleasant – so chatty & smart. Thinks our national ruin & disgrace complete – no faith in it, yet I can't lose all.[87]

Our two stranger soldier guests came again to tea, spent the evg. Robert Garvin of Miss. whose father moved from this state as a prominent lawyer – years ago. A pupil of old Dr. Waddell – a famous old teacher in this State – taught him here. He inhereted the strict discipline, told many jokes of his whippings &c. Was a wild youth. Left the University of Ala. Ran off to the war in Central A., Nicaragua – under Walker – failed – had cholera, yellow fever &c, yet was preserved. The fourth man to volunteer from his state in this war. Been through many hardships & dangers – hardened to it – hopes to be the last in the field. Must struggle for freedom &c. Yet all this may be a deception, for last night I took him to be a saint, tonight – a sinner. Fast. Jones, the clever, ruddy chap, who I thought too gay & wicked, but he is more pious than the other – it seems, but both carried on great jokes of camp phrases (a real new dictionary). How they love the wild, free soldier's life & dislike even the rest of home – its beds &c. Oh how demoralized our men will all be – shocking![88]

He was in the University of N.Y. with R – came home when S.C. seceded. Wanted to see him, but disappointed. He is of a rich family at Huntsville, Alabama I guess. Carried on nonsense & jokes. Jones wore a new suit made today, the other laughed at him as a hotel keeper – old kit &c. Garvin stayed over to have one made. Both consider And. the most quiet place they entered during the war, but we think it full now.

87. Mary Keith of Pickens has not been identified.

Ella L. Allen of Greenville District was the daughter of stonemason James M. and wife Elizabeth (*1860 Census,* Greenville District, 408).

88. Robert Garvin of Mississippi was indeed a colorful character. Garvin was evidently one of William Walker's "immortals," a private paramilitary expedition that captured Nicaragua in 1855. Walker declared a republic, became dictator, legalized slavery, and was ousted within a year. In 1860 Walker was executed, while trying to take over Honduras.

Both Garvin and Jones were attached to Morgan's Cavalry, a unit that often passed through Anderson during the war.

I was disappointed again that R didn't come. His boy Alfred or Manuell came – the notorious scamp, yet he was faithful to his master – wouldn't go to the Yanks – after all inducements & is now safe home.

Friday April 28th A refreshing day of sunbeams & shadows – a heavy rain at noon – slow & sweet in evg. I spent the morning in my room – arranging my clothes for summer & to meet R. Read newspaper account of the assassination of Lincoln & Seward by J. Wilkes Booth – son of the actor – almost insane.

Lincoln died on the 7th of April. Anniversary of the fall of Ft. Sumter – Seward will survive. Others on the occasion wounded & died &c. Shocking tragedies. The North filled with mourning &c, yet rejoicing for their triumphs over the South complete in every instance now. They consider the war ended. Stopped their draft for soldiers. Our expenses – a million dollars. They can afford to offer liberal terms now to the South as they consider, but 'tis rumoured they were refused & hostilities will begin. We have nobody & no means left to fight. They may offer no more peace, so what will be our fate? Horrible. The soldiers still come, but no rejoicing – badness enough I guess, but how mortified & unsettled they all must feel.[89]

Aunt Anna & Will here all day busy sewing & chatting. Arranged flower wreaths in evg for Cora & Mamie & Rosa Webb to wear at night, but the rain kept kept them home from their Club. Mary went home to Grandpa's – baby so sweet & pretty. Gloomy evg – I felt sad. Pa came home from Greenville – no quorum in the Legislature – gloomy about the times – infectious!

And at last Robere came home! Pa came on the cars with he & Johny from the army in N.C. Talked with them & spoke their forlorn condition. Ragged & dirty & worn out as are all the soldiers nearly who return from that hard campaign. Said R had not changed clothes for two months. Fed corn & starved nearly for a month – no rest – long march here to Richmond nearly – feet sore & weary and gloomy I guess. Though coming home to friends & loved ones. Poor fellow! He could scarcely look at Pa straight – wonder what he was thinking of me – no inquiries. Peter McD came home too – not here. Will I see them – my two correspondents & what then?[90]

89. Abraham Lincoln was shot the evening of April 14, 1865, and died the next morning. Secretary of State Seward survived multiple knife wounds in the ensuing action.

90. Peter McDavid, "Pete," or "P. A." McDavid was Emmala's cousin from Greenville, the son of Allen and Caroline Acker McDavid. McDavid served shortly as a private with the Palmetto Riflemen, Company B, Fourth Regiment, South Carolina Volunteers, and later as a lieutenant with the South Carolina Second Rifles. He married Fannie Sullivan, daughter of Dr. J. M. Sullivan, at Greenville, South Carolina, in May 1867; the couple eventually had three children. A year before, in April 1866, Pete's sister Nellie married Fannie's brother Richard Sullivan (*Time Capsule,* 57; Salley, *South Carolina Troops,* 581; Lucas, *Early Anderson,* 66; Reed, *Journals,* Appendix F; Evans, *Confederate Military History,* 723–24).

His boy Manuell was over here in morn – telling me of their hard time & the solemn occasion of the surrender. He saw Gen. Lee with his own eyes & heard him say "no use to sacrifice his men &c" but the Yanks couldn't get him off. He was glad to rest & his master had enough of war, was sick & worn out. Poor Robert – could I cheer him? Not like his dear devoted Mother perhaps. They must have a happy family meeting over there now – six sons in the army – all spared – all here but two (they not expected now) & the two sisters here & parents. How much they will all talk on.

Aunt Anna sent to know of R – the fate of Tom Carter – could hear nothing. But all this day & night he is thus near me – almost in sight but for the trees & heavy foliage that hides his window now. Yet how far apart we are – almost forgotten the other features – 'though always together in spirit. Congenial mates perhaps & are we to be more? I thought he would have sent me a note, but none came – disappointed. He will be closely watched now – may we act openly & honourably – when & how will we meet I wonder!

I wandered at night in the dark piazza – raining without – thought of such times when he used to come. Wondered of what he was thinking &c and there was a man on the steps ere I knew it. My first thought was – "'Tis me." I felt inclined to melt into his arms – should I or not & will he expect such or would he be shocked! Then I feared 'twas some wild soldier & I screamed out "Who's that?" He told me (Frazier) Wilson & called for Miss Eleanor. She has been on every hand – three today. All admire her & why – few care for me & are they as they should be? Some others think not! A sleepy night. Give us happy dreams & happier morrow!

Sat. April 29th A variable pleasant day of smiles & tears – busy at home. Becky Webb & Eleanor ready with baskets of lunch to go to a picnic, but all parties backed out – boys & girls couldn't agree. We ate lunch at home.

Mrs. Pinkind here – we sang duetts, then to our surpize a soldier friend entered – Cousin Tom Carter. One of the captured army of Va., yet wouldn't surrender – escaped & hopeful still & brave. Had a hard time wandering about there. He looked right handsome – delicate form – wavy black hair, bright eyes & rosy face. Good & moral & so lively & blunt. Had a cold & could scarcely talk, but he & I sat chatting all day of the times &c. He said Tom & Jim Hamilton & one Charlie Jones of Abb. were all anxious to learn if I was single – wanted to visit me &c. In evg he walked down to Grandpa's – where they will be glad to see him. He reminded me of Alfred today – his voice & ways. Fear he may go the same way – with consumption – hope not.[91]

91. James "Jim" Hamilton was quartermaster for Phillip's Legion, a Georgia unit under the command of General Wade Hampton. Hamilton may have been kin to the former governor of South Carolina of the same name, making Judge A. Prioleau of Boscobel Plantation, between Anderson and Pendleton, his uncle (Vandiver, *Traditions,* 159; see Emily B. Reynolds

Guests came from Pendleton on the cars too. Helen Smith & Fannie Adams – dined here & sat some time talking Fan is fine looking – smart & stiff – talks much. I sang for them some. She went to see the Wilkinsons – spoke of their brother Joe coming home soon – having my likeness. She would send him to see me &c.[92]

Helen stayed with Eleanor – 'though nobody was much pleased, only cares to collect beaux around her. Gus Van Wyck came along, Keys McCulley with them in aft. Called this morn & at night again. A good looking merry chap! Frazier Wilson & Nick Whaley – two Charleston gents, called on them too, so they are highly entertained tonight whilst I was deploring my false or constrained lover – so near – so far! He & C went to their brother Ed's today – have so many kin to see. I can't see much of him, wonder if he is not thinking of me &c and what will be the result! All here wondering why he comes not – they will tell him tales of me I guess.[93]

In the soft – hazy – dewy moonlight – the fragrant flowers & myriad roses – dripping with pearly drops – I sat in the piazza – knitting & dreaming so sadly. For every step I thought was his and my heart would bound, but sink back more depressed – as I found he would not come! And always before when he came from trips he called on me the second day or night &c and now when most interested – he comes not & I get no message even and what does he think & feel? Direct us for the best oh God! He is weary & worn – no clothes – has to stay home with all the collected family. He would cause too much excitement were he to seek me already. He fears all of us down here & some of my letters – or tales he hears may offend. Still he will surely came ere long – or I can't stand it – late –

---

and Joan R. Faunt, comp., *Biographical Directory of the Senate of the State of South Carolina, 1776–1964* [Columbia: South Carolina Department of Archives, 1964], 229).

Charles Jones (age 24) of Abbeville was the son of teacher Joshua W. Jones and wife Ophelia. The Joneses lived in Calhouns, South Carolina (*1860 Census,* Abbeville District, 10).

Alfred evidently refers to a deceased friend or relative.

92. Frances "Fannie" S. Adams (b. April 9, 1839) was the daughter of Placida Mayrant Adams, widow of the Reverend Jasper Adams (d. 1841), first president of Hobart College in New Jersey, where Fannie returned after the war. Mrs. Adams was a planter who had assets totaling $30,000 in 1860. Her siblings included Elizabeth, Carolina, and Joseph. Elizabeth wed Archibald Campbell, from New York in 1859, and the Adams girls traveled north to see their sister as soon as the war was over (*1860 Census,* Pickens District, 58; Simpson, *Old Pendleton,* 146; Smith, *Book of the Dead,* 61; Lander and McGee, *A Rebel Came Home,* 74, 98).

Joseph Wilkinson was a Charleston attorney.

93. Lydia Ann Maverick married New York attorney William Van Wyck, and the couple had seven children. Daughter Lydia was about seventeen years old in 1866, very close to Mattie's

Sunday April 30th A delightful day at church & S.S. Some couriers came from Greenville to say they expected a Yankee raid there & warn us to be ready too – but no one seemed much excited or to believe it. We little thought the storm was about to burst upon us so soon.[94]

All that day & night & next I looked in vain for R – or a messenger – can't understand him again – mortified &c. Theodore with me in evg – singing – quarrelling &c.

---

own age. The oldest Van Wyck child, Dr. Sam Van Wyck (1835–61) married Margaret Caroline Broyles (1834–1923). "Maggie," sister of Oze Robert Broyles, was a cousin who had once been close to Emmala Reed. Dr. Van Wyck was killed in Kentucky while serving with General Nathan Bedford Forrest. His sons left South Carolina and prospered. Robert Anderson Van Wyck was a New York City judge and the first mayor of greater New York City. His brother Augustus or "Gus" was a New York State supreme court justice and a democratic candidate for governor of New York.

Lydia Van Wyck's brother, Samuel Augustus Maverick (1803–70), went off to Texas in 1835 during the Republic's war for independence. Maverick was taken prisoner and was awaiting execution when the United States minister to Mexico, General Waddy Thompson of Greenville, South Carolina, a close family friend, obtained his release. Emmala Reed was named after Mrs. Waddy Thompson (Emmala Butler Thompson), a close friend of Mrs. Reed's (Dickson, *Journeys,* 71–74; Simpson, *Old Pendleton,* 107–10; *1860 Census,* Anderson District, 296; Vandiver, *Traditions,* 68, 118–19; Everson and Simpson, *Far, Far, from Home,* 98; William Watts Ball, *The State That Forgot: South Carolina's Surrender to Democracy* [Indianapolis, Ind.: Bobbs-Merrill, 1932], 105–6); see Reed, *Journals,* Appendix F.

William "Nick" Whaley was part of a family of refugees from Edisto Island, South Carolina, staying with William B. Smith, a Charleston banker and the father of Helen Smith, to whom he was married at Pendleton's St. Paul's Episcopal Church on August 29, 1865 (Edwin H. Vedder, *Records of St. Paul's Episcopal Church of Pendleton, South Carolina,* [Greenville: A Press, 1946], 38).

94. Federal cavalry under the command of Major James Lawson rode into Greenville on May 2 (Huff, *Greenville,* 144).

THREE

MAY

Monday May 1st 1865 Dawned as bright and beautiful as every Mayday before – but we little expected it was to be so desecrated here! All schools & young folks of the village went out on picnics in the woods – with lunch and dances & fun – many of our village soldiers at home & some strangers. I was not invited to any – strange. Eleanor & Helen went to one – Mamie to another and thus they were all scattered – when the enemy approached and flew home amongst them in the greatest alarm. We were terrified 'till they came – for by this time we begun to realize it.[1]

Rumours of their approach came all day. Cousin Tom Carter was here with us – we sat chatting nonsense, but he was so calm & collected – didn't believe a word of it – laughed at our fears. But Pa came at noon said it was positive – advized us to pack up our clothes & valuables for moving off in the country somewhere that night 'though we could think of no place of safety. We went to the plantation to order the mules & wagons brought up quietly thinking we were a day ahead any way. Ma began to tear up drawers to pack clothes & silver &c in boxes, but I hadn't the energy or heart to do anything. Felt petrified & despairing.

My greatest grief being that I could not see Robere & perhaps never might again, until some awful change had swept over one or both. Destruction of property, of persons, or change of heart that might alter our whole after life, but I never

1. The Yankees were in fact on the way. It is somewhat remarkable that Andersonians went right ahead with their May Day festivals, regardless of the imminent danger.

An excellent source on "Brown's Raid" is Thomas Bland Keys's article titled "The Federal Pillage of Anderson, South Carolina: Brown's Raid," *South Carolina Historical Magazine* 76 (April 1975): 80–85. Keys wrote that one celebration was "a large group of juveniles" supervised by a Mr. La Far at Silver Brook and the other a school outing on the Rocky River. Both locations were a few miles from the courthouse square.

Federal troops commanded by Colonel William J. Palmer and General Simeon B. Brown invaded Anderson while pursuing President Jefferson Davis and the Confederate government's gold he was believed to have with him. There were cavalry troops from the Eleventh Michigan, the Fifteenth Pennsylvania, the Eleventh and Twelfth Kentucky, and the Eighth, Ninth, and Thirteenth Tennessee, totaling two brigades or about 3,600 troops.

Brown had to fight off two skirmishes with home guard units in the district, and his arrival in Anderson was delayed until late afternoon on May 1, 1865. This first wave of invaders stayed for about three days. Also see Robert Underwood Johnson, *Battles and Leaders of the Civil War,* (rept. 1970; New York: Thomas Yoseloff, 1956), 4:479.

thought we could forget or neglect each other! Fannie was going up there to see them to get some money of hers from the Dr., her guardian, so I couldn't resist writing a wild note to him, which it is fortunate she did not deliver perhaps – no chance.

Mrs. Wilhite was here & went there much alarmed and Dr. W sent her to hasten home – the enemy were at hand. So Clif & Tom Carter came from town to tell us – they saw a man who was their prisoner 8 miles from here & escaped. Then we hurried around wildly, but in a few minutes more they were upon us & all was wild terror & confusion!

I had just torn my clothes out of my trunk &c when many horseman galloped by – shouting & shooting. And for a moment I did not dream, it was the foe, but then it came – "the Yankees, the Yankees!" And all of us rushed together screaming. Ma & the children – white & black – & we girls – negroes all willing to help us bring & hide clothes & silver &c – some of them crying in terror.

We found they were pursuing some of Wheeler's & other S. cavalry passing through & taking up all the men prisoners – paroling some – passing by those who had paroles from Lee's army, but confining many in the C.H. for a few days. Clifton was so excited & rash – rushed out toward those who were rushing madly past exclaiming "what does this mean?" &c.[2]

Several stopped at the gate – calling him to come out with many oaths or they would blow his brains out – with arms pointed towards him & one shivered a sword on the gate, of which I have a scrap. They made he & Tom Carter walk before them, to town, as prisoners. They observed Tom's parole, but Clif had some trouble in getting them to "respect his stump," but at last an officer let him come home. They hurried back to our delight, for we were all in terror here. Eleanor had screamed at them, for she & Mamie had just rushed in from the picnic in alarm. Fannie followed him to the gate & would have gone on with him had he allowed. Stood about there coolly 'till his return.[3]

Then three great ruffians in blue suits & fully armed rushed in the back way to Ma's room – calling for arms – took an old gun & shivered it. "Knew we had more" – we had just hidden two & saved them, but we had to get out three elegant little

2. General Joseph Wheeler fought in 127 battles, was wounded three times with sixteen horses shot from under him, and rose to the post of senior cavalry general, C.S.A. Wheeler's cavalry units often passed through Anderson in the preceding years, but they were gone by May 1. In May 1865 Wheeler was captured in Georgia; he received a parole in June (Stewart Sifakis, *Who Was Who in the Civil War* [New York: Facts on File, 1988], 708; Wakelyn, *Biographical Dictionary,* 434; Warner, *Generals in Gray,* 332–33).

3. According to Louise Vandiver, the townsmen without pardons were kept on the second floor of the courthouse. Clif escaped by simply slipping to the rear of a massive column, then making his way home, a few blocks away (Vandiver, *Traditions,* 240).

pistols & give them up. Yet the key to the drawer could scarcely be found. Ma was excited, but talked cool – tried in vane [*sic*] to find the key awhile, they impatient – threatening to break it open, but at last they got them & marched off. One had primped himself before the glass. So cool & impudent.

I felt so humiliated & alarmed, but calm. Wouldn't go near them – though the others all stood amongst them, ready to talk or protect each other. Then a crowd came in the other way & called for liquor – had to get a jug full, which they got & dashed off with. We feared much danger from these drunken wretches. But all these were in terror of being detected by officers – we could see – for they were so hurried & just then an elegant looking young officer – Captain Patterson – Adj. Gen'l of Brown's Division – Stoneman's corps – came & rang the bell politely. He asked "if we would have a guard – sorry it had not come before we were molested &c." In a few moments sent one who proved a most faithful & invaluable sentinel & saved us much danger!

But ere this – a gang had taken both of our good old carriage horses from the stable – "Pearce & Derry" – ordering Emory [a Reed family servant] to give them up. We were too sorry to see them going off – rode through our yard afterwards. What will be their fate? To be rode to death very soon I've no doubt. How we shall miss them – no more riding for us!

Still Pa was in town amongst them & we didn't know what his fate might be. We saw him come to the gate with an officer, ask if we had a guard & go back – then soon return alone & unharmed, thank heavens. He had been in his office beginning to remove notes, money &c from his safe & just had all strewn around when they rushed through town. Our citizens dispersed in all directions. He stood there alone amongst them – for as Mayor of the town he went right out to meet them & ask for terms, but a ruffian had already dashed up & threatened to shoot him if he didn't open his & another door there, which they did, but the man rode off.

Pa advanced to meet the Gen'ls Brown & Miller of Stoneman's cavalry raid of over 2000 men – who had at last come to sweep our little unprotected village! They had been trying to get up some defense before, but 'twas well that none was attempted or we would have been destroyed! We hear they said "They hoped some defense would have been made here, for this was the hotbed of Secession & they wished to ruin us."[4]

4. General Simeon B. Brown was a tall man of fifty-three years, who wore a brown hat with the brim pinned up in front. Brown hailed from St. Clair, Michigan, where he owned the City Hotel. He resigned from the army on June 11, 1865, and died in 1893 at age eighty-one. John K. Miller, in command of Brown's Third Brigade (Eighth, Ninth, and Thirteenth Tennessee Cavalry) was still a colonel at the time.

Vandiver relates a story that the identity of Brown and his brigade was intentionally obscured after the war, when Andersonians sought redress for grievances regarding the May 1

We were forced to be submissive – humiliating as it was – for our little militia force – few arms &c – could have done nothing here – now that Lee's & Johnston's armies have surrendered. We have no further means of carrying on the war & could only have reaped desolation now at the last & of course "self preservation" is the first instinct.

Gen'l Brown seemed to be rather a hard – indifferent man. Said they were ordered to collect horses – arms & tithes of provisions as we did – from the Commissary stores and they had soon robbed the place of all these things. Pa pointed out to him a building where were stored quantities of liquers of Mr. Guardine of Charleston – wine merchant. At least $200,000 worth of splendid old wines – brandies &c considered invaluable by these men, but ought to have been destroyed – to prevent drunkeness & ruin here which was visited upon Columbia. He promised to keep his soldiers from it, but didn't try. They were soon breaking in & drinking madly & all trembled for the effects. Happily – night soon came & then strict orders drove them out to camps in the suburbs. Only the patrol guards left to ride the streets & a guard – one or more at nearly every house. All was soon as quiet as though no hostile foe occupied the town & human hearts throbbed in terror.[5]

The soft young moon shone sweetly down on the fragrant earth & all was calm & lovely, but how the earth quaked with dread & horrible suspense in fear of worse things! Pa came safely home & we were all together. Helen Smith & Tom Carter here besides. Both very cool. A forage master came with orders to take our fodder for the horses & soon that was all gone, but no corn. He promised to come back & stay with us as a kind of protection, which he did – faithfully. Another wretch, "a Galvanized Yankee," who had deserted on both sides kept here as a cooper at work six months & married here. He joined them, rushed here demanding a saddle (guard protected it) and threatened Pa with much danger. This alarmed all, but nothing came of it. (We ate supper in quiet with two Yankee's as guests – enemy's & robbers – but ostensible protectors & so they proved bearable.)

---

raid (Keys, "Brown's Raid," 80, 81, 86; Vandiver, *Traditions,* 241; Mrs. William H. Overman and Flora C. Keith, "May Day in Anderson, South Carolina, in 1865," in United Daughters of the Confederacy South Carolina Division, *Recollections and Reminiscences, 1861–1865 through World War I,* vol. 4 (1993), 366–68.

5. Mr. Henry Guardine (Gourdin), a Charleston merchant, must have thought his valuable goods safe in a remote town like Anderson. The 3,600 bottles were stored in the basement of B. F. Crayton's store on the courthouse square. Judge Reed, in all likelihood, was trying to avoid further destruction and possibly divert the attention of the raiders by allowing them to get good and drunk (Keys, "Brown's Raid," 83; Vandiver, *Traditions,* 239; Stevenson, *Diary of Clarissa Adger Bowen,* 67, 73; Lander and McGee, *A Rebel Came Home,* 84).

The guard was a dirty, stupid youngster from mid Tenn., was wounded in Longstreet's corps in Va., then deserted or was freed to go with the enemy. Has no choice either way I think, but wants to go back home. Seemed very contented to sit & walk around here & sleep. Yet, no plunder – though he needed a horse & clothes &c. He never left the place – walked about whistling or singing merrily (the native talent). Had a right good face. Talked with us all – too much if anything, but seemed earnest & took good care of us. Many villains asked if we had a guard – or came in & were repelled. So we were glad little "Hinton" – stayed so closely here with his "two story horse," which he promised to give us if he could get another – did not.

The officer was a real cute & impertinent downEaster from New York – near the lakes. Red hair – florid face – hooked nose & nasal twang of the Yankees & their broad pronunciation. He tried to quiz us much & Pa was rather too obsequious. He would communicate nothing, a sly, mean – exultant look. I feared to speak to him – we could have quarrelled &c. (Lt. Wood, who lived in New York – near the lakes) talked loudly & freely of everything. Got few replies from us & fewer smiles, though his were profuse, with many impertinent glances from cynical eyes. (He was a married man, he told Pa) Rather gallant to us. Presumed once to ask me if I were single & guessed my age (26) exactly (Oh the cute Yankee!) and urged me to guess his. At last I said 30 & he added three, but I felt disgusted!

He told us "they were Stoneman's Com'd." Left Knoxville Tenn. some weeks ago – many thousands strong dashed on through N.C. & here. Came from "Ceasar's [*sic*] Head" – the grand view in our state – marked it "their headquarters – April 30th/65" Left there only yest. at noon & rode rapidly here in a day – Over 70 miles – the strongest brigade – Palmer's – going through Greenville. He couldn't tell us their force here – or their destination. Was guarded & suspectful of his words – not insulting, but prophesied that in two years Robt Lee, our southern hero whom they venerate, will be leading the Union armies to Mexico to whip France &c. Will it be so, with our fickle, humiliated people? Perhaps so.

He slept under our roof, giving us every assurance of protection & the guard lay outside, under a tree, near their two horses feeding, but we all sat up – or lay around in the parlor – undressed & fearful. Ready for an emergency – a long, weary night. I lay on the floor near – Ma & Pa. – slept fitfully – heard the patrols passing through sometimes. We were mercifully preserved.

Tues. May 2nd dawned at last. A long day of terror. All up & watchful with the early dawn. Three ladies came early to ask Pa to help them get a guard. Mrs. Belcher, Mary Waller & Catherine Gadsden – saying Mr. Brown's house was near a picket post, but no guard, was fearfully robbed of provisions &c. Then later – came Maggie Van Wyck & Tom Broyles on the same errand – to get a guard, but both parties had to go & apply at hdqurts, Gen. Brown at the hotel.

They (the Broyles) had been searched – horses, arms, the vegetables in the garden taken and their father's watch. The faithful old time peace, by which he had connoted pulses – 30 yrs – snatched from him – to the regret of all. Maggie grew eloquent in describing the excitement there once more. One brother, Wm Newry in Tenn. She & her two little boys. Sallie & child with Mr. Williams & brother Tom – just arrived. Gus (Broyles) & Tiny Bacon fled from the Enrolling office in Greenville & that day had just entered the house and been thus suprized. Robert & Tom & John, the three youngest brothers, just from the Army. The two just paroled from Lee's army & could have stayed at home safely, but all were taken by surprize. Thought it was Kirk's desperate raiders & so all started at the first alarm & rushed to the woods & swamps for safety.[6]

The Williams mounted their fine horses & leaping the fence, were gone like a flash & escaped all. John & Gus – too late to mount – horses taken – ran off on foot one way, but were captured next day & paroled, 'though they threatened to take Capt. Gus on to Tenn. He & all the Enrolling office here escaped after much pleading. Robert & Col. Edward B. ran towards their farm on Rocky River – pursued & shot at, but escaped throughout by lying in swamps several days. (Manuell feeding them). And all that time I had no token from him – only my fears & suspense. What did it mean? Tom & Tiny Bacon were too late to escape – stayed at home unharmed from the shots around. Sallie thought her husband was shot & fainted. All was confusion & alarm there![7]

Maggie was the same smart – noble – interesting woman I had long known & loved, but so estranged to me. Tom resembled her, was a fine looking – stately – commanding looking person – rather haughty & irritable, but a man to love & admire & influence by some fond, noble woman. Who will it be? He seemed nervous & excited 'though by the insults at home he was powerless to act or resent. Seemed so fond of his sister and I know they are all so happy at home now. So intelligent a family – must enjoy this reunion.

I did long to be with them, as formerly or as R & I might have dreamed, yet is it all over forever & what does he mean by this silence & neglect. So near – yet so

6. Tiny or John E. Bacon was an attorney in Edgefield, South Carolina, before the war. He was thirty-four years old and served in the commissary for the Seventh S. C. Infantry (*1860 Census,* Edgefield District, 109; Hewett, *Confederate Soldiers,* 17).

7. James Thomas Bacon, son of E. L. and Sara A. Bacon of Edgefield Court House, South Carolina, attended Union College in Schenectady, New York, and the University of Leipzig, Germany. Bacon taught music at the Johnson Female University in 1854. Later he was editor of the *Edgefield Chronicle,* a name Emmala evidently miswrote. Garlington states that Bacon was a "well-known writer and lecturer" who never married; "Tiny" Bacon was his cousin (Garlington, *Men of the Time,* 10; Vandiver, *Traditions,* 112; *Le Bas Bleu,* vol. 1, no. 5 (Aug. 1854), 2.

far. After all his late professions &c. Strange creature! He knows they oppose, is afraid to venture openly in this uncertain state of affairs, but is he unhappy about it? He might at least write to me. They soon departed. Will they ever come again?

We all sat talking the day away in anxious suspense – a long, bright, sunny day. Stragglers would come around – with evil intentions no doubt, but were repelled by the guard. Our Lt. took every meal with us – talking much. Meanwhile the ruffians were let loose & were throwing open the stores, public & private, in town – pillaging everything, assisted by poor whites & negroes who made themselves rich for once. Quantities of cloth & thread & a variety of articles, fancy & useful. Bacon, flour – salt & sugar were cast away.

All our negroes & everybodie's were there, taking off loads. Some shared with their owners. We got some fine thread & writing paper only. They all roamed about free & careless for several days & no work done. They no doubt thought the year of Jubilee had come. All dreamed of freedom & discussed the prospect, no doubt, but were too sensible to go off with this wild raiding party, save the reckless boys – who dashed around armed on horses. Proudly & defiantly! Dozens went off from here, but many were sent back or willingly returned to good homes & owners and get on now as usual. We thought some of ours might go, but didn't care much. Let them choose their own fate. May it be for the best!

The wild crew tore up everything in the depot – cars & R.R. – fruit &c. Then on to the University – the Treasury Dp't now, which no doubt attracted them here. And then we could hear the destruction all morning, as all the iron presses & works were broken to pieces and confederate paper money scattered all over the earth – books &c burned up. All totally demolished! Much of the money was not signed & valueless, so it all will be soon. Every negro & child had piles of it. Hundreds of dollars which we took as worthless, but 'tis so useless & so humiliating now to think that this is the fate of our currency & our Gov't! All of our old school relics were destroyed up there, except Mrs. Daniels tablet – safe here. Did her pure spirit look down on such a scene & Dr. Johnson, our old Chancellor! Both spared much suffering here![8]

8. Johnson Female Seminary was established in 1848 by Daniel Brown, J. P. Reed, and Stephen McCulley. The Baptist minister William Bullion Johnson was named chancellor and J. S. Murray president. The school averaged six hundred students a year, many boarding on campus or at a variety of locations all over town.

The central structure of the school housed the printing presses of the Confederate Treasury during the last year of the war. Invading federal cavalry destroyed the treasury hardware and occupied the grounds as a temporary camp. Later the First Maine Infantry took possession of the building and grounds, using the university buildings as headquarters, barracks, hospital, and the district Freedmen's Bureau offices.

So the work of destruction went on all day. Many houses were entered & plundered of clothes – silver, jewels, provisions & everything, but it was because the wretches had broken into the stores of liquors which we should have poured out & drank so profusely. Many drunken demons did fearful damage – with oaths & insults to many poor creatures without guards. [W]e feared our town would be destroyed but the drunken mad-men as was Columbia, but thank heaven – 'twas spared!

The Tuppers lost everything & suffered much. Three women alone – Dick in the woods. The Silcox's were plundered & alarmed – poor Tillie sick & fainting. The old man hidden out & half crazy. Mr. Myers, who suffered so much in Columbia, had spasms since, was hung up until nearly dead, to make him reveal about their gold – failed. Dr. Cater's place & clothes torn up. He hung up for the same purpose. So at the Winthrop's Dr. W. was hung up & beaten with a shovel. Even good old Mrs. W. threatened with hanging. The Ruccor's house, being empty, was sacked – furniture & all destroyed. Whitner's house threatened with burning. Mrs. Glover & other ladies made to play the piano for them.[9]

Old Nancy Hammond lost much – was shook & injured. Frank Hammond's folks (absent) lost everything at home – nearly – clothes of all the family taken.

Soon after the federal garrison left, townsfolk created the coeducational Carolina Collegiate Institute, with W. J. Ligon as president. This move was clearly a reaction intended to avoid turning the old college into a permanent school for freedmen and their children. In 1889 Col. John B. Patrick opened the Patrick Military Academy, which closed its doors in the 1920s.

Johnson Female Seminary (often referred to as a university), Emmala's alma mater, was quite close to Echo Hall, yet the presence of Yankee sentries made the school a place to be avoided, at least by the ladies of the Reed family (Elizabeth Belser Fuller, ed., *Anderson County Sketches* [Anderson, S.C.: Drake House, 1969]; Vandiver, *Traditions,* 111–18

9. Mr. Myers has not been identified from the information available.

Dr. A. P. Cater was indeed strung up by his thumbs and questioned concerning local outlaws and hidden treasure. When the torture proved fruitless, the raiders left and Dr. Cater was cut down. A local Anderson physician, Dr. Cater (age 50) was married to Martha Postelle (47). The couple had four children: Enoch (17), William (23), Essie (25), and Tom (19) (Vandiver, *Traditions,* 198, 240, 259; *1860 Census,* Anderson District, 260).

Sixty-two-year-old Dr. Henry Winthrop stayed at the Pendleton home of Dr. Henry Ravenel. His niece, Caroline Ravenel, was present for much of the incident. The old doctor was hanged from his bedstead until his toes just barely touched the ground. He was beaten until he disclosed the location of some hidden gold (Stevenson, *Diary of Clarissa Adger Bowen,* 51–52; Keys, "Brown's Raid," 83; Caroline R. Ravenel to Isabella Middleton Smith, May 18, 1865, in Daniel E. Huger Smith, Alice R. Huger Smith, and Arney R. Childs, ed., *Mason Smith Family Letters, 1860–1868* [Columbia: University of South Carolina Press, 1950], 213; James A. Hoyt, "The First Day of May, 1865," *Anderson Intelligencer,* May 3, 1866).

Those of the departed, Josie & Ben with their ambrotypes most regretted. We learned afterwards that at Grandpa Hammond's much harm was done. He had hidden out with his horses, but drunken crowds came & stole clothes & all little useful articles – pictures – clothes of Nick & Alfie – the dear departed.[10]

Built fires in the floor & piled on clothes several times, but one of the party begged for them. One vile wretch spit at dear Lucie, yet I don't know yet how they took it all. Elias Earle's family suffered most perhaps – pointed out as rich. Palmer's Brigade – coming from Greenville – had camped there. He & staff in the house, but protected nothing. Destroyed all the provisions & clothes. Took negroes & made them give up jewels & silver & gold. Shot at the ladies & made them produce the buried treasure or would burn. Started to hang up poor Preston, but all stood out bravely, said burn or hang I won't yield.

On the whole no lives were lost & everyone can manage to live I guess. Many horses were taken, but they left mean ones behind & gave to other people. So some crops can be made, perhaps. A fearful prospect still, but thank heavens it was no worse.

At noon – our Yankee Lt. came & brought some of the fine wines & brandy as a present to Clif &c, to my regret, for he & Tom loved to drink it too well. 'Twas old & very fine & may serve us in sickness yet. Then we heard their band of music playing in the C.H. finely. Many stirring airs, which we couldn't help admiring. It seemed so strange to hear the four discussing – Dixie – Yankee Doodle &c in our streets so triumphantly & my heart thrilled sadly! It broke sweetly on the calm – sunny air of noon – filled with bloom & fragrance, but I wept sadly.

10. The identity of Old Nancy Hammond remains obscure.

Benjamin Franklin "Frank" Hammond (age 54) was a farmer who had a $54,000 estate in 1860. He had a large family and moved to Florida with wife, Mary C. (46) and children William, Benjamin F., Catherine, Garand, and Oscar (*1860 Census,* Anderson District, 163).

Ben was Benjamin Franklin Hammond. A Private B. F. Hammond appears on the roll of the First South Carolina Rifles (Orr's Rifles). He was twenty-two years old when he died May 23, 1864, at Lynchburg, Virginia (South Carolina Department of Archives and History, *The Roll of the Dead: South Carolina Troops, Confederate States Service* [Columbia: n.p, 1994], 204).

Elbert Marion Ruccor (Rucker), was born at Ruckersville, Georgia. A graduate of the University of Georgia and Harvard University, Rucker was a member of the 1851 State's Rights Convention in Milledgeville, Georgia, and he served in the Georgia State Legislature. "E. M." married Sarah Francis Whitner, daughter of Judge Joseph N. Whitner, in 1853. According to Garlington, E. M. Rucker did not actually move to Anderson until 1872 (Garlington, *Men of the Time,* 368–69; Simpson, *Old Pendleton,* 171; Vandiver, *Traditions,* 117, 262, 270, 281; Bailey et al., *South Carolina Senate, 1776–1985,* 3:1718).

Nick and Alfie Hammond have not been identified.

Our Lt. promised to bring the band to serenade us, but did not fortunately or it might have been spoken of.[11]

As he & guard sat talking to us – Theodore Smith came down to see what had become of Helen & all of us – talked nonsense awhile. His room had been entered. As they approached him to search his person for gold &c He fell back on the pitcher with a view of breaking it over his head & threw his gold eyeglasses at them, which they were mean enough to take. He couldn't hear their approach, then they left him.

A gang offered him tobacco, wines &c, but he declined. 'Though his manner pleased them & they said "We like you." They stole his pocket book containing a little money & my tress of hair. All his treasures were gone & his talisman. He begged for more but I declined – not his to have again.

At last that weary day had dragged over and brought another long sleepless night. Our Lt. had talked much & asked me to play & sing, which I didn't like to do – but did. Sang a few tame songs. Didn't care to attempt any national air & provoke words &c. He said nothing – asked Eleanor for Dixie. He & the guard were both to watch us again, but suddenly about 10 o'clock there was a bugle call to mount. They started up in surprize & wouldn't tell what it meant – settled down to stay anyway, as we hoped, for we feared it was a signal to burn or something, but it wasn't repeated. They were sent for by a young bugler – who ate supper and then they went – saying they expected to march on but wouldn't say why or where they were in such hot haste. Gave hints that it was in pursuit of Pres't Davis as we heard he was passing through with many guards to the Trans. Miss & we hope they will escape.[12]

Our Lt. rode off in haste, saying 'my love to you all!' and he would return if they stayed. Our guard lingered about for some time, willing to stay & protect us, but

11. "Dixie" was a song written by Daniel Decatur Emmett in 1859 with the original title "I Wish I Was in Dixie's Land." The song took on political lyrics, and the South took it as their own battle hymn. The popular tune was played at the inaugurations of both Abraham Lincoln and Jefferson Davis (Diane Ravitch, ed. *The American Reader: Words that Moved a Nation* [New York: HarperCollins, 1990], 139.

"Yankee Doodle" was a popular tune of the American colonial era, when the British used it to poke fun at the American colonists and their provincial manner ("Yankee" was a derisive term for a New Englander and a "doodle" was a fool). The Americans played the tune as an act of defiance, much as the Union troops did in Emmala's description (Ravitch, *American Reader,* 11–12).

12. Jefferson Davis and his entourage were passing very close to Anderson. They were in Abbeville, S. C. on April 28, and by May 3 President Davis had crossed the Savannah River and entered Washington, Georgia (Denny, *Civil War Years,* 563–74).

he too mounted his tall Rosinante[13] & rode off with some rations for our thanks. We listened then to the different bugle calls & orders to mount! Forward! March &c, whilst their band played "Yankee doodle"

We heard the dull, heavy tramp of retreating thousands at the hour of midnight, until all was silent. We knew not their object & trembled for the result, thinking they left orders to burn the public works. There were many threats made about Pa's & Col. Orr's houses & we trembled. ([T]hey robbed & tore up his house terribly. He lay out for many days & nights. They might have injured him & the C.H. was full of prisoners whom they treated to cognacs &c, then released on Weds.)

All night long we watched in suspense, hearing still the dashing of patrols I suppose, but many houses were robbed & threatened. We just escaped several times we fancied by their arrest – thank heaven! At last that weary night was over! Clif & Tom Carter & some of the servants by day went out to their camps to try & pick up some horses or mules, as all of ours were stolen, but they had all been taken up, to our regret – 'though we afterwards managed to borrow several for the farm – none to ride yet. We slept some after another bright & peaceful dawn!

Weds. May 3rd Was a calm, lovely day – for awhile no tramping, cursing foes, no rattling of vehicles & of citizens, but all resting from the excitement & robbed of their treasures. Yet, ere night it waxed higher than ever for 'twas said that Kirk's terrible raiders, or outlaws from the mountains, were coming down to burn & destroy. Some thought that Sherman's or Thomas' armies were near. Many wild rumours afloat – so we all packed up clothes to move out in case of burning & hid bundles at obscure houses &c.

Our negroes went out to camp & brought in sacks of corn. Many bushels were gathered up by the people & other valuables. We had thought that several of the men had gone or wished to go off, but all were faithful. Yet some confessed that it was because they were too old & had families they couldn't leave behind. They couldn't go. Some talked a little pert, were idle & free a few days, but all soon settled down to their usual routine. Very respectful as far as we can see, but I rather dread them yet. Henry took our jewels &c off & buried them that day (got them all safe afterwards).

We heard such bad reports from Grandpa's that Tom Carter had to leave us in the evg & go to them. We missed him much – were alone that awful night – for we heard wilder rumours than ever. All the men in town nearly hid out in the woods for fear of being "hurt" as was threatened. Pa was pursuaded to go – as a

13. Rosinante was Don Quixote's faithful mount.

prominent "Secesh" with many home enemies too. He with Dr. Broyles & several Charleston men stole out at dark & remained safe in the woods all night.[14]

In the aft a parcel of the provost guard & other rash boys here. Came to Pa to get arms to go out & arrest some stragglers, but he pursuaded them not to do so – it would do only harm. (It was reported afterwards that he encouraged it & was marked for it – we trembled for that!) But they would go their way & a small squad arrested two Yankees. A small party came up. Some threats & shots exchanged in town. One youth was shot dead or left to die there, alone in the streets, whilst all scattered.[15]

"Theodore Parker" of Charleston. Nephew of the Perroneaus here – a boy of 17 – very rash, but brave. Dick Tupper was knocked in the breast by a gun – almost fainted, revived in the hotel. He & Joe Hyde pursued home by pistols several times, (hid). A negro man shot accidently, his leg was amputated & he died, probably from too much chloroform. So that was the sad tradgedy of the war in our streets. [W]e feared they would take vengeance that night, but thank heaven we were spared. We sent for Capt. Daniels' from Reeves' to come & stay with us. He limped over, but became much alarmed for his own safety, as well as ours. Had a presentiment of evil – as when he was shot – couldn't sit up – so he wouldn't stay. Had a servant to go home with him – then we were all alone. Clif was unwell – so we slept on the sofa & Fan & I watched, going out often to listen.[16]

About midnight heard many troops marching through. Palmer's Com'd perhaps & a negro Brigade. All went through quietly several nights – in perfect control, with flags of truce – disturbing no one. They went on through to Ga., where they were garrisoned at Athens & different towns, we hear – for they consider the whole South subjugated & it virtually is.

We can make no further resistance, but what is to be our fate? The order was promulgated that Sherman & Grant were making terms of peace & hostilities were to cease, but we don't know the particulars. Only hope that old Andy Johnson won't be allowed control, for he will give no mercy we hear. Rumours of Foreign

14. The threat of terrorism remained strong, especially for men like Judge Reed, who had signed the ordinance of secession. Federal troops frequently invaded Southern towns in widely spaced waves to keep the citizens in a constant state of fear.

15. "Provost guard" is a military term for a police unit. In this case, a group of young men, most likely veterans, were about and looking for trouble by detaining stray federal troopers. They hoped to obtain sanction from the local civil authority figure, intendant J. P. Reed. Reed placed James Hoyt in command of the hastily formed home guard unit.

16. Thomas Keys identifies this youth as McKenzie Parker, who had served with the Marion Artillery. Parker aimed a pistol at one of Brown's troopers and demanded the man surrender. He pulled the trigger twice, misfired both times, and was subsequently shot in the chest (Keys, "Brown's Raid," 80–86).

aid & recognition keep coming, but we don't know the truth. There are no mails, we have no money, no means, no gov't, no hope scarcely! Are a ruined – humiliated people! Awful to contemplate.[17]

Ga. & we perhaps deserved it for sin & imbecility – a falling off from just principles. The civil & military authorities corrupt, desertion, speculation, robbery, drinking, mismanagement & the loss of confidence in the Pres't & civil authorities – ruined us – whilst a powerful – perservering – cunning – cruel Yankee nation have outnumbered us & overpowered us, but what will the end be we fear to know. All feel subdued, but bear our calamities as cheerfully as possible. That third sleepless – weary night was gone & we safe again at home. E.T.R.[18]

Thursday May 4th No more raiders had come and we began to be at peace, but all of us were listless & fearful & unhappy. Some boys began to call on the girls. Nick Whaley, Frazier Wilson, Keys McCulley, Dick Tupper & Joe Hyde here many times during week – Eleanor & Helen delighted.

In the aft. I ventured out to the Bap. church to attend the funeral of young Parker. Many there who had passed safe through the storm. Very dusty streets seemed polluted still by Yankee steps & breath &c! And there lay their young victim, covered with flowers. I had made one wreath of white roses. No near relatives of his here.

Next day another youth (Majors) was buried there – had shot himself with one of their broken guns – accidently (sad) & died at the hospital. A Yankee lies there now wounded, shot in the country by a bushwacker as several were. We are glad they were not molested here or all might have suffered more. I stopped at the Wilhites coming back. They talked rather pert – get up so many rumours there. Displeased with us for not running after to help them &c.

I came home & found Theodore Smith here with the girls & he remained all night to protect us. Chatted nonsense with me awhile. Sang for him &c. We all slept rather peaceably that night. Still fearing some danger. He sat in his chamber all night as usual – reading Carlysle's Essays – enjoyed them – found no foe. He was cool & brave 'though effeminate – rather.[19]

17. President Andrew Johnson felt little remorse for the Southern aristocracy, yet his plan for Reconstruction was considered quite lenient, and he soon created provisional state governments all over the newly defeated Confederacy. South Carolina's provisional governor would be Benjamin F. Perry of Greenville, an old law partner of Judge Reed's.

18. Emmala provides an interesting assessment of Confederate rule.

19. English author Thomas Carlyle (1795–1881) was strongly influenced by the American Transcendentalist movement. The "essays" may refer to a series of lectures titled *On Heroes, Hero-Worship, and the Heroic in History* (1841).

Friday May 5th I was down early singing. Theo came down & joined me – his bright earnest eyes – so long sleepless – sat down & enjoyed the music, but sang for him & talked nonsense until I grew tired & dismissed him rather abruptly. Didn't know then he felt it so much, but I was sleepy & sad, longing to see R.

Young Whaley & Wilson &c here with the girls and my former friend, Tiny Bacon came to see us – a handsome – chatty, clever fellow, but so practical & unimpressible &c. Played some very nice, correct pieces for me on the piano, but mechanically – pronounced my best songs & sweetest flowers &c "only nice or right pretty." So different from his enthusiastic cousin Jim B., my teacher once.

But Tiny was made a practical man of (far better) by the stern duties & losses of this war. Lost his leg & his brother, his horse & arms & employment as As. Enr. officer at G. – has nothing now to fall back on. Still uneasy about his father & mother & two little brothers &c – trying to get home & can't – poor boy.

But I am sorry that I was so far ruled by my impulses as to send the note I scribbled on Monday to R in my alarm & excitement, by him, a stranger, but I have it – unaddressed – as if a relict of "somebody's." That he would understand & Tiny was to make no inquiries & he had no curiosity. So I thought it safe, but was ashamed of the prevarication & subterfuge and soon I was heartily ashamed of the trick all together. And the feelings I had manifested. As I feared they disgusted him – I most wished to please. Would that I had more judgement & pride & could control myself better – or that I was not such a fool as to love him, when he seems so indifferent now – or treats me so strangely, even if sincere!

He had been my only love for years – the only one I had looked to, to make the future happy, perhaps. He had always been so true & devoted – 'though mysterious. I know he cares for none other – wrote so often & lately – so devotedly and after three years absence – of course I expected to see & hear much of him now. And amidst all these dangers – when I didn't know the fate of either – I had heard he was sick & worn out – then had to flee & knew he was miserable about the state of our country as he is always so gloomy.

Then he had no late answers to his letters or not favourable ones. I didn't know why he hesitated, only knew I couldn't bear the suspense & so rashly (not boldly) sent him this note, which Tiny handed him in private, but awakened other suspicions I fear and what did he think?

On the whole – he has no clothes yet to wear out I guess. He is so devoted to his mother & all. Cares only to remain there & he is afraid of their opposition. So many of them together. His love is not strong enough to stem the storms of their disapproval & the trying future responsibilities. So he is unhappy I've no doubt.

What does he mean – I long to know! Would that I had not sent a message & bided his time to break the spell. He might have respected me more – for now he thinks me over anxious & silly in my frankness to strangers – thus disregarding his wishes. I scorn secrecy as mush as he does candour – will we ever agree – & ever meet as old!

I reread "Jane Eyre," the strong novel by "Curren Bell" these last few days, to try & make me forget the dark present, but nothing could drown "the voice of my heart" – as he once called me. Mrs. Murray & others here in evg.[20]

Sat. May 6th Lovely day & night & all calm again, thank heaven! We all slept quietly at last. Helen & Tom with us still – Dick T. after many narrow escapes – Joe Hyde & Tiny Bacon here in morn – Nick Whaley, Helen's present flame – a nice fellow & Keys McCulley here in aft. with the girls.

Mr. Wm. Smith came down from Pendleton on a hand car, to see Helen – had escaped up there entirely. A small body of Yankees had gone near Pendleton and been frightened off by a comp., only a few houses entered – not his. He hurried off.[21]

Theodore followed him here – glad to see some of his kin again he said. Seemed to be feeling especially lonely & said he had been "miserable since yest. when I treated him like a dog," but I was not aware of it. He came early & said "he would spend all evg – he didn't care how much I gaped or was weary." I pitied the poor fellow. He is capable of entertaining me better than anyone I know & cares more for it – just now.

He can't fill my heart as one does. Strange & he indifferent it seems, but I know he is not. His soul cannot so soon forget! He seemed happy to sit & listen to me sing some of his favourites to the piano – then we went into the "pretty room" as he called our parlour – enjoyed the vases of bright roses I had arranged there. I sat

20. *Jane Eyre,* a classic romance by Charlotte Bronte (1816–55) under the pen name Curreh Bell, has been a perennial home library favorite since first published in 1847.

21. The Pendleton Home Guard Company, under the command of Captain Jones, fought a short skirmish with a federal unit near the Pendleton Factory (modern-day La France, S.C.), about ten miles north and west of Anderson. Floride Clemson notes that the Yankees did not enter Pendleton because of Jones and his fifty to seventy-five men, aged sixteen to seventeen years (Vandiver, *Traditions,* 244–45; Keys, "Browns Raid," 82, Stevenson, *Diary of Clarissa Adger Bowen,* 51).

Pendleton, South Carolina, was founded in 1790 and named to honor Revolutionary War soldier Judge Henry Pendleton. The village was for many years the only settlement west of Camden and served as the seat of government for the Old Pendleton District (established 1789), later parceled out as Anderson, Pickens, and Oconee Counties. The Pendleton courthouse square attracted schools, merchants, and manufacturers.

When the Anderson District was created in 1828, the little town was not well located to serve as seat of government for the new district. Lowcountry gentry found the location a pleasant retreat from the coastal climate, so Pendleton continued to thrive, largely owing to the presence of the Blue Ridge Railroad line that ended just beyond the village (Edgar, *WPA Guide,* 442–44).

listless, glad to dream in silence whilst he read to me part of "Thompson's Seasons" & Wordsworth's "Extension." That sweet, simple story, so elegantly told in polished verse.[22]

He read it too so well – we understood it – comments scarcely necessary – for we've long been good friends. More congenial minds than many others. The young folks in the next room – no doubt thought us lovers. I was almost indifferent. He urged me to sing to the guitar. He would join in some – then sit & look at me with quiet satisfaction, his soul in his eyes. He compliments my small hand – scarce daring to touch it any time – full of respect for me. Says "my smoothe placid brow – shows I've never had a care," but even then my heart was wrung for another. He begged for another tress as his talisman, but I always waived the subject.

We stood in the piazza in the sweet twilight. I scribbled some on white rose petals – "a fairy thought" – to his wonder. He says write "Je vous aime" (I love you) & I did it for pastime. He tried to get me to sign one, but I wouldn't. He took that as a momento. We strayed among the shrubs & flowers – for our garden was a fragrant little wilderness of bloom & beauty – a variety of sweet roses, honeysuckles &c, of which he plucked some. Enjoys them more than anyone I know. Such delicate – refined tastes for beauty. Though bad morals I fear.

He thanked me for having beguiled one weary afternoon for him in this Elysium – with "his only charmer," but said "I was a heartless woman" – couldn't be moved. So I had not been moved in the least by him – yet felt gratified for he appreciated me as few do & his was a mind. He had some feelings that harmonized with mine – of which I find few & may never meet more.

But my soul still craved the companionship of love & protection. Oh Robert – why do you neglect me thus! I saw some of his family often. All see him but I – the most interested – why is it? It is because there are so many of his kin at home now, he will be too closely watched. This is such a want of manly courage, so degrading to me. Then, I'm sure he has no clothes to be seen in yet. But when will it be that we can meet – if but once to understand each other. I can't bear this suspense.

22. "Seasons," the most popular poem of James Thomson (1700–1748), consists of four separate works recollecting each of the seasons. Thomson revised the work throughout his life (Markham L. Peacock, Jr., *The Critical Opinions of William Wordsworth* [New York: Octagon Books, 1969], 367–69.

"The Excursion" (1814) is a long poem, in nine parts, by William Wordsworth (1770–1850), poet laureate of England. Wordsworth drew direct inspiration from Thomson's "Seasons," which had apparently covered much of the same ground generations before (John O. Hayden, ed., *Poems by William Wordsworth,* [New York: Penguin Books, 1977], 2:90, 95).

He has always reproached me for being absent during the two weeks after his coming last year – then he seemed much more anxious to see me. Now, when we had gone farther – he lives within sight near two weeks now & we've not met – nor has he sent me a message. Afraid of responsibilities &c, but his honor is implicated now and I thought his heart, but what does it mean? Teach me to bear it all & both to do their duty Oh God! Pride should make me repel him now forever, but he must have some good reason. I cannot break it off yet – my only dependence for love & earthly happiness 'though it might not result thus.

I saw some of his brothers & Maggie near the gate & stopping to look at them – thought 'twas he. Theo asked me "If I'd seen the Dr.?" How it grates me to hear that question now from many – I feel forsaken & scorned &c. I abruptly turned away as if I didn't hear & he left me – feeling my indifference it seemed.

In the bright moonlight after tea, when he might have come, "Hannah," their servant came & brought me a note from him "out of the Yankee lines" she said – so sly. I don't like that and I felt mortified but glad to see something from him once more. Couldn't realize it was the same man who had written to me so ardently before – who now wrote me this cool reply?

(Indignant that I had trusted news to Mr. Bacon, a stranger. Had various reasons for not leaving his home – rather he would have died before the fate of his country was known – too dark to discuss kindly &c) Not a word of apology. No wish to see me – nothing, but cool indifference and perhaps disgust for my boldness as he may think.

I long to know what he thought, but I should rather hate & scorn him perhaps for these feelings – 'though for my life I can't. I read as one petrified. I sent no reply – none since. Could only wander off alone & sigh at the faithlessness of man – or his cruelty! He loves me yet perhaps, but his strange nature is unaccountable!

I had gone up stairs to bathe when called down late Sat. night to see some visitors – Rev. John Elliott, the idol [*sic*] parson here & Miss Lavinia Seabrook – as he is staying there now. Had protected every house from Yankee intrusion where he went. A charming man – his health bad – has six months recess from preaching. Gone down to meet his father's family on Coast now. We all sat discussing the raid in the bright moonlight & I gave them some sweet roses when they started. Pa had gone in the country with the William's foraging horses.[23]

23. Rev. John H. Elliott was a Charlestonian who served as rector of Anderson's Grace Episcopal Church in 1861–62 and at St. Paul's in Pendleton. Elliott married Catherine Ann Sadler. Rev. Elliott's brother was General Stephen Elliott; his father was Stephen Elliott, Episcopal bishop of Georgia and Florida; his grandfather was a well-published naturalist (Vandiver, *Traditions,* 197, 242; Thomas, *Episcopal Church in South Carolina,* 235; "Centennial Program and History of Grace Episcopal Church, Anderson S.C.," passim; McGee, *A Rebel*

Sunday May 7th A bright, calm Sabbath day – of rest & peace. At last, the long sad week was ended. I went to S.S. & Bapt. ch. Mr. Murray gave us a plain sermon, as usual – on "one thing needful." Nothing very appropo. But I was conscious that I did not enjoy religion & holy thoughts as I should, for they centre only on that one erring – faithless man – whose kindred soul shuns mine now – that he ever sought before & for no reason that I know.

All of his family went to Epis. ch. that morn – he absent. Maggie & Tom were writing notes to Helen about her going up to Pendleton with them. Loving her money, the sordid spirit, 'though they scorn her as being fast – strange! No messages for me & I always loved him so! Maggie went home that aft. with Gus Van Wyck in a buggy.

I went in the aft. to the Epis ch. – heard Mr. Keith – sweet singing. The Yankees had broken the organ we hear – shameful desecration of the wretches! Tom Carter was with me (excluded Theo) as the other boys were with Helen & Eleanor, but I was sad that moonlit eve too. Couldn't talk or sing with the others – wandered alone among the roses & in my room. Sleep, my only relief. No pleasant dreams. How weak our hearts. How full of sin & folly to cling thus to each other! But 'twas "hope deferred that sickened my heart." Reality would have been less painful!

Monday May 8th A cloudy day – rained a little – not enough, for 'tis very dry & dusty. Tom Carter here all day – a queer, indifferent chap – seems to care for nothing & nobody, but Eleanor shuns him, as usual – poor boy. Frazier Wilson & Dick Tupper &c all fell victims to her bright looks & winning arts – within those few days. Frazier's diamonds rejected too. She is a confirmed little flirt, but why is she so honoured with the disregarded love of so many hearts and I so few, when I prize it so highly? She numbers her lovers by scores, I but a piteous few & they – unfaithful. Well, it is all right some way!

Nick Whaley &c were with the girls today. I was reading & forgetting all day – or trying to. At night George Brown came in to spend the night – had been hiding around Belton – the same tall, lank – queer creature! Teazed me about R & I

Came Home, 76, 87, 169; Simpson, *Old Pendleton,* 168–69; Evans, *Confederate Military History,* 390).

Miss Lavinia Seabrook has not been identified.

Sarah Ann "Sallie" Broyles Williams (1840–1928) married William Dickson Williams (1826–1906) in August of 1860. Bill Williams was an Anderson dry goods merchant from Greeneville, Tennessee. The couple later moved back to Tennessee and raised seven children: William, Jr., Lucius T., Margaret D., John Quintard, Marie Lanier, Que Lucille, and Emmett (adopted) (Smith, *Book of the Dead,* 420; Vandiver, *Traditions,* 93; Simpson, *Old Pendleton,* 134; Boyd, *The Broyles Ancestors,* 21, 57).

would confess nothing – he crazy to know – thinks me changed &c Bill Hammond was here too that day!

The soldiers & poor people around were raiding our tan yards & public stores – nothing was safe – a state of anarchy & ruin. Some threatened Pa – as he had been active in regulating provisions &c. So, when called out by some men to discuss their stills, we were alarmed – fear much evil yet! A guard around the Commissary stores that night.

Tues. May 9th George Brown lingered awhile – played the violin sweetly & I sang "my soul is dark" for him. He went home then. I was sewing in morning. Tom Broyles called on Helen (not me) to go up to Pendleton with her, but they can't get off. She still lingers here longer than we wish – to see Nick Whaley &c, silly girl – is too fast I fear.

Clif – Fan, Mamie & Tom went down to Grandpa's for the day & all came back at night. In the aft. to our surprize, Uncle June & his nephew, Tom Jones drove up to see us – the first just from the army – looked nicely, but changed. Older & hair gone. Talked as lively as ever, but gloomy about our country now. Spoke of the garrisons stationed in Ga. – Andy Johnson's vile orders for removing arms &c, awful! Tom Jones was a fine looking – dignified – nice young man – whom all liked. A half cousin of ours. He went up to see Mrs. Sloan. They went back home to Grandpa's – were just from Elberton, expected soon to return. A Yankee garrison there – shocking![24]

A crowd of young boys here with the girls & Tiny Bacon – we had music & nonsense. He is crazy to get home, they anxious to go to the Trans. Miss. to fight, but 'tis folly. Every pass is guarded we hear.

John Peter came & spent the night to exchange experiences as to the raid. A gang went to their out of the way place – took horses – saddle &c – not much harm done. Left them two mules & a horse. Julia met them very cool. I'm glad they escaped as well. I wrote her a long letter.

Tom Carter & I promenaded in the glorious moonlight among the roses awhile, but I was miserable about R. Could only steep my senses in sleep's sweet oblivion – couldn't write – sing, read – talk or anything.

Owe many visits to suffering friends, but can't pay them – sinful waste of life & soul now. What are his feelings? I hear every day of his going out to their farm to guard his father's mules as they plough &c, for many are being stolen everywhere. This is only an excuse for his absence. He could come & write. Better for being in

24. Tom Jones has not been identified with the information available.

Elberton, Georgia, was about twenty miles south of Anderson.

Mrs. Mary L. Sloan (age 35), widow of John B. Sloan and mother of Tallulah (17), Curran (15), Thomas (14), and Luella (10) (*1860 Census,* Anderson District, 157).

Va. – we would be happier. We could correspond, hope. Here, he always tortures me with suspense & cruel neglect – why is it? Just that fear of his proud family! Ah – well – how will it end – heaven direct!

Weds. May 10th Bright – brilliant day, but a shaded one to me. John Peter left. Then Tom Jones & Vie drove up to spend the day. A very nice, pleasant fellow – George Dean came to the door awhile. Spoke of five Yankees having been killed by some of Wheeler's men in Townville. Shot in the woods after parole. I fear somebody will suffer for it – 'twas wrong.[25]

Then a Confed. officer passing by attracted our attention & stopped. Came to the house & sat chatting with us awhile in the piazza – asking after Grandpa's house – glad to hear Miss Vie was here. All that time I thought his face familiar with the long ago. Could scarcely identify it with that worn soldier as "Jim Hamilton" – Alfred's best friend, whom I used to know years ago. He seemed almost to love me then – as he stole a lock of my hair once. We were at least good friends awhile & here he is again – on his way home from the wars, to his mother & sisters in Ga. – refugees & had lost much.

He had been Q. M. in Phillips Legion since the war – was with his comrades now – afraid to pass about alone – so had to hasten on with them, paused here a short while & at Grandpa's perhaps & then on. Will we ever meet him again?

His figure & firm character reminded me of "Rochester" in Jane Eyre. As such I might love him as a rock to cling to – rough as it is – but scarcely has the depth & polish to attract me. So another old dream neither long nor cherished flitted through my mind! Strange to see so many men here again & so many old acquaintances, but none of them have yet brought me joy. Will I ever have more? What is to be my fate? I tremble.

Nick Whaley here awhile to see Helen. Wonder if he is as devoted in earnest as she is just now – or is it a flirtation. She is rather demonstrative. He may think her fast. He is a nice fellow, called on me to confirm many of his opinions. Will take her to walk this aft. So she won't go home as expected & indeed they sent her a bundle from Pendleton as if to stay here (to our regret), strange!

25. George Roswell Dean was born January 25, 1844 in Anderson District. He was captain of Company A, Battalion of State Cadets, until the closing days of the war. In 1865 he married Hattie Camp, and the young couple lived in Belton, South Carolina, until 1867, while George taught school and read medicine. He later attended medical school and grew to become a prominent surgeon and practitioner (Garlington, *Men of Our Time,* 109; *1860 Census,* Anderson District, 499; Vandiver, *Traditions,* 108; Evans, *Confederate Military History,* 126).

The incident near Townville, South Carolina, cannot be verified and may have been just one of many "raids" on lone federal soldiers in the countryside. Bushwackers, deserters, stragglers, and soldiers returning home made the upcountry dangerous territory.

We all sat chatting – with cards & music all day, but I felt too restless. Have scribbled all this nonsense which I may one day regret. Vie teazes me about R – thinks I should notice him no more & so it seems – direct me, oh God – what is best to do! May he not judge me wrongfully. May I commit no more folly & imprudence, but be a woman of dignity & honor & truth, but pray he act as he should!

In the aft Mr. Whaley came again – with Keys McCulley – chatted very pleasantly with all, but took Helen to walk & stayed with her late – must be in earnest. Tom Jones & I had a nice time with the guitar, albums &c, then took Eleanor to ride with his nice buggy & horse – so they had a charming time. So I sat around moody & unhappy still. No one to care for me, yet Eleanor met R in the street for the first time & exchanged bows. Yet I saw none of him. Watched awhile in vain – grieved & almost vexed. Vie & Tom went home late. He didn't like to leave. Tom B. sent Helen to ride with him – called at the gate on her a moment. Tiny passed by – neither spoke to E. or I – strange!

At night I sat alone in the shadows – whilst the glorious moonlight gleamed on flowers & trees without. How happy I might have been with a little trust & devotion. The household all silent – wonder at me – & how will it end? Can only sleep & dream.

Thursday May 11th A clouded day, without & within. I arranged lovely vases of roses & clipped off all the old blooms (so soon withered) to bring out the new – until my fingers were blistered. Up with the early dawn sweeping to try to forget. Sewed some & then read through a sweet little novel "Vara or the Child of Adoption" – a missionary's daughter – adopted by the Stephens in N.Y. to be educated – married Rhodene Grainger, a cousin – Both became missionaries. Many true characters & pretty fancies in the book. This whiled away another long, lonely day without seeing him until late at night.[26]

Mr. Smith came down on a handcar in the aft. for Helen, but a heavy gale of wind & rain came up – darkness covered the land awhile. We were glad to see the rain 'though not enough to assist parched vegetation much I fear. Our country in its present ruined – helpless condition. No doubt to be made worse. I too grew miserable at the prospect & hope deferred. He went off to spend the night with Theodore as they couldn't go home – to Helen's delight.

He was rather snappish to her; she worries him much I guess – her mother very ill, but she can't bear to go back to "that vile hole in Pendleton." Wants only to stay here in idle nonsense with Eleanor & "the boys" – cares for nothing else – talks outrageously, laces to death, expects it to kill her, don't care. Cares only for Nick

26. Jane Hornblower (1797–1853), *Vara; or, the Child of Adoption* (New York: R. Carter, 1854).

Whaley now. She is very pretty & rather smart & good hearted, but selfish & vain & silly &c. Poor girl, what will be her destiny? Some "lucky catch" I guess. She is so rich.

We had a dull night of it. I sang some of our old favorites, which needled, but drained my suspense. What suffering cold & cruel thoughtless men can bring to true, clinging women's hearts – alas! So undeserved too!

Friday May 12th A radiant morning after the shower – earth glitters – cool winds – up rather late. Busy sewing nearly all day. Practising. Boys with Eleanor & Helen as usual – I alone. Uncle June & Willie & Aunt Anna came up to spend the day – a clever, funny fellow! Teazed us all much. I always liked him, with all his faults. Sad – lonely evg to me, but I whiled it away reading aloud to Cora & Clif at night, a story book.

The Broyles had a picnic on the river that day – had invited their guests – the Keiths, Munros &c and Helen had a special invite – no one else here. Eleanor was with her near their house – not spoken to, even by R – who stood near & he scarcely speaks to Clif. What does it mean? Wonder if he went & how enjoyed it & what thought of Maria K. If changed toward me, hope we may understand it anyway. Both be blest – separately – for I can't think bitterly of him. What thinks he of me? Unjustly perhaps? I was miserable, but weakly so – & confessed too much to Lucie, my only sympathizing friend – by note.[27]

Sat. May 13th A lovely day again, but cool for the season. [W]as sewing for the children all day & trying to get grease out of old silk with camphine – which removed it, but left stains – too bad. This all worried me, but kept my thoughts from dwelling too sadly on my false lover.

Helen was happy with Nick all day – morning & aft. – for he is a nice young man – really devoted to her. After two weeks acquaintance, they have become engaged to be married soon they now think! Strange! She does look very fair & lovely – a smart, nice girl, but silly about beaux. Wonder if they will be true & happy? He is dignified & sensible & rich. May suit her father – hope they may marry & do well.

That morning Mary Ann Woodson here awhile – always half witch – told my fortune in my hand, as she has so often done & hit the truth. Today – she said "my

27. Judge Robert James Munro and wife Margaret arrived in Anderson before the Civil War and settled there with six of their seven children. Mrs. Munro died during the war, and the Judge moved into Miss Benson's Boarding House. He met and married Lillie Roper, a widow from the lowcountry. The Munro and Reed families had once been close friends. The family included Robert, Jr. (age 39), Margaret Munro, Jr. (36) or "Maggie" or "May," Sarah (27) or "Sallie," James or "Jim" (20), Edwin (22) or "Willie," Theodore (18), and Harriet (14) (*1860 Census,* Anderson District, 258; Vandiver, *Traditions,* 22, 23, 263, 308).

lover was near – I would see him soon – there was a cross between us – not caused by me. He couldn't pass letters, he loved me deeply – more than I loved him – he would urge me to marry him." She wasn't certain there would be a wedding. His folks not so much opposed as formerly. "Several persons loved me – I cared for but one." She guesses well in some things. Wonder if all – does he love me so truely? Is he worried? When will we meet?[28]

Lucie & Waller Nardin stopped in to see us awhile in the evg. he was just from Johnston's army – paroled, but so blue about affairs. He don't want to hear it mentioned. Only wants to go to work, but can't see what at – no home or means – his medicines even disturbed at home – not by raiders. He seemed dark & cross enough & Lucie looked so queenly & sweet. Can she be happy? Hope so. "[L]ove hides all defects" – as I've discovered. She sympathized with me & blames him some. He had seen R – wonders that I hadn't. How will it end? Mused sadly.[29]

At night a camp of Johnston's soldiers in the woods near us – singing lustily. Wonder what feelings the associations awakened in R near by – when he heard "Lorena" &c as they sang it. Guess he didn't care to be there or in camps again. What will he do with himself? Tom told Clif today – "he would marry no woman without gold – might court Helen – cares little for her." (It will be in vain too – good!) but how heartless. They are all thus sordid, unless 'tis R. Will he prove so & is he seeking to give up because we have no gold? True – we would be poor enough, but true devoted hearts could endure all![30]

28. Mary Ann Woodson was a local Anderson fortuneteller and the wife of David A. "Dave" Woodson, a master printer and compositor for the *Anderson Intelligencer,* who died in 1878 at 69 years old. Mary Ann passed on a few years before her husband (Wilkinson, *Early Anderson,* 240).

29. Lucie (Lucy E.) Hammond Nardin (1840–1927) and Dr. Waller Hunn Nardin (1837–1905) lived on Fant Street, near the railroad depot. Lucie's parents were Dr. Herbert and Elizabeth Hammond, making her Emmala's second cousin. Lucie and Waller were married October of 1860 and she eventually gave birth to eight children, five girls and three boys. Dr. Nardin, Sr., and Dr. Nardin, Jr., both practiced medicine in Anderson.

Waller Nardin was the son of French-born Dr. Frederick Nardin and Charlestonian Eleanor St. Clair Nardin (Brown). Nardin graduated from the medical school of the University of New York City in March of 1860, making him a classmate of Robert Broyles. In early 1863 he joined Orr's Rifles and was appointed assistant surgeon for the 25th South Carolina Volunteers. Dr. Nardin operated W. H. Nardin & Co., a mercantile establishment, and later in life taught hygiene and chemistry at Patrick Military Institute (Vandiver, *Traditions,* 55, 120–21, 123, 234, 258, 260; *1860 Census,* Anderson District, 160; *Cyclopedia of Eminent and Representative Men,* 350–51; Evans, *Confederate Military History,* 772–73).

30. "Lorena" was possibly the most popular tune of the era, due in part to its hauntingly sweet melody. The lyrics allude to a familiar wartime theme of young love held for a moment then gone forever, but only in this earthly plain, because "'tis dust to dust beneath the sod;

Sunday May 14th A bright – beaming day – fleecy clouds, flitting over bluest skies. Off to S.S. & taught my little class & sang – heard Mr. Murray's very good sermon from "Revelations" on the joys of heaven. "He shall wipe away all tears &c" And I felt some consolation in view of the thought that I might suffer no more there, but be blest forever – after all our trials here & I might know him there in peace & love &c. If we were both so fortunate as to go there & may live for this end!

His servant came to me this morn to say Tiny Bacon was off to Greenville & would take any note &c. I sent one to Miss Lizzie Johnson & he came by to say adieu & hurried off. As a young friend he had neglected us much – kept away by them I suppose.[31]

Not one message from R – even by this confidential boy of his – but as I sent no answer to his note last week, save the message "so strange a note deserves no answer" – knowing from his strange nature, this might offend however much I was wronged.

I couldn't resist writing a few lines to send him. "[M]ost unaccountable! Most mysterious! Most inexcusable! You have sought & won all reproach!" What will he think of it – how act – was I wrong? Forgive me if so and may all end for the best! may we understand each other & be satisfied.

At noon Aunt Anna & Uncle June here to dinner – had all been to hear Mr. Jones preach – wish I could. In aft. went to Epis. ch. – heard Mr. Porter in a very good sermon, but I wish they were all more forcibly impressed on my mind & soul. Singing very sweet, by Hattie Bruce. Organ broken.[32]

I looked in vain for R – the third Sunday here & not been to church yet I guess – strange. I hear he won't come to see me until he gets some new clothes. He is ashamed of this excuse – so he gives none. Poor fellow – when will he have any and what will be our destiny? I became better reconciled to his absence then, having faith in his long, true devotion & respect shown even in his seeming neglect, but is it all true & what next!

---

but there, *up there,* 'tis heart to heart." Authorship and date remain unsure, but H. D. L. Webster and 1850 are the most probable answers. (Henry Steele Commager, ed., *The Blue and the Gray: The Story of the Civil War As Told by Participants* [New York: Random House, 1950, 1995], 586–87; Parrish, *Confederate Imprints,* 600).

31. The 1860 census shows an Elizabeth R. Johnson living in Greenville District, but it is uncertain whether this is Miss Lizzie Johnson of Greenville: the census entry lists Elizabeth Johnson's age as eight, though it is possible this is a mistake for eighteen (*1860 Census,* Anderson District, 327).

32. Mr. Porter, Episcopal minister, may be the Rev. J. A. Porter of Charleston (*1860 Census,* Anderson District, 218).

Hattie Bruce has not been identified.

Theodore S. joined me from church – looked badly – been suffering with pains &c. Seems miserably alone in the world – no one to talk to. Even longs to be with some relations. The first time he ever acknowledged it, I'm sure. I advised that he should go & see his sister, Mrs. Kuhtman, in the mountains. So he ought to – for recreation. He asked me to accompany him – which I, of course, declined. He discussed some of the foibles of marriage & humbuggery – as much to say he would never try it. Teazed me about "the Dr." Which I didn't notice. "Glad to hear I hadn't seen him" Begged me to kiss the flowers he was inhaling. Was off early, teazing Helen & Eleanor about their important "secrets," for they had beaux, as usual. Drove them off – to their chagrin – all right. Quiet night musing.[33]

Monday May 15th All up with lovely dawn, to arrange the house. Early breakfast – sewing &c – which I kept up all day 'till tired. George Brown here awhile – played violin sweetly – awakened some familiar thrills. John Peter here to dinner. I wrote to Julia – wish she were here.

Rumours all day of more Yankees coming & at noon four – or six came in to town From Ga. – to mail letters they said. But of course to look around & see how affairs are getting on – for they had heard of the home raids on property & might settle in. Then perhaps they had heard of the public meeting in the C.H. this morning – where he urged "submission & acquiescence to the Union &c" It may have been a political speech – to save his neck.

At noon Mr. Wm. B. Smith came down for Helen. He & Pauline stopping the Phaeton a mile or two out for fear of losing the horses. Pauline came to dinner, a sweet, modest girl. Her father came to see Helen & Theodore to hurry them off. Yankees in town &c.

Dick & Nick been here all morn. He & Helen made all arrangements. She wrote & asked [her] Pa, then he went to see [her] Pa – made his acquaintance & asked for his lovely daughter. Trying moment I guess – to both. He replied "Yes – with pleasure" thinking it a fine match no doubt. Whaley – a good family – well connected & well off I guess. He is a prepossessing young man & seems devoted to her – 'though I wonder if it isn't more her gold.

Tom Broyles was bent on accompanying her to Pendleton. Winning she & the gold too, I guess, but there was never a fellow so taken down as he was. She wrote

33. Mrs. Anna Smith Kuhtman of Walhalla, the sister of Theodore Smith, was probably the wife of "H. W." Kuhtman, a very wealthy miner from Bremen, Germany. In 1860, Kuhtman claimed $50,000 in real estate and $50,000 in liquid assets for his gold mining operation in the "Cheokee" section of Pickens District, South Carolina. Mrs. Kuhtman and her children resided at the Daniel Brown home in Anderson at the time of the 1860 census. The family included Anna (age 14), Ina (10), Lenora (8), Bennet (6), Richard (4), and William H. (1 mo.) (*1860 Census,* Pickens District, 23, Anderson District, 157).

for them to accompany them home by agreement – he came, much primped, with his saddlebags. To pay a long visit to his beloved Pendleton kin. Looked to[o] haughty to enter the house & could scarcely speak to any of us. He looked as if he hated me. Answered my questions stiffly. Never looked at me – his face flushed with pride & passion or anger. I guess – no doubt thinking of me as connected with his brother. I felt indifferent to his opinions – told him "he was sick here in Anderson, because there was no one here congenial I supposed." He muttered out something about the fair sex & refugees especially. Evidently he cares only for them, the proud wretch!

After all that he didn't expect to be taken down before us! To walk so far in the hot sun to lug her baggage – behind Helen & her beaux, of which he must have been jealous. Vexed – he stood hesitating for some time – as to whether or not he should go. A hot face & just mortification!

Mamie & Pauline ran on ahead. Eleanor & Dick. He slighted. Nick come for "his Helen" of course. Seeming very happy and poor Tom – the late rival joined them & prevented all private talk & arrangements for the future. But it was good for him. We laughed at his chagrin! But why will they hate me so – how should I act – how will it end? Sad.

At last we were free from guests – Becky Webb here awhile in aft. – sweet girl. Lida Pickrell called to say goodbye, but I missed her. Off to a strangers home near Montgomery, Ala.. Going in an ambulance all the way – with a strange man – Col. Wood – who married her cousin. A bad face too & here she is to travel with him so far. No telling what may happen – horses to be stolen &c. The smart lovely girl will be missed here – but I hope she may soon rejoin her own family & be blest evermore! Wish I could keep up with her destiny. R will never know her now.[34]

In aft. – soft twilight I roamed about thinking as usual – of my "false lover," though his boy passed to say "hoped it wouldn't be always so &c." I fully expected him tonight – fewer people here & there, but he came not. Ma & Mamie went over to see queer Mrs. Wilhite, as she begged. Late & sleepy now – must rest & dream, yet we ought to watch & pray! Our good little maid Louisa fell down with another spasm – alarming!

Tues. May 16th Fair & bright & calm – as usual. All quiet & busy at home. Dusting & sewing &c. Too busy over common drudgery it seems to me – the everlasting round of house cleaning, sleeping, eating & working on mending clothes to wear – I detest it all, but 'tis necessary thus to live.

Though there are mental & moral actions I covet more and I pine for more sympathy & love than I get. felt especially today how little I have, how few to care

34. Colonel William J. Wood was a member of Hagood's Division, First South Carolina Infantry.

for me – no one congenial & fond and I grow daily more cold & hardened and old maidish – as I have nothing to save my warmer, better impulses. No one here cultivates it much & disappointment makes me morbid almost. What will become of me? A will to overcome & live for better things – independant of this is all I can do. So I worked on – all day. Made Cora a spenser waist.[35]

Lou Wilkes came to dinner – chatty & clever as ever – full of the "raid" &c. In aft. Jane Fant came – could talk only of her many beaux & friends. So many nice gentlemen. Former acquaintances in Ga. had called on her in passing through. Many make love to her – she refuses many good offers, but always unfortunate in her attachments. Strange fate that denies me the pleasant acquaintances & love, such as she casts away!

I sang for her, had no conquests to relate. [W]e gathered a few of the fading roses, for all have disappeared suddenly – it is so dry. Clif gathered the petals today to make rose water. Yearning to be useful about home – no employment in town – hope he may be kept out of mischief & happy at home always & useful. Is beginning to read more too. I had to try & teach Lucie & buddy [J. P., Jr.] today. Find it a hard task, they are so willful.

As I stood hidden behind a rose bush, near the gate at dusk, I looked up & saw three horsemen passing – elegantly mounted & talking gayly. In one rapid glance – found that it was one Capt. Williams, John & Robert Broyles – nearest me & not looking toward the house even. As far off & indifferent looking and so much a stranger to me now – as though our hearts had not filled for years with only the others image. Dreams of future union – how strange!

I noticed he had a large moustache and looked rather different from our last meeting. It all flashed over me – what M. Ann W. told me in my fortune on Sat. "that I should see him within five days – unexpectedly – with strangers. He would look rather changed to me – by beard or something!" All just true – singular! But does he love – will we meet as said? It seems not, from his studious absence & silence. What can he mean? Oh to see him – to understand it all!

But several times today I have felt so humiliated by their wicked scorn & hatred of me & mine & attentions to others & love for money & rank. His want of boldliness – feeling my own equality in many respects. That I was worthy of better love & better fate than to get into such a nest of vipers, as they would prove to be perhaps – however charming within themselves – as I used to & might still find them.

I scorned myself for clinging to any hope or faith in him or that I would accept it on any terms. Should I scorn him & all; yet again faith & love would say "he is acting only with caution – afraid to risk all, yet knows how much depends on it –

35. A spenser waist was a woman's fitted jacket, usually of waist length or shorter, often called a waistcoat.

afraid of my future happiness." So he wisely refrains awhile and my heart would cling to him as its only congenial mate! Strange thing is woman! What is to become of me & of him?

Tonight – he & all the brothers were singing with Sallie in chorus – happy at home, yet he has professed to be so anxious to hear me. In his last letter – said "he had heard none other since me & cared for none &c" And now what? I read over those full, free, ardent, noble letters yest., where he expressed such devotion from childhood & felt happy that it had been so. Wondered more at the present & sudden unaccountable change; 'though his heart is unchanged I'm sure! Oh my Robert – when will you come to me & all be well with us!

At night I was gloomy awhile, with my knitting in the piazza as usual. Then read aloud to Mamie & Cora some. Felt more cheerful. Came up late & in the bright twilight heard many distant sounds of music – the Maj's staff most boisterous. He hears too & what thinks he? Eleanor had beaux this aft., as usual. Andrew Moreland. Late now – I can rest & dream – God willing.

Weds. May 17th Bright morn – music lessons for Cora – practiced myself. Sissy's troublesome spelling. Sewing & knitting &c. Thus the weary hours flitted usefully, but not profitably on the whole I fear. Some boys here to see Eleanor. I sat in the damp piazza trying to read at dusk, but my thoughts would wander to faithless – cruel R.

Then I saw him pass by (as of yore) from town – his arm linked in a friend's (Tom Williams of Tenn.) and he never glance[d] towards the house or me. 'Twas the first time I had been visable when he passed – or seen him. He used always to search for me then & bow & throw over flowers & notes in boyish folly perhaps. What does he mean now by this studied avoidance? Would that I knew all his feelings & home influence & our future!

My faith in his love & honour & return to me is beginning to wane, for he might have acted differently in many ways. I blush that he perhaps exults over my two candid avowals of feeling. What will be the end?

All call him proud, as they all are. They entertain other & better company – they think & they scorn us. Does he mingle with the ladies & how feel towards them? I know he has long been & will be true to me at heart, unless he hears falsehoods of me, but 'tis his place to seek & reveal the truth any way! But my sighs & tears were all in vain! Give me strength to act a worthy part Oh God & forget him & crush out all weakness if need be. And to live for better purpose! Save & bless him forever!

At night I read aloud – a story book to Mamie, Cora & Clifton – all much interested. Well written – of two young naval officers & their fortunes during the American & British War of 1812 to 15. Frederic Stanley & his self conquest over all passions & errors that made him a noble man. Rewarded here & hereafter with honours & love of Ella Manners &c. But poor Arthur failed to conquer himself & was well nigh ruined by self indulgence. So may we all take warning! Late & dark – rest.[36]

Some Yankee stragglers through the country here – all report that they have captured out Pres't – Jefferson Davis – in his escape with all the Confed. gold left. The $140,000 reward offered by Yanks will accrue to his captor! Awful if true! Such a downfall for our proud little Gov't & its bouyant leaders – after such a run of good luck at first. The tides all turned against us – from his obstinacy & mismanagement they say – but who can tell. I fear he may meet a cruel fate, hope not. What have us all to expect? A dark future – I tremble

Thursday May 18th Pleasant morn – stormy evg again – same stupid routine of sewing – reading – music &c. Besides I picked the green peas for dinner, which I relish so. Much now in this dearth of rarities, but I've not had much taste for anything lately – in my sorrow.

In evg, my work all went wrong and I became so grieved & worried thinking he would never come, because Pa had said Eleanor & I were both "well faded." Fearing it was so. The only relief I had was to take a walk – as I hadn't been out in weeks & nature looked so radiant & beautiful – leafy roads, beautiful fields of grain, but all desecrated now by Yankee rule. Near twenty in town today – to send off mails, get horses shod &c – they said. very peaceable, but they steal horses in the country.

Fan, Clif (darling, beautiful, good, little baby sister) not gone into short dresses. Such a pet with us all. Lucie & J.P. all racing along with me to Mary Ann Woodson's. They to get out some of their hidden goods & tobacco and I to hear more of my fortune. Crazy for any relief, any grounds of hope – since she had proved somewhat true so far. In my hand & in the coffee or rye grains – she read "that he & I loved deeply – some crosses – he watched & kept back, but would break through & visit me soon – or notes, boquets, walks would soon come – there would be tears shed by someone – he she thought – wouldn't be surprized if I married in less than six months. We were near together – soon to meet &c" Oh can it be true? I fear not![37]

36. Frederick Stanley was indeed a hero of the War of 1812, but the identification of this book remains a mystery.

37. Coffee was in short supply by spring 1864. The coffee substitute of choice was rye grain, roasted and brewed, common and simple to make. See Mary Elizabeth Massey, *Ersatz in the Confederacy* (1952; rpt. Columbia: University of South Carolina Press, 1993), 72–73, which describes how people survived the shortages of the war in the supply-starved south. See also F. Farmer, "The War Work of the Women of Pendleton District," United Daughters of the Confederacy South Carolina Division, *Recollections and Reminiscences, 1861–1865 through World War I,* vol. 1 (1919), 386–91.

I stopped in at Reeves on my way home. Chatted idly a moment. He teazed me about him & said that John B. had asked him "What we had quarrelled about?" What does that mean – does R seem vexed at me – what do they all think of it now? Just then at dusk John & R passed by the gate very near me – yet so far. (Is that the only way we shall meet according to my fortune? But she guesses little things well)

All the Reeves made some exclamation "There!," which I'm afraid he observed. They spoke of how mad he looked all the time. Or is it sad and miserable as I feel, that makes him cross too – poor fellow! Thus we were brought this near, after more than a years absence. I was happy to see his tall, erect form & manly face, which others call plain, but embodies all I care for. But he looked straight on. Wonder if he knew I was there & how felt? In passing alone in aft. he heard me singing I guess. What feelings did it awaken. Does he not wish to hear me sing as of yore the songs that made him so happy – he said! Surely – the fates cannot keep us apart – we must be mated spirits, but may heaven direct all for the best!

It rained at night – he came not. We all sang sweet home ballads &c.

Friday May 19th Cool, pleasant day – had rained some – not enough. Still the painful monotony & pleasant comforts of home, for which I am grateful and may one day have cause to regret its ease – 'though my heart now idly – mainly pines for one worthless object I fear – which might afford me only grief &c! God direct me for the best!

I made vases – was sewing, teaching, singing & reading, as usual – but alone & silent, for none of us talk easily here & I can only dream sadly! Eleanor Belcher & Teresa Brown called – talked so much of people & things & the times – not agreeable to me. They had long predicted our downfall & think others silly who were hopeful!

Yest. Andrew Moreland was here – with E – of whom he thinks too much – his angel Carrie scarcely cold. he is very respectful and a noble souled man we fancy from his sentiments expressed. He is going to Charleston now to his mother & sisters, but longs to go West if we ever do. Thinks us his model family – Pa & I & all. "I am a noble girl" Eleanor is perfection to him & she may never get as true a heart & as good a protector! may all end for the best![38]

I walked in the garden & sighed in vain – not even a glimpse of him & he has been here three weeks today – what can he mean? Thus he acted after his trip to New York & what a miserable time to us then – four years ago. Now, when we had more hopes – how must they must be crushed! How does he feel & act? When will

38. Andrew Moreland wed Miss Sallie Fuller of Charleston in December 1866 (see Reed, *Journals,* Appendix F).

I know all & can I excuse him? Felt almost impelled to write him a note demanding explanations – he may be kindly saving my feelings from future wrong. Two of his brothers – Gus & John – passed near me. Scarce speaking & scornful. I fear raised suspicions. Dark, dreary night – can I not dream of him & will he not come? I did dream sweetly of him – saw him & conversed.

Sat. May 20th A pleasant day. Sent some of the last fading flowers of Spring to Kate Tupper, but we agreed that "nothing seemed as sweet now as formerly." Is her heart too disappointed – along with our public trials? I was mending then until called down to see Uncle June & some boys. George Brown & Erasmus Broyles, who stayed to dinner and amused us highly.

George – lank & lazy, gifted & clever, but worthless. Played the violin sweetly and talked queerly "Ras" is a wild, rowdy chap from Miss., but can't get there. Lives with his uncle Witt now – wanders about over the country in mischief raids on Gov't property. Don't want to surrender or take parole, but fight to the last. Has encounters with Yanks, yet brave & daring I guess. Has an effeminate – pretty face, but manly spirit it seems – soft voice too. Chats all the time, telling his war experience. Very varied under Stonewall Jackson, Longstreet &c. A prisoner near a year. Tried often to escape & failed. Dared everything, safe now. What is his destiny?

He can't be really bad, but only lively – amused us much – delighted with my music. We played a game of "seven up," which I have not done lately. They diverted my mind from the old channel some hours – I had just concluded I could stand it no longer & was writing a note to R – hope I will resist this impulse – for it will be all wrong![39]

But we were all shocked today by the arrival of the Yankee garrison, which some of our own men went off & brought us as a protection they said. "They Unionists" Bob Hubbard – shameful! A company of them – mostly negroes, gay looking soldiers on an equality with the Yankees – rode into the University grounds awhile & about town. Two came in here to dinner – gave no thanks – did no harm. They say they will be punished if they do now. They will stay here – about the C.H. to enforce the civil laws &c – they say. One Lt. Summerby in Com'd – they say. A fine fellow apparently. Pa chatted with him as the "Mayor" here – socially. How they must triumph in our downfall!

They were giving all men paroles who had none & are very civil – so far, but there is some bushwhacking of them going on in the Dist. I fear we may suffer for it. Hope they may all be removed & not molest us. Our negroes will feel their influence. It is too humiliating to see them amongst the free & equal. Playing cards in the C.H. Clif says. How bitter the pill we have to swallow! They assert that they

39. The card game Seven Up is also known as Pitch, or Old Sledge (Walter Gibson, *Hoyle's Modern Encyclopedia of Card Games* [New York: Doubleday, 1982], 14, 15).

have captured Davis – Lee – Gov. Brown & all of our prominent men & sent them to Washington to be tried. Can it be so? Was ever a nation so completely down trodden & degraded? After such a gallant defense? Poland & others may be similar, but this is wonderful & what are we to expect in the troubled future?[40]

Clif informed me that for the first time – R.B. came up to him & had a chat this evg – on our terrible condition – this "reign of terror just beginning." I know he feels it much. That he has nothing in the world & never expects to have. Claims now a watch & chain & pistol only. No money – no clothes; will try to "leave here some day & never return."

All of this he wanted repeated to me. I'm sure as a reason why he shuns me and I am sorry for the poor fellow! This may prove his noble feelings in regarding mine, with his hopeless nature – he sees nothing in the future to entice. Knows it cannot support another as it is – fears to encourage it farther. Still – we have both committed ourselves too far to stop without better understandings. Can it end thus?

While Eleanor was entertaining four young beaux – I felt so weary & sad. Went with Clif & Fan to walk towards town. When half way – who should we meet but R.B. face to face on his way home! I was much confused. I'm sure he felt so. He gave a peculiar bow – meant to be very gracious. Smiled & said good evg &c but his glance rested mostly on Clif & Fan. I felt almost paralyzed, but was conscious that I gave him a calm look of wonder & a slight bow & no words! Thus was our meeting after a cold parting over one year ago and after all the years of devotion. I know there were peculiar heart thrills in each and is he satisfied? What thinks he of me now?

He kept looking back, but in the distance. I scarce know how he looked, but he was my same old Robere – my only love – a tall – manly form that seems made to protect me & I long to meet him as I should. I know he felt tenderly towards me. Now will he not come or write soon? I felt as if I could sacrifice all for him. We might go forth together to the west & struggle to live in love at least, for all have to begin anew at the South & this place suits us not. But if our souls are as congenial as we imagine – then surely fate will not always divide us. May heaven direct for the best!

40. Jefferson Davis was indeed captured in Georgia and sent to Fort Monroe, Virginia. General Robert E. Lee was not "captured" and was often seen in Richmond. Governor Joseph Brown of Georgia was imprisoned but was soon released and eventually pardoned.

The reference to Poland notes a contemporary situation in Eastern Europe where the Polish serfs (slaves) were emancipated in 1861, sparking the Second Polish Revolution in 1864. The Poles fought the Czarist Russian oppressors as partisans and eventually won considerable autonomy. Judiciary reforms followed, and the serfs learned to govern certain aspects of their own lives (William L. Langer, ed., *An Encyclopedia of World History: Ancient, Medieval and Modern, Chronologically Arranged* [Boston: Houghton Mifflin, 1960], 704–5.

I trembled so, I could scarcely walk home – felt happier for the meeting, but it will make me more anxious again. Was he at all triumphant – over my feelings & my letters & his late neglect? Surely not – he must be too noble, but he should have explained. Would that I knew all. I know he is ashamed to visit me in such clothes & can get no more now. He thinks he is sparing my feelings many trials, but no – I can never be satisfied without seeing him & owning his whole heart! Must dream of him again. 'Though Yankees are in town.

Sunday May 21st A pleasant morn- warm afternoon & night. The first time I have felt oppressed. Taught little class in S.S. Mr. Murray gave us a long, rather impressive sermon on "consider your ways" – oh that we would! But the Yankee Lt. Summerby came in & sat down amongst us – very quietly, but it made us feel badly.

I saw the Broyles going home from the Epis. ch. and R was there – to my surprize! He has the excuse of no clothes to be seen in, but goes everywhere, but where I can see him it seems. Used always to go to my church – not now – was with his mother & brothers. She & daughters used to be Methodists – now turned Epis it seems. I didn't think he would, yet he is proving a deceiver in all things it seems. He wrote once of going there to see Maria Keith. Was that his object now? No, I'm sure he thinks of me, but circumstances overrule & he may not have the moral courage to overcome – or he doubts me from stories. What is it? I felt grieved. Four Sundays here & we've not met scarcely. Just so he did after coming from N. Y., but what does the queer chap mean? I ought never to notice him again, but my heart rebels. I thought he would have written me today, but was disappointed.

Ed B., Bill & Tom Williams wrote for Pa to go up there – afraid to leave the house himself. Wanted him to get paroles for them – so they always want his assistance, but none of our company &c!

Beans & peas for dinner, nice. Doze & reading some of Spurgeon's fine sermons in aft., then went to Bap. ch again. I grew tired of the monotony. Would that I could listen to a Spurgeon – would that we had more fine preachers, but that vocation seems to almost have given up. No religion in the land – alas! Mr. Murray gave us a very good exposition of the 3rd chap. of Hebrews.

On my way to church I encountered Theodore S. accidentally and he deliberately turned to go with me, as he always does when we meet – so he did and wanted to sit by me, but I declined & ran in. Mrs. Leitch & Mattie sat with me – well dressed & smart. Theo came home with me & sat till dusk as he always does, talking of many things – interesting, but wicked, abusing the parsons &c Complaining of his sufferings & bad health. Wishes he could die at any time to relieve him – but he doesn't fear the hereafter – never thinks of it – but that can't be true.

He abused the South & proved slavery was wrong – ought to be abolished. This is why he is glad the enemy has triumphed and so it must be wrong, but what can follow? He speaks of going to some Sulpher Spring – his Bethesda. He wants me to be the angel to "stir the waters." Speaking of his being half blind, deaf. Wanted to know if I wouldn't be eyes & ears for him. I treat all as jests. Then he is crazy to know about "the Dr." – so interested to know all about it Hears "he is the only man I ever loved" Repeats poetry very appropo, about disappointment & youthful love, but I confess nothing (half sigh).

He spoke of my "elegant negligence" of manners & arranging my hair &c. Begged for a curl as his talisman, I declined. He believed he would turn shoemaker – if he could have the privilege of shoeing me. So much nonsense! Loath to leave – wanted to come very soon to hear secular music. Made me sing many hymns for him & seemed to enjoy all.

George Brown stepped in very abruptly on us. Had come from Belton & left Ras. Afraid to go home. [N]o parole. Stayed all night, talked much as usual. Theo wondered if he was my beaux. Ted Tupper with Eleanor – chatted with us at the gate. Theo admires his brother Fred as smart. I recommended Kate to him. Says he will visit them. Hopes Ted won't visit me – too agreeable & smart. Late & warm, but my heart is sad for Robere – what will be our future?

Monday May 22nd A brilliant – dewy morn – for it had rained a refreshing shower in the night. A long – busy – weary day at home – for 'though every moment is comfortably occupied and I am gareful for many blessings. Yet, my heart still idly sighs.

Saw R pass by home several times without even glancing here – strange. George Brown saw him return & teazed him about me, to my regret. He denied all. What does that mean? Yet, he was always to secret for my fancy & I too communicative, which he don't like. But he acknowledged that "we corresponded" as George told him of the letter he took out (never rec'd) Said "he had no clothes decent to visit in & wouldn't have met me Sat. for a thousand dollars" – his usual extravagant speech.

He smiled with evident satisfaction at talking of me, but how does he feel about his conduct I wonder. When will it be otherwise? I shall begin to have a contempt for him, grow indifferent if he doesn't show more honor & manly courage. 'Though he may think is all for our good & it may be so – God Direct! I can never cease to think of him and the old love & pray for his destiny.

George came home & worried me awhile – wondering what is between us. Played the violin for me sweetly – got him a parole & went home abruptly. The queer chap – long a good friend of mine, but good for nothing.

Aunt Lucie, who is at Mr. Brown's now, came in to see us a moment. Blue & cross about the times & she can't get a home anywhere now. Abused R's strange conduct & sympathizes with me, as none other. Then I was making collars for Pa – reading – teaching sissys lessons, practizing &c till night – when I knit & walked & mused & all sat chatting in the piazza together.

The hateful Yankees still here & our citizens forced to sit amongst them & doing nothing – no business. A dreadful state of affairs. They go off & steal horses in the country. Julia wrote me a long letter today of their taking Mrs. Brown's horses, threatening danger to her. Brown's Brig. of 1000 men passed back through there yest. to Pendleton (on their way North perhaps), which they will punish severely we fear, because they were fired on by Jones camp there before. Bush-whacking has been common around. They will try some of the citizens for the offense they say. God preserve them.[41]

Tues. May 23rd [A] lovely morn – must arouse to action! Sewing & lessons &c all day – the dull routine of duties, but I ought to learn more active duties I know.

Some excitement again about the Yankees – for two companies passed by here with the U.S. flag flying. Many negroes along – part of them paused in front of our house awhile. Soon moved on. About 600 had camped near our plantation last night – robbed & threatened Milford Burriss. His wife came here for redress. All distressed; one of these companies had stopped & worried Grandpa's folks again. Fed away corn & fodder & scattered it over his place. Took meat & vegetable & a mule (Wallers), so Uncle June walked up here & they went to the officers & got it back – so they are stealing & doing much harm generally.[42]

Today all the negroes & people were made to bring in the plunder from the stores. Nobody returned all & nobody was satisfied I guess. Wonder what is being done in Pendleton. All kinds of rumours of men killed, but we hope that all of the Yanks are on their way out of the country – then what?

This aft they had a horse race in the school grounds, which idlers went to see! Dick Tupper & Joe Hyde called on Eleanor. Uncle June here to dinner at night.

41. The potential for open combat was past in Anderson District, but ambushing Yankee troopers, black and white, was a fairly common practice in the remote regions of the newly conquered south. Travel was dangerous for everyone during this period. Pendleton was not punished for the defiance of Captain Jones's brigade of student soldiers (Keys, "Brown's Raid," 82).

42. Milford Burriss (age 50) and wife Vashti (37) were farmers and merchants. In 1860 Burriss's assets totaled over $100,000. The couple had a child named Vashti who was about nine years old in 1865. Milford Burriss died after a stroke in December 25, 1873; at the time of his death he was sixty-nine years old and a Baptist.

Louise Vandiver writes that settler Joshua Boroughs (an earlier spelling) came to Anderson County in 1724. His sons each owned land along Generostee Creek and each spelled the name in a slightly different manner. Vandiver told that by 1906 the original Anderson District family of Joshua Boroughs had grown to "1,313 descendants in 11 states." The family flourished, and Burriss eventually came to be the most common variation in Anderson County (Vandiver, *Traditions,* 146–47; *1860 Census,* Anderson District, 203; Wilkinson, *Early Anderson,* 96).

Marion Hall (Charleston) came in to see us – a queer creature – intended to eat supper perhaps. Almost a stranger too – but a poor soldier – who has no home or books or acquaintances & don't know what to do here. Still he is so pert – one can't feel like treating him with politeness. Has some good moral traits too I guess. Drawled out about the uncertain destiny of each one. Is right good looking, reminded me of his brother Ned's devotion [to] me long since.[43]

Saw R pass this morn without turning. We seem complete strangers now & wherefore – miserable! I long for some congenial companionship – no one even talks to me at home – or enjoys music, books &c with me. Clif busier around with the poultry – flowers &c. Now someone gave him geraniums & beautiful hex plants, which he had Myers, a gardener, to plant out today. He & Fan went to Dr. Broyles in evg for something else – "Citrena" Saw no R. Will we never meet & how & is it all over forever? How he always tortures me when at home – pride should forbid me ever renewing it and should long ago have prevented it, but fate will draw us together. I cannot resist – cling only to him, the false & queer – dreams now.[44]

Weds. May 24th A bright – calm day – sewing quietly. Making short clothes for our sweet darling, bright, good, beautiful, little baby sister – eight months old & nameless – pet of us all. Aunt Anna & Uncle June & bad little Will came up for the day. She in one of her tantrums – morphine &c – frightened & disgusted us. He was mortified – not so funny as usual.

We heard this morn that all the Yankees had left here. Ordered to Tenn. & thence to Mexico to fight the French – they say. We fear all may soon become involved in general & make war again, but it may end for the best. Now we tremble in uncertainty under Andy Johnson & such villains – for they threaten further vengeance to our State. It is to be a "negro territory" – God Forbid. A number of negroes tried to follow them away today – gals (shocking), but they pretended to drive them back. We know not whether more will pass through or not. Felt relieved today, but can our people ever settle down to work in peace again?

Ed Hanahan called on Eleanor. Becky Webb here in aft. – sweet girl. I walked halfway home with her. Far enough for R & I to catch a glimpse of each in town & I turned back. Stopped in at Reeves & as I sat talking to them, he & Bob Williams passed stiffly by – never turning, yet he must have known I was there. What thought he of all? How strange that he should pass me thus after all we have been & expected to be. His fine form & stately walk and even the face which few

43. Marion and Ned Hall of Charleston have not been identified.

44. "Citrena" is most likely a brand name for citronella, or essence of citrus oil. It is purported to be an insect repellant, but it was also used as a base for cosmetics.

admire are all to me, but should not be now – for they all add insult to injury. His mother & sister passed me without bowing.[45]

His brother, Gus & others paused here to get a fiddle & would have it to a frolic at their house at night. Sallie Munro with them & others perhaps – what does he do & feel in the midst of all – is he wholly changed & mean? I have every ground to doubt & give him up forever, but my heart still clings to shadows. His boy Alfred here today – talking freely to the negroes & they all say too much I guess & he may not know now. "Said he loved me much – often saw his darling when she didn't know it. Was determined to take her away from here some day – no child to be ruled by his folks – wanted to visit me. Had no clothes that I should see" &c &c. Even if all is true – he acts too inconsistently & strange. How can he love & how can I forgive, but we may never meet – Strange creatures!

A sad, lonely night – Eleanor & I communed rather more freely than usual on our disappointments &c. Doubting false men and false friends – since we have none who seem really to care for us. Of all the crowds of acquaintances & professed friends I've had – all false – none intimate now. Why is it – strange – human nature! My soul pines for companionship. Can we do nothing but sadly dream & scribble.

Thurs. May 25th A pleasant morn. Spent, as usual, undisturbed – fitting up old clothes for Eleanor &c. In the aft read & sang to drown the blues – heard R had gone off on horseback – wonder where?

Ma & I determined to pay some visits, as we had not in months, but we little thought it was the worst time we could have chosen! We went up to Col. Davidson's – where we had long been owing a visit. Nina D., a nice – clever woman – many children. The Col. was out. The Misses Julia & Minnie Robinson came in there, talked much of their experience with the Yankees, which we all had to relate – will provide talk for a long time.[46]

45. Edward J. Hanahan was a student at a Columbia, South Carolina, military academy in 1860. He enlisted and achieved the rank of lieutenant in Parker's Company, Marion Artillery (*1860 Census,* Columbia, 41; Hewitt, *South Carolina Soldiers,* 204).

46. Colonel James Wood Davidson (1829–1905) of Newberry County, South Carolina, graduated from South Carolina College in 1852. He was adjutant of the Thirteenth Regiment of the South Carolina Volunteers, strongly represented by Anderson County men. Davidson spent ten years as a staff writer for the New York *Evening Post.* He published two books in 1869, *A School History of South Carolina* and *Living Writers of the South.* Davidson died June 15, 1905, while in the process of compiling an unpublished dictionary of southern writers (*Davidson Family History,* 74–75).

Julia and Minnie Robinson have not been identified, though Emmala's journal (see Appendix F) notes the marriage of Minnie Robinson to James McFall in Anderson on November 8, 1866.

And just then a heavy storm of wind & rain came up – refreshing to nature, but detained us there. Then a crowd of Yankees came dashing by and we thought we were well caught! They were so well equipped, in blue [cloth] suits & oil cloths &c, so well mounted. All the horses in the South are gone – awful!

They dashed into town & alarmed some by saying they had come to stay, but Lt. Davidson (a son of theirs) came in with them – rode in & relieved us. He had been to Greenville on business. Came with them for protection & they wished him along to guard against bushwhackers. Lt. French & 20 men from Tenn. sent out to order Palmer's Brigade & all other troops to return to Tenn., to be disbanded – thank heaven – having no garrisons.

But we know not what may remain for us, as 'tis confirmed now that they have ordered our Govs to Washington & Pres't Davis & family have really gone too. What will be his fate – to be tried perhaps for instigating the murder of Lincoln. How awful! A full account of his capture rec'd today in Augusta paper – not read. But the rain was over & the earth looked gladdened.

We went into the Murrays awhile – Mrs. M & Jeffie – clever. Mr. Murray planting out potato slips – said "this is after the war!" And so we may all do soon. Coming home Mrs. Sloan came out to abuse the Yanks – hoping the air would be purified and one rode by who may have heard her. She & her children are very determined in hatred. Home late – met no one. Passed one Yankee officer, who raised his hat – we never looked at him. After tea, Reeves & his wife came over & chatted awhile – dry, clever fellow.

I actually rec'd two letters today – one from Fannie Smith, which Nick Whaley brought – having been up there to see Helen for a week. His first visit, but they were all so mutually delighted. Hope to consumate the early engagement ere long. She & Helen both wrote advising Eleanor to accept of our lowcountry beaux – that we might move down there when all go. Called me "Aunty" & says I better take Theo – at once if he thought so. I could never do that & don't care to live there by any means – somehow my heart will cling, but to the one false idol. I was sad that night again.

Friday May 26th It rained nicely in the night, reviving all nature! I was quietly sewing most of the day – had some company. Mr. Fred Tupper called on me – a fiery looking bachelor. Red hair, beard &c – sharp. Hates the Yanks so desperately – no gentleman amongst them. A mean, malignant people who will injure us in every way. So he thinks it our duty ever to hate & injure them. But he feels so unsettled – thinks of moving to Louisiana – people so free & social. The girls so unaffected & frank. He talked much of the times & is very smart & fiery. Rather critical – managed to bring in that no one ought to marry now. He had no idea of taking in a wife when he had to paddle his own canoe – so I guess they all think now! Left abruptly. Wonder what is his opinion of me & if I shall ever see much of him![47]

In aft two Hanahans & Nicky Whaley came to see Eleanor & the last came to see me & talk about the Smiths awhile. Admires Fan so much and she writes me of her cruel destiny in coming up here & hating Pen. & Helen always so fortunate – so it seems with all, save I. I caught myself making several impudent speeches to N – about what others said of his match – so thoughtless – hope no harm will result. He seems to be a nice gentleman – young & devoted.

Old Mrs. Porter came to see Ma & I – discussed Yanks &c. Didn't owe us a visit. Sallie Gibbes & her brother "Jupiter" – two queer – ugly looking creatures, who walk daily, came in & chatted awhile. Would have me sing – airs of Byron, Moore &c. Seemed to enjoy them. I have so few people now who care to hear my music.[48]

Aunt Anna – Uncle June & Willie came up to spend the night & several days – all discussed the times at night till we were miserably blue. Pa had seen the military orders for the Gov't of N.C., so terribly severe – such a system of tyranny as was never conceived and our fate may be worse. So we tremble & pray. Heaven avert it, but the worst feature of our case will be that it is such a terrible revolution in character & feelings of people & our affairs – that our faith in all things good & righteous will be shaken and the reign of infidelity begin again. For many hardened creatures who argued that we alone were in the right – will say no God assisted us & there is no God &c

Fred Tupper argued this morn "that the righteous cause has never yet prevailed" in all the annals of history – from the time of the Jews & Christ's unjust death – fate of Poland – Hungary. Even in our first revolution we were wrong – commenced fighting for nothing, especially the favoured royal colony of S.C. – the history of which I read every day now! But it is to be a reign of terror in every sense. We have not helped ourselves enough – so many failed to do their duty – all have survived.

We were overpowered my wicked myriads. May one day arise in might as F. Tupper thinks – the "Northwest will next rebel & we join them or else Mexico

47. The 1870 census records that a Fred (age 34) and spouse "S. R." (29) Tupper lived in Charleston's Ward 1 district (*1870 Census,* Charleston County, 32).

48. Mrs. Porter was the wife of Mr. Porter, an Episcopal minister.

Sally and James "Jupiter" Gibbes cannot be positively identified. The Gibbeses were a family of lowcountry lineage that had come to build upcountry plantations, like Ashtabula in Pendleton, South Carolina, a town situated fifteen miles west of Anderson on the Blue Ridge Railroad line where Andersonians often lived, traded, and retired. Floride Clemson writes about a "Professor Gibbs" teaching in Pendleton in 1866; this is most likely Dr. Lewis Reeve Gibbes, a medical doctor who held graduate degrees in mathematics, natural philosophy, and chemistry (Lander and McGee, *A Rebel Came Home,* 113).

& whip the North!" may all end for the best, but we can't foresee & we all must suffer any way! I felt miserably blue & sad.

Sat. May 27th A cool – damp morn – clear & reviving! The usual home monotony & variety of occupation. Ma & I made buddy a suit of clothes. Beaux with Eleanor all day – I none.

Waller & Lucie here awhile in aft. She is my only friend now it seems. I couldn't help confessing some of my feelings, asking advice &c. She thinks him the greatest mystery living as I do. We can't doubt his honor & sincerity, but what does he mean and when shall I know better? How had been gone away – I feared long, but was in town today.

Uncle June talking with him much – well pleased, but says "he is not worthy of me" Loves to drink & asked for it today, 'though he wrote to me of stopping it. They & Clif made arrangements for a grand fishing trip next week. All this going on & talking of his going to Pendleton, yet he can't visit me – or write – after being at home one month – today. All that we have hitherto felt & professed seems so queer & inexplicable! I should never think of him again, but cannot help it. Loved to hear Uncle June talk of him today so much of his "soft hand" – which I long to clasp in my own – as once – but ah – will it ever be?

I was sewing 'till weary – then walked up the hill with Lucie & Waller near his home – his window was closed, but on my way back – met he & father & brothers &c. All walking along talking. Didn't seem inclined to notice me. Knowing how they have all treated me I thought it best to take no notice of them & passed by without looking up. Don't know if he glanced at me or what they were all thinking. He will make it a further excuse to be vexed, but I was right I'm sure. It may look more suspicious – or be a triumph to the rest, but will we ever be reconciled & will it be well?

I felt miserable to see my spirit's mate who has been so near me thus afar and thought of all that has been & must be – I sighed all evening. Then must write to him – demanding an explanation, but does he not think of me or why not write. God direct us for the best!

I sat singing to the guitar at night – sweet ballads – that recalled him – in vain. Uncle June listened awhile & talked of R & prophesied it would all end right – like Guy Hartwell & Beulah and wished me dreams of him – that our soft little hands had met in a fervent clasp. Will it ever be? I've concluded that we women are queer creatures & so are we all – strange phenomena. Late & cold, but a mocking bird is trilling a serenade.[49]

49. *Beulah* (New York: Derby & Jackson, 1859), a novel by Augusta Jane Evans, includes woman-to-woman dialogues about religion, and life in general, that provide unusual insights into a Southern woman's point of view on the eve of the Civil War.

Sunday May 28th A splendid morn – bright & very cool for the season. All up too late. Went to S.S. & church – a crowd there, but Mr. Murray preached a very good sermon. Appropriate to the times – about the skepticism of the age, which is fearfully on the increase I fear. But from the 73rd Psalm he proved that we cannot understand God's Providences now – for it will take all Eternity to comprehend the truth. We should not now doubt his goodness & mercy and we may yet come out for the best! Whatever storms sweep o'er us – the Christian may be happy in view of the rest to come and "whom he loveth he chasteneth."

Wish I could remember all, but it was too long & much repetition. Then we had bad singing. Ought to have a choir & practice, but Mr. Hall don't approve & is spiteful about it & because I would sing a little faster in S.S. fear I've provoked him.

The long, bright afternoon – I sat in my room scribbling. Crowds at the Epis church. I wrote to Julia and a note to R which I fear I shall have cause to regret. He has treated me so strangely for a month – after all that has passed between us – so I thought perhaps 'twas right to demand an explanation and I hope that I did it prudently. Confessing & yielding – no point – but my impulses & feelings always influence me too much. I sent it by Elbert, who gave it to him very quietly. What did he think of it? What will be the result? I tremble – fear it may prove evil! God protect & bless me.

At night Uncle June & Clif were relating their war experiences – about which soldiers will always have tales to tell. Uncle June can talk big. Has been a veteran, but missed all he could; yet been in some rough scenes & escaped well! Terrible to think of the destruction & sacrifices we've made in vain! The loss of our best men & brave leaders, yet all of these are blest now – we are yet to suffer!

Eleanor & Dick walking as usual. Late – read – dream & pray to be better & more useful & wise.

Monday May 29th A dark – cheerless day – rained a good deal, yet the sun shone out some. Couldn't disperse the shadows from my heart, for it was disappointed & mortified & tried – intensely! As I sat sewing on the children's old rags – hearing dull lessons, receiving no kind words or love from any source. I mused many gloomy fancies in silence – no congenial heart to sympathize! Uncle June teazed me some – a good hearted – genial, affectionate soul. Aunt Anna is kind hearted too – unwell herself – cares only for her husband & boy 'though. All seem to have some nearer ties to gladden than I. Joe Hyde called on Eleanor.

I sang & read a little to cheer me, but watched all day in vain for some tokens of him. Even an answer to my appeal. Nothing comes – 'though he passed by to town. Does he mean to insult me – or is he crazy as predicted or what? Will my suspense never be relieved? Why am I so tried? Yet it may be well! I walked the garden in voiceless agony awhile. (Heard he had even stopped at our fence & pulled off cherries today – such cool indifference) Expected a note – or him – but nothing came. Then I heard all the others chat & some of us sang old choruses together. Felt in a melting mood over those sweet old melodies, until a startling clap of thunder made us all think the enemy were at hand with their artillery. Each started in alarm & the rain poured in torrents awhile. Now we've scattered to rest & dream. Write letters to Aunt Lizzie in Augusta by hand tomorrow.

Tues. May 30th The last day of the bright – mild month of flowers to my regret. Unseasonable weather – it rained & was gloomy & in the aft, a dark – heavy storm came up – much thunder & lightning. Calm awhile at night when Uncle June predicted some beau of mine would call. For that was the very night to "go courting." That was why R used always to choose such nights I suppose.

I thought he might come perchance & when I heard the bell ring at night my heart trembled with anxious expectation – for a servant had just told me "how faithful he was to me – had been waiting to get his new suit of clothes made before he could visit me & they were nearly finished. He was having trouble at home – 'though they all loved him much – said he was the best one & he wanted to leave there with me &c" Still that is all idle gossip – gave me one moment's pleasure & was over, for if he loved so much he might write or seek me any way! However, all may be best as it is!

In the morning Aunt Anna & I drove to Georgia Brown's to try & get our bonnets fixed (can't yet). The little smiling creature talked to us pleasantly – a cheerful little widow 'though so lonely – tries to be independent & happy – hope so. A good friend to R & I, wants to find out all about it, but I told nothing.

Sewing & reading at home as usual. Looked over some of his old letters & ardent professions, but a few short months ago & felt the change deeply. At night we all sat singing, trying to revive old times. Uncle June merry, but Pa so gloomy that he can't bear to see us enjoy music, company or anything – silly! He reads everything. talks none but to scold – unhappy nature. Wish we all could do better!

Theodore S entered and amused us all with gossip awhile, then they all dropped off & he stayed with me 'till 11. (Too late these times). Would have me sing & play much & as he appreciates my music of course I like it. We seem to understand each other very well. He says many nice little things, but expects them to be laughed at – teazes about R & tries to discover the truth, but I will not admit, 'though I can't deny all. Yet he is puzzled – would like to know all – so should I! He was not very agreeable – learned or sentimental that night. Always remarks on my very small, pretty hand &c. Pa scolded about his long stay & the poor fellow had to go in the rain – he was injured I fear, with his rhumatics &c.

Weds. May 31st A cheerless day for the opening of summer! Half sunbeams & shadows – a little rain – earth much washed! Busy with little things all day – weary

& worn with waiting & hoping in vain! Uncle June & Aunt Anna at last returned to grandpa's – Eleanor with them. Pa was too unreasonable at noon, made us all feel badly.

I was determined to dream away another evening over a novel & letters – as I have no happy realities. Saw R pass by in rapid unconcern, never glancing at the house. Is it indifference or despondency – scorn or shame – when shall I know? Why don't he write & come! I almost hated him then – yet my heart kept repeating over the sad lines from Mrs. Heman's

"Woman's lot is on you!
Patient tears to weep through suffering hours
And sunless riches from affections deep
to pour on broken reeds – a wasted shower –
And to make idols – but to find them clay –
And to bewail that worship – therefore pray!"[50]

Alas! my fate – why – and I love such a one & in vain. To what end is my life given & what his – for he loves none other I'm sure. What will be our fate? Direct aught oh God!

Wrote to friend Fannie Smith in evg. She too feels young hopes blighted, but she will yet be blest I guess. A soft sweet evg. Lovely moonlight eve, when I sat alone in weary waiting – in vain, until blessed sleep came over as a relief for which I am thankful, but no pleasant dreams came.

50. Felicia Dorothea Browne Hemans (1793–1835) published her first book of poems in 1808 at age fourteen; *Domestic Affections and Other Poems* (1812) became her best seller. Her early work was dedicated to the sentimental poetry Emmala reveled in on this occasion (*Columbia Encyclopedia,* 931).

FOUR

JUNE

Thurs. June 1st A bright – lovely day – sufficiently cool & warm. A little sewing & teaching, but it was whiled away in forgetfulness of self & all around as I grew absorbed in a novel. "The Belle of the Levant" or one in a thousand – by G.P.R. James – very exciting & pleasant narritive style. Scene – France during the troubled times of 1500. The wars between the League, led by the Guises' & the royalists – Henry's 3rd & 4th, the noble Henry Quatre of Navarre. Days of intrigue & passion & poison & crime. Just after Catherine de Medicis.[1]

One of her attendants, Beatrice of Terraza – an Italian Princess – passed through all unscathed. A pure & noble woman – brave & brilliant – the noblest passion in her heart crushed by the false man she love, whom she destroyed. Fair, sweet Eugenie de Hunaneau was happy at last with the noble marquess of St. Real, the dwarf page & Philip St. Aubin. All passed away unlamented. How strange to think of these lives & people & their fate. What will be the end of the parts we are all playing?

I was trying to forget my own care all day – for his cruel indifference & insolence grow almost insupportable. He & the rest send here for our buggy, but can't visit or scarce speak to us. He passed, very well dressed for the first time, 'though I heard that was his excuse – scarce glances here – sends no message. His boy here several times today. I said to him "Tell your master he surely is crazy" He wrote to me once he expected that fate & he heeds my notes at least – so silently I can't understand it all. This sudden change – for he has loved me. I feel ashamed of my continued interest. All reproach me with it – white & black – & expect better of me, but I can't help it yet. I must become used to our fate. I haven't firmness & pride enough to meet him. Aught, but all may yet be well.

Lizzie & Mr. Bleckley here awhile – clever as ever. Ate fruit – green apples – cherries, raspberries. Friends to R & I. Mattie Leitch (little sister) a sweet, pretty girl called. Night came & no social joys to home – the same sad moonlight regrets, 'till I came up & finished my novel. Late now – all sleep. Nick Whaley & Dick Tupper here with Eleanor today – needs time.

1. George Payne Rainsford James (1799–1860) was an English novelist who wrote historical romance novels just as such stories first peaked in popularity. Here, Emmala provides her synopsis of his *The Belle of the Levant* (n.p., n.d.).

June 2nd Bright, busy morn – as I weeded the garden, picked beans & raspberries &c – hard work – to me. Will I ever be reduce[d] to such continued drudgery? I made a pair of pants for buddy too & then – worried over the false one – for I saw him pass several times. Apparently well dressed & vain. He & all the Broyles, Williams, Munro's &c went to Seneca river in wagons. Fishing for a day & night. Clif & Uncle June intended going, but the last had rhumatism & didn't come by for Clif. Very well too, I guess – as perhaps they all wanted to hunt up drink – as vile men will do.

In aft Joe & Pheme McCulley called – nice girls. Dick Tupper & Albert Maury on Eleanor – elegant boys in their own opinion – talking of "first families." Tried to sing some with me & couldn't. I went over to the Wilhites & talked with the awhile. Mrs. W seemed much pleased to gossip about the news & her work – since her maid left. And her friends – the Broyles. They had some boarders – Mr. & Mrs. Kirkwood & Mr. Gordon. Scotch people belonging to the Treas'y. They all made me sing for them a long time. Seemed delighted with Scotch songs. Pa & all the children & Clif had gone to the plantation in the wagon to pick cherries. Came back very late.[2]

Our girl "Maria," who had been run away a week came in – half starved. Poor thing – where else can they go for sustenance, but to their Masters. 'Though thousands are being freed to die. reports of Yankee garrisons – emancipation &c – grow worse from all around. Make us feel badly enough, but we can't learn the truth. Blue at night.

Sat. June 3rd Bright, warm day – all of us busy seeding cherries to preserve. Can for pies – pickle &c. I tried to take an interest in it all & cooking vegetables. Very necessary accomplishments I know, but I can't like it. Vie H. came up for several days – mostly to help us all, but tart as usual. Seems to have a distaste to my music that always offends me as it is rare to me to hear such opinions.

I went to the Methodist prayer meeting in aft, but few there. Rev. Sam Jones spoke very sensibly – encouragement for the times: 'though we lose all else & retain God's favour we are blest. In the midst of our trials now, if we would stop & ask "Why art thou down oh my soul & why art thou disquieted within me" considering the mercies left us, we would be happier. I must try it, for I sigh continually now & am so unhappy. Cling only to thoughts of R too faithfully & he so faithless & cruel. Deserves only my contempt. Still, I can't lose all faith in him – will

2. Albert Maury has not been identified, but talk of "first families" presumes southern gentry, and thus he may well be a relative of C.S.A. naval commodore Matthew Maury.

Mrs. Wilhite's guests were C.S.A. treasury workers stranded in Anderson.

expect his return yet & his truth. Yet, what if all is in vain – what then? All right – but oh the trial.[3]

I invited Mr. Jones to tea here, but he declined until Monday. Vie & I went on to Mr. Brown's to see the family – all very blue. Miss Mary & Teresa talked to us much. The Gadsdens & all came in lamenting their losses &c.

As we came home we met Theodore just at Dr. B's & he turned & joined us, with his usual nonsense, but my thoughts were all of R. If he saw us – what thought & felt. When should we ever meet – for they all got back from fishing. Eleanor met him & had a bow. Theo came on home & sat there to smoke out his cigar before calling on anyone. To enjoy the enchanting scene are calling for the faeries he said. "Decidedly cool!"

He got some cherries & flowers & marched off – came on with me talking nonsense of how my "garden & music & society had afforded him his only pleasure during his sojourn in Anderson." He might soon have to leave here & "how could he leave me" – unless I bid him &c &c, but of course all was stuff. We sat talking to J.P. – whom he pets, but he hurried off in the dusky moonlight. Would have stayed, had I asked.

A dull evg – as Vie wouldn't tolerate the piano. I soon came up stairs to rest & bathe & muse sadly on the absent & faithless. So near, yet so far. A storm at hand – thunder, lightning &c – late now.

Sunday June 4th Very warm & bright today – felt more like summer than it has before. Went to S.S. & Bap. church singing &c. A very good sermon from Job – consoling – comparing – his afflicted condition to ours. To try our faith & we can't foresee what may be the end. I enjoyed it & felt impressed by the singing &c.

Came home & found company to dinner. Col. Orr & Dr. Tom Evins were here with Pa, but his face was flushed with drink – trying to drown thoughts on these sad times and his ultimate fate perhaps. He expects confiscation, arrest & maybe death, but he had better be preparing differently. Hope such won't be true, yet I am beginning to pray for Pa's fate & all the leaders.[4]

3. Rev. Samuel Barkesdale Jones (1825–94) was a long-lived Methodist cleric who served most of the state's larger congregations during his lifetime. Vandiver wrote that "Sam Jones, once a noted evangelist" was possibly involved in stealing horses from some black union soldiers up near the Savannah River (A. M. Chreitzberg, *Early Methodism in the Carolinas* [Nashville, Tenn.: Publishing House of the Methodist Episcopal Church, South, 1897], 355, 364; Vandiver, *Traditions,* 251).

4. Dr. Thomas A. Evins was thirty-nine years old in 1865. Captain Evins served with Orr's Rifle Regiment as a regimental surgeon (Vandiver, *Traditions,* 93, 259; *1860 Census,* Anderson District, 260; *1870 Census,* Anderson County, 695; Brown, *A Colonel at Gettysburg,* 315).

They all sat & talked of our calamities & became very blue! Dr. Tom has lost all and after he has endured in the war – feels so embittered – can't give up to our oppressors & violent against the men at home & all secessionists. He is a brave, high minded man – too excitable! Yet smart & energetic. I always fancied him, as many do. He appeared very indifferent to us all at first, but after dinner came in – sat & talked to me a long time, very pleasantly, of all the times & my experience during the raid. How I employ my time these days. Was I having to be domestic – did I wish to emigrate – he was determined to do so – 'though he had lost all & would have to begin life anew!

Wonder if he cares for a helpmate – said he feared Southern ladies would marry Yankees to better themselves & would not smile on the poor Confed's who had lost all in the struggle. Yet, true hearts will not do so and I think the men don't seek to avail themselves of the smiles left – for the course our hearts longs more for sympathy & to sympathize. Yet, as he says "the men don't like to drag any woman down to their fate now. Yet, since we are all dragged down already, better struggle on in love" – with congenial hearts – it seems to me. Tom is a noble man & cares for none I guess. We were quite interested in our chat whan the bell rang for the church & he departed (to come again I hope).

I went again to Bap ch & Col. Orr laughed at me saying "I must be very bad to require so much church going." Poor man fears I might not see him again. We hear that Gen. Robert Toombs, a Ga. statesman, has committed suicide to keep out of Yankee clutches – dreadful! Our Pres., Gov's & other public men kept confined in Northern prisons – garrisons coming – awful![5]

I was sick at heart & sad all day about these things & R's cruelty & falsehood. I saw him not & heard no word of him today. Not a word of reply to my note a week ago – demanding an explanation. What does he mean? Read over some of his recent letters today & thought how changed, yet I cannot think he is – but what

5. Robert Augustus Toombs (1810–85) of Washington, Georgia, noted lawyer and statesman, wed Julia Dubose ("Mrs. T") in 1830, and the couple had three children. Toombs was a Georgia legislator, a U.S. senator, then the first secretary of state for the Confederate States of America. In July, 1862 Gen. Toombs resigned his government post to command troops in the Peninsula Campaign and the battles at Second Manassas and Antietam.

Toombs was not, in fact, dead as Emmala surmises. He fled to London via Cuba in May of 1865. Upon his return in 1867 the northern press pushed the issue of an amnesty oath and pardon. Toombs replied, "Pardon for what? I have not pardoned you all yet!" He never again held public office and never swore an oath to the Union. Toombs died at home in Washington, Georgia, at the age of seventy-five (Wakelyn, *Biographical Dictionary,* 413–14; William F. Amann, ed., *Personnel of the Civil War,* vol. 1, *Confederate Armies* [New York: Thomas Yoseloff, 1961], 358; Andrew F. Rolle, *The Lost Cause: The Confederate Exodus to Mexico* [Norman: University of Oklahoma Press, 1965], 227).

is it? We hear they are fighting west of the Miss. Kirby Smith & Forrests forces – with the French &c. What will it effect & what will be the end?[6]

As I went to church – I met Theodore & he turned right round to go with me – 'though I didn't like it at all. He would go into the church with me too & sit there to criticize poor Mr. Murray's humourous sermons – the singing &c. The wicked wretch – we quarrelled much.

The lecture – from Hebrews – was very good – on the rest remaining for the people of God, which I long for. We all sang with spirit too! It rained a shower. Theo would come home with me & in the house & join me & talk nonsense & have me sing hymns & flatter. Yet talk so much to distress me in ridicule of holy & pure things. I felt peculiarly devotional & tender.

Wanted to weep, but was thinking only of R & why was he not there & shall I meet him in the blessed hereafter – if not here? He is forgetful, or else jealous of Theodore perhaps – from stories. Won't seek me – hope not! He tired me out – 'though I appreciate his regards – of course. Still, he is no real – true man – digusting in many ways. We do not think of marriage only to entertain each other I suppose, though he says "he is miserable when he leaves me here" Poor wretch! He appreciates me – few do.

Marion Hall came home with Eleanor & sat here until late at night (got his supper). Drawled out so much nonsense we became sick of him. Albert Maury – the nice little stranger, came to say goodbye – being struck with her usual & she might do worse. He seems to be a fine fellow – off to Charleston & his plantation in Marlborough now. What will be her destiny with all her beaux? Seven boys wished to gallant her from church this aft. None of them worth much. Wonder if Ben will never come? Shall I not see R again. Direct for the best oh God! Vie took Mr. Jones home with her this evg. Sweet, soft moonlight night. Late & sleep & a day badly spent I fear.

Monday June 5th Sunshine, half hazy & very sultry. My brother Clifton's 20th birthday. Yet he has a wife & the responsibilies of a man & family & no means. One year without his arm – sad. Looks more mannish & is happy – I hope – so far. Busy at home, but did little. Sent various things to Julia by John Peter, who was here. She writes, begging some of us to come to her lonely home, where she has so many cares, I guess, but none of us feel that we can yet. I can't leave here until I lose all hope of seeing R again – false as he is, for my soul clings only to him.

6. Lt. General Edmund Kirby Smith (1824–93) surrendered his western forces on May 13, 1865, the last Confederate Army to surrender. General Nathan Bedford Forrest surrendered in April at Selma, Alabama. Emmala alludes to a vague hope for French forces in Mexico, under the Emperor Maximilian, to intervene on the part of the Confederacy.

However unworthy! He was passing here all day & all saw him – save I. J.P. talked with him. Not of me & am I wholly ignored?

Mr. Murray called on us this morn – chatted on the times. Raz Broyles & young Lewis came also to dinner – bad scamps – not very welcome, but the first to enjoy my music so much. Then Witt Broyles & Dr. Jimmie Brown came also to dinner. He is an upright, worthy man – I hope. Commands some respect. Brought me a sweet note from Emma – she writes so well, all of the sisters thus gifted. The crowd left after dinner. I sent a note to Peter McDavid or has he too forgotten me since our long correspondence in the army – what will he think of R? But all men are faithless.[7]

Reading in evg – then Betsy Danson came in grinning as usual. A buxom lassie. Then Rev. Jones came to tea as we invited – a fine looking, pleasant man. Intelligent & independent. Sat discussing the news with Pa & I. Enjoyed raspberries much at tea, but he left soon after – being unwell & tired. He reminded me of the day when he & the Capers & Broyles all were here together – all changed now![8]

After he left, Becky & Rosa Webb – with their cousin Charlie Webb – a fine young man – came & sat awhile, talking nonsense & singing. But the sad, sweet songs I sang brought back thoughts of Robere & vain regrets for other days & I was miserable. Wish to weep all the time & I fear Eleanor & Theodore have missed me this evg – rejoined her & walked on talking much nonsense of me & my "sewing society" Idle flattery of both of us. As if he were so intimate.

Robert & Dr. Tom Evins – the two Internes – went walking behind & heard it all. R never spoke to her & what do they think of us both & all of our experience? I know he scorns him & thinks there has been flirting &c 'though we discussed him in our last letter. But what fate is this!

Soft – dreamy moonlight. I wandered in the piazza & thought of it all & heard R & Dr. Tom pass again towards town – late. Talking busily he hurried home alone by here – pauses not to think of Melodia these days – nor to speak or look at me – nothing. How can he do so after all the past between us. What will the end be? Yet I hear of his talking of drinking &c. I fear he is falling, but my heart will cling to him. It seems forever – regardless of all! Oh to meet & talk with him & sing for him once more, or for a letter from him & what can he mean? God help me & bless him, it may all end for the best!

Tues. June 6th Sunny & sultry – most miserable day for me! I heard in the morning that R & all had gone to Pendleton for a long visit perhaps, I was still

7. "Young" Lewis was most likely a Broyles relative from the Pendleton area, possibly the son of Andrew F. and Susan Sloan Lewis (Simpson, *Old Pendleton,* 168; Lander and McGee, *A Rebel Came Home,* 94).

8. There were no Dansons, and no Betty Danson, in South Carolina at the time of the 1860 census.

ignored – even my note. After being here near six weeks – so all his excuses about clothes &c were false; then from the Keiths I gathered how he went with them to picnic & party at Judge Munro's. Was specially devoted to Maria, whom he wrote to me about wishing to know. I've no doubt he is captivated – for she is brilliant, pretty &c. 'though this is the first time I've heard of his seeking other ladies. I never before doubted his constancy to me – on these grounds.

All together feeling the whole dream of my life run past. Its hopes all crushed by this one cruel, faithless man, who might have at least treated me with respect &c. I was sinking in the depth of despair & misery and wept & prayed for hours in agony I've scarcely ever known before. Read over all the sweet, soul speaking poems of Mrs. Hemans – "Arabella Stuart" Prayer at girls school. No more poems of love. Mrs. Hemans – who probes to the very depths of love divine in the human heart & exhibits all its truth – holy – sad emotions and they soothed & purified my feelings. Only fed the love I would crush – or that I should tear out & supplant with scorn.[9]

Yet, for my life I cannot yet. I must have some faith still 'though I ought never to receive him or apologies again & may I never have an opportunity. Yet, if he continues thus – it is perjury to his own soul – with all its love of years & professions to me thus boldly cast away – leaving me to suffer alone – with the scorn of his family. The pity or congratulations of my friends who know it. My own forsaken, bleeding heart, which has all my life pined for devotion – trusted in this alone & find it false. Yet he must be the true man, the honourable gentleman he has pretended & I imagined. If so, how can he do so – 'though I daily hear of more faults of his & he certainly lacks moral courage! When & how shall we ever meet & what will be our fate? God help us & help me to bear it!

Sewing & reading as usual then during the day. Mad. Pinkind called in aft – going from Abbv. on a visit – home to Pen. Gave all the news & gossip afloat – amusing account of a wedding she had attended. Spoke of their family – the Gerrards – a noble family of Poland – only them left & their only brother, whom she thinks a star – her mother in Charleston. She talked boldly to the Yanks in Pen. I went out to pay two sad visits – not feeling inclined otherwise.[10]

To the Tuppers first – whom I found buried in grief for the death of their father lately – an old man – half crazy – in Charleston – almost alone. They wept & talked

9. "Arabella Stuart" and "Evening Prayer at a Girl's School," two poems by Felecia Hemans first published in 1828, appeared in an anthology titled *The Records of Women; with Other Poems* ("Felicia Hemans" in John R. Greenfield, ed., *British Romantic Poets, 1789–1832, Second Series,* vol. 96 of *Dictionary of Literary Biography* [Detroit, Mich.: Gale, 1990], 130).

10. Charles Gerrard of Goose Creek Parish, Charleston, was a baker. The 1860 census notes his German birthplace.

sadly. Kate & Cordelia – two thin, sad creatures. Feel their accumulation of distresses. The property of a large family – father & seven brothers – all living in affluence – swept away. All become paupers with no hopes for the future scarcely. They long to leave the country – feel in a dungeon here. They would sacrifice all to get their two brothers to Europe to a better life there. For Dick to be educated there &c.

I would scarcely be equal to that sacrifice. To see my brothers & loved ones go & leave me behind with all these trials & a wasted life – no love – no joys evermore! Who can endure that & which is best? They seem almost despairing, but are noble Christian women – willing to undergo labour, but not the loss of independence & friends. I think Kate is grieving much for the fate of her wounded cousin Fred – of whom they know nothing, perhaps they are engaged.

So others have greater trials than I and I felt grateful for the many blessings of home – health, comforts & family. Yet to have no love & meet only with false lovers – to be deceived & triumphed over – seems to me hardest of all! And to go on from day to day in mortifying suspense is awful! The truth however bad – is more consoling – or we can learn to abide by it & school ourselves for the future – 'though I doubt not but that were he all mine under any circumstances – my fate would be more unhappy.

I always open to the verse in the Testament as a fatality almost. "She is happier if she so abide &c" True of me – no doubt, yet the heart will pine for earthly love & congeniality! Only a dull monotony of drudgery & unsatisfied longings lies before me now – when others can enjoy so much. It is all right & I can be content with the assurance of God's love & protection & hope of heaven – love & peace to come![11]

Kate & Cordelia & Eliza Hyde. Three noble girls were there – all sad. Then I came to the Keiths to inquire after Nannie, the fair young sister who was very ill. Found the noble old father (Epis. minister) & son – Dr. Keith – a splendid young man & Dr. Rutledge in the parlour. All elegant gentlemen. Talked awhile of the times &c, then Ella & Maria came in to see me. Pretty girls – sweetly dressed – discussed the news, but she caused one pang in telling of the picnic they attended with the Broyles four weeks ago. How charmed they all were. "Dr. Robert helped me catch a fish" & the privilege of being with him.[12]

11. Emmala refers to Paul's advice in 1 Corinthians 7:39–40: "The wife is bound by the law as long as her husband liveth; but if her husband be dead, she is at liberty to be married to whom she will; only in the Lord. But she is happier if she so abide, after my judgment: and I think also that I have the Spirit of God."

12. Dr. Rutledge may be Henry Middleton Rutledge, who would have been in Pendleton courting Margaret Seabrook.

Conversing freely such as I have not had in years, 'though long my professed lover & attentive to no other. Now he comes from the wars and seeks others. Forgets me & can I have not even a word or look? He is not worthy of this devotion & regret, but I can't help it yet. Hence I am miserable. I longed to hear more, but couldn't ask – soon left. Now he has gone in the midst of Pendleton gayety with his Talliaferro relatives & I've no doubt hears me discussed & abused by many. Alas! Poor me – would that all were well!

I met Mrs. Dr. Borland going in there – so fair & sweet. Lamenting the losses by the Yankees, yet more hopeful of the future than many. As Maj. Jim Whitner, just from Richmond, a wounded prisoner – says the Yankees are behaving well everywhere. Their policy will be more lenient, but that Kirby Smith has a large army fighting west of the Miss. How will it all end? I met the Gibbes, but no R. His house all deserted looking & for how long?[13]

In the soft moonlight night – Clif, Tom, Eleanor & I went to Mr. Webb's for variety. I to kill one more lonely night. Found a merry houseful there. Mr. & Mrs. W. very glad to see me. She & I discussing our society & the six sick men in the hospital with no attentions scarcely. Her bother William Waller has been straying off for 13 yrs or more – four in the army. Back here to rest with his relatives again – tall & sunburnt, but rather a lively bachelor of 35 – remembered me & will be rather social I fear.

Old Dr. Evins right agreeable – Becky sweet & quiet & their cousin Charlie – perfection – they think. Cousin Lou there for a night – quite a gay young widow, longing to marry. An old beau came from Atlanta Ga. to see her. Mr. McDaniel's – a teacher. Tall – slender – slow old man of 60 – four sons & grand children. Wrote to her as a stranger – comes now to woo & she will reject him I guess as too old – queer doings.[14]

13. Nan Keith was in fact the newly wed Mrs. Dr. Borland.

James H. Whitner was the son of Judge Joseph Newton Whitner and Elizabeth Hampton Harrison. Private J. H. Whitner enlisted with Company C of the Palmetto Riflemen in April 1861 and rose through the ranks to major in the Fourth South Carolina Volunteers, then the Twenty-second South Carolina Volunteers. He had four brothers and three brothers-in-law all serving in the Confederate army at the same time. An attorney before the war, Whitner returned to practice when the hostilities ceased. James married Ellen Stovall of Augusta, Georgia, and they had no children (1860 Census, Anderson District, 156; Vandiver, *Traditions,* 223, 232; Simpson, *Old Pendleton,* 170–71).

14. Dr. Alexander Evins (1802–76), one of Anderson's earliest doctors, studied medicine in Kentucky, then moved to the Pendleton District in the early 1820s. Evins served seven consecutive terms in the South Carolina state senate (1842–53), representing both Pendleton District and Anderson County, then retired to the home of Dr. Tom Evins and his family in Verenne's Township. In 1872, suffering from consumption, he moved to Spartanburg County

Marion Hall had invited himself there for the evg. Too slow & disagreeable as ever, but I had to entertain the crowd with music of every variety for hours. They all seemed to enjoy – laughed considerably – seeking forgetfulness. I spent some happy evgs there with R – in days now gone forever. Came home late & mused sadly in the sweet moonlit piazza & find sleep the only relief! Thank heaven for quiet, happy repose – 'though troubled dreams sometimes come – does he dream now & of whom?

Weds. June 7th A somewhat breezy – clouded morn – but warm. Jobbing around lazily – seeded cherries for pies &c. The last of them, so many stolen & eat the first plums – nice. Grandpa's carriage came by with Lucie & children moving to the hotel rooms – Miss Mary Waller going to assist. Children left here. Eva & Dessie – Lucie & Waller came to dinner with us. Mrs. Murray happened in then also – so we had a very social time.[15]

She was glad to hear that R & I were estranged. Said he was not worthy of me, but I can't feel thus. Uncle June & Vie rode up there in aft. We all went round to Lucie's rooms in the old hotel – very neatly fixed up, yet a disagreeable place to live – visitors came at once. Mrs. Sloan, Liz Bleckley. William Waller was there helping good naturedly – had been sighing about "Miss Emmily" all day. Lucie said & wouldn't take several millions for me – if I was his &c – stupid.

We all some variety stirring around there & coming home together when old Theodore would join me in the street – to my chagrin. He disgusts me these days – too devoted. Came & sat on the steps till dark – as usual. Repeated some of "Mothergooses melodies" – laughed too much. I was in no mood to enjoy any – he called me "an iceberg." I was glad to have Lucie & Waller, my two good friends, stay with us, but they were so blue & absorbed in their own cares & can't care much for others now. I longed for their sympathy about R, but they only abuse him & scoff at my charity & faith in him yet. For my heart only clings more closely, seems harder to sever – when I know I must.

Lucie & I read over some letters & chatted. We wondered in vain "What he means" & if I can do nothing he will feel. Is he enjoying himself in Pendleton. I suppose trying to forget me – how can he. Waller & I only exchanged a few words about it. How he used to tell him of "being desparately in love with me" He knows he has been – so do I, but we can't understand him now. Only that he acts very ungentlemanly to say the least & I should demand an explanation or return his letters by some responsible person. He would do this favor for me with pleasure.

---

and died there May 14, 1876 (Vandiver, *Traditions,* 19, 23, 130; *1870 Census,* Anderson County, 695; Bailey, *South Carolina Senate,* 493–94; *Anderson Intelligencer,* May 18, 1876).

15. Mary Waller (age 41) lived with her other brother C. M. (43) at the time of the 1860 census (*1860 Census,* Anderson District, 157).

When I hesitated – he reproached me for "want of spirit" & so I felt crushed indeed at the idea of giving up my only treasures – which will only gratify & estrange him forever I suppose. They will be destroyed hopelessly – every relic of our long romance & his war experience & the tender words I prize so highly and I will never have more.

Then there have been no vows. He hasn't mine to return – being destroyed in the army – so perhaps I need not senses or what would be the result! The very thought was agonizing, yet the necessity was almost forced upon me – so I tossed wearily on my bed & dreamed of it. Of consulting his brother Edward – who abused him much – about it. He was cold & hopeless. This may be a fortunate change for us – I may waver, but feel now as if I never should! Lonely moonlight night.

Thurs. June 8th Very pleasant – reading, knitting, sissy's lessons – sweeping & making Pa's shirt – my occupation – sad enough. Pa read Andy Johnson's amnesty proclamation today – severe – confiscation &c. To many classes – hard oath to take, some excluded from it – all men of property to be levelled – horrible! The yoke will be pressed upon us ere long too we fear. Immediate emancipation &c. I tremble for Pa's fate, but he is hopeful.[16]

Poor Clifton is going to have a hard time too – saying no business, no means, arms gone, family &c. He is beginning to realize his condition, but I hope he may get along somehow in the future. I felt quite depressed about all this & my own sorrow.

Mrs. Sloan & Liz Bleckley called – nothing subdues her cheerfulness. The first is just coming out after her husband's death three years ago. I stopped into Reeves awhile late – talking nonsense – a happy pair in their cottage, both busy & content & useful. I promenaded awhile in the brilliant moonlight at home to muse – then company came.

Tom Osborne & Lt. Davidson to call on us – (first visit at night in an age) very pleasant fellows. Tom ugly & bad – a teaze. The other a right good looking, nice, young man & sensible & practical. Talked well about the times – past & future. Entertained me pleasantly & enjoyed some of my songs. Late & sleepy & sad now.

Thurs. June 8th Very warm – sewing &c. I didn't take time to think much. Mrs. Sloan & Liz Bleckley here in evg. At night Tom Osborne – an ugly – silly boy & Lt. Davidson called. He entertained me with war stories &c & a variety of themes. He talked well & has seen good society. Been to Richmond when his father was

16. President Johnson's "Restoration" plan was actually quite reasonable, though former Confederate officials, high-ranking officers, and those with 1860 assets over $20,000 were not allowed to take the oath until they had received a declaration of amnesty.

in Congress &c. He expects to remain here & share the fate of his country & countrymen – I sang a little for him – they left rather late.

Standing then in the moonlit piazza I heard a gun fired & a scream afterwards. I thought it may be a tradgedy, but didn't realize the fact till the next day – when we heard that a negro man had been killed in town. Taken out by a band of disguised men at midnight. An innocent, peaceable negro all thought, taken from his frightened wife, taken out, tied, the house searched & then he was shot & left lying in the street next morning. The intention being to warn other negroes of danger perhaps. A written threat found as to two others. 'Though one of these was reported killed & Alfred – Col. Orr's carpenter – a very upright, worthy negro had been taken out & whipped & fired at. That was the gun I heard. No one knows who perpetrated the dark deed – nor for what reason – all excitement. We hear that other negroes in the country have been treated so & others running away have been shot or hung. A horrible disorganized state of society, crime on the increase – people so hardened – all better things done away with – shocking![17]

Friday June 9th Showery & refreshing. Uncle June came & brought Vie to stay several days. He & Clif went off in the rain – on a grand spree I fear – with provisions & traps &c for catching fish in Seneca river – expecting a crowd of other men – all to stay out two days & a night. Hope they may get into no mischief. June very gay. I finished making Pa a shirt. Did other jobs – read &c. Then went out in aft. First to Dr. Holland's to get a feather fan which he had made for me – as I once asked him in the street to pick me up a fan in his wanderings. So I was bound to take it & pay 25 cts in silver – all I owned – to my regret. It was a neat – substantial fan, but not as nice as I desired. Stout Mrs. H. & clever Dr. – very cordial. I went by to see Jane Fant awhile – always a crowd there – of beaux. She had been up in the hospital nursing the sick – feeds them &c. Has done everything for them lately. No other nurses, yet they all talk freely I fear.

Pa was organizing a police force of 150 men in town today to guard against future troubles. A Capt'n & 20 men to patrol the streets every night – pretty hard service I guess. I felt timid about going through town, but ran up to see Lucie awhile. Very cozily fixed up, but feeling badly about the murder committed at her very door the first night & Waller having to patrol. Anne Gadsden & Carrie Waller there. I was determined that Theo shouldn't join me again – 'though he stared very hard so Waller walked with me through town.

17. This type of racial terrorism was evident immediately after the war and preceded composition of the "Black Codes," which confined the activities of freedmen. This incident also predates Ku Klux Klan activities in the South Carolina upcountry.

A quiet night at home – Vie & I walked & talked in the garden – enjoyed a rare & lovely moonlight. The full silvery orb was struggling amidst clouds – lighting them up with beauty and reflecting on the eastern sky a lunar rainbow – in faint – white tracery – with a tinge of varied hues. Very pretty & rare. I had heard of & never seen it before. Mrs. Daniel – our loved teacher used to tell us about it, but I never saw one before.

Then there was a fine sprinkle of rain – all the time in the moonlight, which was charming even in feel. I thought of other days & scenes forever gone. How R was now in Pendleton with his gay relatives attending parties & finding new friends &c. Forgetful of me & all the past. I talked of him till my heart melted tenderness & sorrow – even 'though so mortified I ought to hate. Yet this is woman's way – always too ready to excuse & "Oh to love through all things" Strange that we should be so estranged – who have been so intimate for years & is it always to last! I read over some of his letters today & wondered if I should send them back. Can't bear to give them up, but help me to decide aright – oh God!

I sang a few sweet, sad songs. Came up stairs & read some of Mrs. Heman's lovely poems, then dreamed that I rec'd a long letter from him beginning "cruel Emmala" & going on to explain all. I was so crazy to enjoy its contents even in dreams – when the morning bell – daybreak (C.H.) awoke me. Rather Vie screamed out that it was an alarm of danger (as in the plan) & we were all quite startled, but dozed again until Pa aroused us blustering below.

Sat. June 10th A dark – damp, dreary morn – such as I love for home – quiet & reading – scribbling – novels &c. I gathered some sweet fresh jessamines & white roses to send Kate Tupper – with a note claiming her friendship – for I do admire her exceedingly & she is going away now to Ga. I hear, but she never answered my note. Has not answered – strange to say, but I'm always slighted by people – even by those I care for.

Busy all day – it rained – gloomy evg. Vie & Eleanor went to Reeves. I alone & sad. Pa talked to me about R & his treatment & the way his family treat us all, yet the old Dr. is so intimate with him – he concluded that he should call them to an account for it all. Though I want some kind of justification – fear this won't be well – so I trembled.

Pa did not know the nature of our long intercourse & correspondence – thinks him such a strange fellow. I determined to let him see some of his late letters as I may have to return them soon. We may never meet again & I will be the injured party! Hope I was not wrong, yet fear R would be very much offended if we ever were friends again – however, I felt that 'tis right my parents should know all & console if possible – for I am almost despairing.

Sunday June 11th 1865 And is it possible that I have lived 26 years in this sinful world! Thank heaven I have had so many comforts & health – friends & pleasure & blessings, with but few trials. Yet they may be yet to come. Then, I have always pined for more love – and R – my only love has caused me all the sorrow I ever knew. Many heart pangs lately, but will they not soon be ended? I have always wept as younger years swept away – now I am becoming more reconciled to my fate, whatever it may be. Teach me to be better, more resigned & happy – oh God – & to do thy will evermore!

I went to S.S. & heard my little class. Mr. Hall rather impertinent to me in the singing, but that is his rude way. Other girls felt like revenging it, but never do – haven't the spirit of many more! A long – tiresome sermon from Mr. Murray. Vie & Grandma home to dinner with us – enjoyed plums, cherries, apples &c and an Apricot peach Dick Tupper gave to Eleanor.

In aft went to Epis ch – full house – sweet singing – Mr. Keith preached on "Be still & know that I am God!" Impressive! Theo was behind me & I knew he would come home with me, but didn't spend every Sabbath evg in such nonsense & sin. I wanted to be alone & sigh for my R, then I was tired of Theo's attentions now – so I slipped off first & ran home a back way. He hurried & caught a glimpse of me & knew I was running away from him. He followed me home – came in & asked Ma & all – if I had come in & he sat till I came, but I was by then, out.[18]

I learned from one of the servants that one of R's had been there. Told how mad I was about Theodore's attentions to me & so he wouldn't visit me – had run off to Pendleton – didn't know when he would return. Attending parties, so I wondered when we would ever meet again, but jealousy was part of this excuse. Hope of his love still. But I had to go out & join "my bore" as he confessed he had been & vowed he wouldn't worry me with his presence again soon – I hope not until desired if I am lonely again.

Poor fellow – I am sorry for him. He displayed more sincerity & feeling than ever – worried me so much to find out if I really did run away from him today & Friday & why. He had heard of running away with men but not from them. He didn't believe I cared for a living man (how mistaken) but I should know this is the way to get men to follow me! I wouldn't deny or assert anything – only laughed jokingly!

He talked of his improving health – wished he had a country home & a wife. Advized me to marry – it improved all ladies &c. Much stuff that I didn't fancy and left at supper time as usual because I didn't urge him to stay. perhaps he will be vexed good, but I guess not. I would be glad could I have my R, yet rather than

18. The minister's text is from Psalms 46:10.

none I would like to be entertained by T – who is so well informed & spicy & devoted to me. Yet so wicked – hating his bro. & sister &c.

At night Pa told me about reading R's letters, which he seemed to admire – him & his ailments – don't blame him, but me for his conduct – as his letters proved my suspicions & accusations & telling so many people, but he don't understand our natures. That I had to deal thus with him, owing to circumstances, but it may have been wrong yet he has treated me with shameful neglect this time & my notes. Has he changed entirely & forever – with all the new charmers he is seeing at parties in Pendleton &c. I dreamed sadly that night!

Monday June 12th A cloudy – sultry day – jobbing around – reading & knitting &c. Couldn't work much. So sad about my R's neglect. Wept again bitterly as I have not for one week. Sigh continually & foolishly.

In aft Uncle June brought Cora & sissy home & a basket of nice pears. Some to preserve & pickle – which I helped skin. Vie stayed all night & this may have prevented a visit. As we stood in the piazza – to my surprize & joy I saw Robert pass twice to & from town – so he had come from Pendleton in less than a week. Without all his gay relatives there, whom he hasn't seen in so long. I know he was thinking of me & worried!

I saw him once more – whom I feel my soul's companion – now so far – will it ever be otherwise. He was well dressed in black. A splendid form and oh I longed to meet him again. He passed slowly at dusk, gazed in here – thinking of me then & I was sure he would come at night, but Eleanor & Vie laughed as if in sport when he passed – so his oversensitiveness may have felt it – or thought 'twas I. Perhaps he has to go on guard tonight? I couldn't help expecting him & sighing in vain! What are his feelings – how will it end? Direct for the best oh God!

Clif & Fanny went up to Julia's. Broyles today on a visit – I sent cape jessamines. Dick Tupper here all evg – a fine youth – robbers at their house last night. Dick tried to get Eleanor to go to ride with him, but it rained. His brother Allan's horses – which four robbers tried to steal the night before. Alarmed Dick & all – who drove them off. Kate Tupper was to go to Ga. with her brother – wrote me a sweet note.

Tues. June 13th Very warm day – rained all evg. Vie, Eleanor & I were silly enough to go down to Mary Ann Woodson's to have our fortunes told. Dave bothered us with his stories for awhile – but we got him off, after grumbling a good bit & my giving her a basket of apples. So – she finally began – turned the grains in a cup & looked in hands. Told Eleanor many truths about her many beaux. "One she preferred loved her – would yet come – another girl in the way – her flirtations & marraige – 8 or 9 children &c."

She told Vie of having a bachelor beau & one with light hair. They would marry – have 8 children. She seemed much interested in the subject. She told me the same tales of R's devotion to me – some horses – he loved me to the soul – trusted me in every thing – our families opposed but all would come out right – we would marry, he believed all I did was right – would make a devoted husband, he would come to see me today or soon. I had other loves, but neither of us had cared for any other for years. I felt relieved & hopeful all day – because she had told me some little facts of our meeting before &c.

Uncle June & Aunt Anna here today – I sat reading, knitting, sewing & practising, but it was a long – sad day to me – busy as I was. Jeffie Edwards here in evg – nice girl – rain at night – poor guard out. Mr. Murray &c. Maybe R is in it. Saw him pass this evg in haste, but he saw visitors again & every foolish fancy keeps him away – 'though I'm sure he came on purpose from Pendleton & left the gay crowd of relatives & came home to see me I know. Will he visit. I was miserably lonely waiting & watching for him again in vain. God save him (& bring us together!) Vie & I sang some sweet airs – she & Eleanor talked much. I dreamed of battles last night – may I dream of love & Robere tonight to the rain serenade for surely we are not forever estranged.[19]

Weds. June 14th A brilliant, fresh day – pleasant breeze – sultry night. A long, weary day to me again – spent in my usual occupations until tired out – for he came not. Passed by in cool indifference – I couldn't even catch a glimpse or tone & others could in the street. I sighed in vain all day – ashamed of my weaknesses, yet I can't help it – for all my young life seems gone! No friends, no sympathy – nothing congenial or elevating. No one to appreciate.

Anna Gadsden here awhile in morn – to see Vie & I. A nice, chatty girl. We ate fruit – pears, plums, cherries, apples &c. A warm quiet eve & dull – sad night to me – what does he mean & how employ himself – & how feel! I am forgotten now – when every thought is of him? Strange fate!! I must have strength to overcome! Help me oh God!

Read an instructive Sunday school book this aft – as to overcoming all self will & evil feeling & passions & loving God supremely! I must profit by it. Late & bright starlight & sultry – fine vocal – no other sound.

Thurs. June 15th One of the warmest days I ever felt – a sultry morning – I scarcely had the spirit to get up or try to do anything but engaged in my usual occupations. Had my new bonnet fixed – or rather an old straw bleached & remade & trimmed with white tarleton by Georgia Brown. Eleanor added black lace – buff & blue crape &c. Very neat bonnet for the times, but the change of seasons always

19. Jeffersonia Edwards was twenty-one years old in 1865. Her widowed mother, Nancy (age 65), raised "Jeffie" and her three siblings, Angeline (30), a university teacher; Eliza (24); and Agnes (19) (*1860 Census,* Anderson District, 155; Vandiver, *Traditions,* 112, 122).

worries me – with my bonnets &c for which I care so little & it seems all useless to me now – no one appreciates me.

Eleanor & I were called in to entertain Marion Hall & Jupiter Gibbes. Two queer – awkward Charlestonians – well educated, but disagreeable! M – rather good looking, but tiresome &c. Yet he was dignified & pleasant enough today – is going soon to teach in a family at Greenwood – showed us a sketch of his – very pretty.

Gibbes was very ugly, but intelligent. Converses very well & repeats poetry exquisitely. Has memorized all fine poems for his own pleasure – 'though he pretends to scorn the character of a poetizer &c Yet was willing enough to make the display. Edified us all highly by his delicate, vivid – dramatic recitations. Showing the powers of an actor & an appreciation of sentiment such as one would scarcely suspect & rarely sees.

First – an anonymous description of what a wife should be – exquisite! Then – "flowers" by Timrod – our own poet. Very pretty piece – then "Hoods' Bridge of sighs" – with its deep humanity – splendid, but not too delicate for our ears. Then a Roman story of Virginius & _____ – same character by McCauley – grand – yet painful these two.[20]

I would like to hear him render much more of the magic of verse into realization! Music & poetry blest charms of earth. The combination too exquisite. I sang many true old airs for their benefit "Moore's Farewell" &c – most touching. I thought of how R had once seemed to love it. "Would take it away in his heart" to the army, yet seems to have forgotten all; he passed here this evg – without gazing in – looking so cold & taunting &c. I almost made up my mind that it was my duty to hate & scorn him – after all his strange conduct – yet this morn my heart was near breaking to see or know of him again & it will often yet feel so! Alas, yet time may cure all![21]

20. Thomas Hood (1799–1845) was an English poet, magazine editor and humor writer. Many of his poems, like "The Bridge of Sighs" (1844), expressed great compassion for the poor and destitute (*Columbia Encyclopedia,* 1314).

Henry Timrod (1828–67), poet laureate of South Carolina, was born in Charleston, where he attended the prestigious Classical School. "Flowers" was an early Timrod work. Timrod's success as a poet came as a result of the Civil War. Few of his war poems are concerned with the martial aspects of the conflict; rather. he wrote of loss and anguish. He died in Columbia, South Carolina on October 7, 1867 ("Henry Timrod," in Joel Myerson, ed., *Antebellum Writers in New York and the South* (Detroit, Mich.: Gale, 1979), 339–42.

Lord Thomas Babington Macaulay's poem "Virginia," a tragic ballad, or lay, concerned with rape and tyranny, appeared in his *Lays of Ancient Rome and Miscellaneous Essays and Poems* (1854).

21. "Moore's Farewell" was a dirge written by Thomas Moore (1779–1852), an Irish patriot who was equally comfortable writing verse or songs (*Columbia Encyclopedia,* 1893).

Pa & the children all rode to the farm for plums. I couldn't work – so determined to dress & go for a wander. My main object to meet R & have some kind of test. I dressed & looked unusually well – I know & what thought he (Eleanor had three beaux in the parlor!) I saw R sitting in the hotel piazza lazily as I passed – how does he employ these long, weary days at home – save late evenings. Of what does he gossip in town? Does he dissipate? He had a full view of me passing up & I never glanced at him. Met Theodore as I passed – the only two who think of me at all I guess & they no longer kindly perhaps!

I went to Mrs. Benson's to see Mrs. Whitehead. A sweet – chatty creature. Martha Washington too came in – very pleasant – both elegant! I came to see Lucie in her sunny rooms, ate some nice cherries Theodore had brought & sent her, but couldn't talk much – late. Met Maria & Ella Keith – Mrs. Hall & sisters just from home. All chatty & pleasant, but my heart was in a tumult then! In the middle of the street I had met Robert Broyles for the first time since his return – seven weeks ago. He & someone walking & meeting me – whether intentional or accidental – I don't know but he looked red & rowdy & careless – as if drinking.[22]

Perhaps each wished to test the other & were filled with vague suspicions. We looked at each other quietly a moment – expressed nothing, but neither bowed – for of course he should have done so after all that's past. Yet he may accuse me too unjustly! But how can we be so estranged forever & why can't we understand? Uncertainty is the worst of all – if really unworthy & indifferent I could hate & forget him – but if he has grounds he considers just, why does he not seek explanation! Yet this may all be for the best – for our happiness! Heaven grant it & direct our destinies!

I scarcely felt so miserable as I feared, had goaded Theodore again too. Vexed him perhaps and is this the last of my two lovers & the last I'm ever to have? I suppose so & life will be a dreary blank, but I must be more amiable & useful & happy & pious now! May I ever find some congenial, appreciative spirits & meet the loved & pure in heaven!

It rained at night. Vie & I sat in the piazza chatting over the mysteries of human hearts. We can't understand this case, but she urges pride & scorn & silence, or patience on my part! She is a high toned girl. Late & alone – what dreams may come to he or I?

Friday June 16th A burning hot day – half cloudy, but sultry. I couldn't sew nor work much – did but little, no visitors – no joy. Dick to see Eleanor. Nice boy – on guard at night – went by singing &c. Clif & Fan returned from their trip to Julia's & Whit Broyles – chatted freely. Waller & Lucie & the children were here

22. Martha was the twenty-year-old daughter of Francis Washington, a wealthy Charleston widow (*1860 Census*, Charleston, 284).

awhile. Vie & I walked with them late. Saw R pass late with John Keith. Heard the sound of his voice talking first time, but not to me & never may again.

All of them at home abused him & Pa said "he was not worthy of notice" and I must return or destroy everything & demand the same of him & be strangers evermore! And can it all be? I am growing more reconciled, but I will yet feel it & will he? He was up town all this day in idleness. Why was he not at work or reading or doing his duty towrds me? Even Theo is vexed and now what – hereafter. We heard the boy on guard going by singing to Eleanor as she is very popular amongst them all! Lonely, sultry night.

Sat June 17th Sunbeams & shadows – showers refreshing. I felt sad again at R's strange conduct. Determined to write once more as my last resort – demanding an explanation – so I reread some of his & wrote one to visit me – combining two constructions as I always do – he says. What effect will this have? I tremble to know – for I don't know his & may excite further contempt. Yet, how can he have so soon lost all tender, honourable feelings and it may bring satisfaction.

Vie & Fan & Eleanor would read & criticize & say 'twas not severe enough or I should never notice him again – so unworthy of me. I should destroy or return his letters. I know that my woman's pride should make me scorn him in silence, yet for my life I cannot yet and must still cling to hope that he is worthy. 'Though we are thus severed forever perhaps! Heaven direct for the best! I gave it to Uncle June to hand him, but they didn't meet – providential perhaps – so I have it still.

Aunt Anna & Uncle June here all day. He was rather gay, but clever & good natured. Teazes & admires me, "just the right size" – too good for R. If a young man he would court me & get kicked he knew &c. It is pleasant to find anybody appreciative. I was sewing &c. John Keith came in to see Clif. Chatted with me pleasantly awhile. Dick T. & Norton Leitch here with Eleanor. Fine mist at night – sad & lonely – with music & promenading. Damp – pleasant night! Saw R ride by on a fine horse. Not a glance. Utter indifference now. What can he mean? Yet this may be well for us both![23]

Sunday June 18th Warm still. Went to S.S. & church as usual. Heard class & sang. A new child – Sallie Cook – smart – interests me. Never went to S.S. before. I noticed Fred Tupper in church. Didn't feel much of Mr. Murray's sermon, for I am growing too thoughtless & callous I fear. For my mind will wander off to the absent & faithless R.[24]

As I knelt & prayed that all might be well with him – little did I think he was there gazing upon me and with what feelings I wonder. As I turned to leave after

23. Norton Leitch's relationship to W. Y. Leitch remains unclear.

24. Sallie Cook is most likely the ten-year-old daughter of Joseph and Fernese Cook, from Walhalla, South Carolina (*1860 Census,* Pickens District, 39).

service – our eyes met. He had been sitting that near me all the time (yet so far!) in the place where he used to come to hear & see me years ago. He was there now for the same object, I know – could resist no longer seeing & hearing me sing &c. We had been breathing the same air, hearing the same things & how felt towards each other & all?

Had I known he was there I would have been more confused – it was as well! He turned & gazed at me quietly – an earnest gaze – which I returned with one of wonder, memory & love. Doubt in each I guess & sadness. His dark eye – black waving hair – fine form & all impressed me as finer than ever. He as the man of my destiny. What will be the end? Oh God direct for the best!

He turned away talking & stood outside until I was out of the way – foolishly. Why could he not walk boldly with me, as my own? He walked alone at a distance gazing after me I guess, then slowly home – thinking of what? I dreamed of him all day – shall I not see him soon? We will surely meet. He was on guard in his father's place last night with Pa, but avoided him until morning. They spoke & this aft he bowed to Pa & Ma riding from the plantation – so what next!

Grandpa's folks up to church – took Vie & Lucy home. I went to Bap. ch. Heard Mr. Murray's lecture on Hebrews. Mattie Leitch sat with me – sweet, pretty girl. The Earles all elegant! Sultry evg – I read some of Spurgeon's fine sermons. Part of Job "the sublime & human" sweet, touching powers, such a soul – deep & pure! I sympathize truly.[25]

I read over a few of Willie East's pure, beautiful letters of long ago – so holy & now he is a blessed angel no doubt realizing true bliss. Shall I ever have such congenial spirit friends again? Even Sallie – his widowed bride – my friend once forsaken me! Theo's feelings wounded still I guess. Not at church anywhere. Poor, lonely creature! What does R. read, would that we could read & talk & feel together! Clif on guard with Gus tonight – Fan sad. I looked at stars through spy glass & dreamed – so warm[26]

Monday June 19th Rather pleasant today – tried to sew & read &c. Went over to Reeves in the morning to see Dr. Jim & Lou (Burris) McFall & baby girl. She used to be a sweet, loving girl friend of mine 2 years ago – not met since. She was a wife & mother – devoted as both – talking of her Jimmie & to the baby – funny. They have been living in Milledgeville Ga. since the war. Want to go to South

25. Mattie Leitch was probably kin to W. Y. Leitch. In early 1867 she married a Mr. Marshall of Charleston (see Reed, *Journals,* Appendix F).

26. William "Willie" Washington East of Laurens, South Carolina, served with the Palmetto Sharpshooters. He was twenty-five years old when he died at the Battle of the Seven Pines, May 29, 1862 (S.C. Department of Archives and History, *The Roll of the Dead*).

America. He was a slender, good looking fellow. A happy pair I guess – so are John & Mattie Reeves.[27]

I came home to my sighing for the faithless R. Saw him pass at dusk & will he never come? Liz Bleckley here in evg & Hattie Bruce – a noble girl – smart & appreciative. It rained gently – so she spent the evg with us & her brother Willie came in for her – a clever boy. We had plenty of music. All of us played & sang. She wonders at our talent & she played for us exquisitely. Perfect style. Looked over some of my formals in evg. I am always too thoughtless & confidential. Happy to get with any congenial spirit, but keep few friends I fear. Dark, dreary night. No R – yet![28]

[The following entries, which appear in various locations throughout the journals, are placed here in their proper chronological order.]

Tues. June 20th Pleasant day – but I felt sick & sad – couldn't work – so I read all day to beguile the weary hours. "Vale of Cedars" – by Grace Aquilar – the English Jewess writer. Wrote well – this a stirring tale of the court of Ferdinand & Isabella in Spain. With some proceedings of the horrible Inquisition & persecution of the Jews by Catholics – their secrecy of worship – undetected 'though living in high life. Ferdinand Morales – their favorite courtier – a hidden Jew – married his lovely cousin Marie Neusigney. yet she had loved before – the British stranger Arthur Stanley (Earle of Derby) then fighting for Spain. Her persecutions by Don Luis Garcia – awful. The murder of her husband. The trial of Stanley & his escape. Her fate & death – all sad & thrilling! I was absorbed in this & some old journals of mine all day.[29]

27. Dr. James M. McFall was the son of William and Rachel McFall, a planter family from the Broadaway section of Anderson County. The other McFall children were Carrie (age 32), Lucretia (a schoolmate of Emmala's who died May 29, 1866, at the age of thirty-one), and William or "Willie" (23).

Dr. "Jim" McFall was a medical student when he enlisted in the Palmetto Riflemen. Captured at the First Battle of Manassas, he must have been exchanged, because records show him being promoted to sergeant major in February 1863. His last promotion was to adjutant (captain) in 1864.

The McFalls moved back to Anderson County by 1870, when the census recorded a physician, Dr. McFall, living in town with his wife Lou Burriss McFall and their three children, Livinia, J. C., and R. T. After moving to Pickens County, Dr. McFall died suddenly on March 20, 1875, at thirty-two years of age (Salley, *South Carolina Troops,* 581; Hoyt, *The Palmetto Riflemen,* from *Time Capsule,* 57; Vandiver, *Traditions,* 62, 192; *1860 Census,* Anderson District, 198; *1870 Census,* Pickens County, 434; Lucas, *Early Anderson,* 164–66).

28. Willie Bruce has not been identified.

29. Grace Aquilar (1816–47) was an English author specializing in dramatic fiction with a religious theme. Her works included *The Vale of Cedars* (1850), which Emmala synopsizes

Tommie Wilkes here all morn. A nice, handsome boy – Mid. of the naval school in Richmond – over now – a dignified sweet chap. Sad, quiet night – I almost felt that R thought of coming, but did not & wondered if he ever would now – for all the Pendleton crowd had returned and he was no longer alone & free to do as he pleased perhaps. I felt sad – but sleep brings hope always.[30]

Weds. June 21st Mild, breezy day – smiles & tears. Jane Fant came & sat all morning chatting – both of us sewing. I singing some for her – pleasant. Billie Hammond came at noon to dine. Rough, clever chap – not so congenial. Not much done today. Saw R at dusk & hoped he would come tonight, but he went on guard – I think.

Heard of him today – his boy told Becky how he was bent on coming here last night, but something prevented it – wonder what? That his parents attacked him lately about being engaged to me – he proudly confessed it (surely not as engaged – for we are not – 'though equivalent) & said "he would wed me in less than six months at all hazards & they could not prevent – had a right to make his own choice &c."

Yet he does not treat me as if determined – two months at home & no meeting – no letters! Awful! How sad & weary the moments he has caused me & has he too suffered? Why has he not come – for I know he is true to me & our hearts cannot forget, yet in reading over some old journals I see how he was always cruel & mysterious to me. I should not have trusted – much as we really felt! What will be our fate!

Eleanor & I went over to Dr. Wilhite's after tea as she had begged – but to my reluctance – found three Scotchmen boarders there. All rather pert & one too garrulous – half tipsy I think – disgusted me – all anxious to hear me sing. I had sung only "the Newfoundland dog" – at their request when I was sent for to go home – thinking maybe R had called, but it was only Theodore Smith. I knew he couldn't stay away longer. I didn't care much to go – it was 9 – he stood reading patiently – glad to see me & in a jolly, amiable mood – he said.

I sang & played all his favorites – he thought so graceful & sweet. Talked much flattering nonsense, but was not very interesting or personal. Gossiped, discussed

---

(*Encyclopedia Britannica,* 11th ed. [1910], 428. (Aquilar apparently passed into obscurity and does not appear in later editions of standard reference works).

30. Tommie Wilkes was a Confederate Naval Academy midshipman under the command of William H. Parker, one of many who accompanied Jefferson Davis during his retreat from Richmond. Twenty-two midshipmen were dismissed, paid, and dispersed near Abbeville in early May (Davis, *The Long Surrender,* 25, 33–34).

Humbolt & South America & its rare charms. Almost made me wish to go there, each grew weary & gaped & I drove him away – near 11.[31]

Meanwhile R – my real heart – was passing on guard. Heard me singing – must have suspected the cause & will he be still kept away by that or come soon. What thinks he of me now? Will he take leasure in guarding around my house tonight ? Even Pa & all excited when they thought he had come tonight & disappointed. Surely he will yet come & all be well! Late & quiet now. About 11, as I retired, I heard the guard walking by here talking. Wonder if he was one & what he was thinking of me then – he could not be otherwise.

Thursday June 22nd Very warm & sultry again – gentle rain in evg – not very cooling. I was sewing busily all day – new jacket for buddy – bonnet for baby. Knitting & reading various things & teaching sissy & napping a little. Thus this long day wore off. Becky Webb & Lou Wilkes here late. I was all alone – saw R pass with seeming indifference and yet, perhaps a crisis has come in our destiny!

Pa met Dr. Broyles at our gate (there R passed them – wonder what he thought) the two fathers walked off together & had a regular confidential chat on our affairs. Said far too much I fear – for Pa & I are both rash & imprudent! Dr. asked Pa to walk home & see his garden. Pa declined & began to ask why his family treated us all with such silent contempt & for years – since we were equals – he thought he stood higher – had done much service for them all. He heard they were having a row with Bob because of me. He went on to tell how he had written to me for years, but since he had come home – had not called or spoken – for two months now! And that I had written & demanded my letters & an explanation & rec'd no answer. What did he mean by it?

He had intended to call the gentleman himself to account. Spoke of negro news. Dr. denied any rows with R – save on another subject. wonder what? Nothing has been said of this, but they had suspected it & were of course bitterly opposed to the relationship! (I blush!) Gus came up & chatted with Pa all up on the news at the gate, but what will they all do & say now? Has R heard it & what will he think & how act! I fear he will blame & lose respect for me for telling so much. Or is he destitute of courage & the true spirit to merit my love; should my pride not dictate now a final farewell to him – my only love – but what is best – Direct us oh God! May no harm come to him – but good to us both. May I see or hear from him & know all our destiny soon. May he think kindly, may we act wisely & yet be happy! Pa told me of it all – feels it! I looked vain for him this night & evermore perhaps – all sat quiet – may I dream sweetly.

Friday June 23rd Quiet, busy day at home – visited in aft – alone. Went to see the Gibbes (Miss Louisa pleasant) – Fannie Earle – she & Preston agreeable.

31. "Humbolt" referred to Brazil in particular or eastern South America in general.

Florence unwell – they've moved down to study from Prof. Gibbes of Charleston – fine scientific advantages. Wish my sisters could & would avail themselves & I too.[32]

I encountered Maggie Munro there – she, Fannie & I. First time since old society squabbles – queer – all gracious now, but I'm not disposed to get too social with the fiery family of Munro's. Remember old scenes too well – 'though they are very clever & pleasant when they like. Broyles specially intimate. She managed to tell that "William M. had been on a visit to them" Young widower in Macon now. Ah, my how many unfortunate scrapes I've been in – unwittingly! Fannie E. so intelligent – too proud! All more humbled now by our national fall & losses – dreading confiscation now.

I went in to see Baylis Earle's family too – Eugenia stiff – talks much of Dr. Cooly. Tense & children – Joe Adams – a prisoner who took the oath while living in the North. Queer changes in a few years! I went on to see Lucie & Waller a little while, but all the Halls came in. I left – was hurrying through the streets from Theodore, but he pursued & caught me – amused many no doubt. I was glad that R was not in town – though I longed to see him. Shouldn't care for his opinion, but can't help it & this would affect him. T & I walked on chatting of common places; I turned aside to visit the Seabrooks & sent him home from the door. They were amused & I fear that they may think us engaged![33]

32. Fannie and Preston Earle were the children of Elias and Harriet Earle.

Louisa Gibbes has not been identified, though a familial relationship to Sallie and Jupiter is evident.

33. Major Joseph Manning Adams (1836–77), son of Rev. Jasper and Placidia Mayrant Adams, attended the Citadel, entering at age fourteen and graduating at twenty. He served as regimental quartermaster for the Fourth South Carolina and was a prisoner at Johnson's Island, New York, for eighteen months. He returned home, read law, and started a practice in Pickens, South Carolina.

Joe Adams married Eugenia Postelle Earle, daughter of John Baylis Earle, in December 1866, and returned to teaching school in Anderson. He died at his Oconee county plantation. The couple had a son named Quincy (*1860 Census,* Anderson District, 159; Simpson, *Old Pendleton,* 146; Vandiver, *Traditions,* 116; Evans, *Confederate Military History,* 426–77; see Reed, *Journals,* Appendix F.

Dr. Hiram C. Cooly (1831–73) attended medical schools in Philadelphia and Paris and established a practice at Anderson Court House in 1857; he was a founding member of the Anderson County Medical Association. A Captain Cooley was a surgeon with the Fourth South Carolina Infantry for the duration of the war (Vandiver, *Traditions,* 171, 227, 259; *1860 Census,* Anderson District, 155; Wilkinson, *Early Anderson,* 139; Hewett, *Confederate Soldiers,* 103).

Louise, Margaret, and their parents Archibald and Caroline Seabrook Hamilton were refugees from Charleston living in Pendleton. Margaret wed Colonel Henry Middleton Rutledge

While talking to Louise S I saw R pass up town late with other boys. We saw each other hastily. How does he feel now? How they all discussed the subject at home since Pa's revelations. (A negro woman of theirs was here today telling our Becky tales of him & his devotion to me) crazy since "he saw his darling at church last Sunday – wants no other, will have me, he will come soon – note – don't care for what old folks say" Yet, if true its true that he loves me thus, what keeps him away? What does he mean & how will it end? I long to know! Long to see him & talk over all these things. Long for his love & protection if he is worthy, but surely he is not to act thus & speak of me only to negroes) A quiet night at home.

Sat. June 24th A long, dreary – wet, cool, day – but I enjoy such now & then. Had to sew all day – rearranging old dresses. Couldn't read & dream enough to please – felt thankful for blessings, bit pined for R. Saw him pass home late alone. I can only remember his fine form now & hereafter perhaps. There was a light shower in the early morning sunlight & a rainbow in the West – rare & queer – struck us all! Pa was robbing a bee queen, nice fresh honey. This dark – wet night he is out on guard – heaven save him – perhaps R too.

Rumours of a negro garrison coming – dread it. New Troubles & no Robere to sympathize as I had vainly dreamed – he too is sad & lonely I'm sure. So – when shall we meet!

Sunday June 25th A strange, variable day of smiles & tears – dark clouds & light showers all morn. Cleared off during churchtime. I started to S.S. – no one there & Mr. Murray gone, so I was glad to attend preaching at the Methodist church & hear Mr Jones – who gave us a sensible rendering of the young man's scruples who came to Jesus to know what he should do. Is he saved – had been so exemplary, yet "one thing thou lackest" – he couldn't give up his riches for Christ. So we all have one besetting sin which we cling to & should root it out & guard against it.

Wonder what is my besetting sin! What idol we should destroy. It must be my vain thoughts of Robere & clinging to him through all things, especially as we were so near today for the first time in 14 long months. Yet more widely severed than ever it seemed. Not even catching each other's eye, not daring to look or speak, but how felt each?

Vie & Waller were there – I guess he thought of our confidences in the two last. How he had written to me envying their happiness & as they sat before me one & we apart. Did he sigh then to have my darling? – too bad – the false wretch who dare not come & claim me, when he knows our hearts sigh for each. We all sung

---

and they raised a son, Archibald Rutledge, a future poet laureate of South Carolina (Lander and McGee, *A Rebel Came Home,* 97).

with a spirit "Oh for a closer walk with God" Mr. Jones sings well. What thought R of my voice now. He used to love so well! I know he loves it still & loves me still however changed he seems! Queer creature!

To my surprize Theodore Smith was there. Saw me enter & came in – sat behind & then Robert came & sat just opposite him where both could gaze on me & see neither – my two queer lovers & what were they thinking of me after all our varied intercourse? T knew nothing of R & his presence. In his vanity – may deem himself secure as far as he wished to go – much as I've tried to slight him! But R was thinking savagely of T – I'm sure.

Perhaps had a contempt for the poor, weak fellow. Maybe admired his talents & wished I might accept him as a riddance. Perhaps was really jealous & imagined that I was encouraging T. He walked with me. Wonder how he did feel about it all. If he gazed on me with love or scorn or indifference after all these years of romance & all we have professed for each other & all we might have been.

I trembled with the excited state of my feelings – wept at the sad change – prayed for strength & blessings upon both. His bowed head so near me with its dark curling locks – did he pray & is he not striving to be a Christian still. Are we never to know each other's feelings – love & be blest! It seems too unnatural that we are forever estranged. It must be – we must meet soon! He came there alone, he must have wished to meet me today! Vie & Lucie laughed at my excitement for I didn't wish to go out knowing that Theo would walk with me & what would R. think – but it should have made no difference! But R. rushed out wildly & home in haste – never looked back. What did he mean? – indifference – shame – fear – jealousy – or what – I can't imagine – when that manly form of his should have been my protection – now & always! What is to be our destiny?

I avoided Theo but joined Eleanor & Jupiter Gibbes – the ugly little monkey came with me, but we had few words. I left him at the back gate – shocked Theo & Eleanor who walked on & only bowed to him. Fear I offended both, but my heart was in such a tumult from conflicting emotions. Hope I didn't vex either – I have cut Theodore so often lately he will be quite estranged – perhaps hope all may end for the best!

I sat alone all evg – read some of Spurgeon's spirited sermons & the Psalms. Wrote letters to Julia & Emma Brown. Have no R to write to now. Overlooked some of his letters & my journals regarding him & our stormy past – wondered as to our future. I see that years ago when he was so ardent – I did not respond, but now my heart yearns in vain for he seeks me not, but he loves me as ever I'm sure & can never forget! His servant Alfred here this evg. Wanted to see me, but I didn't know it in time to learn what he wanted – sorry! Why sends me no note? Told Becky of his new boots & clothes – was coming to see me soon – ashamed of himself &

longed to see me. Determined to win me, but it didn't seem so, yet I must see him again![34]

John & Mattie Reeves here to supper. Clever – went home early – happy pair! It has rained fitfully all evg – dark & dreary – cold & damp – thunder & lightning – storm at night. R got wet going to the Epis ch this aft – poor boy! Is he dreaming of me now? I dreamt last night that he married Ella or Maria Keith, but I was not invited. He came & rode with me later & said it was a "mock marriage," but I was miserable. Shall he & I ever be one? Mary Ann in my future was sure of it – saw the wedding bridal room she said. Will that ever be? Too strange to realize! Yet we might be happier thus than we shall ever be apart!

Pa on guard last night. Brought in three men – Dick Tupper &c to cut a bunch of Ham, honey, bread &c – after 1 oclock. Clif is out this dark stormy night. Fannie staying with Fan. I read some poems to the girls, but they won't appreciate them. Eleanor took a blue pill – always complaining. I am thankful to thee oh God for health & a cheerful, hopeful spirit, the comforts and many blessings given me – even the vain longing for human love may be denied me in mercy! Thy will be done oh God![35]

Monday June 26th A brilliant, breezy – lovely day – all nature refreshed! Busy, but did little – finished reading Ramsay's History of S.C. In afternoon Eleanor had visitors – I none. Went our to pay some visits – no one at home. Met no friends scarcely. Felt neglected – disappointed & miserable. Ran from Theo – saw Lucie awhile. Met Robere with others. He stared & smiled & bowed. I – sadly – looked too flushed – my heart ached – wondered & loved in the soft moonlight. He came now – will he ever? Read & rested – bright stars – End.[36]

[There is a six-month gap before Emmala's journals resume on January 1, 1866 in a new journal.]

34. Emma Brown was Julia Reed Brown's sister-in-law.

35. Blue pills, or blue mass, was a mercury-based medication. Prescribed for an assortment of ailments during the nineteenth century, the treatment could result in mercury poisoning if taken for an extended period of time.

36. David Ramsay published *Ramsay's History of South Carolina from Its First Settlement in 1670 to the Year 1808* in 2 volumes (Newberry, S.C.: W. J. Duffie, 1858).

Part II

January – April 1866

FIVE

JANUARY

Monday – January 1st 1866 [w]itnesses the dedication of my new journal to a new season of joys & sorrows – hopes and fears – though alas! the shadows prevail and there gleam but few sunbeams across my pathway these bleak and cheerless days! I scarce know why it is – for I am surrounded with many home comforts – good health – a large – wicked family and many blessings; but of course "there are skeletons in every household" and trials in every life – with disappointments in every heart!

With my cheerful contented nature I generally manage to make the best of every circumstance, forget the ills too soon sometimes and become reconciled to every fate. Yet tis best for my own happiness no doubt! Strange that I should have been so often deceived in my friends, or in those who professed to be my friends and lovers – nearly all of whom I have found false and forgetful – until finally estranged! But thus it is – each day we live but proves the inconstancy of the human heart brings new cares and sorrows – so that nothing earthly can be relied upon for permanent happiness! Thank Heaven! we have better promises in the future for those whose faith and works continue steadfast! Yet I fear tis my lot to always be deceived – as with my impressive sensitive nature I am always pleased – am too candid and confiding – hence the more likely to be imposed on and to suffer from changes incident to less faithful hearts.

With our large household white and black there is much labour connected – responsibilities & anxieties and of course the faults are all sources of trouble to each of us. I try to do my duty towards all yet fall very far short I know especially in my domestic avocations and amiable qualities – when I allow myself ruffled by my younger sisters who are impudent and self willed yet I know tis my place to set the best examples & do my duty faithfully. We are all lacking in affectionate demonstrations too – however much we feel

Our Sister Julia who married so young and unfortunately – is settled near us with her large – helpless family and is the source of many trials to herself and us – as yet – by her weak husband's faults – heaven deliver and save them! Our brother Clifton – so young and dependent on my father – who has no good education or profession or means with one arm lost in the service of his country – a fair – loving wife who has been sick for a month and looks as if she might never be quite well – with her sweet – chubby – good little Helen – none of them knowing what the future can have in store for them! Yet I am thankful that he seems to be avoiding temptations and is becoming more useful and better at home. May he continue to improve and succeed in becoming a noble man and his young family be blest! But my father seems to be so despondent about business affairs and the many persons he has to support – no provisions and no money and no resources – he thinks.

Yet whilst feeling that tis all very bad, I must acknowledge it might be worse and many others are not so fortunate, so I will be content and hope for the best[.] It is a trial to see our old servants being scattered, but a greater to keep the useless ones here to support with their new ideas of freedom, yet we may be thankful that emancipation has been received by them in such a quiet – sensible – humble way generally and can only pity their hard fate in their new life of freedom – which to some will be a sad change! Four of our coloured families are settled on Pa's plantations – may be of some profit to us but very little I fear – only an expense. Those in our yard are not yet properly distributed. too many children no good cooks etc. yet. Hope all will be better arranged. I was sorry to see our Becky go – with whom I had been raised and she grieves to come back, but it may be best so – God grant it![1]

Our Father is sometimes sad and cross but lately has seemed more submissive to fate – more genial and kind than formerly and we hope all may be happy and prosperous just now has a great fever to emigrate to Mexico or South America – we talk of it – but will effect nothing. I guess for new manias continually arise. I doubt if we would profit by the change and tis always sad to leave one's home and break up all the associations of life! May heaven direct us all for the best for we really would all like to emigrate from here thinking it would be better for our young family to grow up elsewhere than in this selfish – unsocial – sordid place – this dull little village where there are few inducements to improve our minds – nothing to care or hope or live for hardly – and so few families living in unity & concord – no spirit of improvement – amusement – or religion – one continual humdrum way of living to eat and sleep – and dress a little – labor on at petty things continually – yet this too may be all well – 'though I aspire to greater and better things and a wider field of action and enjoyment! Want to see more of the

1. According to his will dated September 7, 1880, the plantations owned by J. P. Reed consisted of a 152-acre farm "three miles from town," likely the vicinity of the Hammond, Jones, and Carter places as well. This property was in Varennes Township. An 1877 map of Anderson County by S. M. Pegg places the "Old Hammond Place" about one and a half miles south of town; there are also noted three "truck patches," and a twenty-acre possession called the "Julia White tract," which I believe to be in Rock Mills Township, west of Anderson Court House, where Emmala later raised her own family (Alexander, *Pendleton District Records,* 189).

Becky was a servant for the Reeds.

wider world outside with its many phases – live to some wider purpose – see and enjoy all thats best 'though as we have to encounter too much evil perhaps "where ignorance is bliss T'were folly to be wise"[2]

So again I'll be content whatever my lot – even though it is only to live thus from day to day – eat common food (I enjoy all but don't see enough to its preparation.) Sleep too long perhaps – sew and knit much for the family – read scraps of everything – but don't study and think enough – enjoy all books but don't have enough time to devote to them or teaching my young sisters – brother, nieces & nephews as I should nor the young blacks or others around whom I ought to benefit! I don't devote enough time to music or other accomplishments perhaps but no one appreciates it in me to any extent – admire for a moment & all's over – I have few persons here to visit me or to visit socially & freely – no congenial spirits really – there are no beaux here to (visit) drop in and entertain or escort one in a gentlemanly friendly way – none worth wedding – who value me and so we'll drag on thus this dull life – dependent on Pa I fear to the end. Though I am glad never to have been caught in the net matrimonial before – with all its cares – might never be suited to it – better so – yet sad to have met some few heart trials in my time – even this however has been & may be for the best, and I'll rest content.

The first week in January 1866 was cold and wet and uncomfortable! We all stayed quietly & busily at home enjoying books most – pining most for true friends! Such freezing cold nights and mornings as I ever rarely felt – and never like!

Sunday the 7th of Jan Heard Mr. Murray preach at the Bap ch in morn & Mr Keith at Epis in aft. Enjoyed both – the music of the last most – the organ played by Sallie Williams sweet touch – the Broyles and the Capers voices united & in fine chants & which were splendid, but the old memories which surged through my heart connected with some voices & one dark pair of wandering eyes thus was painful – even whilst feeling it best! Ah Robert! one year ago we had far different feelings I fancy – when you were a soldier in Va. and wrote so constantly and warmly – now we are estranged for ever more and he has acted a shameful part. He was attentive to others – may be devoted – yet he is wholly unworthy – though it is hard to learn complete resignation and oblivion! Other eyes and voices have

2. Venezuela, Brazil, Mexico, even New Zealand came under consideration as potential refuges for ex-Confederates with no desire to be "reconstructed." This phenomenon transpired between 1866 and 1868 (Foster, *Ghosts of the Confederacy*, 15–17).

Emmala quotes Thomas Gray's poem "On a Distant Prospect of Eton College" (1742): ". . . where ignorance is bliss, / 'Tis folly to be wise."

sought & have partly influenced me at different times and but lately the fascinating hero of Cokesbury awoke far different hopes.[3]

Yet all have proved fleeting and false & I have sighed and wept over my fate at meeting those so unworthy, when there must be better creatures in the world and I surely deserve better. Yet even here I will confess "all's for the best" and the future may prove it – if not by an earthly, a heavenly reward! I must live to do good for others no selfish ends! Lula Broyles was here with Mamie & nursing poor sick Fannie that week. Some little parties in town at which we were not expected – no visitors – no love, only the cruel news of Whit's falsehood to me and of the grand Christmas trees in Greenville & Cokesbury. The joys elsewhere contrasted with our own dullness. Mollie Brown here one night, nice woman. I went to see Murrays and Bleckleys – my good friends – sickness there – trials at Lucie's and Julia's & Webbs – all our intimates – & at grandpa's as they hear he is sick in Ga. – away from his family – but we hope he will get safe home – Cora & Lucie went home with Uncle June on Sunday.[4]

Tues. Jan. 9th Very cold but bright and calm – for the first time this winter devoted to visiting to try and retain & make friends – pleasantly spent & – I hope with good results! First to Julia's – to cheer & sympathize & help a little – must do more. Then to mantuamakers to fit a dress. To Gov. Orr's plain mansion – saw his plain clever wife, very kind to me & Mattie our friend, a noble smart girl too – fond of gayety now – hope we may all be friends forever. Mary Waller there to see

3. General Ellison Capers (1837–1908) graduated from the South Carolina Military Institute (The Citadel), where he later taught mathematics and rhetoric. Wounded three times during the course of the war, Capers became South Carolina secretary of state for the Orr administration at age twenty-eight. In 1893 Capers received an appointment as the Episcopal bishop of South Carolina—interesting given the fact that his father had once been the Methodist bishop of the same state. He married Charlotte Rebecca Palmer, and the couple had seven children. His autobiography is titled *The Soldier-Bishop Ellison Capers* (Wakelyn, *Biographical Dictionary,* 124; Faust, *Historical Times,* 35–37; Sifakis, *Who Was Who,* 105; Brown, *South Carolina,* 423; Garlington, *Men of the Time,* 73–74).

Cokesbury, South Carolina, was a village of schools and colleges, situated on the high ground between Augusta, Georgia, and Greenville, South Carolina. In 1834 residents named the town to honor America's first two Methodist bishops, Thomas Coke and Francis Asbury.

Contemporary Cokesbury is the epitome of rustic simplicity, a rare historical diorama. The town is a viable modern community that possesses a faithful nuance of antebellum bucolic life in western South Carolina (Edgar, *WPA Guide,* 358; Francis Walker, *A Compendium of the Ninth Census* [June 1, 1870 Census] [Washington, Government Printing Office, 1872], 324–25; "Historic Cokesbury," pamphlet published by the South Carolina Department of Parks, Recreation, and Tourism; "Cokesbury College, Greenwood, South Carolina," pamphlet published by the Cokesbury Historical Commission).

4. Miss Mollie Brown has not been identified.

Marion. Mrs. Hill lately moved here from Ga. – so cordial & clever & chatty and sensible – defended me (against enemies in our old soldiers aid society!) She & her children glad to see me. I ate plain dinner with them unexpectedly – hope to be very social.[5]

Then to Mr. Smith's the poor tailor just moved in town. Many troubles caused him to lose mind & health. His wife, a clever woman & old Mrs. Magee also. At Mrs. Sloan's I found a disconsolate widow who had lost her all, with husband and negro property complains sadly, but is a smart woman with clever children. Lula a nice girl – At Mrs. Jolene V. Morris a gayer widow once more disconsolate, very pretty & very independent! Her widowed mother there & two sisters. Sallie plain but smart – is to teach school here. Jenine pretty & lively. engaged to marry soon – all very cordial to me. Mrs. Whaley boarding there – her sons all off for Charleston.[6]

5. James Lawrence Orr was the newly elected governor of South Carolina, sworn in on November 29, 1865, to succeed provisional governor Benjamin F. Perry. In January 1866 the governor met with the new secretary of state, General Ellison Capers, Judge Sam McGowan, ex-governor Perry, and his law partner Judge J. P. Reed. Emmala is being facetious in her description: the governor's "plain mansion," called Arlington, displayed wide porticos, frontal columns, and a golden cupola. In January 1866, Mattie Orr was eighteen years old, pretty and witty, and her father was the new governor of South Carolina (Leemhuis, *James L. Orr,* iv–v, 12–3; *South Carolina Biographical Dictionary,* 240–42; Faust, *Historical Times,* 549; Wakelyn, *Biographical Dictionary,* 334–35; *1860 Census,* Anderson District, 159).

Marion Allen Gaillard Hill (age 34), wife of druggist and Baptist minister Richard S. Hill (43), served the Confederate cause by assisting the committee of women who met the train with refreshment for the soldiers. Mrs. Sylvester Bleckley recollected how she once brought a pitcher of milk and Mrs. Hill a bottle of liquor. After a long pass through the train, as the two women walked back into town, Mrs. Bleckley still had a full and rather heavy pitcher, while Mrs. Hill carried an empty and light bottle. Mrs. Bleckley vowed that next trip she would also bring the more popular, less burdensome beverage (UDC, *South Carolina Women in the Confederacy,* 364–65; *1870 Census,* Anderson County, 458).

6. The tailor shop of Clark and Smith was situated near the town square. In 1866 Jesse R. Smith was fifty-two years old, with many children. Mrs. Magee could possibly be Mr. Smith's mother-in-law (Vandiver, *Traditions,* 24).

Mrs. Jolene V. Morris has not been identified.

Martha M. Whaley of Charleston is mentioned in connection with the activities of the Soldiers Relief Society. She was the wife of Colleton planter and Charleston attorney William B. Whaley, whose family refugeed in Anderson until it was safe to return to Charleston. The Whaley sons, attorneys William B., Jr. and B. J., were off to Charleston to be present for the reopening of the city court system (UDC, *South Carolina Women in the Confederacy,* 114; *1860 Census,* Colleton District, 313; *Jowitt's Illustrated Charleston City Directory and Business Register, 1869–70* [Charleston, S.C.: Walker, Evans, & Cogswell, 1869], 217; *Charleston Courier,* Jan. 9, 1866, 3).

Then to Mr. Craytons – his daughter Kate Maxwell the pretty bride – with her young husband. Another Dr. & Mrs. Maxwell whom I used to know – pleasant – their father also. Dr. M thinks of moving to Mexico! Then to the Gibbes – Saw only silly Sally – & bad Bessie Washington & the poet brother "Jupiter" a moment. At Mr. Earles – found the three sisters Fannie, Mary, & Florence all very pleasant & social. [F]ixing up their loved & only brother Preston to leave for college in the morning for the University of S. C. in Columbia where I hope he may do well – a moral noble youth – Mr. Stratton the little deformed but genial Pres. Minister there awhile & pleasant, expected to have called on us before, they asked us both to tea. I declined with regrets, but hope to see more of the pleasant family![7]

I went on and shopped a little. Many Yanks and blacks everywhere a nuisance and strange men. A few familiar faces, but as strangers to me – R B's – Dr. Tom's etc. No bows, wonder why! At the hotel I found Bessie Webb out soon to move to Charleston. At the Fants – Jane & Rosa Lasard out – but Amanda there – delighted with her new wedded life – fortunate for her! and they all manage to have more fun than we! At Baylis Earle's – Eugenia a nice clever girls – Annie, Sallie etc. I ought to be more social with everybody & might enjoy life better here![8]

At home I found Milton Brown for tea; a rough bumpkin, but some good ideas and aspirations I hope – a little music & very cold & late now, when I ought to be at rest with the sleeping world. The bright stars as sentinels in the cloudless sky and a merciful great Ruler o'er all, but no warm loving hearts to care, Specially for me

7. Elizabeth "Bessie" Washington was forty-five years old in 1866, the wife of John B. Washington, accountant for the South Carolina Railroad; they had a home on the corner of Radcliffe and Coming Streets in Charleston. A refugee from Charleston, Bessie had two young children, Harriet and John B., Jr. (*Directory of Charleston, S.C., 1860,* 139; *1860 Census,* Charleston, Ward 6, 440).

Wallace H. Stratten, a Charlestonian and Presbyterian minister, arrived in Anderson in January 1865 after church attendance ceased in the fall of 1864. Officially installed as pastor in September 1865, Stratten "served for four and one-fourth years." In the spring of 1870 he was released by the church for reasons of failing health, then moved "to the Southwest and into another field of work" (Eleanor L. Cathcart, et al., *Yesteryears: The Heritage and History of the First Presbyterian Church, Anderson South Carolina* (Anderson, S.C.: First Presbyterian Church, 1987), 60–62.

8. Jane and Rosa Lasard have note been identified.

John Baylis Earle and Jane A. Earle had five children at the time of the 1860 census: Ortense C., Eugenia P., Sally F., Annie W., and Samuel. In 1866 Eugenia was twenty-one, Sally nineteen, and Annie seventeen, the same age group as the Reed girls. In 1860 Baylis Earle registered as a farmer with property valued at $35,000 and other assets totaling $175,000, making his family among the wealthiest in Anderson. Baylis Earle served Anderson as a lawyer, judge, and solicitor (*1860 Census,* Anderson District, 158; Vandiver, *Traditions,* 12, 200, 262).

below. Yet all's well I hope with my own conscience and spirit and content! Heard some boys go by singing familiar songs well tonight, but fear they were rowdies.

Weds Jan 10th A serene sunny day that I enjoyed very much after the previous cold clouded skies. Again I spent the whole day in visiting, as there was nothing special for me to do at home and wished to pay up old scores – though I accomplished but little that day I fear. Went first to Elijah Brown's nice residence, where I saw dainty little Mollie & Lillie who looked and talked so well. The house so well kept, with every comfort and two charming boarders. Rev Mr. Elliott, the tall & elegant Epis. divine. Little Stratton, the deformed but interesting Pres Gen. Newton Brown & others eat there![9]

They must have pleasant meals with everything to minister to the physical mental and moral pleasure, wish I could share them! The sisters were grieving most for their departed sister Hattie Earle who died in Arkansas in Nov as poor Dock wrote – after his hard times in the army. Wounds and imprisonment and absence of three years. His sweet bright little bride of a year struggling on among dangers and strangers in the far West – To be cut down thus in the midst of their united happiness. Their only child the bright little boy to follow his mother in few days to the grave Was too sad! She was a noble girl – whom I had seen graduate here with distinction and wed some years ago, then go forth with the brightest prospect & this is her fate. Never to return amongst her old friends or relatives again, though she found many to love her there! Sad fate but all may be best![10]

9. Joseph Newton Brown (1832–1921) hailed from Townville, South Carolina, a village fifteen miles northwest of Anderson. He graduated from Brown University in 1854 and was admitted to the South Carolina bar in 1858. Colonel Brown commanded McGowan's Brigade at the battle of Spotsylvania's costly Bloody Angle. Twice wounded, Brown was captured at Petersburg, Virginia, on April 2, 1865, and released soon thereafter. He married Elizabeth "Lizzie" L. Bruce on February 28, 1866. After serving one term in the state legislature, Brown organized the first Anderson National Bank (Garlington, *Men of the Time,* 54; Vandiver, *Traditions,* 88, 139, 229, 246, 262; Vandiver Report, Item #14; *1860 Census,* Anderson District, 161; James F. J. Caldwell, *The History of a Brigade of South Carolinians, Known First As "Gregg's" and Subsequently As "McGowan's Brigade,"* [Philadelphia: King & Baird Printers, 1866], 72, 90, 96, 105, 125, 137, 148, 156, 200, 219, 224; Crowther, "Anderson's Boys," 530; Varina Brown, *A Colonel at Gettysburg,* passim).

10. Elizabeth "Hattie" Hubbard Earle, first wife of Francis Wilton "Doc" Earle, died in Arkansas. The couple wed in September of 1859 and immediately set out for Arkansas. When the Civil War started "Doc" joined the Confederate Army. The couple's newborn infant died on November 12, 1865, and their four-year-old son three days later (obituary, *Anderson Intelligencer,* Nov. 20, 1865; Lucas, *Early Anderson,* 54–55; Harry U. Earle, Jr., and Samuel James Earle, *The Earles of Evergreen* (privately printed, 1984), 42.

I called in to see Constance Simmons, but she met me at the door saying her uncle was too ill for them to admit visitors, so I stopped next at the Tuppers. Admitted into their cold – elegant parlor – but they soon had a blazing fire – where the old lady came & excused herself as being very busy. Cordelia next the youngest but so old in her habits & tastes. So timid, but so pious, indeed almost fanatical, as we should be on the subject of religion – and desire to save souls – of which alas few seem to think these days. She would be a true and devout Nun or Saint and I hope can accomplish good in this sinful region. I felt that I do not feel nor exert myself enough for my Saviour, yet cannot see what I could do! Make me wiser & better – Oh God![11]

Then came in the buoyant brilliant Kate or who was hitherto characterized by the greatest vivacity – which has been almost crushed out of her by misfortunes during the war – loss of property in all their large family – their father's death, brothers wounds and the death of her favorite cousin or lover perhaps, Fred Tupper. From all of which it seems she can scarcely recover. But she is so smart & cultivated – reads & teaches & talks so well – Might do so much good & be such an ornament to society but she selfishly excludes herself from all now – Cares no longer for her old friends or new. Won't go out & don't care whether or not they visit her but she entertained me delightfully. Smiled with some her native brightness – Her dark eyes, fair hair & rosy cheeks & elegant form – beautiful and I would love to claim her as a friend – but don't know that I shall see much more of her. She urged me to stay longer, (but not to return). Spoke of letter writing, but not as if she would write and I would like nothing better than to correspond with her – Wonder if Dick and Eleanor will ever consumate!

I went then to Dan'l Browns – a household of women who do their own work Mrs. B & Elvira Belcher making a coat & poor Teresa – wrapped up & complaining of the world's coldness in general. I wish she were a more fortunate person – with love & home of her own. Strange fates are marked for people. I paused then at Rev. Mr. Keiths passed the old "Johnson University" – my Alma Mater, now used by our vile Maine Garrison – as a Yankee hospital – desecrated.

Past the Broyles old home, where I once spent such merry days & found such congenial friends, now all over forever! But Ella & Nan Keith has found them all I ever did – and could speak of nothing but their charms and their intimacy – their admiration for Robert especially and wishing they could win him. Such smart pretty lively girls – They might succeed perhaps, but lack music to win his heart supremely, for he can never feel the same toward any other woman. Ella evidently loves him & tried to quiz everyone about mine & his affair. Says he admits "his

11. Constance Simmons is possibly the daughter of Baptist minister David Simmons of Townville (*1860 Census,* Anderson District, 268).

admiration for my music" at least – I – no more. He is worthless to me now I think, but hope he may be blest!

Maria K the favorite – of his & mine & all – I think was absent to my regret Nan is engaged to Capt. Borland – still in college – Old Mr Keith came in to chat with us awhile – very interesting old man. We discussed "affairs of state" He predicts a war with France or England. The U.S. very easily crushed the South, liberated &c – but tis fallatious I think! He goes soon to his old church in Charleston "St Michaels" the family remains here longer.[12]

Next I stopped at Wm Webbs nice home. The John Webb's family there previous to removing to Charleston next week. Bessie came in to see me, a bright pleasant girl, whom I asked to stay some with me, but she declined – Miss Matthewes too was very pleasant – at the Winthrops I found only Miss Mary. Nice maidens & widow ladies there only. Home to a late dinner afterwards. Cora accompanied me to Mr. Hyde's – a happy household & cozy little cottage home. A perfect state of training, the parent so clever & quiet, the children so useful & smart. Eliza a noble girl, teaches the younger ones regularly advanced studies in which their good brother Joe assists. Wish I could do so at home. We talked of many things, then I had to sing from some of their old music books. Favorite songs for the girls & Mrs. H. who used to be quite a musician herself. I hoped to have finished my visits, but didn't get quite around.[13]

Stopped at Wilhites & found only simpering Mary. Heard that Bill Humphreys their boarder had gone near Belton to attend the marraige of Warren D. Wilkes that night to Miss Telfourd, an uneducated country girl! How strange, after his brilliant career, or rather his talents & attainments. The society he has been in – the field he might have filled – all thrown away in dissipation – now improved, but wrecked perhaps. Aspires only to a country school & home with the comforts supplied by a plain old farmer & his domestic daughter I suppose & it may be best for him now – as his best years & talents & prospects are all gone, and it may prove

12. Captain Borland has not been identified, beyond the knowledge that he was from Charleston and a medical doctor who wed Nan Keith, which made him a brother-in-law to Robert Broyles.

13. Mary Winthrop and her family were Charleston refugees, where all the South Carolina Winthrops lived, according to the 1860 census. The 1870 census records forty-seven-year-old Mary lived with parents, Dr. Henry and Elizabeth Winthrop (*1870 Census,* Charleston County, 102).

Miss Matthews was a child of either J. R. or W. R. Matthews, and therefore a grandchild of the Charlestonian planter family of Joseph F. Matthews, who lived at 98 Rutledge Street (*Charleston City Census, 1861,* 182; *1860 Charleston City Directory,* 100).

Rev. E. F. Hyde taught school at the Townville Academy in 1872, but little more is known about the lowcountry family (Vandiver, *Traditions,* 204).

his salvation, but will she be happy? Hope it may be well for I always felt interested in his career.[14]

Home late – found sweet Becky Webb here with Eleanor – for the night – to reveal the great secret of her coming marriage – to Jim Hoyt etc queer taste in her too. And my own destiny was almost decided that night forced upon me unexpectedly. First Col. Newton Brown called – who hadn't been here in some time – Pa admires him so surely for his worth – 'though he is a queer genius – I like him but could never love I don't think – particularly as his brother is in the family and so worthless – he feels this I think – shows his preference for me "which he will not reveal," but uneasy about the claims of others – he came in saying "he wanted to see me especially if I was frozen up – thought of writing to know etc"

Becky & Eleanor threatened to leave the room – but he pacified them – & I hinted for them to stay – as just then Mr. Theodore Smith entered as my visitor & I couldn't entertain both beaux – strangers to each other – one with a longer claim and his slighted advances hitherto – to be healed – the other hesitating I think – with all his moral worth and amiable qualities – a greater prize than the others talents and ardour perhaps – yet – two such eccentric characters – such grotesque manners and bachelors of such names as Smith & Brown – neither of which I could assume with pleasure – being ambitious to soar above my own common sphere – with my rarer gifts I flatter myself I scarcely knew how to receive them – but was compelled to throw Newton upon the girls to entertain – to his chagrin & theirs perhaps – sorry I couldn't chat a little more with him & not neglect entirely as I did – until he sprung up very abruptly to leave – thinking T & I – engaged – no doubt and 'tis the last of his visiting perhaps Yet I must try to retain him as a friend – hereafter.

I was of course pleased to see Theo again – my constant devotee so long who has entertained & appreciated me above all the world and 'though rejected he returns to me with generous feelings to bid me farewell. He's going down to Charleston and thinking we might meet never more of course, I devoted myself to him then his four month stay with his sister – Mrs Kuhtman in the mountains – above Walhalla – with all the physical & intellectual comforts there enjoyed –

14. Warren D. Wilkes (d. 1883) continued his legal career upon returning from the war. Corporal Wilkes served with Company J, Fourth Regiment, South Carolina Volunteers. Wilkes married Isabella Telfourd of Belton, South Carolina, in January of 1866 (Salley, *South Carolina Troops,* 665; Vandiver, *Traditions,* 233, 262, 266; Jesse Walton Reid, *History of the Fourth Regiment S.C., Volunteers, from the Commencement of the War until Lee's Surrender* [Dayton, Ohio: Morningside Press, 1975], 17; *1860 Census,* Anderson District, 261; *1870 Census,* Anderson County, 410; Lucas, *Early Anderson,* 55).

rendered him a better man I think! His health was reinvigorated – his spirits more cheerful – by the genial companionship he met there.[15]

Having always lived so alone – he had grown more gentle & amiable – his temper & tastes improved I think – no chances for dissipation in which he had once plunged I fear & almost wrecked his health – but for this fact – I might love & resign myself to him – willingly perhaps – Yet, if perfect reformation is possible I might forgive & forget it seems & he had many excuses – the death of his idolized brother & thrown on his own resources with his rare tastes and unpractical attainments – living a forlorn life – little sympathy with his "sordid brother & frivolous family" he says – so he yielded to temptations & subsequent misery no doubt – became too a skeptic of all pure & holy things I fear yet seems to have recovered somewhat from this greater stain – to be more seriously inclined – and less sacreligious & profane – I hope. At least he disguises it from me – and I think he has been sincere in showing me his real self – where I find the good counterbalances the bad!

He is learned in many books & languages & sciences – is capable of writing – much – as an author in almost any field – could accomplish much for the literature of the South – good to himself & others I hope – yet he lacks energy & ambition to excel here I think – pretends to scorn literature & will prove himself a practical worker. I know not in what hire – I wish he could mingle the two – and be all that I desire! He has the deepest – feelings of love & honour I hope – true appreciation of music and of beauty in everything – but not so much of good.

[I hope(crossed out)] & fear he is too much of a sensualist but after laughing so much at my prudery hitherto – he yielded it due admiration now. [S]ees with purer eyes I think, But he is jealous & sensitive & excitable – would be exacting & cross I fear – but could he be cruel to a woman he fairly loved as I know he does Me? [H]e is too generous at least for it to last I fear yet I can't tell how it would be and would ever dread. He came "once more to sit at the feet of her – whose lightest tones are melody to his ear" – he wrote once – 'though considering himself rejected he had never quite despaired – he honoured my scruples my sincerity & candour – and would always have an affection & respect for me though I had made him suffer tortures – the bitterness was passed he had been plunged in depths of woe – which he never more could sound – and now he would live with some new hope

15. Walhalla, South Carolina, has long served as a mountain retreat in far western South Carolina. The little planned community, founded in 1850 by the German Colonization Society, was the Blue Ridge Railroad Line terminus. Walhalla was a true frontier town during and after the antebellum era. An added wartime danger was the huge number of deserters turned outlaw hiding in the mountains to the north and west of town (Mary Cherry Doyle, *Historic Oconee in South Carolina* (Clemson, S.C.: privately printed, 1935), 47.

& energy – which I was glad to hear! But my slightest encouragement seemed to afford him new joy!

I scarce knew how to feel – with my undecided nature – at which he always laughs & it is a misfortune! Yet I am strongly tempted to yield to his generous delicate appreciation of me and superior qualifications which I can find in no other man – notwithstanding his faults & the mutual objections we might have of family & connection & limited means – health & temper & as Pa too seems to cherish some strong predjudices against him, which may not be groundless owing to his physical & moral defects – the mean sordidness of his brother towards him as even Fan my professed friend so long – proves false but the Kuhtmans far more worthy – value me I hope he brought a kind letter from Anna to me – saying how much they will miss "dear Uncle Theo" &c and I might find them delightful friends some day – will be cultivated – live in some city – go to Europe perhaps &c &c may heaven direct all for the best![16]

I have no desire to marry anybody – shrink from the very thought & might be miserable on the approach of the reality with any man – I may never have loved with all the true – lasting fervour of which I am capable & never may – not finding the proper object or return – yet I have wasted feelings on worthless objects which I can never recall I fear hence whilst Theodore was all "passion and precipitancy" – "I was all cool indifference" – repelling all warmer advances and sudden plans &c

Then is it well that I should admit him as an accepted lover – or is it decreed that I should ever even prepare to marry as all other women do & covet? I never expect to unless to him – as I am getting beyond attractive youth – so few persons are met suited for beaux or husbands – here – and I know that I am more comfortable and happy at home than I could ever be elsewhere with the intimacy and cares – and new relations and duties of married life – however I might be agreeably dissapointed!

Better though among strangers – seek this fate if I ever yield – not here or in Charleston – too well known, both of us would be too freely discussed &c I have no other lover now & may never have a more congenial one – books & music & all fine arts & social cheer – are our chief joys, yet we are not practical enough I fear – 'though he vows he is! [H]e entered with a dignified air – his fine face & dark flashing eyes – with a new stylish "tout ensemble" – that was striking! After some commonplace general remarks – he urged me to sing & play for him as usual –

16. The 1870 census identifies Fanny living with husband Hazel A. and young children William B. and Georgianna. The Heywards lived with banker William B. Smith, his wife Fanny S., and nineteen-year-old Pauline in Charleston. Hazel Heyward averred no occupation to the 1870 census-taker.

seeming to sit entranced – but hopeless – for during his favorite airs – he seemed to suffer real pain in thinking of my cruelty and final parting. [W]ould lean down & brush away tears – then with smiles & witty sallies respond: Oh he is a rare jewel!

In the midst of the greatest sentiments he would exclaim with some ludicrous similes and jokes not always delicate – laugh nervously & heartily at everything whilst despising all frivilous & gay things! – with his dark – gloomy feelings it is well he can mingle the humor which all such affects & saves him from madness which counteract or dispair! He argued though that dark eyed people were never crazed "I thought otherwise," & only the grey eyes of genious – or tender blue – "like mine with their soft inner circlet of beauty" &c were liable to insanity!

What pleasing flattery he heaps upon me – who find so few to appreciate I fancy – is it vanity though? I hope not. If he were always as kind and tender – surely it would not be happiness to live for him – sing & read and work with him evermore – yet there would come changes and crosses and mortifications I am sure – he seemed pleased to be with & hear me again – yet to expect nothing – though he asked after my ultimate decision which I couldn't even then give – but waived – and he seemed to respect each freak of mine – after they all left – sat with me as long as I would permit (near 10) with his sentiment & poetry & love & humour flowing from his lips & eyes – but treating me with most delicate respect.

At last he went – promising to return next day for last time after bidding other friends goodbye – packing up & selling what furniture &c he had here but since then I hear rather [a] bad story on him – of his requiring so high a price for his carpet & refusing to let Dr. Holland have it for his debt – as the latter had cured him with rare medicine but I suppose now he wants money to start on – he told me of how those sharpers here wanted to swindle him & he prevented – but which is wrong & he is too sordid If at all dishonorable I should despize! and Pa gives him credit for only bad traits – I'd have scarcely strength of mind & will to resist home influences – as my heart has no powerful promptings – though my fancy & vanity may be flattered & pleased & yet I hope all may end for the best!

Thurs – Jan – 11th The weather is becoming again o'rcast – but I spent this day selfishly in doors Reading & scribbling in morning. Bessie Webb called a little while – a nice girl and then in the aft. when I had waited for Theodore's coming – until I had almost pursuaded myself that he too was false – (as is ever my fate) and that I did love & respect him truly – he entered – very elegant & bright looking – but with a halting gait as if suffering with rhumatism – (his besetting sin –) gout or corns – or something – I don't know what – though he assumed all the appearance of health and strength and a brave resolution to battle with the world and conquer! I hope that he may be a sound & happy & successful man & all that I could yet wish in the man who claims me for his own – who values me most highly, & whom I may choose as my protector & friend!

I gave him a note with my feelings candidly expressed which his kindness deserved – he seemed overjoyed to receive a token from me – even though unconscious of what fate it contained & kissed my hand rapturously – whilst I drowned my confusion on the piano – singing & playing all of his many favorites – pieces & songs – to which he would hum & gesture & seemed to enjoy frantically – and though he enjoys music properly – not for the idle words of sentiment – but for the subjective influences it has on all the finer senses – which I never saw anyone appreciate & exhibit more intensely than he – And he seemed to revel in the very thought that my voice which soared so sweetly & to please so many – could be brought down to form the chief joy of his life alone in reading our song – or words – every one of which he cherishes as no other man has or ever will regard mine perhaps!

I wrote that my depths of love were yet given to noone Duty would alone develope it perhaps – but he was entitled to all I now could offer – with the promise that when he had got into business in some city – Baltimore or New Orleans preferred as he spoke of them (Charleston I fear) if his health & prospects & truth & purity admitted &c – I might welcome his coming as never before – during the coming year – if agreeable have I promised too much? Will I never be reconciled to its fulfillment!

But he seemed not half satisfied – though rendered very "glad & happy – had a new lease on life – excess of joy" yet wherefore – for I promised so little & was so indifferent! I felt his reproaches that he met with no fit return of feelings & hopes & thrills of pleasure & anticipations & though I was not indifferent & "blushed in pretty confusion" he said – couldn't bear to talk on the subject – as I never can quietly on such delicate themes & trembled in view of the very "intimate relations of married life" of which he spoke – but he once asked me to go with him now – his prospects were as good as any man's – I was too philosophic & calculating – he all fire &c But of course I wouldn't listen to this plan – even were I resigned – to yield all for him – my preparations were not sufficient & his plans not settled enough – for of course I want to be sure of a comfortable home & I must learn to be more domestic & useful so I can adorn any home!

Our refined taste & requirements cannot serve us altogether for real life alas – if so we might indeed be happy & blest together for he does not know much of life's practical duties & did not even know our cereal grains which I pointed out in my vase! We found out some nasty little faults of temper &c even in the other I fancy – each flattered the other's mental gifts – which might produce books & fame yet – are too lazy or unambitious for their developement – or haven't the means & would not be appreciated South! At the North this would have been his vacation – but will it be now he hasn't yet determined – though he seems resolved to do something and with strength of purpose & ability can't fail to find it – I hope twill prove so!

He longed 'though for me to offer inducements that he might remain here some days longer to enjoy my society – to present me a ring &c but I would hear to nothing because I want him to break from this wasted life of three years he has led here (Out of the war & business – an invalid – addicted to opium &c I fear) to seek a newer – wider – more active, better life I hope & improve in every way if he is to be my husband – then I don't wish it known by anyone for many reasons yet so uncertain – my own feelings so unformed & his future &c and would not have him tempt me to yield to any "lovers priviledges" which he wished to claim – for I am not yet wholly reconciled to it all and don't know that I ever can be. Time must prove! Heaven direct!

After hearing me sing to the piano & guitar a great deal – partaking of a nice little bonded tea together & talking of many things – which I would bring up to waive the more serious theme – which at last prevailed however he urged that I should give him a lock of my hair & I could not refuse this – as he goes away so far & our fate so uncertain & he so true – he thinks my hair so beautiful too – so I let the curls fall & allowed him to clip off the end in ecstasy it seemed & kissed it fondly – saying it should be enshrined in gold &c

He values too an old glove of mine he has – would fit it on my hand & claim it all at once – but I wouldn't permit much of this must preserve my prudery to insure his respect – and so after he had kissed my hand in a passionate adieu – and came back to ask "If I would not seal the compact as an engagement" opening his arms to embrace me – I fled in alarm – crying "no-no!"- and he was stunned by my cruelty – "why Miss Emmala What do you mean! you are so precautionary" & walked away highly offended or mortified perhaps

Perhaps to give me up entirely thinking I can never love him &c but I guess not – it would be well anyway – perhaps – I felt sorry for him – but must need to protect myself in his esteem & others – knowing our uncertain fate & his former reputation for amours &c! He wanted to come up before summer &c but I didn't agree – Not knowing what my feelings or our mutual condition may be then – can write decisively hereafter – for we will enjoy each others letters I'm sure & I'm afraid he will place me under many obligations which if my lot is so decreed may my heart be turned to him alone & our future blessed!

At last near 11 – he tore himself away as I said looking remarkably well in his nice new cloth suit – large stylish cravat, neat little felt hat his dark eyes sparkling beneath – & I might be proud of him as mine – wish he were a little larger & had a different name – and reputation! I shall feel his absence I am sure – and prove far better than Whit or Robert would have been – or anybody I may ever win & city life a happier one for me – May heaven direct! I sighed over his final departure and wondering what our fate would be – prayed for the best! Did he rest as peacefully afterwards as I did or was he restless & unhappy – packing &c – I gave him a candle for his use at the hotel as he could get none at that hour & when shall we meet again!

Friday Jan 12th A dark – dreary – rainy day – alone – sad one to me – for I really missed him – now that he had gone – "It may be for months – it may be forever!" – The early morn was pleasant enough – but this dismal night he may be joggling along in some hack – in danger & discomfort – blaming me for my coldness in driving him away & yet I pray not – though I almost regret it & that I didn't see more of him & yield more kindly to his warm devotion such as I may never meet again – and his own devotions cooled down when I most wish for them! Pa was disposed to criticize him still – yet I hope all's well – I sat scribbling this nonsense all morn when I should have been at work perhaps – but couldn't accomplish much in that line today

Jane Fant came in awhile – took some of my music home with her & begged that I should go & sing for them in the aft I was going to afford that pleasure if I could for they really appreciate it but it rained too much to our great suprise Grandpa Hammond rode up – to let me know he was well and had returned safely from his trip to Georgia – where we heard last of his being sick – pleased with his prospects there he will return sometime but left Uncle Dr. H & family settled there – the Griffins nearby &c

We were glad to see the dear good old man again! In the aft – whilst trying to knit & read – I was worried with the bad boys – J.P. – Fred & Sumter sport each other – uncontrollable & what will become of them – Julia here awhile – everything goes wrong with her household it seems – owing to trifling J.P. & will I ever get into such a bad scrape? I went and sat with Fannie awhile – who has laid in her bed so sick – a month – suffering the same pains everyday & has to take morphine which sickens her &c dreadful will she ever be quite well again? Mamie is indefatigable in nursing her so kindly[17]

I feel with shame that I am not useful enough at home – went off to dream alone – a long time & at night to write and read alone – my greatest pleasures now (Eleanor & the children making groundnut candy won't read &c would I be

17. Frederick "Fred" Garlington Brown was born October 28, 1860, at Anderson, South Carolina, the oldest son of Julia and John Peter Brown and a rambunctious six-year-old at the time of the journal entry. Fred was a few years older than his uncle J. P., Jr., and they evidently made a troublesome team when placed together (Vandiver, *Traditions,* 312–13; Garlington, *Men of the Time,* 55–56; Hemphill, *Men of Mark,* 39–41).

happier to have one congenial spirit with me or thus free! I scarcly know wether the pleasure would counter- balance the evil – yet I miss the merry voice and tender words & glances from Theo – last night and so often in the three years of his sojourn here – gone now forever and when & how shall we meet again – and what our mutual destinies? Heaven save & direct us and bring us in happiness together if tis best! Have R & W quite forgotten? False – Worthless men! Will none more true or worthy never fall to my share? Late & dreamy hour – the rains lullaby delightful – may sweet dreams attend my senses & all who love me!

Sat Jan 13th The earth was filled with mist & moisture penetrated every nook – but soon all shades dispersed – leaving the struggling sunlight and mild atmosphere I sat reading papers &c stupidly – as our little willful brother J.P. ran off to Julia's before breakfast where Cora found him & Pa gave him his first switching but with much regret I fear he won't mind it & be all we wish! I was sewing then till noon but I should have gone to Julia's as she expected

I went afterwards to the Fant's – clever folks so far as I see – modest & love music devotedly &c Jane & Amanda (Mrs Swords & Rosa (Webb) – nice girls all glad to see me & when I assented to play & sing – all delighted Miss Mary Milling came in – Charley Webb & John Smith a chap whom I used to see here at school – very comical – whom I thought was killed – passed safe through the war – all sat listening to my many choice songs and speeches – Charley told us of having been at Warren Wilkes marraige – many quests – good supper – right nice affair but till [illegible] the sober will teach – all pleased &c[18]

In town I bought some paper & envelopes – to write to Theo &c saw the Bleckleys & cousin E. L. Earle from Georgia friends to me – the last urging me to go down to see them – will send for me – entertain me with turkey &c have a beau &c so I ought to go – a nice place his mother is lately dead – but he was drinking – too bad On his way to Charleston – as witness in the Keys trial – how will it end for the poor fellows – accused of murdering three Yanks at Savannah River – guarding their cotton [T]oo bad – plenty of negroes & yanks in the street

18. Amanda Fant, along with six siblings, lived at the boardinghouse of her mother, Esther. At nineteen years old, Amanda and her twenty-seven-year-old sister, Jane, were Emmala's contemporaries.

Mrs. Swords could be Ruth Swords, who later married Willis Newton of Pendleton (Simpson, *Old Pendleton,* 185).

Mary Milling has not been identified.

Charles Webb, son of Elijah and Rosa Waller Webb, could have been little more than twelve years old in 1866 (*1860 Census,* Anderson District, 258; Vandiver, *Traditions,* 13).

There are several likely John Smiths, but none can be verified.

associating freely – shocking – near 30 new troops here – very trying – how long will they all remain?[19]

I meet few friends to speak with over in town – Came on to Julia's – busy & children noisy – sorry I didn't go today – I ought to see more & do more if I can for my sister with her many cares – A quiet night at home with Cora Wilhite romping with the children until Maj. Humphreys called to take her home. Pa & I sat selfishly reading or knitting Ma sews or nurses the troublesome baby – sweet little Sissy who said "What's that – hear that &c" but won't try [to] say anything else &c – J. P. asked to be put to bed by Pa tonight as usual nobody reads or works much Poor Mamie has to sit with Fannie so sick now all together in my room – must rest pleasant sunlight outside – but no letters & no love What is Theo thinking of me now – or W. or R. strange – May they be blest!

Sunday Jan 14th Sunbeams and shadows alternated today – calm & mild – delightful! I went to my church prepared to enjoy the services & the holy Communion – which we take so seldom – and I did – but not as much as I wished, there was one mortifying circumstance – J.P.B. sitting in our pew – half tipsy & spitting tobacco everywhere. Calling & starting disgustingly! I was in the same pew and felt so horrified – but he got through better than I expected yet is so wicked & bad – left before communion – feels that he is not worthy but what will ever improve him? This has distressed us all today! Eleanor came in with her stylish new dress – so pretty &c but taken down by him

19. The Bleckley-Hammond-Reed kinship placed some families in both Georgia and South Carolina. This also holds true for the kin E. L. Earle and many other Andersonians.

The "Keys Trial" was actually two murder trials conducted by the same military commission in Charleston, South Carolina. Francis Gaines Stowers of Hart County, Georgia, was tried first; his is the trial Emmala refers to. Later in January 1866 came the trial of Crawford Keys, Robert Keys, and Elisha Byrum.

Three sentries of the First Maine Battalion were murdered on the evening of October 8, 1865, as they stood guard over fifteen bales of cotton at Brown's Ferry on the Savannah River, fourteen miles north and west of Anderson. The cotton belonged to local planter James Crawford Keys; F. G. Stowers owned the cotton barge.

A military commission sentenced all the defendants to be hanged, but the sentences were soon commuted to life. Appeals to President Andrew Johnson came from Governor J. L. Orr and William Trescott. The case was overturned on November 17, 1866, when a U.S. District Court found the initial trial by a military tribunal exceeded its jurisdiction over the state's civil courts (*Cincinnati Daily Gazette,* Dec. 1, 1866; Vandiver, *Traditions,* 170; *1860 Census,* Anderson District, 230; L. Mell Glenn, *Keys Family Sketches: Four Generations in Direct Line from Peter Keys [1761–1835] through J. C. Keys [1882–1935] and the Story of a Sensational Trial* [Greenville, S.C.: Keys Printing Company, 1965], passim).

The Broyles Home, Anderson, S.C. Home of Ozey Robert Broyles, M.D. Courtesy of Pendleton District Historical, Recreational, and Tourism Commission.

Peter Keys McCulley (b. 1845). Courtesy of Pendleton District Historical, Recreational, and Tourism Commission.

Waller Hunn Nardin, M.D. (1807–1905). Courtesy of Pendleton District Historical, Recreational, and Tourism Commission.

Claudia Murray, wife of John Scott Murray and a teacher at Johnson Female Seminary. Courtesy of Pendleton District Historical, Recreational, and Tourism Commission.

James Lawrence Orr (1822–73), attorney, Unionist politician, and the first governor of S.C. elected after the Civil War. Courtesy of Pendleton District Historical, Recreational, and Tourism Commission.

Anderson Courthouse Square. Courtesy of Pendleton District Historical, Recreational, and Tourism Commission.

The children of Judge Jacob Pinckney Reed and Teresa Hammond Reed. (above) Judge Jacob Pinckney Reed (1814–80). (left) Courtesy of Pendleton District Historical, Recreational, and Tourism Commission.

Emmala Thompson Reed, ca. 1867. Courtesy of Pendleton District Historical, Recreational, and Tourism Commission.

Mason S. "Manse" Jolly, leader of an upcountry outlaw gang after the Civil War. Courtesy of Pendleton District Historical, Recreational, and Tourism Commission.

Lily and Teresa Strickland. (left) Johnson Female Academy, established at Anderson by Jacob Pinckney Reed in 1845. (below) Courtesy of Pendleton District Historical, Recreational, and Tourism Commission.

Arlington, home of James L. Orr. Courtesy of Pendleton District Historical, Recreational, and Tourism Commission.

Echo Hall, the Reed family home in Anderson, S.C. Courtesy of Pendleton District Historical, Recreational, and Tourism Commission.

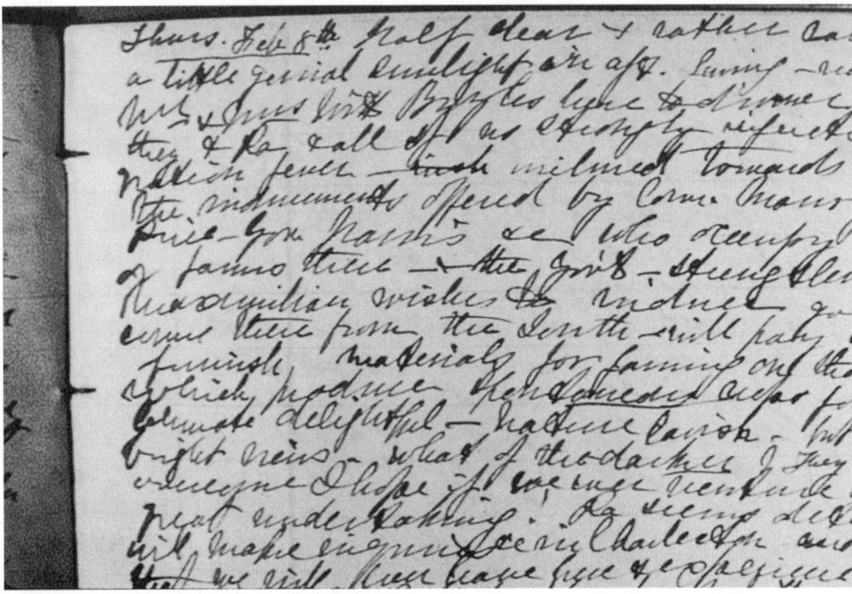

Sample page from the journals. Courtesy of Pendleton District Historical, Recreational, and Tourism Commission.

Francis Kingsley Reed (1845–1924). Courtesy of Anderson College Library, Anderson, S.C.

Clifton "Clif" Augustus Reed (1845–1924). Courtesy of Anderson College Library, Anderson, S.C.

James Reed Miller (b. 1845). Courtesy of Anderson College Library, Anderson, S.C.

Sara "Cora" Cornelia Reed (1853–1929). Courtesy of Anderson College Library, Anderson, S.C.

Mary "Mamie" Eliza Reed (1850–1932). Courtesy of Anderson College Library, Anderson, S.C.

Teresa "Pet" Hammond Reed (1864–1939). Courtesy of Anderson College Library, Anderson, S.C.

Jacob Pinckney Reed, Jr. (b. 1862). Courtesy of Anderson College Library, Anderson, S.C.

Teresa Hammond Reed. Courtesy of Anderson College Library, Anderson, S.C.

Eleanor "Nell" Caroline Reed (1847–1909). Courtesy of Anderson College Library, Anderson, S.C.

Julia Susan Reed (1842–83). Courtesy of Anderson College Library, Anderson, S.C.

Captain William Hammond, Emmala Reed's maternal grandfather. Courtesy of Anderson College Library, Anderson, S.C.

Victoria "Vie" Hammond,
Emmala Reed's great-aunt.
Courtesy of Anderson College
Library, Anderson, S.C.

Mr. Murray preached a very good sermon – on the solemn engagement as Christians we were under – to serve God – wish I could have been more impressed! But few members to commune – not a half dozen males & these so worthless – no deacons scarcely – no religion no choir – no comforts – nobody being brought in to the church – the old falling off – till we are broken up – Mr Murray – never paid for preaching never was a good pastor – ought to visit and talk – pray & stir up the church – or it will die out & half the blame be his Then the debt for the building & $2000 is mainly due my father & a few others responsible – who can't pay it always too large – & no stoves or salaries &c choir to improve it – even Sunday school died out!

I was distressed about it all & wondered what could I do to stir up the zeal & warmth – don't exercise enough influence on anybody around me – help and revive us all Oh God! Mrs Sloan & I talked but could do nothing yet! We used to be most flourishing & now have so declined! My father & mother used to take more interest in such things – but they too have fallen off – J P & Julia so indifferent – so the young children of our families are all growing up without God – indeed neglect all duty – I ought to lead them – but have no influence – it seems they are so bad & self willed – but what is to become of us all?

Newton Brown poked home with me in his queer way – right pleasant – but I don't like the gossip that will arise – (he was quite personal too – talking at the gate – Pa well pleased) disgusted with J.P. and humanity in general wants to move off alone somewhere – I anxious to move among strangers to some city perhaps – so we compared notes! We met R. B. driving a lady – no recognition – what thought each! Grandma H, Vie and Tom Carter came in here awhile, but I had promised to dine at Julia's – or they all insisted – so I went there too – but J. P. silly & so lazy & mean! Poor Julia has awful trials! May God help her to bear them & worse times which I fear must come! A worthless – ruiness husband – so many bad children – trouble with hired negroes – cook sick &c awful! Are such trials to be my fate? God forbid – yet I'm thankful to have been spared – surely she deserves a better fate.

All of us at home lamenting the condition & prospects of our family and longing to move away from our freedmen poor kin & bad influences – pay debts & depart in peace & credit – to find a newer – better home with strangers & make a start in the world – so many young children – three men with no means of making a support scarcely and no care for religion I fear – too carnal and fussy. And we would not be improved by the [illegible] those respects – so what is to be done – we can't tell! Heaven direct us for the best!

I talked with Julia & all as best I could – came on to the Epis. church – heard Mr Elliott deliver another beautiful, elevating sermon on the importance of action – activity in religion – beautiful words & thoughts – wish I could remember better & profit by them! The full choir was sweet – three Broyles boys sang – Tom,

John & Bob – not much improvement but such a change in them who were so timid &c but are so worthless – yet R's dark eyes & mellow voice again awoke too many memories of other days our fancied devotion one year ago & the sudden change his attentions to the Keiths (Ella & Maria there, so pretty)

My other beaux – my compact with Theo – What does he think of it all & are we to entirely forget and be estranged forevermore? Better so – but sad – my heart sighs in foolish sadness with all these feelings today & I was glad to weep a little – 'though to sing those glorious hymns relieved me somewhat! Dick Tupper a nice youth walked on home with Eleanor & I stayed with her late R. B. & Dr. Keith – walked after us a little way but I am alone here now – miss Theo's Sunday visits & company. What is he doing now & what's to be our fate!

I wrote some letters to old friends though I can claim none I fear – so false & indifferent. Sallie Brown & Sallie White & Anna Kuhtman must receive my remembrances – but where are Cora & Sallie Whitmire Hattie B. & all who used to love me & whom I loved – lang syne – & false Whit so lately & Robert![20]

Soft – starlit night! All sat in Fannie's room some trying to cheer her in this protracted spell of sickness Clif must be disheartened – so helpless! Cora and I sang some hymns to piano – sang with sweet baby sister & all scattered off selfishly – to read &c I scribble this unnecessary nonsense which I fear will do more harm than good but I am so worthless can only dream these days & live for self – the girls won't let me read to & improve them – Pa reads alone – no religion I fear make us to improve – Oh God, direct our future ways – give me the love of true noble hearts – and may all be well with us here after!

Monday Jan. 15th The darkest – dreariest of days, cold and wet – hard to keep comfortable even by a fire – where I sat – trying to sew – knit or read – save that I went with Nell (Eleanor) to the Epis. church in morning to attend the funeral services of Mr. K. L Simmons of Charleston who died here leaving a wife & many young children – a helpless family – and he unconscious of his hereafter! Awful! We saw no emotions manifested but their burial service is impressive the full choir

20. Sallie P. Brown of Abbeville was the wife of Dr. Ben Brown of Williamston, the first son of Daniel and Rhoda Acker Brown and the first child born in the town of Anderson. In 1860 Sallie was twenty-two years old and had two children named Waller W. (age 2) and Sally A. (6 mos.) (*1860 Census,* Anderson District, 156).

Sallie White is possibly the daughter of Tom White, who owned the local marble yard (Dickson, *Journeys,* 137).

Cora and Sallie Whitmire were the daughters of Nathan and Eleanor Whitmire of Newberry. The Whitmires were a wealthy planter family whose female children most likely attended school with Emmala or had kinship connections in Anderson (*1860 Census,* Newberry District, 286).

sang in solemn measures – yet I noticed most R. B. as pall bearer – singer in the choir & quite an active person there now – (though I hear not his voice) he looked well – & a consciousness of being of some use – made him more manly looking I fancied – And I've no doubt he gazes on me with as much interest as I on him – (he kept looking back at me) though his ardour is cooled – his feeling not unselfish and pure as mine I fear yet I cannot tell – would that I knew.[21]

But what would Theo think of all this! My mind was worried by these two things all evg – and am I kindly remembered? At night Pa brought home a new cheese – tries to find home comforts 'though our minds are troubled with the number of idle negroes we have here (21) wages to pay – which we need to refit our house in some respect &c – Poor Fannie still quite sick – then Julia's baby has the fever – terrible misfortune with all her other trials – we hope it won't spread there J. P. B. came in here awhile – but so worthless – what will become of them? Pa read aloud the ridiculous burlesque of Spanish chivalry "Don Quixote" to Ma & I – too absurd to laugh at! But cold & sleepy – I must rest – thankful for freedom Many mercies still yet fear I am too selfish & not of enough use or influence or purpose in this working world. Must do better! Cold but comfortable nights of rest & dreams – Thank heaven![22]

Tues Jan 16th The clouds dispersed – the glad sun gave forth re[in]forcing the earth – clear – cold evg. – I was sewing all the morn – but felt cramped in doors – so I went out in the aft – to see the McCulleys – where I enjoyed that pleasant party (a happy month of "conubial felicity" to Carrie since – she said) nice clever girls – Joe & Pheme disappointed I think! I then went all round the stores for vanity – looking for dress trimmings – found none suitable – a number of people out – men & women some pleasant words and bows for me but R's eyes on every corner were most haunting after some dodging by both – we bowed at last as he stood talked to Bill Humphreys – his old friend I wonder what they said or what he thought of me? Mr Walters came & spoke cordially – &c[23]

21. According to the 1860 census K. L. (age 40) and Anna (32) Simmons of Charleston were merchants with a home and some savings. They belonged to the Episcopalian church. The children were all babes and toddlers in 1866. The Simmonses were most likely refugees with business associates or kin in Anderson. K. L. Simmons died January 12, 1866 (*1860 Census*, Charleston District, Ward 4, 359).

22. *Don Quixote de la Mancha* (1605, 1615) by Miguel de Cervantes Saavedra (1547–1616). Judge Reed's choice of reading material is interesting. Perhaps the judge was working a poignant analogy of the recently lost Confederate cause and the futility of jousting further with the new establishment. The character Carrasco's admonishments to return to a less enticing reality would have rung true for a self-deprecating Confederate.

23. The McCulleys were a large family of merchants who operated a general merchandise store. An Irish immigrant, Stephan McCulley, like so many other Anderson merchants, exercised

I went round to see Lucie Nardin a little while – feeling "poor" & bad Vie there – neither very cordial, wonder why, but I don't pay them enough attention. Lucie indignant at Theo for sending for his carpet trunks &c so abruptly without thanking her for care of them or calling to say goodbye – it was mean! He left many books there – yet what does he mean by all? I hurried home late – met Eleanor & Becky Webb in close conversation the last to be married – so soon – queer She is miserable because so opposed – she surely loves much to counteract it – sly cruelty loves much to counteract it!

I had met Joe Hyde going to see Eleanor – a nice fellow – Dick had been there in morn (John Whaley yest. – to say good bye – off for Charleston – Dr. Keith gone!) So we have few upper beaux left here. John Keith & R. B. followed me closely home – (Maria & I met & bowed – his two favorites I guess What thought he & why spoke we not? Alls well![24]

Mr Poppi had spoken of coming at night so all day found me missing with the violin – well that he did not – Fannie had been quite sick all day or suffering with such violent pains neuralgia we think – many doses of morphine don't relieve her

---

a diversity of investment interests, primarily the railroads. Elmira McCulley ran a home full of her own children and friends or kin attending school in Anderson.

Newton A. (age 26) and Carrie Fretwell McCulley were married on the evening of December 12, 1865. "N. A." rose to the rank of second lieutenant with the Palmetto Riflemen, Fourth Regiment, South Carolina Volunteers, companies B and C; McCulley was wounded four times, captured at Frazier's Farm, and surrendered at Appomattox Court House.

Josephine (22) Margaret Euphemia or "Pheme" (20) married Andrew H. Osborne in July, 1866. There is a wonderful record of their respect and love for each other; the January 1960 edition of *South Carolina Magazine* has four wartime letters between Andrew and Pheme, edited by Paul T. Noland and Amos E. Simpson (4–7, 21, 22).

Other McCulley siblings included Peter Keys, "P. K." (20) Palmyra, "Pal" or "Pallie" (17), and Ulney (6). Carrie was widowed and later remarried. Mrs. Carrie McCulley "McC" Patrick was considered by Louise Vandiver to be Anderson's "leading woman politician." She helped found the local League of Women Voters and gained a wide local readership as a newspaper reporter for the *Anderson Daily Mail* (Vandiver, *Traditions,* 90, 182, 315, 316–17; Lucas, *Early Anderson,* 54; *1860 Census,* Anderson District, 260; Salley, *South Carolina Troops,* 574–75, 581; Hoyt, *The Palmetto Riflemen,* from *Time Capsule,* 54).

24. Joe Hyde was the seventeen-year old son of Charleston merchant Lineas Hyde and his wife, Anne. (*1860 Census,* Charleston, 195). The Hydes were a large family of refugees staying in Anderson. Joe ardently admired Eleanor Reed.

John Whaley of Charleston was another refugee.

John Keith does not appear to be one of the children of the Reverend P. T., but may have been a familiar visitor or refugee.

Maria Keith's sister Ella married Robert Broyles, but Broyles evidently enjoyed the company of the other Keith sisters as well.

– Holland's many visits & remedies, uneffectual – So Pa became excited and determined to prescribe a course of medicine that cured him for similar sufferings some years ago in the stomach Dr. Fair of Columbia prescribed hope will be successful in her case for the poor pale creature lies there suffering impatience and despair almost worried about her child but it flourishes. A sweet fat baby – Helen – & Mamie takes good care of both. Clif very attentive & upright but I wish he could be more active &c[25]

Poor Julia must be suffering the greatest trials – a noble devoted woman of sense & taste & soul can endure! Her worthless – brute of a husband – (a willful love match both young & promising) reduced to a large family & no means & he won't seek or can't find employment rushed madly on to temporal & eternal ruin for himself and family perhaps! God forbid! Been on a spree – drank till nearly dead & she came once for wine to revive him today (as a secret) bore it nobly as a <u>true</u> woman will & yet – to no purpose – for he only rushed back into deeper perdition perhaps – but if she could only be relieved of him it would be best surely but may it end for the best – awful now! It will reflect upon all of us alas!

Eleanor & I were agreeably surprized by a pleasant visitor – James or "<u>Jupiter</u>" Gibbes – as classically dubbed for his vanity & attainments! An odd looking little man – but good manners – bright eyes – converses well – and has really fine literary tastes – read much – memorizes remarkably & <u>recites well</u>! he <u>volunteered</u> – Tennyson's "Palace of Art" for our edification – very fine word painting & impressive – showing that "beauties & comforts of sense alone must weary the human soul divine &c"[26]

25. Julius Poppe's store had "the most delightful dolls and other toys at the front, whatever may have been in the funny stone bottles, half-white and half brown." By 1870 Julius Poppe was a barkeeper and grocer who played some fiddle and had an assortment of unusually talented animals around his property. Julius Poppe was from Saxony, and his wife, A. H., was born in England (Vandiver, *Traditions,* 268; Dickson, *Journeys,* 137; *1870 Census,* Anderson County, 696).

Dr. Samuel Fair (1805–70) studied medicine in Paris, then established a practice in Columbia, South Carolina. The ladies of Columbia established a hospital at the fairgrounds, and Dr. Fair was designated "local Confederate Surgeon." "Mrs. Dr. Fair" nursed sick soldiers at Columbia's Wayside Hospital, but during Sherman's raid the Fairs, who resided at their own tenement, were burned out and made destitute (Meats and Arnold, *Writings of Benjamin F. Perry,* 2:236; UDC, *South Carolina Women,* 83, 91, 271; Richard N. Cote, ed., *Dictionary of South Carolina Biography* [Easley, S.C.: Southern Historical Press, 1985], 111; John A. Chapman, *The Annals of Newberry* [1892; rpt. Baltimore, Md.: Genealogical Publishing Company, 1974], 41.

26. Alfred Lord Tennyson's poem "The Palace of Art" depicts "art" as the central aspect of a noble society that lasted about four years. The society was destroyed, but the essence of art survived by being absorbed and passed on through the folklore and folkways of the people.

He spoke much of Theo – his friend – appreciates his talents – brilliant wit & acquirements &c teazed us both no doubt – he might be our friend at least – & a pleasant companion! I sang some ballads to the guitar at his request – but he can't pursuade me that he loves music strange too with his practical tastes! A good friend & would make a fine lover in devotion &c but not do for us!

Eleanor – Mamie & I – had a little chat wishing to cultivate more literature &c – (Theo and Gibbes both ask why I don't write more – I ought to exert my self to do so used to aspire to & love it – best not perhaps unless I could accomplish great acts – fail as other southern writers & many women do – and not steady habits or thought enough They ought to be real literary – too idle Late & cold – stars gleaming – must seek rest!

Weds Jan. 17th A bright frosty day – more mild & clouded eve. Poor Fannie suffering much sickness & pain – Morphine & all remedies failed her so far poor soul – hope she may soon improve Dr. Holland here three times today – Julia & children here in aft – I sewing – knitting &c as usual read a little but at night I try to influence my sisters to read & improve but they won't – Eleanor read some fairy tales to the crowd of black & white children at night

I was wandering with Prescott in the wilds of Yucatan & Mexico – amongst those semi backward early tribes who have left such marvelous relics [illegible] to European civilization! Late – starry hours – for dreams – thanks for a home of peace & comfort now – 'though I lack much love & congeniality![27]

Thursday Jan 18th Snowy frost and sunlit morning – but mild & clouded eve dismal boding! Company all day for a rarity! Aunt Anna, Uncle June & Willie Jones for the day & night both looked better & more agreeable than formerly – quit some bad habits perhaps he full of life – but despondent about the times & his own idleness – rather anxious – but a clever fellow! pets us &c Then Tom Carter here awhile – plain – unsophisticated good fellow – goes to Ga again soon

Miss Ella Gaines called on me in morn fine looking but full of airs gossiped enough of her young preachers Round & Hodges &c both agreed in disliking this selfish town &c wish we could move elsewhere! Mrs Hyde & Eliza called – sweet & social – Mrs J B Sloan – anxious to get some provisions, wood &c supplied to

---

The poem was written in 1833, but analogies to the fallen Confederacy are obvious (G. Robert Strange, ed., *The Poetical Works of Tennyson* (Boston: Houghton Mifflin, 1974), 43–46).

27. William H. Prescott's *History of the Conquest of Mexico, with Preliminary View of the Ancient Mexican Civilization, and Life of the Conqueror, Hernando Cortes,* 3 vols. (New York: Harper & Row, 1843), is considered a nineteenth-century historical classic.

Mr Murray's needy family our pastor whom we neglect so much – dreadful – yet we all feel poor & can hardly help each other – must try. Mrs Elvira Belcher called last very gentle, nice woman – the children rode some on horseback! Fannie a little better – I was busy as usual sang some to the guitar &c for Uncle June after tea – he seems to enjoy it[28]

A week ago tonight Theo with us – devoted half plighted What of him now & when will I hear? I felt a little blue with old unkindness I sang tonight unsatisfied of my future! Direct me Oh God! One more letter rec'd – Sue Sifley my sweet cousin in Orangeburg writing most of troubles with the negroes and demoralization of them by the Yanks there – smallpox there &c too bad Late must read some but am quite sleepy! I wish I could accomplish more each day![29]

Friday Jan 19th Pleasant day – Aunt Anna & Uncle June Jones here – for the day She & I went to the stores & on to see Lucie awhile – out of sorts Rather busy Came home & found Mr Witt Broyles with his two daughters Lula & Mary

28. Ella Gaines (age 30) taught school in Anderson in her younger days, when she lived with her sister, Mrs. J. C. Whitfield, and her husband's family on South Main Street. Later she married a Mr. Hudgens of Honea Path (*1860 Census,* Anderson District, 154; Vandiver, *Traditions,* 122).

George Round of Cokesbury was a twenty-six-year-old Methodist minister. His father, John A. Round, also a Methodist clergyman in Cokesbury, hailed from New York, and mother Marion was a South Carolinian. The family included four younger siblings. Reverend George Round wed Julia Hammond (Emmala's cousin) at Anderson in March 1867. In the late 1860s George Round taught at the "Carolina Collegiate Institute," a new school opened by Mr. W. J. Ligon at the old Johnson Female University (Vandiver, *Traditions,* 117–18; *1860 Census,* Abbeville District, 83; see Reed, *Journals,* Appendix F).

William A. Hodges (1840–89), a twenty-six-year-old Methodist minister from Cokesbury, was a close associate and friend of George Round. Hodges was the second eldest of five children raised by planters Gabriel and "Phebe" Hodges. The Rev. Dr. Hodges wed Cassandra "Carrie" Hardy of Anderson County on October 4, 1866 (see Reed, *Journals,* Appendix F; *1860 Census,* Abbeville District, 81).

The minister Murray and his family were not transient clergy or wealthy refugees with reasonably solid resources. There was no money, hard or soft, and the lack of extra provisions, especially in middle of winter, placed the Murrays in potentially dire circumstances.

29. Susan F. Sifley was twenty-six years old and the wife of minister John L. Sifley. In 1866, the couple had one child, Juanita (age 4) (*1870 Census,* Orangeburg County, 246).

Swiss and German farmers settled Orangeburg, South Carolina, in the 1730s. The area has long been one of the country's most prodigious cotton-growing districts. The town received excessive punishment at the hands of Sherman's marauders, as did Columbia, forty-one miles to the north and west (Alexander S. Salley, Jr., *The History of Orangeburg County, South Carolina: From Its First Settlement to the Close of the Revolutionary War* [1897; rpt. Greenville, S.C.: Southern Historical Press, 1994], 1–25; Edgar, *WPA Guide,* 320).

brought here as boarders to go to school – nice, clever girls – Dr Jim Brown here to dinner a tall – queer fellow, good & easy – seemed to enjoy my singing – & inclined to stay all night with us – but did not. A crowd to dinner however.

At night Newton Brown called on me – the eccentric – practical – student of sterling worth – but no fascinations! He seems to appreciate me highly – and I shall value his friendship – under some circumstances – he might offer – & I prize his love! Time may develop!

He chatted with me pleasantly of many things – said he couldn't talk to the other girls – seemed really to like my songs to the guitar – wanted to have the pleasure of escorting me at night again – would insure me that the man I marry would never drink &c from the enobling influences I would have on him &c Tried to find out about Theo – & R – had watched all our proceedings at the party & thought we were "negotiating for peace" but that was the end strange to say! He was slow to go – and I shall ever remember him kindly! we were both distressed about J. P.'s spree now! &c

Sat – Jan 20th A dark – rainy morn – mild & delicious to me. I was busy sewing all day – making undershirts for the children – as I have to do all the sewing & knitting here nearly. Vie here part of the time – And Scott Brown was kind to run in & see Fannie – bring her jelly & loaf bread – has taken quite a fancy to her – She is improving under Pa's regime – of quinine & light diet &c[30]

It was clear & cold by night – all very busy here as usual – winding up the weeks work. We were suprized however by the arrival of Peter McDavid and Milton Donalson of Greenville Dist. – to spend the night with us – two good – fine looking – clever country swains Pete – a jolly cousin of ours – whom I shall always cherish kindly as a soldier friend to R & I – and feel an interest in his welfare – he scarce knows what to do with himself now – Milt is a tall, delicate – most exemplary young man – smart & moral with refined tastes and well to do in the world! He has been an admirer rejected by Eleanor – to her regret & ours – for I fear tis the last & best offer she may have – Pa likes him so much – he enjoyed my songs to the piano & guitar much[31]

30. Scott Brown (age 28) was the brother of merchant Samuel Brown (*1860 Census,* Anderson District, 257).

Judge Reed may have suffered from occasional bouts of malaria, a fairly common ailment of the era. The use of quinine was widespread because it eased the fever and pain associated with malaria.

31. Milton "Milt" Lafayette Donaldson (1844–1903) of Greenville County was the son of Nimrod and Sarah McCollough Donaldson. Milton's siblings included John, Texanna, and Casper. Donaldson enlisted in the Sixth South Carolina Cavalry and achieved the rank of

They came in late – from town where he had been to get his wedding suit & new buggy – for he is to marry this week – Miss Lou Ware a plump – pretty – stylish girl – whom I saw graduate at Greenville two years ago – they have long been lovers – but broken off sometimes when he seemed to care most for Eleanor – all over now and they will make a happy couple in a country home I guess. He was here & all we girls in the parlor at night had a right pleasant evg. with them, but I confess there's not the same charms about young folks who are in the market – or full of personal preferences &c![32]

I guess they thought us a crowd of unmarriageable girls – and Pa is quite troubled at the idea of never getting rid of us – for our chances have almost diminished it seems – Even Dick Tupper, Eleanor's spirited young devotee for months, paid her a farewell visit of policy today considering that he was too young & so poor & would leave to struggle on for years helping to support his mother & sisters – So uncertain when he could ask her to share his fate – unjust to her – when she might be more fortunate – very trying – but advisable! I never thought this would end otherwise – older advise concerned too I guess – both young folks shed tears – and she may feel it too deeply – yet – alas! we have both met dissappointments that grieved sorely!

I wonder why it is with personal and other attractions – equal to any girls almost we have failed in securing valuable or lasting friends or worthy mates – and have been each deceived by several – and no future prospects now we fear – unless we move away from here any way where family influences are against us! Letters to me that night which I hoped would cheer me only saddened – as I felt they were purely selfish Mrs Dr. Miller of Pen. writing to ask if I knew of anyone going to Charleston who could escort her daughters down to visit Fannie Smith as urged (and she has never written a line to me after all she has professed – how false!) They will go & have a brilliant time I guess – rich, handsome, smart pretty girls – very aristocratic feelings just entering society! Grand!

---

sergeant. After the war he engrossed himself in farming and eventually became one of the state's most renowned agriculturists.

Donaldson served in both houses of the South Carolina legislature. He was president of the South Carolina Farmer's Alliance (1891–92) and a life member of the Clemson College board of trustees (*1860 Census,* Greenville District, 430; Reynolds and Faunt, *Biographical Directory of the Senate of the State of South Carolina, 1776–1964,* 206; Bailey, *South Carolina Senate* (1985), 400–401). Emmala insisted on spelling the name "Donelson" while the census-taker used the more conventional "McDonald," but Reynolds, Faunt, and Bailey all use "Donaldson."

32. Margaret Louisa "Lou" Ware, daughter of state senator for Greenville Thomas Edwin Ware and his wife, Margaret Pendleton Gaines Ware of Laurens, married Milton Donaldson on January 23, 1866 (Bailey, *South Carolina Senate,* 1677; see Reed, *Journals,* Appendix F).

Alas! for poor we – yet it may be best and I scarcely need complain of my own advantages &c in the past I wrote notes to Maria Keith, Kate Tupper, & Bessie Webb – three Charleston girls I would like to call friends – to know about their friends going down – learned but little – Jim Townsend for the first time, wrote me since the war an old correspondent & pretended – friend & cousin – settled at 96 teaching school & studying law – wanted me to suggest the course to be pursued &c and in a very painful way spoke of W. C. – not having trifled with me – had the character of a flirt – ought to be killed devoted to Miss Cunningham now &c![33]

Of course tis mortifying – he made many advances – I was fascinated & encouraged them – yet am thankful that I didn't commit myself made no promises &c so what can he say or think of me the wretch? To forget entirely as I do is best – at least he doesn't trouble me now – nor does R – or anyone, for I am fortunately constituted – impressions easily erased or rather I learn to be contented & resigned to every fate – prefer my personal freedom & comfort at home to every thing else selfish therefore! Eleanor will grieve more I fear cares nothing for books or religion & few people alas! I wish she could go away to school somewhere new scenes & new interests best for her. Wish I could exert a better influence on them all! We slept late

Sunday Jan 21st A bright, cold morn of frost & ice work! We keep to late breakfast hours here – nice this morn – chatted a little while with Milt & Pete – then they were off to town on business before going home – wouldn't stay to church Pete came back first had been adopted by a married man who admired me to try & win me himself – absurd! He concludes that R & I will always care most for each other – He went to have a chat with him outside the Epis. door (where he always goes here hence – has ceased to care for me I guess) but I would like to know the result of that conversation – What will be our fate – & what he thinks of me! Fear he is worthless drinking &c

I went to Bap. church twice today! In the morn Mr Spalding – a zealous little man tried to stir us up to some life and fervours for religion – speaking of the past

33. Ninety Six, a midlands trading post, was established in 1731; its name is thought to have been the estimated number of miles from the closest Cherokee town of Keowee. The contemporary village of Ninety Six, many miles distant, was founded in 1855 (Harry L. Watson, *Ninety Six: Landmarks of South Carolina's Last Frontier Region* [Columbia: University of South Carolina Press, 1950], 5–7; Walker, *Compendium of 1870 Census,* 324).

"W. C." has not been positively identified, but is apparently also the often mentioned and much maligned "Whit."

Miss Cunningham, a Charleston refugee, has not been further identified.

old year. Its regrets and hopes of the New Year – o'er which spiritual interests should prevail – but "the world, the flesh & the devil" seem to reign now supreme – alas! His text was queer "Farewell" – of the ever crushing word – some felt more than others by (as I well remember!) but the most heart rending will be in the final judgement – in the severence of good & bad to all eternity – When loved ones must part forever! we cannot realize such a terrible truth now but may God grant that there may be happy reunions with all my dearest ones in the better world![34]

We sang very well today Respectable congregation – but so lukewarm! Newton B saw me I'm sure! In the aft but few there poor Mr Murray so slighted – his sermon seemed shorter & better but I was there late – Fannie Earle & I had a social chat – I walked by to see Julia – Clif there – found J P there – looking awfully – had been near death with drink – restored now but will go over the same path forever I fear & accomplish only evil! Too dreadful! Julia & I both scorn him I feel but can have no influence – he reads only seemed pleased to see me & the children delighted.

Home to write & read a little – also at night but accomplished little! Pa had been to see Mr & Mrs Murray about teaching all the girls here made satisfactory arrangements, and we discussed studies at night – all of them excited on the subject & I hope will learn well – We urged Eleanor to go too & thus interest & improve herself – the best thing now possible, but I fear she won't. Wish I could have time & opportunity for more study & reading – or could get the children all to assemble & let me read or study with them but they won't do it! A disorderly household – servants impudent & untrained so many burdensome labor heavy on a few!

Ma has too much drudgery & no mental or moral or social pleasures scarcely – Pa don't try to improve us by reading to us explanations on practical things as he might & they never show affection or speak to us of religion but are very kind & generous – & 'tis from early habit they can't overcome – not from intentional neglect of this vital point I fear – but we children are all growing up in the same cold, dull way I fear when we ought to do better! Not useful & amiable & congenial enough – Help us Oh God!

Little J. P. – learns his first lessons well to Pa & always says his prayers to him & bids us good night – an interesting child spoilt though – baby Sissy so pretty & bright & mischevious & sweet pet of us all! Fan unfearing Helen a good dumpy child Clif handsome & up-right & sensible & practical I wish he was smarter &

34. Baptist minister Mr. Spaulding and wife Mollie were possibly from Lexington County, South Carolina.

able to help himself along in life better – with one arm! Late brilliant night – stars & moon radiant – but so cold All sleep now – I too must rest & dream and awake to new life & energy and usefulness & goodness & happiness for us all I hope!

Monday Jan 22nd The bright beginning of the week and school days renewed for our household would that I too could fly back along their fresh & flowery pathway – gathering the sweets of knowledge & innocent joy and even the hardest trials they offer – rather to go on – with the daily strivings after nothing and so many disappointments! Yet 'tis all over for me – and I must only try to act my part better in helping and encouraging others – always improving myself by books &c

Three sisters – Mamy, Cora and Lucie – with Lula and Mary Broyles started to Mrs Murrays – quiet little school – where I hope they will study & do well! I was busy sewing &c for them – all day – no pleasures of social intercourse for me these days it seems – Pa grows more argreeable – talking to us of many things (when he don't scold) & reading scraps of many books – today on "hallucinations" – We have now the Mexican emigration fever – Capt. Maury's report of the rich haciendas there enticing![35]

We will try and learn more about them & perchance we can go someday – hope so! I gave two music lessons after dinner – at night helped the girls with their studies – but slept early. Vie H. – was here – Uncle June came to take her home – but fell out of the buggy in the street in a state of beastly intoxication! horrible – and

35. Commodore Matthew Fontaine Maury promoted a colony for ex-Confederates and sent out public letters with the promise of land measured in leagues, haciendas, sugarcane, tolerance, and a plethora of other inducements, all widely published in southern newspapers and magazines. The Reeds, though touched by a fleeting desire to act on "Mexican emigration fever," opted to make the best of a bad situation and rebuild their future in Anderson (Foster, *Ghosts of the Confederacy,* 16, 20; Boatner, *The Civil War Dictionary*, 520; Wakelyn, *Biographical Dictionary,* 315–16; Rolle, *Lost Cause,* chap. 14, "Agent for the Emperor: Commodore Matthew Fontaine Maury," passim).

The enticement Emmala referred to was a form letter entitled "Ho For Mexico! Notice to Emigrants 'The Forn's Colony,'" which opened with an announcement from J. O. Forn, sanctioned by the imperial commissioner of colonization, to dispose of 108.5 acres, or 25 square leagues, on the Panuco River, at two dollars an acre, plus a gratis donation of enough land for a town (later named Carlotta after the Empress) and a central road. Next, M. F. Maury, imperial commissioner, added some details such as location (thirty miles upstream from Tampico on the eastern Gulf Coast and within fifty miles of the Tropic of Cancer). The letter touted a three-crop climate where cotton, tobacco, and coffee, as well as staple crops, would grow in abundance. Ex-Confederate immigrants passed through the port of Tampico duty-free and were urged to bring along portable sawmills and "seed of all sorts" (Rolle, *Lost Cause,* 223–24).

another disgrace for our family alas! Why will men not do better! Vie & I most mortified I guess Eleanor in a scrape with Tuppers & Hydes worried [illegible]!

Tues. January 23rd A Spring like morn – all full of new life – girls off to school – they were too fussy about dress &c I must to work! And then I sat in the corner stitching all day a variety of garments for the children Julia's & Fan's included – Julia was here nearly all day Scott Brown spent the day here socially with Fannie Who is improving – fast friends now, devoted to little Sumter too She is an intelligent – enthusiastic woman her predjudices rather strong – I sang for her some A mild, pleasant day – soft moon at night – but I didn't get out at all. No visitors & no cheer for me forsaken by all who have ever seemed to care for me – is it really so – or only the periodical blues I take and find all the world so false! Yet tis only then I realize the truth I think & feel how forlorn I really am with all the comforts of life

I care more for worthy – noble – true friends such as I can never meet alas! I fear that even Theo is forgetting me – not a line yet & gone ten days – he may have thought me too indifferent &c & will forsake as others have done before! Letters from Edwina and Molly Hodges prove that they are all a heartless set down there, & care nothing for me after all their pretentions – and that Whit is utterly false & unworthy – a consumate villain! Devoted now to Miss Cunningham – wonder if they will make a match? Oh the wretch![36]

But I am not by any means heart broken – have learned to heal all ills with complacence I think & to expect nothing! Dreadful! Mollie and Fletch are happy in their new cottage home – the beaux all scattered off Cokesbury Mill!, Edwina a true simple hearted girl I think, – but who can I claim as my friend in all the heartless world! After I had collected the scattered comely girls – I read along to them the hist of English Literature for improvement but they don't have much heed – lamp out – must sleep!

Weds Jan 24th A mild – showery day – much company & no work or reading today – Aunt Anna & Willie & Tom Carter walked up to spend the day – She for money & opiates I guess – and for no good – strange to say – Uncle June had at last gone to Ga – but I fear for no good. Mr & Mrs Witt Broyles came down to see Fannie – & the girls – but the last had to be sent for late noon – all departed after dinner Lizzie Bleckley called then – my clever old friend – spoke of her relatives the

36. Edwina Hodges and Molly Hodges were old friends from Cokesbury, South Carolina.

Burts & Griffins &c of Edgefield whom I once knew – as having moved to Galveston Texas[37]

Wish we could go somewhere but fear we'll never attempt it – Pa is too rational – too fixed here – though there are many reasons why we should change our place & manner of living! I wrote letters to former friends – Uncle Dr. Hammond & wife – Kelie Whitman & Georgia Carter – for Tom to take out with him tomorrow – but all my letters are of no avail – for it seems I am forgotten by all – I can't tell how it is![38]

I went with Liz over to see Julia – she & children & J. P. – all looking very well again, he at work in the garden & I hope may do better. I stopped to see Mattie Reeves on my way back – a clever woman – coming home I found a fine carraige at the gate with Josie & – Mrs Newton McCulley – to return bridal calls – both well dressed, & quietly pleasant – I was reading at odd times during the day – so worked none![39]

At night it was warm and stormy – thunder, lightning, and heavy rain – suprized us – but my new friend Col Newton Brown called on me again to my surprize. [H]is visits are becoming rather frequent & serious I fear – 'though it is pleasant to have somebody come regularly – whom you feel cares much for you & whom you can trust! As a friend I desire none better – for he is a most exemplary man – but has unfortunate manners – & our relative ties &c – don't admit of my viewing him otherwise – I don't think 'though he seems to care more for me, & desire more I fancy – from his hints!

We talked of many things but he will speak of marraige & his desire for it – A few personal hints – enjoyed my music somewhat – though I played principally to teaze him – & also about Miss Mary T. & Lizzie B – to whom he has been assigned

37. Eugene Burt (b. 1800) of Edgefield married Sarah Dozier, and they had five daughters. Burt's second wife, Leila Griffin, accompanied him to Galveston, Texas, then to Louisiana (Robert B. Mathis, comp., *The Matthew Burt Family of Virginia and the Deep South* (Privately printed, 1976), 95–99.

Edgefield County, South Carolina, established in 1798, is seventy miles south of Anderson and borders on the Savannah River to the west and Anderson County to the north (Writers' Program, *Palmetto Place Names,* 14).

38. Kelie Whitman has not been identified.

Georgia Carter may be a sibling or other kin to Tom Carter, who apparently maintained contact with kinfolk in nearby Elberton, Georgia, about fourteen miles from Anderson.

39. Emmala most likely refers to Mary E. Reeves, the twenty-seven-year-old daughter of music instructor Mathew and Ellen J Reeves. In 1860, Mary and her seven siblings resided with their parents in Charleston's Ward 6, though the family name was always represented in Anderson (*1860 Census,* Charleston, Ward 6, 422).

by rumour – of whom he speaks very candidly! but I can't tell how it all stands – or what will be the result! He would to be a man to trust – & perhaps to love but gradually & with some disqualifying circumstances – but never to marry here by me! Yet I must be careful – for I wouldn't encourage & worried his feelings – or lose him altogether – & my last hope of – a lover perhaps! for I don't know that I shall ever hear from Theo or any other![40]

Milt Donelson & Bill Watson two nice young gents married this week – Pa thinks beaux getting very scarce for us – he went to a R.R. Meeting in Greenville – I sent a note to Sallie East too – from whom I've not heard in so long! I can't imagine why my friends are so false to me for I know I am worthy of a better fate Eleanor & Dick quite made up – exchanged types &c[41]

Thurs. Jan 25th It had cleared off beautifully – Ma & Mrs Wilhite for a wonder – drove out to see Mrs Crawford Keys – in her distress – about the trial of her husband & son (Robert Keys) now in progress in Charleston for the murder of three Yanks! A critical affair! All absent I wasted the morn reading some strange facts to me – horrible truths in reference to our human organization & the insecurity of human life & happiness! then I wrote to Mollie Hodges trying to prove that

40. Mary T. has not been identified from the information available.

Elizabeth "Lizzy" Bruce of Townville would marry J. Newton Brown. The only child of farmers Thomas and Nancy Bruce, Lizzy was twenty-seven years old in 1866, making her about the same age as Emmala (*1860 Census,* Anderson District, 279; Vandiver, *Traditions,* 139, 158).

41. William A. Watson made his home at a very old place called Orange Grove. By 1870, the Watson family lived in neighboring Edgefield County, where twenty-six-year-old William listed his occupation as farm laborer and wife Martha Allen Watson (whom he had wed in January 1866) kept house, rearing Louisa (age 3), Henry (2), and infant Joseph (Rudolf Edward Lee, "List of Old Time Suburban Homes in the Vicinity of Pendleton, South Carolina and Other Clippings, Letters, etc. from the Scrapbook Kept By R. E. Lee, Head of Architecture Department, Clemson, S.C.," unpublished scrapbook held privately by the author, 20. The Lee scrapbook contains a newspaper article by "Helen McFall—'28" though the date "April 1927" was once written on the page before it was copied; *1870 Census,* Edgefield County, 362).

Judge Reed was on the board of directors of the Greenville and Columbia Railroad, incorporated in 1845, completed in 1853, and its 152 miles of track "so poorly built that South Carolinians expected the rickety line to be swept away by some spring freshet" (John F. Stover, *The Railroads of the South, 1865–1900: A Study in Finance and Control* [Chapel Hill: University of North Carolina Press, 1955], 76.

Sallie East of Greenville was a sister of William East. Emma East, twenty-three years old in 1865, was a teacher in Anderson during and after the war (*1860 Census,* Anderson District, 258; Vandiver, *Traditions,* 122).

I was not a sufferer by the faithlessness of W. C. – only a week's fancy on both sides – for it causes me only a little mortification now![42]

A greater trial was renewed this morn – as Pa handed me a letter from Pete McDavid who saw his soldier friend R. B. the day he left here & wrote some of their sayings! Many queries of me – but expected to meet no more – had intended to woo me for his wife – but circumstances changed & my notes of daring estranged him &c spoke highly of me to all – would never wed Miss Keith – "yet proved by all that he loved me sincerely – but was a mystery still!" What does it all mean – & what will be our destinies? The bitterness has all past – but memories will always assail us cruelly – Yet I wish we had a better understanding – or he would go far away & be successful evermore & I more fortunate!

I was sad this bright day & accomplished nothing but all these vain scribblings – No friends or visitors today – Pete hinted that he wished to win me himself – nonsense! I was knitting & dreaming sadly in the twilight – but the bright moon and stars came out – and to my surprize Cora Wilhite came over to say that her mother desired me to spend the day there – with music &c so I went over and spent a pleasant evg – with a small crowd that had happened in – They are becoming quite gay and fashionable at the plain old Drs & Mrs W – lively, Mary right pretty & interesting – considerably admired – Cora a bright child without any trouble they have plenty of company and fun – a few friends every evg – which must be delightful – whilst at our house we have nobody scarcely and always with too much troubles! So many children &c I wish it could be otherwise!

Lizzie Osberne – a plain good girl was there to tea – played piano very well – her brother Andrew very handsome & pleasant – is engaged to Pheme McCulley they say! Bill Humphreys – the tall slender – red headed – Commissioner in Equity – boards there – they all seem to be fast friends ; he lively & pleasant – devoted to music, made me sing and play much for him – "I'm Afloat" – his especial favorite &c he put his mark on one other song of mine too – I thought of the days when he & R – were fast friends & of mine too – all changed now![43]

42. During much of the trial, taking place in Charleston, Louisa Keys (age 48) stayed at the Keys Spring plantation to supervise the farmwork and the care of her own children, a niece and nephew, and a full complement of free laborers. Son Robert (28) was on trial with husband Crawford (52) (Glenn, *Keys Family,* passim).

43. Elizabeth Osborne was the eighteen-year-old daughter of farmers Thomas A. and Jane Osborne. Elizabeth's twin sister, Sue, died in her teens (*1860 Census,* Anderson District, 258).

Andrew H. Osborne (1842–1929) was twenty-four years old and a veteran of the Palmetto Riflemen, Fourth Regiment, South Carolina Volunteers. He was wounded at Seven Pines, May 31, 1863, and never rose above the rank of private (*1860 Census,* Anderson District, 258; Smith, *Book of the Dead,* 293; Hoyt, *The Palmetto Riflemen,* from *Time Capsule,* 57; Lucas, *Early Anderson,* 60).

Then old Gus Broyles stopped in – poor old fellow withered miserable bachelor I've no doubt – a great friend of the Wilhites – perfectly at home there – goes in to play cards – teazed about Cora for whom he is "waiting" or I remembered too when he used to be a firm friend of mine & loved my music – we only bowed & he talked lustily over his cards as I sang – none but Bill seeming to care for music, but I noticed him much more attentive than he pretended – & he spoke of being carried away with it &c as we sat partners in whist afterwards – we passed a few words – and he called "Miss Emmala" – as flat as formerly surely he respects me & how can they all have changed so entirely! he left quietly & abruptly – no good nights and I guess we'll meet no more soon – if at all[44]

After many jokes & nonsense – we scattered – Bill H accompanying me home with dignity – used to be Julia's lover – rejected by her for JPB too bad & they loved too – he has had none since I think & them indifferent now! Don't call on them – I wish we had more friends here – girls all chatting lively mood Fan most merrily – cold & late Pa back Friday –

Friday Jan 26th A fine bright day but I had to sit sewing all the morn – Some suprize – Aunt Mary Acker & five children came up to see us – a forlorn widow with many children & limited means – has hard times I guess – good woman too – Grandpa Hammond came in too and dined with us all – the dear old man – he & I having a considerable chat about his prospects – Negroes all gone from here & in Ga – he must sell one & settle somewhere more suited to his small family &

Equity is a branch of law necessary to litigate complex property and business disputes, in which the court must anticipate future implications of the action before it. Given the difficulties of such litigation, equity courts are composed of panels of judges with specific legal experience, in lieu of a jury (Jack C. Plano and Milton Greenberg, *The American Political Dictionary* [New York: Holt, Rinehart, and Winston, 1978], 256.

"I'm Afloat" was a popular tune of the era attributed to [London vocalist and songster Henry] Russell (Sears, *1870 Sheet Music Catalogue,* 59).

44. Augustus "Gus" Taliaferro Broyles was a thirty-six-year-old bachelor in 1866. He graduated from South Carolina University in 1848, then read law and began practice with mentor J. W. Harrison. A. T. Broyles joined the Fourth South Carolina Infantry at Columbia June 7, 1861. Captain Broyles soon retired due to an extended illness. By December of 1861 he returned to Anderson and spent the rest of his life at the Broyles homeplace, which was nestled in a cedar grove on the corner of South Main Street and Hampton Streets (Vandiver, *Traditions,* 149, 150, 261; Everson and Simpson, *Far, Far from Home,* 34, 59, 93; Salley, *South Carolina Troops,* 586–87; Reid, *History of the Fourth Regiment,* 53, 64; *1860 Census,* Anderson District, 158).

The card game whist is the predecessor to a similar game, bridge (Gibson, *Hoyle's Card Games,* 375–77).

advanced years – but we all bewailed the state of our country more than ever, as the Yankees seem more disposed to crush us out! [T]he radicals all united against us & forced even the Pres't to succumb I fear – unless he is playing a double game, & I fear they will yet hang Davis & other leaders – establish negro equality &c – awful trials coming yet heaven preserve us![45]

We are more anxious than ever to emigrate – grandpa wants to settle Aunt Mary in Ga – she rather hesitates – but surely it would be better for her large family – In aft all the children went out shopping took Julia's sweet little Carrie – I went afterwards & joined them in the nice fancy store of Bill Williams – who assailed me as having never been in before – and tried hard to induce me to buy things – which I hadn't the money to spend for – he is a nice – stylish man rather my ideal of "Rutledge" or "Rochester" in *Jane Eyre* without their strong characters – had a pretty baby too there – well dressed![46]

Sallie Broyles husband & child – and strangers to me – when we used to be so intimate – queer! none of the boys there during my visits! I went on to see Lucie H. who sat with Becky – the sweet gentle bride elect – sewing for the occasion – a blue merino & the white swiss dress – two sweet women & good friends of mine – though they don't invite me to the wedding!! Becky seems happy in her love of Jamie – so I hope all of her dreams of felicity may be realized!

45. "Aunt" Mary Acker was apparently one of the many extended family members who came to the Reed home seeking help after the war left so many destitute. The 1860 census notes that a Mary C. Acker (age 31), wife of William H. Acker (36), and five young children resided in the town of Anderson Court House (*1860 Census,* Anderson District, 194).

Emmala's astute observation bears closer scrutiny. By January 1866 the future must have looked increasingly bleak to South Carolinians and most ex-Confederates as Andrew Johnson attempted to compromise with the Congressional Radicals. Deposed president Jefferson Davis was still in custody at Fort Monroe, Virginia, and he presented a dilemma: they could hang him and create a martyr, imprison him for life and create a martyr, or release him, stripped of property, and constrict his civil rights.

The Freedmen's Bureau, the Civil Rights Act, and the Fourteenth Amendment all contributed toward political equality for blacks, and that represented a serious threat to the continuity of life in the South. Emmala—indeed many Southerners—held out hope that president Johnson was in fact "playing a double game," and the great deception would end in a passive Southern repatriation and a return to the social status quo (Carl N. Degler, *Out of Our Past: The Forces That Shaped Modern America,* 3d ed. [New York: Harper & Row, 1985], 228–34; George Brown Tindall and David E. Shi, *America: A Narrative History* [New York: W. W. Norton, 1996], 764–66).

46. William D. "Bill" Williams of Greeneville, Tennessee, was a local dry goods merchant and the husband of Sallie Broyles. Sallie Broyles Williams raised seven children, the first of whom was William, Jr. (Vandiver, *Traditions,* 93; Simpson, *Old Pendleton,* 134).

I dread the thought for myself more & more – could never be reconciled to matrimony I don't think, – so free & easy now! Home late – quiet evg – chatting with Aunt Mary of her school days here – &c – the children amusing themselves – a little music – bright moon – then beclouded – a huge halo around it – cold late – I read a story aloud to the girls the two Mary's at Julia's tonight – for reading – must rest!

Sat 28th Jan A quiet morn – but Ma & Cora – went with Aunt Mary & children to Grandpas for the day – I sat knitting & reading & sewing a little – but the week was gone & I had not accomplished much – Mattie Orr (the Govs daughter!) called in aft. She & I very social – she seems fond of me & I admire her much – a stately brunette full of life and fun – quite smart, talks well but rather consequential now & anxious for beaux &c & indifferent to friends &c 'though frank & social – hope we will remain friends but I am losing all hope of retaining any! She had just spent two weeks in Pendleton with the Van Wycks – Simpsons &c Will have fine opportunities now in every way![47]

47. Martha "Mattie" Orr (1847–89), the oldest of the Orr children, spent the war years in Richmond, Virginia, before removing to the relative safety of Greenville, South Carolina. Mattie was a polished young Southern lady about to enter into a higher society, at a time when the survival of that society was in question. Floride Clemson wrote in her journal that she spent the evening of March 11, 1866, with Mattie Orr in Anderson—curious since two months before, on January 15, she had written that she would prefer not to stay at Governor Orr's because "such men disgrace the state." She apparently stayed in the upcountry, or returned later, because on March 7, 1889, as Mrs. Martha Orr Patterson she became a charter member of Greenville's Thursday Club, a salon instituted to further local culture (Leemhuis, *James L. Orr,* 32–33; Lander and McGee, *A Rebel Came Home,* 99, 100).

The Simpsons lived at Mount Jolly, a plantation outside of Pendleton, South Carolina. Richard Franklin Simpson (1798–1882) married Mary Margaret Taliaferro (1808–98) in 1836. Richard Simpson served as Laurens County state senator, then United States congressman (1842–49), and later signed South Carolina's Ordinance of Secession as a representative for Anderson District.

The Simpsons had five children. Taliaferro N. "Tally" (1839–63) attended Wofford College in Spartanburg, South Carolina, and died at the Battle of Chickamauga, Georgia, in September 1863. Richard Wright "Dick" Simpson (1840–1912) served in the Adams (cavalry) Brigade. He married Maria Louise Garlington (1843–1910), and the couple raised ten children. Richard was an attorney and personal advisor to Thomas G. Clemson, founder of Clemson University. He presided over Clemson College's first board of trustees. The Simpsons have been immortalized by Guy Everson and his kinsman Edward W. Simpson, who edited the Civil War correspondence of the Simpson brothers entitled *Far, Far from Home: The Wartime Letters of Dick and Tally Simpson, Third South Carolina Volunteers.* (Simpson, *Old Pendleton,* 135–37; Vandiver, *Traditions,* 87, 223, 281).

I feel that my career of pleasure & youth is well nigh ended & no friends or lovers left me – 'though I've done nothing to alienate & have some attractions I know – yet so it is – & I am sad – but resigned I hope – if for the best! A note from Mrs Miller again at night Urgent for her daughter to get to Charleston – could stay here the night before & tell me their errand – Fannie Smith must be going to marry & has never written me a line – another false friend. Strange! Theo too must be estranged with his absence, their influence, the charms of a new society or my coldness &c so that I doubt if he is heard from again – Well! Bright night but all dull!

Sunday Jan 29th A cool – Sunny day – when all were pleased to attend a church somewhere. At Bap in morn – Mr Murray gave us a very good sermon Christ, the hope of them that believe &c – I enjoyed it – a church meeting called afterwards by good old Mr Nevitt – (Mr & Mrs M. left) to discuss the necessity of trying to pay him something as our pastor – or some provisions – so needed by them – we are shamefully negligent – but all the members are delinquents I fear – all poor & worthless – have neither means nor desire to do better – yet Pa made a very sensible little speech as he always could & they resolved to try & collect something[48]

Julia's Carrie went to church for the first time – a sweet little "Red Riding hood" – but bad & had to be taken home – I met there a girl I used to know with the Burriss' – from Due West – Pal Sharp – the bride now Mrs Coffin I believe- her husband from Charlotte N.C. she a pretty little thing – nicely dressed – glad to see me several brides there &c Pa lamenting that his daughters had no chance – all so! We regaled ourselves with bell pears & apples Ma had kept & muscadine wine – at noon[49]

Julia's children here – all noisy – I was amused at Fred's excitement & speech – over that large N. S. [Northern States] flag which he first saw fluttering from the

48. This is most probably William Nevitt, an early settler in the town's Broadaway section (Vandiver, *Traditions,* 191).

49. W. Rufus Burriss married Mary Dickson and lived at Acadia plantation on Three and Twenty Creek (Simpson, *Old Pendleton,* 70; Vandiver, *Traditions,* 106).

Due West, South Carolina, just south in Abbeville County, was once the site of a country store at Duett's, or DeWitt's, Corner. The place name simply evolved into Due West Corner, then just Due West, possibly because of the way it simply rolls off the tongue. Erskine College, founded in 1839 by renegade Scottish Presbyterians, ushered in other schools in latter years, particularly the Women's College in 1859. Never a large town, little has changed about the town except its name over the intervening years (Lowry Ware, *Due West: South Carolina's Oldest College Town* [Due West, S.C.: Lowry Ware, 1993), passim; Edgar, *WPA Guide,* 421).

"Pal" Sharp Coffin of Due West, South Carolina, and Charlotte, North Carolina, has not been further identified.

staff in town cried "Come, Aunty & see what this is climbing up in the clouds!" – all of them startled at the show – but alas! poor boys they didn't know it was but the emblem of our degradation – the seal of oppression more firmly fixed upon us – as twas raised yest. with many cheers by the garrison here; – other troops are to be sent too we hear – regarding this as a rebel den A large reward offered for "Jolly" a reported bushwacker &c but I don't know that he had really done much![50]

The Radicals are in the ascendant now we fear & may even overpower Pres't Johnson's milder measures of reconstruction & protection – hang Davis & punish us all worse – we are feeling more uneasy! read the trial of the Keys &c in Charleston – threatening as yet – don't know what fate may await us all yet!

In aft I went with Eleanor & Lula to the Epis. church – many Baptists & Methodists there – one of the last turned parson – Gen Ellison Capers (his father the Meth. Bishop), will be an Epis. Minister I suppose – but the army suits him better I fancy – now teaches here – read the services for aft Mr Elliott – (the divine! a noble man!) gave us one of his sublime – elegant efforts – on "Awake thou that sleepest &c!" – truly stirring to dormant Christians & our unaroused sinners – if they would only heed – for all are so dead in sin here now! Wish I could remember & transcribe all his glorious thoughts & words on the unsatisfactory nature of all earthly things and the unending glory & bliss of the heavenly home to come "The ever freshening morn of eternity's rapid cycles &c"

These impressive thoughts – with the organ's sweet notes as played by my false friend Sallie Williams & her three brothers in the choir – once all my frie[n]ds R – had been more than all the world beside – & I feel will ever be – most cherished & remembered for the past devotion of our young years – who has wrought the

50. The source of Fred Brown's youthful wonder was in fact the American flag that flew over the army encampment. The First Maine Battalion, under the command of Captain William C. Corbett, manned the Anderson garrison.

Unreconstructed rebel Manson S. "Manse" Jolly scouted for the First South Carolina Cavalry. Jolly lost five brothers in the war and declared he would kill five Yankees in retribution for each brother. There are many stories of Jolly's bravery and close escapes, but his cruelty cannot be denied. He was credited with executing as many as a hundred Yankees, many dispatched with a bullet to the brain from close range, much like the soldiers murdered at Brown's Ferry.

Jolly and his band took their booty and moved to Milam County, Texas, where he and Walter Sargent (his second in command) married a pair of sisters and started life anew as cotton farmers and horse wranglers. Manson Jolly died suddenly and violently when he was caught by a flash flood on July 8, 1869 (Dickson, *Journeys,* 117–23; Ball, *The State That Forgot,* 133; Wayne K. Durrill, "The South Carolina Black Codes," in *True Stories from the American Past,* ed. William Graebner (New York: McGraw-Hill, 1993], 6–7; Richard Zuczek, *State of Rebellion: Reconstruction in South Carolina* [Columbia: University of South Carolina Press, 1996], 19.

greatest sorrow of my life thus far by his change – which today was almost unendurable!

His love in years afore the letters he wrote one year ago – the war experience he gave me – all destroyed – strangers since his return & he is living for others wholly – but revelling in sin & dissapation, often I fear – then quitting my church & his mother's & all turning Epis – singing in the choir for effect – yet I hope the influences there, the sermon today & all may make him a Christian – that we may meet & know each heart in the hereafter at least, – Maria & Ella [Keith] – so fair & pretty – his cynosures now – yet can he forget me wholly – & were no sweet – then more painful memories in his heart too – as they surged through my heart – destroying all other emotions sometimes?

He looks better than ever before! Well dressed – and independant intelligent air – his large – fine form – & dark eyes still thrilling me when they searched for mine I saw – for only last Sunday – he told our former friend Peter (McDavid) that "We had been nearly engaged" – he had intended asking me to marry him – but he was changed with circumstances would never visit me again &c but spoke of me highly to Maria K – &c would never marry her (would never marry her – will he wed any body?) his tone proved that he "loved me still dearer than life" but we were estranged forever & can it be so when two hearts are thus most congenial – or feel thus drawn together when everything else forces them apart! If united no more on earth may we not be hereafter? I wept most bitter tears – as all these painful memories rushed over me – as he gazed over so intently & how did he feel? Would that the impressive sermon could be remembered by both! – at night we girls tried to sing some together – but I felt too badly.

Monday Jan 29th A bright lovely day – busy sewing &c a little lecture from Pa on charitable feelings &c but I felt blue about many things – and so was quite relieved when I heard that we were expected to attend a "Musical Club" at Gov Orr's that night – Mattie sending a note to beg me come & bring "Ship on Fire" &c but Dick was going with Eleanor I had some trouble finding a companion – no beaux for me!

Finally I pursuaded Lula Broyles to accompany me – She had first been to her "Uncle Asa's" where they were cordial to her – Tom flattered she & Eleanor but none for me Clifton had concluded to go – hadn't been out in so long So we there with Dick Tupper & Eleanor started out in the bright moonlight on the long walk to Gov Orr's hospital mansion in the old oak avenue – but were nearly broken down on our arrival found a warm reception 'though from Mrs Orr – & Mattie – and a merry crowd besides – with many modes of entertainment in the open rooms!

It was rather a stiff crowd of refugees & old maids & a few others not harmonious to me now the Munros, & Broyles & I feared – a most disagreeable time –

but it was more pleasant than I expected yet more painful – for R & I still met as nominal strangers – 'though "In the eyes there lies the heart"- His sister Sallie – Mrs Williams – my early friend – sat near me a stranger – not a glance of recognition between us & I can imagine no reason why, a pale, thin, a stylish woman smart – & plays the piano remarkably well – her own peculiar touch that I used so to love – but she wouldn't play much – one "Solitary Scotch air" only I enjoyed – strange indeed!

Mr Williams – her husband & almost a stranger to me made himself very agreeable – A short dark – substantial looking little man rather handsome – polished &c but somewhat familiar & dissipated I fear – perhaps they don't agree so well either – as she is not amiable & so queer! He came up at once to Lula & I – with a merry chat, desires to hear me sing – such reports &c An elegant company were seated around chatting socially – mostly refugee Maiden ladies & a few gentleman – Gen Ellison Capers being most agreeable; wearing still his Confederate grey – sad emblem of heroic deeds – and our downfall – a mild pleasant face & fine manners – sang tenor with Bessie Washington & Mrs Winthrop the old ballad Annie Laurie – right sweet[51]

I requested Mr Williams to escort Mattie Orr to the piano & she led off the music with a very sweet piece "Remember Me" – She looked splendidly – in bright pink- with her black hair in curled waterfalls — then they came for me to sing – and I saw R's eyes turn to me wistfully – as he sat by the piano talking to the Munro's – fast friends – but enemies to me perhaps – or rather we were as strangers now – yet began a reconciliation then! I bowed to them generally – his big eyes blazed & then he bowed so low others thought I didn't return it – Mattie requested first "Dreams" – which is his favorite too & I know he was delighted to hear it – but did he think it intentional on my part![52]

Then I sang a song – rather fussy – when I took my seat near Bessie Webb – a sweet girl – Tom Broyles near who asked about the song & seemed pleased & Williams came up to whisper "I never flatter but your voice is remarkable" &c – Gen Capers was introduced and spoke of the old times when he used to live here

51. "Annie Laurie" (or "Lawrie"), a popular air by Brinkerhoff, was published in a series of sheet music titled "The Exotics: Flowers of Song Transplanted to Southern Soil" (Augusta, Ga.: Blackmar & Bro., [186?]) and printed in Columbia, S.C. (Parrish, *Confederate Imprints,* 574).

52. "Remember Me While Far Away" was a popular tune by A. C. Sears (*1870 Sheet Music Catalogue,* 109).

"Dreams" was a popular song, "with reverie by H. C. L. and composed by F. H. Hodges," published in a series titled "Parlor Gems: A Collection of the Most Popular Songs and Duetts, with Piano Accompaniment" (Macon, [Ga.]: John C. Schreiner & Son, [186?]) (Parrish, *Confederate Imprints,* 586).

– when we were each much younger – he used to hear me sing & play then &c crazy to hear "The Ship On Fire" – many others joined in the request So later in the evg – I sang it – much excited with the song & because some baleful or curious eyes were on me & because his dark eyes were riveted on my face reading every emotion as he used to – and my heart thrilled too painfully – yet I felt I did the dramatic song justice

He was satisfied – though I never glanced toward him as I sang – and he would glance toward his brothers with a silent look of triumph – as much as to say "Don't you admire my choice?!" &c yet the feeling of it being all over – would come between! I leaned back in excitement & met his glance smilingly – and when Jupiter Gibbes came up to say "he had listened so intently" & I asked sarcastically – "Is it possible" he felt it as a practical rebuff – but R turned off smiling – thinking "thats her old way" – but once while his sister played – he stood leaning on the mantle gazing at me intently & seriously & listening as Bessie & I talked – but my heart was overflowing with painful emotions – of what had been & could never be again – until some tears welled forth and I saw him wipe his eyes – but with what feelings would that I knew!

Was his heart aching to[o] and did he resolve to do no better – I fear not – for he has no moral courage – was afraid to approach me there – though I know he loves me still – yet he is unworthy! he chatted only with some old maids Maggie Munro & Miss Matthewes who carried on a high game with him & he laughed frantically – even danced as they drew him on &c but in his heart he scorned all this I know & longed to meet with me in free conversation at once – I acted with cool indifference I hope – but couldn't keep my eyes from straying now & then![53]

They danced for variety – the Lancers & round dances very pretty – We gazed on, – then they had some silly games – "The Swedish dance" a serpentine, tortuous – ridiculous bobbing about – & winding around – from room to room that was ludicrous – R seemed to enjoy it & I saw him whisper to Bill Williams to get me in – & he insisted & held my hand until I was forced to join the throng – but would not go through with all the intricate images! In the "Giants Sneeze" – he introduced – he sent "Jupiter" for me – & by looks conveyed all his anxiety that I should partake – smiled, pushed others out of my way & all without speaking yet I couldn't resist an answering smile now & then though I should have been more sternly dignified & cool I cannot repress my truth of sentiment![54]

53. Margaret "Maggie" Munro was thirty-six years old in 1866. Vandiver notes that she taught at the Presbyterian Sessions House, a small private school (*Traditions,* 23, 122).

54. Dancing was a popular pastime at late-ninteenth-century Southern gatherings, which often featured stationary audiences, piano solos, and poetry readings. The popular group dances of the era included complex patterned dances such as quadrilles, lancers, and rounds, which quickly evolved into the American "square dance," with a caller reminding the dancers

We induced Mr Gibbes to recite some poems – but his vanity at once prompted compliance, so he stood up & gave us three splendid poems – Well recited! "The Unknown Dead" by Timrod – "our conquered banner" (I believe) by Requier fine new poems & "Ginevra's" sad fate by Rogers that almost moved me to tears – he listened too intently & what thought of all? Jupiter seemed to seek most my approbation & was quite agreeable to me, but Capers was polite & Williams rather too intimate – yet our thoughts were only for each I'm sure & is it possible that we are estranged forever – & is it best?[55]

To our surprize refreshments were handed after the long walk blancmange & apple float nice cake & wafers – he took occasion to bring around a plate & murmer "good evening Miss Emmala" but could venture no more – & as we started home – he seemed to stand & hesitate awhile – anxious to offer his services &c to me again but didn't dare & so left without a word or look – & when & how are our future meetings to be –

We've had a very spicy evg – altogether & good Mrs Orr – & Mattie so lively & social – continued to make us all content – she has returned from Greenville a graduated & highly accomplished girl. sensible & practical now – full of fun & beaux now – deplores this dull place, 'though she is the Governors daughter. She has few advantages of society now her father in Charleston to my regret

Maggie & Sallie Munro stayed all night there & are very useful to them! We had scarcely spoken since the old society squabbles – but I felt no sense of wrong doing & cherished no animosity – were indifference to them whilst they are trying hard to get in with us all – respect is dictated by a true Christian spirit – they made many advances that night which I met just a[s] freely & frankly as is my nature – (not a bit of deceit) yet I was rather amused &c when they spoke of the truth of

---

of the patterns. The gallop, another popular dance of the postwar era, is best characterized as being somewhere between the stately waltz and the vibrant polka. The origins of the "Swedish Dance" are obscure, though it sounds much like the periodically popular Conga line (Richard Nevell, *A Time to Dance: American Country Dancing from Hornpipes to Hot Hash* [New York: St. Martin's, 1977], 1–26.

55. "The Unknown Dead" was a poem by Henry Timrod. "Our Conquered Banner" probably refers to a poem by Father Abram J. Ryan, though it may be "Our Conquered Banner," an unsigned poem published by T. C. De Leon and housed at Clemson University. (Thomas Cooper De Leon, *South Songs: From the Lays of Later Days* [New York: Blelock & Company, 1866], 143–45).

"Ashes of Glory" was a poem by A. J. Requier that paid homage to the retired battle ensign, the stars and bars (William Gilmore Simms, ed., *War Poetry of the South* [New York: Richardson & Company, 1867], 480–82).

"Ginevra" was a poem by Samuel Rogers (1763–1855) from his *Italy* (1842).

the report that "I was to be lost soon in Charleston" – won by Theodore S – in Feb – &c Where could they have heard anything so absurd!

But what has become of him – & why this strange long silence? False too I suppose – but I can't grieve for it – as nature & conscience all point to my first love & is it not so with him – though so long estranged – & perchance should ever forbid reconciliation? He & all were gone – so our crowd stayed awhile & sang some chorus for the Munros & Orr's at their urgent request – sorry we didn't display them before the crowds

Then we walked on home in the bright moon light near 12 – & so tired! Lula – a sweet – fine looking girl – felt that she had been slighted by her mean cousins – who scarcely spoke to her & some not at all! Hateful! She indignant! Dick & Eleanor had seen only each other I think – though R had spoken to her of my splendid voice – "&c Williams also" and of hearing me sing in the piazza – the last said "he must hear me again" – &c but will he ever? Guess his wife scolded him soundly for his attentions &c but I would like to know what impressions each one of them carried away of me yet I am ashamed of writing all this silly nonsense & minutia of unimportant things – vanity & wordliness make me wiser & better Oh God! & bless them!

Tues. Jan 30th The wedding day of James A Hoyt & Rebecca Webb! (here) bright & beautiful day too Such as all would desire for their wedding day – ominous of good I hope to them & all who undertook then such solemn responsibilities, especially for sweet loving – gentle Becky – our young friend from childhood always so intimate here – we will miss her sadly! Her father [Elijah Webb] & friends were opposed to this match – but her lover conquered I suppose – & she must have married from pure devotion – the plain – poor little man she chose with his pock marks – & poor kin & the predjudice against him with some dissipated habits heretofore we hear

But he is a bright eyed, determined, ambitious young man. Editor of the Anderson paper for years – 'though his family live in Laurens – his father the jeweller &c up here today – a stiff looking old man & ugly daughter "Anna or Lucy" Any way we hope he will succeed in the world & make her happier than she was at home with a step mother & children – father so improvident – bad servants She had first determined to have no company, but her father gradually relented & took in a good many guests at the last moment

I was gratified to receive a sweet note of farewell from Beckie Webb – happy in her anticipations & begging me to come – so late as it was I determined to go – as I love all places of amusements, & wanted to see them married – as well known friends Busy all day – but dressed & with Clifton & some of the children went round to Waller Nardin's where Eleanor & Vie were spending the night – the attendants assembled there & marched over to the Webbs – I had gone in & found a nice little crowd on the small rooms – near relatives only – three parsons – a few girls extra & young men clerks! Clever fellows but uninteresting – not a beau for me – I missed Dr. T[homas] E[vans] & R (we used to spend pleasant evg's there!)

Mattie Orr & I sat together – she looked splendidly in fine dress – luxuriant black hair arranged with rats & mice & curled waterfall behind covered with pearl ornaments! A lively – queenly looking girl – but a brunette – Likes me some I think – we sat chatting all evg – Mr Elliott the fine looking talented, delightful Epis. minister with us awhile – all joking &c he asking if our wedding smiles were ready – asking which of us were E. T. Reed – very gracious but he admires Eleanor much – don't call on us however

Soon "the band approached," Eleanor with Andrew Osberne right handsome pair, she quite lovely – bright face white Tarleton dress &c crimson sash &c white wreath &c on her hair very pretty! he a quiet chap engaged to Pheme McCulley – a pretty little thing Then Sallie Cresswell – a dark – lively girl rather pretty – hair coquettishly arranged – a mixture of curls & plaits – dressed in white & red Annie Hoyt & Vie Hammond – plain girls in pure white – but Vie looked uncommonly well – rather pretty – She with Jim McFall, Anna H. & Charley Webb a little clerk here – rather queer crowd!

Then came the bride so fair & sweet – but calm and happy looking – not the least perturbed 'though I fancied she – the modest timid girl would have been overpow[er]ed, as surely I would be at that hour! In pure white swiss – veil & w[r]eath – & white hyacinth ornaments – she looked pure & lovely he – very nicely in his new clothes – and behaved with calm dignity – very quiet too full for utterance I suppose – I hope with love & joy – boding future happiness – but perhaps he thought of the many girls he had courted in vain – of the [illegible] lust – & maybe she thought too of [illegible] Hammond – the noble youth who died for his country claiming her love – sad! I could scarcely (behold the scene without tears)

Mr Murray performed a long, pretty ceremony – very solemn & binding – yet neither spoke "I will" – to my regret? his mild – genial face & tinged locks made him a general favorite – then his jokes with me &c who will be the next couple married R looking at me suspiciously – but in vain After many kisses and congratulations were over we all chatted very freely – Marion & Dick Hill & Liz Bleckley being very lively & silly I fear but I enjoyed their jokes & talking with John Humphreys "the Yankee" as we all called him, – being just from Yankee land where he was so fortunate as to return to his business begun before the war – as travelling clerk with a high salary – expenses paid &c has a good time – but says he hates them all & doesn't mingle very freely – but he is free & gay enough everywhere I guess though he didn't seem to be quite as dissipated as formerly![56]

He had rather an imported air with his new clothes. The checquered cravat which we called "the stars & stripes" &c he listened to my music very intently – he & his brother William seeming to have really an appreciation for it – but I had quite an attentive auditory around the piano when I sang the many songs called for. Campbells old "Soldiers Dream" was the favorite- Old Dr Evins & others calling lustily for a repetition of it – as Eleanor & I sang that & other duetts Mr Elliott seemed pleased also, mostly with her appearence! Even there he & Mr Murray were trying to form some beneficial plans for this wicked community, proposed a "Young Mens Christian Association" which I tried to encourage & hope will succeed.[57]

Miss Mary Waller came & drew of[f] Mr Elliott home just in the midst of this discussion – to my regret We were ushered in to a very nice supper table, Waller Nardin – my escort – and much we all enjoyed the oysters & other substantials, cakes, jelly &c 'though the men had a far better opportunity of helping themselves afterwards of course – as is the very selfish custom, though of course ladies are too ethereal to care for such physical aliments! After the ministers had departed, they insisted that I should play for them to dance which I did – and they teazed me about reporting it to the church, but surely it wasn't wrong!

They seemed to enjoy a quadrille & old reel heartily, but at last I rebelled & started home – after one o'clock. John Humphreys accompanying me in the bright moonlight – he was very jolly – but most interesting to me because he spoke of his friend RB – & their former intimacy – his devotion to me in the army & he couldn't think it changed – knew it was not tranferred to any other – but he intended to frost me &c – I wish he would, but this is wrong to feel – or to let others talk to

56. Marion Gaillard Allen Hill's first husband was J. E. Allen. They had two children, J. E., Jr., and "Pet," who married Dr. S. "Sammie" M. Orr. Widower and newlywed R. S. "Dick" Hill's children were M. J. (Janie), R. S., Jr., and T. F. In the 1890s, R. S. managed the very successful Farmers Alliance store in Anderson (Vandiver, *Traditions,* 55, 195, 281, 312, 314; Simpson, *Old Pendleton,* 212).

John L. Humphreys (1833–70), the well-dressed salesman, is difficult to identify. A Lt. Humphreys served with Orr's Rifles, was promoted through the ranks, and was wounded and captured at the Wilderness (Vandiver, *Traditions,* 226; Smith, *Book of the Dead,* 196).

57. "The Soldier's Dream" was a popular tune of the era, composed by Fr. Sulzner, with a dedication that read "To Miss D. E. Johnston of Mobile" (Parrish, *Confederate Imprints,* 617).

The Young Men's Christian Association moved south in 1858 when established on the University of Virginia campus. The organization pursued moral and spiritual well-being through healthy activities and community interaction. Greenville did not have a "Y" until 1876 (Huff, *Greenville,* 199). Information regarding the original Anderson YMCA has proved scarce.

me about or to him – may result in no good – yet I can't resist – for I can never forget or cease to feel anxious about his fate & feelings! And can it be that we are estranged forever

Wed Jan 31st A delicious day – bright & balmy for the season – most of us here dressed to call on the bride that morning – even Fannie & Clif ventured out on their first visit since her illness – but it was rather a stiff crowd assembled in the parlor – no beaux – Becky & Jim looking very nicely, but of course had lost interest in all others! I went in to Lucie's (Nardin) awhile & had a social talk with her; Vie & Sallie Cresswell proposed to bring around the crowd to a "surprise" at our house that night for want of other employment – but they came not – Vie came for several days. I came by Julia's on my return – suprized to learn that Newton B. had returned a visit to his affiance Lizzie Bruce near Townville – to be married soon – a sudden arrangement!

In the aft – Marion & Dick Hill called on me – & I never met with such wild, jolly people – full of jokes & laughter especially about "how he & Nance got married" – the widow & widower! I was highly amused – he would have me sing The "Ship On Fire" – &c for him, thought them wonderful, & begged for social visits, from me at their house – Lula & I then walked up town "to see & be seen" such a pleasant evg. – a trick I never perform scarcely – but am always disappointed, don't see the people I wish.

To my surprize encountered Teresa Brown (who had first called on me too – expressing wonder at "my rejection of Theodore" – crazy to know how he addressed me &c!) in a store with her two false lovers? Newton Brown & Dr Tom Evins quandam friends of mine too I suppose, but both bachelors, have another choice & will marry soon we hear! how strange for them! Dr had just returned from a visit to Spartanburg & we teazed him a little – said "he had brought a lady back" – but surely not "Mrs Evins" yet![58]

Said he regretted not being at the wedding – as I was there of course "&c and blushed for some reason I know not what, if for me I should be pleased" – but 'twere not or else he keeps himself aloof I scarce know why – one that he is a staunch Elder in the Presbyterian church – I a Baptist – his & Pa's politics different &c&c – yet I needn't flatter myself that he or any other man feels any special interest in me, 'though I don't see why I don't deserve it as well as many more – then there are so few worthy men to fancy!

58. One of Anderson's many springs bore the name "Miss Teresa Brown's Spring," and it was rumored to have the power to invigorate and even heal those who drank from it (Vandiver, *Traditions,* 110, 179).

We spent the pleasant night alone at home – only Mary & Cora Wilhite coming in a little while & the children boiling molasses candywhich we all enjoyed. Vie & I sat up late & rather too confidential – for I fear she is not very sympathetic – 'though I cannot live without expressing my feelings freely to someone & I have so few now to trust – she abused me for my continued interest in R – which grieved me much that day.

SIX

FEBRUARY

Thurday Feb 1st A pleasant day but I was confined closely to my seat sewing for my younger sisters all day – Vie helping some. Pa & Ma rode down to see grandpa Hammond who had met with another one of many accidents which befall the active old man – a mule having jerked him down – and injured him seriously we feared – but he was soon himself again apparently – 'though we fear he can't stand such misfortunes long – Dick called on Eleanor – She & I were pleased to receive an invite "to a dance at Rose Hill, by Mrs Frank Whitner & the Misses Harrison"[1]

The first regular invitation I had rec'd to that house – On account of the many sectional squabbles &c of old – 'though Bettie & Lucia H – directed it of course – I hesitated about going – because it was the first & I might receive no more if slighted & because I always love company & fun &c especially such elegance as I would find there, but it was well I declined on account of my religious professions – which prohibit dancing or even encouraging it in others I suppose – for it may lead to much sin & folly. 'though it is certainly the most innocent & beautiful of all amusements I should think – & not best that church rules should prohibit it more than many other things – yet I may be growing too worldly – and we should all live more conformably to true Christian principles!

Eleanor is in the very prime of her glory now she thinks – young & beautiful – eliciting much admiration – without having much intelligence to depend on, loves gayety, dress & beaux supremely & inclined to flirt too much 'though – few

1. Anna Church Whitner (age 28), wife of attorney Baylis Frank or "B. F." Whitner, was a native of Athens, Georgia. Anna and "B. Frank" built a large home on Whitner Street. Rose Hill, the Whitner homeplace, belonged to B. F.'s parents, Judge Joseph N. Whitner and Elizabeth Harrison Whitner of Andersonville. The Whitners merit the distinction of being among the first to live in the new town of Anderson Court House. In 1830 they expanded and embellished on a simple log cabin and created a sprawling complex named for the hill's distinctive rose gardens.

The young Harrison ladies, Lucia (or Mary, age 20) and Elizabeth (or Bettie, 22) were daughters of attorney J. W. and wife Mary J. Harrison. Elizabeth Whitner was the girl's aunt. The other Harrison children include Isham (age 18), John (16), Ida (11), Nina (9), Frank (8), and George (7) (Vandiver, *Traditions,* 13, 14, 15, 20, 22, 28, 29, 68, 150, 197, 200, 201, 249, 257, 262, 270; Dickson, *Journeys,* 7, 22, 78, 82, 137; *1860 Census,* Anderson District, 155, 258; Bailey, *South Carolina Senate,* 1717–18; *Cyclopedia of Eminent and Representative Men,* 128–30).

opportunities here! Dresses with taste and enjoys all heartily but not as I might do with my whole soul prepared for my enjoyment that is pure & rational & where hearts are kind & true but I meet so little of this I fancy! She sent for Mattie Orr to come & spend the night & accompany her – both looked elegantly as they dashed off in the Governor's phaeton (after 8) to the Judge's mansion.

Eleanor fair & rosy in a gray silk with crimson trimmings (much of Julia's old wedding finery 'though!) Mattie in lilac skirt & white body – with elaborately arranged black hair & magenta plumes &c to surmount her brunette face & stately form – a perfect Zenobia- dances with regal grace & would be quite an ornament to any society, and is destined for a lucky life no doubt as Governor Orr's daughter for four years to come &c we are proud to claim her as our friend too, for she seems sincere & unassuming – & may never change towards us we hope![2]

The Misses Harrison were the other fair, delicate beauties there & all enjoyed themselves dancing merrily to the music of a colored string band from Pendleton in those spacious rooms – (no refreshments) no one missed me perhaps – Save R – who stood alone & awkwardly as he don't dance & met no congenial company there – he may have speculated on my absence 'though had we met there without speaking &c – it would have been far more embarrassing & painful!

They came home after two – disturbing my quiet slumbers somewhat – Vie & I had spent dull evg. – but I can always enjoy reading & scribbling alone –

Friday Feb 2nd A cooler day – threatened rain The girls gave me full accounts of the party – but as Mattie was preparing to give one at home for the children that night She had to hurry back and I had to sew steadily all day to finish a worsted dress each for Mamie & Cora, Vie & Ma assisting but it kept us all busy! Then Eleanor was invited to another dance at the Robinson's – (so I begin to be left out entirely from their gay throngs!) She would have Lula Broyles go also (though she had been unwell all day we want her to become acquainted here – a sweet, pretty girl – who doesn't attract much attention yet however – as her cousins the Broyles slight her too much – strange & mean!)[3]

Night came rather beclouded – but they were all fixed off after too much primping by the vain youngsters! Mamie, Cora, Lucie & Mary Broyles to Gov Orr's – in

2. Zenobia was Queen of Palmyra (circa C.E. 270), an ancient city-state in today's central Syria. When Zenobia threatened the Eastern Roman Empire, the Romans destroyed Palmyra, captured the queen, and took her to Rome as a captive, where she shrewdly negotiated her own release.

3. The Robinsons most likely refer to the family of Dr. and Eliza Blassingame Robinson of Pendleton, South Carolina, who had seven girls and two boys. Elizabeth, the oldest child, married Dr. Tom Evins. Jane or "Jennie" wed Samuel Owens, one of Anderson's early jewelers (Vandiver, *Traditions,* 25; Simpson, *Old Pendleton,* 214).

a little wagon – henry driving – too far to walk – found a large, rude crowd of boys & girls – had games, dances, music, & refreshments – Juvenile & fun – each full of the little beaux and their own conquests on their return (when they distrurbed me talking half the night) proving that the younger Miss Reeds are likely to have a more successful time in society than I perhaps – hope it may result more satisfactorily to each one of my fair young sisters – so fond of dress & pleasure – smart & pretty & good enough I hope as yet!

Clifton accompanied Eleanor & Lula to Mrs Robinson's (Dick T) & Keys McC, returning home with them) both in blue, buff etc – looked well – found a merry crowd – Eleanor – danced 'till a late hour plenty of young beaux & flattery – (no edibles) R had slighted Lula – the selfish scamp – talked to E. of many silly things – pretended to confound our names but spoke no more of me – (had turned Episcopalian!) yet she insinuated that I was to marry soon & he seemed much worried – a total change of countenance, she said – & how did he really feel – or will it ever be true! he had escorted Ella Keith & talked to her much of course – she loves – does he? [H]e & Tom both pretend to admire Eleanor – but I hope there will be no flirtation there – they are worthless fellows

But my heart will cling to the false Robere – of whom I dreamed that night – that we met in his home & in presence of his mother were reconciled, as he wrote to me – I read his words of explaination &c there, he came & sealed the contract – I saw & felt it all so truly but awoke there to find it all indeed "The baseless fabric of a vision – that leaves not a wrack behind!" – and I sighed & wept myself to sleep again – thinking it might never be!

Tis best not to doubt – but for what else were we created I can't conceive – as these same feelings I know have existed between us so long & cannot die – we are growing older – with no hopes or plans for the future – & must drag our wasted lives I fear until we meet in the great hereafter & what then? I felt very lonely & forsaken after all the gay girls had left – feeling it was but the beginning of the end – I had always been deceived & forsaken by my associates – and it must increase with my maiden years 'till I have few interests in life perhaps and all my wealth of soul be poured out in vain! sad fate!

I ought to try & be more useful & content – & thank heaven I can forget my sorrows so easily sometimes – when I have the least ground for cheer! As I sat singing a few sad songs alone – to my suprize Newton Brown entered – to spend a short hour in social chat 'though there was a great change within a week I fancy. Then he came as my admirer [illegible] – but to test the probabilities &c – I gave no encouragement uncongenial &c and he no doubt knows of my predilictions, – so he went off to woo & win a clever country lass – devoted to him I guess – "to save himself from being an old bachelor" &c and it is far better – I hope may be happy – but it seems very hard to realize that queer old fel[low] is to marry

I shall miss my last visitor & gallant I suppose – the last one who has or may manifest an interest in me – since Theo seems entirely false, so I felt a little blue during his formal visit after all my petty trials! I teazed him a little & he didn't deny anything – advized me "to make up with R" would that it were possible. He seemed to enjoy a few songs I sang – but left early and I was again – all alone – Clif, Fannie & babe together Ma & Pa each engaged in their room – little ones asleep &c but I felt like no companionship – went off to scribble & read – but soon slept & dreamed – for thank heaven I can as yet always welcome that blessed panacea for every ill – undisturbed repose in my comfortable room – in perfect health & security! Long may it continue thus – as a compensation for the disappointments of life!

Not often do I meet with familiar scenes or faces in my dreams – but they were very sweet tonight – of reconciliation with the estrange[d] lover of my youth – which must haunt me forever! May heaven grant a happy termination to this strange affair!

Sat Feb 3rd Clear & blustery today – closely immersed in doors – with my pen all day as Pa directed me to copy his contracts with the negroes – for the Yanks to keep- and I went about it hastily – so that I made several mistakes for which he reproved me considerably but mildly (Fannie had copied two so well – he was well pleased) I felt mortified – for I knew I was capable of better things – only I've written so much & to[o] hastily My hand is almost unreadable &c but my heart was the troubled fountain of many emotions today – beginning with late disappointments & mortifications – the dream I had[4]

4. By the summer of 1865 federal authorities instructed South Carolina's planters to secure labor contracts with former slaves. The sharecropping contract usually involved a one-third share of the year's crop yield for the laborer; the other two-thirds went to the planter, who risked an investment for shelter, seed, implements, and livestock. U.S. Army officers assisted the Freedmen's Bureau, acting as de facto judges during negotiations. The military often prodded reluctant planters into drawing up contracts and coerced suspicious freedmen into signing.

On December 25, 1865, Governor J. L. Orr issued his first official proclamation, sustaining the suspension of habeas corpus and admonishing all South Carolinians to obey the Freedmen's Bureau demands by entering into labor contracts and then to fulfill the terms of the obligation David Duncan Wallace, in vol. 3 of *The History of South Carolina* (New York: American Historical Society, 1934), reprints several versions of these contracts from Richland County, 1865 (pp. 229–30).

Judge Reed continued to take on responsibility for about twenty-one souls, many of whom were camped out on the grounds at Echo Hall and on other property throughout the county. Some freed slaves left the area permanently, but many remained or returned to find work (Snowden, *History of South Carolina,* 865, 876; Wallace, *The History of South Carolina,* 229–30).

Eleanor's account of R – last night so that I felt deserted by all the world – with no future joys before me on earth – and this continued unworthy regret – so I wept most bitter tears, & had no words or smiles for anybody! This is wrong – I must be more cheerful & content and amiable & useful in the house & circle where I am placed & must forget these little things – looking only for higher rewards! I had rec'd letters from Jim Townsend – reminding me of W.'s falsehood; & one from my true, noble hearted school friend Sallie East – so long silenced towards me by later duties. – Yet she wrote as fondly as ever – begging me to visit their home in Greenville next week – as her brother William was to bring home his bride (Fannie Hamby of N.C. – a lovely girl) & they wanted me there to form the happy throng.[5]

It would be pleasant for me to go – a happy change perhaps – but I don't feel like the exertion – or ride alone &c and fear I wouldn't be repaid &c – then Pa says he can't give me the money & I know I have taxed him too often for little profit – so I have despaired of going – and have nothing now to expect! The girls here were busy writing their compositions (for me to correct) recounting last night's pleasures, preparing for more parties – Pa encouraging it – for I fear he cares little for sacred things these days yet would it be wrong for us to get up some little dances and acted charades for amusement – to give a pleasant variety to our dull life here? Surely not – I must get over my blues and become more genial – and why can I not accomplish something with my pen or to establish social & mental & moral reforms around me![6]

I must exert myself more & live for a better purpose – 'though each day drags on the same dull rounds of little duties – & not half accomplished that should be! At sunset Pa came home to bid us prepare for the coming of an elegant gentleman guest – who had brought to him a letter of introduction from his copartner in Spartanburg – (Mr Duncan – lawyer) which recommended him very highly – as Dr Carter of Winchester Va, – now trying to revive his shattered fortunes as a trader in New York city – engaged in a "hardware" establishment & travelling through the country as their "agent" &c[7]

5. William East of Greenville married Fannie Hamby of North Carolina (see Reed, *Journals,* Appendix F).

6. Charades were apparently a new and more sophisticated entertainment than the traditional tableaux vivants, in which participants recreated a still-life scene from history or fiction. Charades required the participants to act out a scene of satire, tutorial, or comedy. The modern game of charades is pantomimed. See Mary Chapman, "Living Pictures: Women and Tableaux Vivents in Nineteenth-Century American Fiction and Culture," *Wide Angle* 18, no. 3 (1996): 22–52.

7. David Robinson Duncan (1836–1902) of Virginia graduated from Randolph-Macon College in 1855, then moved to Spartanburg, South Carolina, where his father taught at

So he came to us a perfect stranger – and we awaited his entrance with some anxious expectation as to his merits and result &c for interesting new acquaintances are always desirable in this stupid little village where one sees so few that are worthy of remembrance, then I always like to hear from the outside world – from cosmopolites who are posted &c! he came – and bearing the stamp of nature's true nobility we fancy in every look and act – we hope that he is numbered amongst our friends henceforth & forever! Of course – young ladies are ever on the alert for beaux; – some merely for idle conquest, others seeking naturally to find that true ideal for which they are born, or to find more congeniality of soul than they have met before – and is it wrong if they don't assume or cavill too much! Surely not!

Of course all we girls primped up & appeared in the parlors – but there are so many of we forlorn females that we are ashamed all to be seen. Vie H. was here – Lula & Mary B – Mamie & Cora – Eleanor & I – but of course we two did most of the entertaining & he scarcely spoke to either of the others – but Nell with her beauty & tricky ways – always affects the conquest in despite of my superior accomplishments &c&c but I am getting too old alas! Pa was entertaining him – both recounting stories of the war – Clifton a silent listener – & I joined then first to add a word now & then.

He was a tall – large – magnificently made man – such as we hear is natural to the noble valley of Virginia where he has always lived – on a rich old farm I guess – for he told much of his widowed mothers plantation – crops & stock &c (spoke later of his five brothers & one sister (6) – Of his school days in the University of VA – & at Washington City where he heard all the fine speakers in Congress &c of his wild pranks – & mischief spoke in every look & word afterwards- 'though he declared he had never been intoxicated, never gambled nor was profane or bad – but a perfect gentleman – religiously inclined – raised in the Baptist Church![8]

Wofford College. Duncan married Virginia Nelson on July 9, 1856, and they had four children. He was admitted to the bar in 1857.

In 1861 Duncan joined the Thirteenth South Carolina Infantry, Company C. Major Duncan was captured at Petersburg on April 2, 1865, then released after a short imprisonment. Upon return to Spartanburg he was promptly elected to the state house and later the senate. Duncan also served as trustee for both Wofford and Converse Colleges (Bailey, *South Carolina Senate,* 1:433–34; Garlington, *Men of the Time,* 121–22; 1860 Census, Spartanburg District, 347; *1870 Census,* Spartanburg County, 406).

8. Dr. Robert Kerefort Carter, son of William and Mary Carter of Winchester, Virginia did in fact have a Baptist mother and six siblings still in the Shenandoah Valley. Dr. Carter, a University of Virginia Medical School graduate, served as an assistant surgeon with the Thirteenth Regiment, Virginia Infantry. Dr. Carter's next assignment was the "Medical Directors Office, Manassas," where he spent the next nine months of the war "in charge of hospitals."

Had been a physician – but as surgeon in the army – 9 months on the field – afterwards in charge of hospitals – lived at ease – but grew sick of it – no means of support at home now – the country impoverished for a time by the ravages of war, – his mother left without servants (or anything) he became very industrious "sweeping – making beds &c at home!" but had gone to New York – into more rapid & lucrative business – where he doesn't intend to make acquaintances – hates the Yanks – likes some places of amusement occasionally – "to see Booth play Hamlet &c"- but has no use for everyday wonders &c is trying to make money for his family I guess – to secure the stand in the world – nature intends for him, and to win a wife someday I guess – who may well be proud of such a man![9]

He spoke candidly afterwards of his loves – engaged once two years – but the lady married whilst he was in the army – regretted awhile but considered best now – doesn't pretend to have any now – but speaks of dear lady friends (Nellie Taylor of Va – in Charleston now &c) will travel through a few other places in this state on business & return by the end of Feb to New York – but hopes to return this way in November![10]

I found all this out gradually – for 'though he talked freely & well – in the most earnest, practical – candid way – he was perfectly unassuming – no vanity but true manly pride, – had tact & fine manners to entertain each one well – much humor no artful sentiment, – but some slangs learnt in college & army I suppose – yet withal – a perfect man we fancy – of which there are but few alas! he was very handsome too! – beautiful black hair, moustache & beard – but laughing blue eyes I think – fine teeth – and a smile like sunshine – a pure, fair complexion – noble brow & form, an Apollo for any woman's adoration; dressed in plain Confederate Grey – but very neat

Had expected to enter no parlors on his tour he said – as strangers are generally received with such suspicion – but he seemed glad to meet us socially & gain us as friends and I hope has given & won the undying love of my gay & pretty sister Eleanor whom he called "Miss Nellie" – as his favorite name – & I – "Miss Emma"

Carter, a traveling "hardware" salesman, represented an unnamed firm based in New York City, and it was there he married Anna Young in February 1867 (T. K. Cartmell, *Shenandoah Valley Pioneers and Their Descendants: A History of Frederick County, Virginia from its Formation in 1738 to 1908* [Berryville, Va.:, Chesapeake Book Company, 1963], 95; *Compiled Service Records of Confederate Soldiers Who Served in Organizations from the State of Virginia,* United States War Department Records, Soundex index, micro copy # 324, roll 536, film E 581.4 C65, no. 536; see Reed, *Journals,* Appendix F).

9. Actor John Wilkes Booth gained a notorious status when he assassinated Abraham Lincoln, but Edgar successfully disassociated himself from his brother and continued to tour the United States and Europe.

10. Nellie Taylor of Virginia has note been identified.

for short – himself – as "Robert Kerefort Carter" (middle name for his grandmother!) It will be a bright episode to have known such a man – wether or not we ever meet again, but he is just such an acquaintance as we need now – & Providence having thrown him in our way surely it will result well – and he not prove a traitor as most other interesting strangers – whom Eleanor & I have met – such as Ben A – Whit C – &c&c[11]

He sat talking with calm indifference – without scarcely looking at us for awhile – at supper was very entertaining – and afterwards – espied my guitar & asked for songs – (Nell regretted she couldn't play I'm sure) but she & Clif sang a few ballads with me – he really seemed pleased – (& argued a great taste for music – which I afterwards concluded he didn't have much of!) listened intently – to "Beautiful Star" Moore's farewell & oft in the stilly night" he liking best old songs for association &c – So he began to turn & view us with some interest and converse more gallantly – saying "When I return to N.Y. – I would be pleased to send you some music" – which I hope he will remember, ('though others have not done so) yet he gave the same promise afterwards to Eleanor as she began to awaken his admiration from the first I think.[12]

We removed to the piano – where I played & sang – but he & Nell – began a little flirtation aside over music &c – and I soon found that "all my sweetness was wasted on the desert air" – as usual – 'though he was very polite & pleasant to me afterwards – didn't disguise his preference for her which increased as he remained here I fancy and so it ever is & I can hope for no more – where youth & beauty are my rivals He left near 10 – for Fant's boarding house near the depot – asking Pa which church we attended – and promising to dine with us next day

Sunday Feb 4th Was a cold – cloudy day – but we went from here to the Bap. Church – a crowd of we girls – not many people but Mr & Mrs Hoyt looked well – and our new friend Dr Carter sat behind us with Maj Ben Sloan – an army acquaintance of his – Mr Murray gave us a very good sermon – comparing the days of Noah – with the days of the coming of the – "Son of Man" – quite eloquent & vehement – & Mr Spaulding's prayer afterwards – very impressive – but our hearts

11. Ben is most likely Ben Adams, but the identity of Whit C. remains a mystery.

12. "Beautiful Star," a popular duet of the era, was written by English composer Stephan Glover (1812–70) (Sears, *1870 Sheet Music Catalogue,* 12).

"Oft in the Stilly Night" (1818) was a popular song with music by Sir John Stevenson and lyrics by Thomas Moore. The editors of *The Great Song Thesaurus* note that it was one of Abraham Lincoln's particular favorites (Sears, *1870 Sheet Music Catalog,* 95; Lax and Smith, *The Great Song Thesaurus,* 338).

are all so cold & unmovable as they were when Noah warned them to prepare for the flood! Heaven grant all may heed ere the last dreadful end![13]

Of course we were all on the lookout for the "Adonis" as we left the church – but making his handsomest bow to Nell he escorted her home – to the chagrin of a band of boys who walked behind, poor Dick Tupper one blazing with wrath & mortification & jealousy I suppose! They had quarreled a little before – & it did her good to make this display – showering all her smiles on the new beaux without a glance for Dick & Joe her young & clever devotees whom she has lost now I guess! I hope she can claim them still as friends – but to gain the Dr would be so far superior! he a real man in size & age (27 yrs old/12th of March 1866) – they nice little boys – yet she should not trifle with their true hearts or any others as she loves to do!

What a lucky girl she is in gaining admiration & true love – but she too has had some disappointments – but not this time I hope! As for me I expect nothing more – & have had but few heart oblations and they so false – when I know I have merited some better! The Dr stayed to dinner & after tea until a late hour Sunday night – so agreeably was he entertained – he said – when yest. he wondered how he should get through this day among strangers We felt already like old friends!

Julia & children were here to dinner – (for we had turkey – cake & wine &c such as poor Confeds can't have everyday!) but our miserable – unfortunate sister – had to leave her worthless husband drunk – as he has been for a week – & came here to seek a little relief in her sorrow with her five helpless children – Whom he can't or won't support – & they will be scorned to the lowest extremeties we fear – horrible thought! He seems to have lost all his senses in beastly sensuality – would take his two boys – Julia's children & drag round the barrooms yest. spending what little money he could get for candy – drinks &c – and soon their rents & negro wages will be due & where will be the money to pay for when they have sold all they can & he drank up the money & lies home like a vile beast – his noble young wife & helpless little ones – beginning to suffer with anxiety if nothing more & her hired nurse ran off & left her thurs – several days – (returned again) Mamie had spent that anxious Sat night with her when all went wrong – even her children

13. J. B. E. "Ben" Sloan of Pendleton achieved the rank of colonel in command of the Fourth Regiment, South Carolina Volunteers, mustered in April 1861. "The Fourth" largely comprised men from Anderson, Oconee, Greenville, and Pickens Counties. Anderson provided three companies, including the Palmetto Riflemen and Orr's Rifles. These units migrated through a number of commands as the Confederacy reorganized its military reserves time after time (Vandiver, *Traditions,* 27, 57, 223, 235; Everson and Simpson, *Far, Far from Home,* 33n, 44n; Reid, *History of the Fourth Regiment,* passim; Hoyt, *The Palmetto Riflemen,* from *Time Capsule,* 45–59; Salley, *South Carolina Troops,* 570).

straggling home after a drunken father so late – against her will but he is getting violent I fear & all love & respect lost – so what will be the consequence! May heaven look down & pity and offer some relief – for it looks like the most desperate case I know!

I don't know anything that Pa or I could do for relief or anybody else! I hope that Dr C – may not hear of him & his doings &c but we can't expect anything here – with such a connexion &c as we have – our own attractions will not be weighed! How unfortune for us – & better had we moved away long ago Dr C argued to Pa how he could make his fortune in some city now – & we all urged that day for a removal to Atlanta or somewhere – surely it would be far better for us in every way & he too seems inclined – but talks still of Mexico &c So I fear we'll never go anywhere! Hope it may be decided best.

We all sat together & discussed many things – but incidents of the war & success in N.Y. – now mostly – until Pa would get him off to get some items on business – he ordering a hardware bill from Dr C – for his shop – 'though he moved to postpone from it until next day – too bad! As Eleanor, Vie, & I sat in the next room – he came & joined us glad to get rid of old folks – but he would have been more pleased had only Nell remained I think – 'though that would have been too pointed – so soon; they soon began to look over a book of poetry & mark sentiments & scribble to each other – whilst Vie & I entertained each other with books he wrote in my album too –

Towards night proposed to go up & mail his letters & one for me – begging Nell to walk with him & when I objected as twas cold – late &c – he said "Oh you older sisters are always in the way!" Said laughingly – but I felt it was true – or that we were considered nuisances & so ran out – but he followed me with apologies &c and we are good friends at last I hope for he seems so free & artless & sincere – and if not my fate to win his love – I should be most happy to see Eleanor in possession and proud to claim such a connexion – & the other advantages it might bring to us all! Pa too would be more than delighted though he pretended not to have much faith as we are so apt to be deceived – & so little claims to such a friend – all considered &c he will meet so many more attractive in his travels perhaps!

They walked & returned to tea – which we had handed in the parlor – and then Vie remained with us – she & I singing hymns to the piano – whilst he & Nell chatted nonsense, – we referred to the Bible to our natal verses in Proverbs – & he alluded to the verse in 2nd John – "Lady – I beseech thee that we love one another!" & looked at her significantly – may it all be well! he seemed to have a respect for sacred things that was commendable for Nell is too bad – & even her influence was counteracted! After dinner the Bleckleys had called for me to ride with them – but I declined – too cold – had company &c – but at last the pleasant day – was all gone & each one dreamed of the Dr no doubt![14]

Monday Feb 5th It threatened snow all day & a few flakes fell – much business done in town – Witt Broyles & Dr Jim Brown here awhile – I was busy sewing &c all afraid we wouldn't see our new friend again – as Pa & Clif wouldn't write him again – thinking it would look too pointed, – & we heard he was to dine at the Sloan's – was to have left that day too he said – but stayed over until Tues eve. Pa & Clif had seen him up town all day – he & John Humphreys had even treated Pa to a drink &c – too bad – for surely he don't indulge thus freely – he says not – but likes a social glass now & then & John whom he has met in N.Y. is a regular scamp – sent word he would like to call on me that night but had a business engagement!

Wish he had if he could tell me of R – but best not for I forget & scorn even him in looking at this nobler man & wondering if there are no such for me in the world! Mary & Cora Wilhite were here in evg. & at dusk – Pa played the violin & the girls all danced – anxious to learn how. It is an agreeable & pretty accomplishment, but will be well for them? But Dr Carter had told Clif he would call awhile at night (having an engagement at 9 – on business – but he forgot or eschewed it – never spoke of it here!)

We should have had him to tea – for he ate his three meals at Fant's that day – & came stumbling up here in the darkness – with a borrowed lantern to guide him – and Pa & all were delighted to greet him again – as it proved some real interest we think! Clifton & the girls were playing cards so after a little merry chat – he proposed that we should have whist also – "wanting to beat the Col." – Pa and he seemed pleased to play 'though we hadn't in so long – So he & I – Dr & Nell won each a game though she had never learned before & was rather shy & awkward – proving that she was rather awed & more deeply interested than usual in his opinion he so gay & free – joking with Pa & I and encouraging her!

But he was glad enough when Pa took his violin awhile & the rest retired, then he went – & Nell, Clif & I sang to the guitar a few songs – which he seemed to fancy – or when I went to the piano & played mostly for my own amusement whilst he & Nell carried on nonsense over cards (fortune telling) & scribbling – he wrote her – "like some love bird without its mate my weary heart is desolate" &c – said to her many personal things – wouldn't flatter but gave hints – begged that

14. Perhaps the Reed children had a biblical passage assigned to them at birth as a family tradition: "And now I beseech thee, lady, not as though I wrote a new commandment unto thee, but that which we had from the beginning, that we love one another" (2 John 1:5).

we shouldn't marry before his return here – for he would come again – and jokingly asked her to go with him to Abbeville tomorrow & on to New York &c told about various romances of his &c but teazed her about "red head" (Dick) following him around &c – but if there's any sincerity in man he certainly evinced some special interest in her – which she fully repaid – and surely they are fated for each other! May heaven direct for the best![15]

He once started to go but sat down – would have been glad to spend the night had Pa urged for he came in to bid adieu – so after 11 – he rose and donning his nice grey Army overcoat, jockey hat & gauntlets & lighting his lantern – appeared a grand specimen of Manhood before us – bidding us a cordial goodnight – saying mostly to Nell "I hope to find an opportunity of calling on you ladies tomorrow!" And surely he will come & we can retain his friendship &c 'though his proceedings reminded me much of Whit's – who was so handsome, so devoted but so deceiving – the villain!

Yet this Virginian is certainly a nobler man in every way! I had withdrawn all claims or hopes to any attractions – and so rested content – not even dreaming – for my future must be a blank I suppose – as the golden days of youth are gone and though I have rather gained in looks & acquirements and my heart is as pure & true as ever – yet all's over with me I think & I must be reconciled – & live for others! Cold night!

Tues. Feb. 6th Half cloudy – & rather icy – a wasted morn over my scribblings – read & knit some – must answer a sweet letter from my old friend Sallie Wideman Brown (Dr Ben's wife in Abbeville Dist.) who is still true to me and I hope I may rely on her ever more – She asks me of R.B. but I can tell nothing – Sallie Arnold came to see me & try to pay a debt she has owed me four years for music lessons – of which she is much ashamed. She is a nice girl – and I'm sorry – feels so mortified – hasn't the means to pay money – but wanted me to accept a nice poplin dress she has (a present to her – not made) but I don't need it specially & declined – reducing the bill – as I hope to get a little money now & then for it – for my own special uses[16]

15. Abbeville, South Carolina, just south of Anderson, was named by early Huguenot settlers in remembrance of a town in France. Abbeville has been called "the cradle and grave of the Confederacy," because a concrete plan of secession was formulated on November 22, 1860, atop nearby "Secession Hill," and the last meeting of the Confederate cabinet was held at the Burt Mansion on May 2, 1865 (Edgar, *WPA Guide,* 446–47; Lowry Ware, *Old Abbeville: Scenes of the Past of a Town Where "Old Time Things Are Not Forgotten"* [Columbia, S.C.: SCMAR, 1992], passim; Writers' Program, *Palmetto Place Names,* 11).

16. Sallie Arnold was twenty years old in 1866, the daughter of Lawton T., a rather successful mechanic, and Mary W. Arnold. Sallie's siblings were named Grace and Mary (*1860 Census,* Anderson District, 154).

Joe Hyde has called on Eleanor I must go to work – ought to go & relieve my sister Julia in her extremity if possible – but tis out of my power I fear. She came & spent the aft. with us looked sad – but Clif brought in this new dancing negro boy from town to amuse us all with awhile – but what will bring her permanent relief?

I sewed a little – but we expected Dr Carter to call in the aft & bid us goodbye as he told Clif he would to leave this aft. for Abbeville – but he didn't go – pretended business – but seemed glad enough to stay over & see us again – though we had given him up as gone for good without an adieux and I lost confidence in him at once – at once – thinking this was the way of the world – but he proved more faithful!

At night Enoch Cater & Isham Harrison two nice – handsome boys came round to see Eleanor about getting up a dance here as the negro band from Pendleton was down for the purpose She was crazy for it – & Pa consented – but Ma opposed & so she couldn't bid them come – but just then the bell rang & our Dr entered with his lantern again – & when I saluted him afterwards as "Jack with his lantern" he exploded with a laugh & "thats complimentary!" All laughed & I felt quite chagrined – but had meant nothing & smoothed it over as "Will o the wisp" &c we were delighted to see him enter.[17]

The handsome form in grey & smiling face – but he descended too much from his dignity – tonight with jokes & freedom of speech & manner – used too many slang phrases – but seemed such a frank free fellow he just displayed his real self & is full of mischief – he sat flat on the floor to chunk up the fire told us about burning up his old socks today because they were holy & buying new ones – no wife to darn for him &c The boys looked & laughed in wonder! but they soon left & he seemed glad to get with Eleanor & I alone – seemed to feel like a brother or cousin – free & easy as you please – but not impudent a perfect gentleman we hope – but full of life – he proved his preference for Nell by every act Urged me to sing & play while they scribbled & talked sentiment I suppose – 'though he listened to a few songs intently – never flattered any!

He handed Eleanor a note which he had written to send but concluded to stay over a very elegant note of thanks for hers & her sisters hospitality & kindness to

17. Enoch Benson Cater (1847–86) was the son of Dr. A. P. Cater, one of Anderson's first physicians. Lousie Vandiver relates the story about how the Caters came to be married. It seems that young Martha Postelle planted two cedar trees in front of her place of residence, the Dickinson Hotel, and named them after herself and her sweetheart. Martha told her young suitor that if the trees thrived she would marry him between them, but if they should die, "why, she might not." The trees evidently survived (Vandiver, *Traditions,* 22, 23, 198, 240, 259; *1860 Census,* Anderson District, 260; *Greenville Mountaineer,* Apr. 18, 1845).

a stranger – hoped we would continue friends – that the two states Va & Ca. were bound together by strong ties since the war – but he hoped there would be still stronger consumated & "hope we may meet again" &c I hope he was sincere in all he said & that they may love & meet again as one someday! Dick & Joe her boy lovers have been here today but surely she suits "Kerefort" better!

Hope he may return soon & all be well with them! he amused us with many jokes – then to our suprize a band of music struck up outside – the boys bringing the coloured band to serenade – very good – reminded me of old times – not much sweetness or sentiment however – we three sat in the parlor quietly enjoying it & chatting away! But then he had to go – and we were sorry to bid adieux to the elegant stranger – our new friend of whom we hope to hear again & meet oftimes for I would prize him as a brother – yet fear it cannot be! he & Pa exchanged kind speeches but he said too little to us – & the bright "Will o the Wisp" – vanished with his bright smiles – forever perhaps as other visions of pleasure have gone before! he seems to regard me with a little fear & respect I suppose – but not much pleasure I fear! Anyway I hope we'll meet again on earth and in the better world above!

Late & cold & dark – can I not dream of some noble "Robert" if the reality is never mine? He really left next morn & we missed him much – wonder what's become of the fine fellow & if he will ever remember us kindly & if we'll ever meet again & how – Pa may see him soon in Charleston

Weds Feb 7th A damp – dark day – which I dreamed away or read, without plunging into the recreation of a novel as I intended, finished the first volume of Prescott's Conquest of Mexico of the noble endurance & strength of the Spanish invaders under brave Hernand Cortez of their discoveries among the Indian tribes in the rich cities of ancient Mexico with wonders of which we never dreamed of the brave, independent [Tlascalans][18] who battled so long for freedom all interesting – the pious forbearance of their priest Omeida – pride of Montezuma – the last Emperor of Mexico (in 1519) I believe – and of the brave – civilized Aztecs & Toltecs in the golden days of Anahuse & good deity "Quetzalcoyotyl" &c

I gave music lessons to each of the girls – who wouldn't go to school today – & Pa scolded them – always ready to blame but often right in his reproofs 'though too harsh! He & all of us are worrying now over the condition of Julia & family – with no means of living & J Peter a drunken dog laid up at home with his fair young wife – my noble sister shelling what little corn they have left – for mill I hear & five poor young children with such a fate before them as they have! How dreadful! But

18. The Tlascalans were a tribe from the Valley of Mexico who allied with Cortez against the Azteca.

may God avert the worst! Mamie went over there this evg. to comfort Julia as only she can & to abuse J.P which seemed to grieve him most from her – & he blamed himself & promised much but what will be the end? Too bad to contemplate I fear!

We are in comfort yet at home – but with so many dependent on my father we can't tell what the end may be! he feels it much but is strong & energetic & capable I hope for many years! Clifton seems to feel the importance of action & sobriety & does all he can now – but is dependent poor fellow! Fannie is nearly quite well & Helen so fat & good & sweet – but we are a noisy – helpless – useless – consuming household – so many females & children! I might be helping to earn subsistance perchance but scarce know how when there are so many more needy out of employment and I have my place here at home too which I couldn't bear to lose yet forever! '[T]hough none of us have a prospect of leaving it by matrimony!

I was suprised to receive a letter from Lou (Burriss) McFall from her new home in Arkansas – with only her young husband & idolized babe – but they will have hard times & bad health – she misses her church & religious advantages & sighs to see old friends again! May she be blest evermore! A true, sweet, pious friend to me whom I hope to remember & meet in the better world above as she wishes too!

I heard too of my sweet old friend Nettie Brockman – (Mrs Sandy Earle) moving to the west – many trials on the way but I hope she may be fortunate – & that we will not wholly forget each other & the happy past 'though she does seem estranged as all my other young friends have been by marraige &c The thought has often grieved me sadly – but in hearing from a few lately after a long silence I find that other & dearer ties & cares have not quite extinguished old memories of school joys &c but alas! All are more changed towards me than I have ever been or could be, & I can't account for all the falsehood my true heart has met.[19]

19. Henrietta M. "Nettie" Brockman (b. 1840) of Greenville, South Carolina, married Alexander Campbell "Sandy" Earle (b. 1837). They lived at Greenville during the war years, and Elizabeth "Bessie" Harrison Earle was born there on February 17, 1864. Nettie's younger sister, Lucy Ann Margaret Brockman, married Julius Earle, Sandy's older brother, in 1852.

When the war started, Sandy was enrolled at Bethany College, where he founded the Delta Tau Delta fraternity. Captain Sandy Earle served with the Fourth South Carolina Infantry, then with the Dunn's Rangers of the Virginia Cavalry. In early 1866 the Earles moved to Ouachita County, Arkansas, where brothers Samuel Girard Earle, Jr., and Francis Wilton "Doc" Earle had gone in 1859. The rest of the Earle children were born and raised in Arkansas. They include Mary Eloise (b. 1866), John Harrison (1868–92), S. Benjamin "Sank" (1871–1946), Irene Adella (1877–1901), and Josephine Rowena (1880–1912).

In about 1908, after their children had died or left home, the Earles left to homestead in Oklahoma and west Texas. After this, they wandered back to Greenville, South Carolina using a small covered cart pulled by a pair of burros. They roamed the country of their youth, selling baskets to make ends meet. Sandy died at the Confederate Veteran's Home in Austin, Texas, in 1916; Nettie died in Arkansas in 1925 (Earle, *The Earles of Evergreen,* 42–49).

One month since Theo left with all his protestations &c – and not one word! I only hope he is not a villain – if I never see him more – Fannie S[mith] wholly estranged too – as many more Cokesbury folk all deceiving &c! Tonight my Whitmire friends in Greenville are rejoicing over the arrival of a brother's bride – & I'm not there as invited by my true old friend Sallie – for I hadn't the means or an escort – yet may not miss much – hope to be remembered! I was reading a little mythology & French this aft – with Mamie (Telemagne) wish I could devour all readable books &c at once – but it consumes so much time I can't give now – ought to study more practical things too –

But Eleanor never thinks of books only of nonsense &c none of them will let me read to them but at night I collected them a little while to read part of Moore's "Lalla Rookh" the Eastern legends – having almost forgotten it – (Dr C said 'twas his favorite!) but I found it unsuited for pure & youthful minds – though many exquisite passages thrilled me as those marked to me by Robere & forgotten long ago – or does he ever read & think of it False one![20]

Lula sang "Lorena" sweetly & reminded me of it all too – until I shed a few tears – but altogether it was a lovely day of selfish pleasures to me! In the dusk we all danced the dope some – when I joined in "chasing the fox" &c as in my free & happy girlhood – as these children now are just beginning to enter such pastimes – they danced a little to the piano – all of them disappointed in not being permitted to have the ball here! I read late all rest so I must with my cold & dream – Milder stars out too Where is Kerefoot?[21]

Thurs Feb. 8th Half clear & rather raw & cold a little genial sunlight in aft. Sewing – reading &c in morn Mr & Mrs Witt Broyles here to dinner – clever folks they & Pa & all of us strongly infected with the emigration fever – inclined towards Mexico from the inducements offered by Comr. Maury & son, Gov Price – Gov Norris &c who occupy rich hacienda's or farms there – & the gov't – strengthening under Maxmilian wishes to induce good settlers to come there from the South – will pay expenses – furnish materials for farming on those rich lands which produce spontaneous crops four times a year! Climate delightful – nature lavish – but all these are the bright news – what of the darker? They are to be met

20. Author Thomas Moore was known for his patriotism and charming nature. "Lalla Rookh" (1817) was a romantic poem set amid the backdrop of Persia and Arabia. Best known for his satires, Moore also collaborated with contemporary composers, such as Sir John Stevenson, to write long remembered songs like "Oft in the Stilly Night" and "The Harp that Once through Tara's Halls."

21. "Dancing the dope" refers to dancers shuffling about with arms and shoulders relaxed and head sagging. "Chasing the fox" has not been identified, though it may be a version of a game known as Red Rover or Ringalerio.

& overcome I hope if we ever venture on such a great undertaking! Pa seems determined now will make inquiries &c in Charleston and can it be possible that we will ever leave here & experience such a new life & will it not be for the best?[22]

The young folks were anxious to have a dance here tonight Eleanor most but Ma & I knew 'twas wrong – & Pa vehemently contested both sides – yet favored it – but as we couldn't agree there was none here – the crowd assembled at Mr Ruccor's at night – the Pen. band down – fine fun I guess – Lula Broyles & I went up street in the aft – in & out stores encountered John Humphreys & R. B., the bad old chums at every corner staring – smiling & talking of me I know bowed but I would like to know the subject of their discussions & thoughts – John won't call to frost me I guess! (wonder what's become of Dr. Carter!)

We went round to see Vie & Lucie a little while, back by Julia's – where she sat worried with her children & miserable husband just getting over his spree – seemed humble &c but will it last? he says he will go away & try to make a support &c and it would be far better for all no doubt yet I fear he hasn't strength of mind or will sufficient – & can accomplish nothing! heaven grant them better times – home late aft. tea Dick Tupper called for Eleanor & Lula to go to the Ruccors looked nicely – talks sensibly – but is a real boy – his sister training him to study at night – he proposed that I should get up some charades for a purpose here &c think I shall – try it – for variety – I read some over at night – late & bright & cold no love for me

22. In 1864, Napoleon III of France established Austrian Archduke Maximilian and his consort, the Belgian Princess Carlotta, as the emperor and empress of Mexico. Meanwhile, the troops of Benito Juarez continually harassed the French troops, and to the north, the American Civil War was in progress. In 1865 Emperor Maximilian invited ex-Confederates to colonize east central Mexico.

Emmala probably refers to General Sterling Price and Governor Isham Green Harris, two men integral to the colonization of Mexico. Price, a native Virginian and a Missouri congressman, commanded a Missouri regiment in the Mexican War. He served as governor of both New Mexico and Missouri.

The plans quickly soured in 1867, when the U.S. government closed the southern frontier to emigration, Napoleon III withdrew his troops, and Maximilian died at the hands of the triumphant Juaristas (Rolle, *The Lost Cause,* 100–13; *Columbia Encyclopedia,* 1789).

Isham Green Harris was a governor of Tennessee and a hard-core secessionist. Harris fought under the command of General Richard Taylor, and when the war ended made his escape to Mexico. The former governor of Tennessee became, for a time, the mayor of Carlotta (the Confederate colony), but returned to Tennessee in 1868 to help oust the Radical regime of Governor Brownlow. In 1877 Harris became U.S. senator from Tennessee, maintaining his seat until he died in 1897 (*Columbia Encyclopedia,* 1241; Rolle, *Lost Cause,* 79–81, 89, 90, 92, 164, 195).

Friday Feb 9th A bright sunny day – reading news & invited to a surprize at Gov. Orr's again at night all of us here invited and we resolved to go if they did dance – for some enjoyment & company &c but we were troubled about getting out there so far – a dark night too. Lula B., Vie H. & I – went in the buggy first & sent it back for Clif – Fannie & Eleanor – found a large crowd of young folks who sat around rather awkwardly awhile before the music came – but I chatted with Mrs Orr & Mattie very socially – and various youthes

Tom Broyles awhile – I invited he & several others, with a few girls to unite in getting up some charades for amusement – they seemed to consent with pleasure – but we were rather a dull crowd – & I felt strangely to see R.B. enter & talk all around to others – never catching my eyes – 'though he followed every movement no doubt! He was the only man who didn't dance & seemed lost, wandering around – talking only to silly Sally Gibbes &c we stood once around the center table looking at stereoscopes – and he never noticed me – 'though I wanted to enjoy the same pictures & hear his opinions once more![23]

A quiet crowd played cards in a corner – I sat about, scarce knowing what to do – whilst the merry throng wheeled in the dances to the music of the coloured band – the lancers & round dances prettiest – of course the men who danced cared for no other company – but they were silly boys scarcely worthy to entertain me – 'though Bill Humphreys made himself very pleasant once – Prue Benson &c – But I gazed at the dancers while Lucie Harrison & Eleanor were pretty & gay – Mattie Orr brilliant & graceful – &c Lucia & brother (Isham) Sallie & Jim Munro danced well together![24]

But I grew weary of everything & sad as R sat by me ever so indifferent but picked up a handkerchief that I dropped & handed to me gracefully but without a word or smile how did he feel! After one the party dispersed and we had a long cold walk home as Fan & Clif had taken the buggy – Dick & Bill – & Maj.

23. The stereoscope was a handheld optical device, resembling binoculars, that presented the viewer with two pictures from two slightly varying angles that created the illusion of depth of field ("3–D"). The popular version invented by Oliver Wendell Holmes was a common parlor toy for many years before the advent of amateur photography, radio, and television (*Columbia Encyclopedia,* 2715).

24. Thomas Prue Benson was a twenty-two-year-old railroad conductor in 1860; he enlisted in the Palmetto Riflemen on April 14, 1861, at the rank of corporal. Benson was wounded first at Frazier's Farm and again at Second Manassas. Promoted through the ranks to become the third and final captain of Company C, he was lieutenant of Company B in March of 1863 when Tally Simpson (Third South Carolina Infantry) mentioned that "Pru" Benson along with George Miller (possibly Emmala's future husband) visited their encampment near Fredericksburg, Virginia. Benson later married Gertrude Taylor of Pendleton (Simpson, *Old Pendleton,* 112; Everson and Simpson, *Far, Far from Home,* 201; Hoyt, *The Palmetto Riflemen,* from *Time Capsule,* 54; Vandiver, *Traditions,* 157, 223; *1860 Census,* Anderson District, 260).

Humphreys with me the tall, clever fellow my sister Julia's old lover – says he has gotten over all old affections – & we agreed that R had – our former friend – who hurried by us so changed alas! Lula B. was sick after getting Vie pleased

Sat. Feb 10th A pleasant day – household busy preparing for company – as we had a letter saying that Misses Carrie & Ressie Miller would be here to accompany Pa to Charleston (but he had gone on that morning train) – they would have to be with us till Monday & be escorted by Rev. Mr Elliott and other ministers on their way down to the Epis – convention I drove to the depot in carraige to meet them – but as 'twas early – drove up to see the Murrays who seemed glad to see me – good friends of mine we talked freely of many things[25]

At the depot again had a chat with Handy Fant – a nice boy – once my Sunday School scholar – who told me of his trip with Pa last summer – meeting many acquaintances of mine, one Robert Wallace of pleasant memories – lang syne – who sent remembrances &c wonder why he don't come to see me again – once the angel of his dreams & he a bachelor off for the West![26]

At last the Pendleton [railroad] cars arrived bringing Dr H Miller & his two stylish looking daughters to return our visits, on their way down to Charleston Monday – I brought them home in the carraige & we were all soon very social. After a nice dinner Mattie Orr called on them, then joined us as we four girls walked up town to Mr Williams store where they made a few little purchases. he

25. The Miller girls, Caroline L. "Carrie" (1847–1938) and Reseca E. "Ressie" (1846–1932), were the children of Dr. Henry C. and Caroline Miller of Pendleton. At eighteen and nineteen years old, the Miller girls were due to learn the ways of Charleston society. Ressie later married J. N. Hook and Carrie married W. W. Simmons, but neither had children (according to R. W. Simpson). Carrie's wartime letters to cousin Tally Simpson make up a large part of Everson and Simpson's edition, *Far, Far from Home.* It was Carrie who managed to develop Tally's interest in the mystery girl, Fannie Smith of Charleston (Lander and McGee, *A Rebel Came Home,* 114; Simpson, *Old Pendleton,* 138–39; *1860 Census,* Pickens District, Pendleton, 190; Everson and Simpson, *Far, Far from Home,* passim).

26. Handy Bruce Fant (1846–1919) was born April 11, 1846, in Chattooga County, Georgia, the son of Oliver Hazard Perry "O. H. P." Fant and Mildred Ann McGee Fant. Both father and son were railroad depot agents for the Greenville and Columbia Railroad, but Handy most likely worked on the Blue Ridge Railroad (Belton to Walhalla) in early 1866.

Handy B. Fant married Mary Eugenia Carlisle (1841–1927), the daughter of Presbyterian minister William and Margaret Carlisle of Varennes Church, in June 1871. By 1873 Fant succeeded his father as the Anderson agent for the Greenville and Columbia Railroad, which was his central occupation until 1891. H. B. Fant was also a Baptist minister (ordained in 1884) and a successful grocer (H. B. Fant & Sons) (*1860 Census,* Anderson District, 160, 261; Garlington, *Men of the Time,* 140–41; Vandiver, *Traditions,* 276).

Robert Wallace has not been identified.

seemed pleased to see us promising to come & see them & we too – but he never comes!

All four of their big Broyles cousins came in to greet them, surprized at their being our guests – no doubt! R first who spoke freely to them – bowed stiffly to me – not a word! but he soon left as Rev. Mr Elliott came in to be introduced by their father – offered to escort them down – Capt Wilkinson spoke to them cordially too, then Gus & John B blustered in and as we walked off upstreet – John joined Carrie & Eleanor all the way – R looked on as if he would like to but could not – & what did he think of his first cousins & I being thrown thus intimately together? Strange! They are his haughtiest Talliaferro kin – of whom they are proud – but know little – & came here as our guest as do nearly all their relatives in preference yet we are estranged! Queer![27]

We spent a quiet evg. at home – chatting & with music – for they made me sing much to the piano & guitar – (Dr M near at the Broyles') Carrie saw some scribbling of R's & teazed me about it – what will she say to him? In their room – they insisted on arranging my hair like theirs – on immense cushions A coil behind – cats & kittens rolled once in front with nets & bows & fancy combs &c Quite elegant & stylish looking – but very elaborate & troublesome – I would never do it – but all told me it was very becoming & I ought to decorate myself more – to be more attractive – yet I never will I suppose as 'tis no use now

Sunday Feb 11th A pleasant day – we all went to the Bap. church in the morning – 'though the girls rather preferred the Epis. their own church yet courtesy prompted them to go with me & to see our church Mr Murray preached a very good sermon – singing & all very good (In the aft.we went to the Epis ch[crossed out]) Dr Miller came here to dinner –

I and Ma & Vie H. were here & to our surprize an Indian & his wife entered – George Bushyhead chief of the Cherokees about 1000 in N. C. a Bap. preacher – on then to Washington as an Agent to present petitions to Congress – for collecting __.000 interest on 7000000 due them for years – to assist in their support He was well dressed in broadcloth and had a finer face & head than most Indians – sad man evidently but short black hair & fine head – a sensible man &c spoke tolerable plain English, his wife an ugly old thing wouldn't talk – nicely dressed in worsted shawl &c long earrings & other bogus jewels – but they behaved very well & as chief &c we felt obliged to ask them to eat at the first table with us but they soon left & after getting some provisions for next day – went off – they laughed at our pronouncing the long lists of queer Indian signatures they had to their

27. J. W. Wilkinson was a Charleston attorney (Parrish, *Confederate Imprints,* 180).

papers! poor creatures – What a sad fate – exiles from home & country & fast being annihilated – hope his mission may be successful![28]

In the aft. we girls & Dr Miller went to the Epis. church & heard Mr Elliott "the divine" preach one of his purist sermons – & the Broyles singing was very good – I caught R's eye several times he smiled – as if ashamed – I felt sad as usual! The girls had promised to go to their "Aunt Sarah Ann's" (Mrs. Broyles) awhile & so after church – R joined Ressie & Capt. Wilkinson, Carrie – & with their father they went over & sat awhile until dark & rain drove them home – Tom escorting them-! I was writing a few notes for them to carry – one to Caro Maverick – which I hope will be kindly rec'd – one to Fannie Smith – another false friend to me – she don't deserve it, but I can't forget or resist old friendships or conceal my feelings – wrote a little reproof & many (which [crossed out]) tempered by good wishes – which I hope will be properly considered, – Not one line has she written me in these three months after all our long intimacy letters & promises &c but she has been immersed in pleasure in her gay city home & bent on catching a beau – has won a Heywood of the old aristocracy as was Whaley – to elevate them – on their money &c so they are exultant – but he is younger than she! Hasel Heywood a fine name & I hope they may be happy. She will have a proud wedding in Grace church 12 splendid bridesmaids of the first families & beauties – of course I didn't expect a place there – but only to hear from her & hope to see her hereafter![29]

Theodore too is false – after all his professions – gone over a month & not a line – so I wrote a short note requesting that my letters & mementoes be destroyed – but with a good wish! What effect will it have? I fear bad as usual – be regarded fast &c the girls may read it, or R hear of it & what will they say? But Ressie promised to deliver it quietly she & I had a long social promenade in the piazza when

28. George Bushyhead, a principal chief of the Eastern Band of Cherokees, first journeyed to Washington in the 1850s to petition the claims of his town and kin, but in early 1866 many Eastern Cherokee empowered Bushyhead to request a reservation be set aside in the southern Appalachians. To finance this project he proposed the government pay off on the interest accrued since the establishment of an 1848 transportation and subsistence fund; the government did decide to distribute the long dormant funds among the Eastern Cherokees (John R. Finger, *The Eastern Band of Cherokees, 1819–1900* [Knoxville: University of Tennessee Press, 1984], 58, 102–8, 113; Charles Sloan Reid, Marguerite Brennecke, and R. C. Carter, *Persons, Places, and Happenings in Old Walhalla* [Walhalla, S.C.: Walhalla Historical Society, 1960], 106).

29. Caro Maverick of Charleston has not been positively identified.

Hazel (sometimes spelled Hasell) Heyward married Fanny Smith March 1, 1866, in Trinity Church, Charleston, South Carolina. Fanny Smith was Theo's cousin but also a close confidant to Emmala in the recent past. Fanny's past love interests included the deceased Harry Miller and Tally Simpson of Pendleton, as well as one Mr. Whaley.

we spoke of R – & tried to pump me – & I fear I always evince too much but said little, said she was sorry we didn't make it out – for if others had objections she had none "knew he never loved anyone else" – &c Carrie repeatedly called me "cousin" through mistake she said – both know of it – & wanted to hear more – but don't know or care much about the B[royle]'s affairs or are very deceptive!

They pretend to be good friends of ours & I hope may so continue for they are elegant girls, – but just entering society – will change They are tall fine forms – fine dark hair & eyes smoothe clear faces low brows but hair rolled back & well arranged – Carrie the prettiest dewy eyes ruby lips & queer coarse nose – Ressie the sweetest I think – both smart, fine manners & well read, will go into the first society below dress handsomely & splurge forget us then & on their return I guess as the gay – false, lucky Smiths have done – & we as worthy out off here in the backwoods with no advantages!

A fine letter from Aunt Lizzie Willis in Augusta today – told me of their gay round of festivities concerts, suppers &c given to raise a cenotaph to the hero "Dead of Augusta" – & small pox raging there fearfully too so the world goes on rejoicing [in] spite of every calamity An Italian Opera Troupe expected there – & she wishes I could hear them & take a sin voyage with her to Cuba &c regrets too that I am beyond the pale of all these rare pleasures which I could so appreciate![30]

Sent the photo paper of uncle Ned's partner in business – Charleston – Col Chisholm a splendid looking – polished bachelor – surely he would do for me – & why can I not win such a man for my protector &c would that it were possible – but no luck attends my lot thus! She reproves me for casting off Theo with his great soul & rare acquirements &c & I didn't think any friends of mine approved him & reproved my weak clinging talk &c I fear surely it will ever be while both remain here unchanged – so I would that some better fate were ours![31]

30. Lizzie Willis, wife of Edward "Ned" Willis, was cofounder of fertilizer and cotton factors Willis & Chisholm, located on Charleston's North Atlantic Wharf. It cannot be determined if they were actually related to the Reeds or whether "Aunt and Uncle" are merely terms of endearment for old family friends. Aunt Lizzie's adventures in Augusta, Georgia, sound intriguing, given the difficulties of the postwar years. By 1870 the Willises were back in Charleston and lived in a home at the corner of Rutledge and Montague Streets (*Jowitt's 1870 Charleston City Census,* 220).

31. Colonel A. Robert Chisolm, business partner of Edward Willis, resided at 17 Rutledge Street in Charleston and was one of the many Chisolm brothers and sons who practiced law, leased property, and traded various goods all over the Charleston area before, during, and after the war. Before the Civil War, the Chisolms were also planters on St. Helena Island, Beaufort County, South Carolina. The family included Mrs. Louisa I. and children Robert Jr., Alex R., George H., Alice C., Elworth, William M., Louisa I., and Fred M. (*Jowitt's 1870 Charleston City Directory,* 220; *1860 Census,* Beaufort District, 7).

She is a noble, brilliant woman wish I could see & hear more of my brilliant aunty – so lucky & merry & happy! A sweet little token from Anna Richtman – a good friend of mine & L's in the mountains – her father Consul for Austria over here! We sang hymns, all talked nonsense &c then scattered for the night as they were to leave so early![32]

Monday Feb 12th We were all aroused before day – to see off the girls to Charleston – with Mr Elliott who had called to see them about it a moment after church yest. – their father had stayed here & we sent them all to the cars – in the carraige – by 8 oclock after a little breakfast & saw the sweet happy girls off in their entrance upon the great world – which they are sure to enjoy but I hope to see more of them hereafter!

I was busy doing little nothings all day – reading – music lessons &c (Dr Holland wishes to send me his boys to teach!) when Mattie Orr came & spent the aft when she, Nell & I read over some charades &c discussed the propriety of getting some up in this dull town wherever anything of the kind usually fails 'though I fear – we found no one else that evg. quiet sleepy night. I read a little to Ma about Mexico &c – glad to rest early – 'though how I love to sleep & dream & rest – thankful for all mercies – but we're all wicked!

Tuesday Feb 13th A splendid – clean, bright day – at home – reading, knitting, sewing, & writing still retain me busy all morn – whilst Clif & Fan, Ma & babies went to eat dinner Turkey &c at Julia's ere a worse crisis comes upon them, for it seems it will come – and nearly the worst now a helpless young family all helpless & dependent wafes & rent can't be paid – Julia's little furniture to be sold for his debts – he a worthless worm – no business anywhere – not useful at home, brought on by his own vile propensity – he promises to go off & make a support & leave them to their fate – Dreadful indeed! Poor Julia came here so grieved & worried

Janie Robinson called – nice girl; but I can't comfort – J.P. seems going crazy too oppressed by his cares & J rependant yet it might be best for all! Sad affairs may they end for the best! Eleanor & I wrote notes to different girls begging them to come & take part in charades (all failed but two – [crossed out]) all declined – too bashful &c but I wonder what are the real reasons of R & the Broyles & Keiths, Tom promised to come but did not!

We sent for Mattie Orr but she would have been faithful to her app'tm't a noble girl – so unassuming! Little Pal McCulley came too – rather quiet &c – Dick T. & Joe H. – Keys McCulley – Jim Munro E. Cater, & came in to select their parts – so had rather an amusing – scene reading over the parts selected &c – hope it may

32. Anna Richtman, daughter of an Austrian consul, has not been further identified.

suc[c]eed – but nothing of the kind can here – so inharmonious! I'm sorry to have undertaken it such difficulties hope times may improve After that I stole over to the Wilhites awhile Dr & Mrs. W pleased, usual gossip – A quiet evg then at home & likely to remain so girls writing valentine's I believe – usual, silly school boy & girl offerings! Wish I could send hints & to various grown up – deserving fellows! I knit & read & must rest now (so sleepy I could scarcely scribble the above!)

Weds Feb 14th A bleak windy day – clearing off very cold to my regret! Ma & I went to town in the morning to procure some trimmings &c for dresses – some pretty goods very tempting – perfumes &c but I resisted! Spoke to a few clever people – & ran home. Ma to Lucies, Julia here awhile I gave music lessons, wrote letters &c in aft dark & wet & gloomy – prevented the young folks coming for charades – Mary Wilhite here a little while – to get a part, children dancing merrily. I read some to Ma – & slept coldly but peacefully!

Thurs – Feb 15th A brilliant, freezing morning – all up too late & grumbling over small fires – but we ought to be more active! Busy in morning – Aunt Anna & Willie Jones here she helping Ma make her new poplin dress – In aft. the young folks assembled to reherse charades – went over two very well for the first referring to their copied parts of course – Liz Bleckley came in & took two characters at my request does well – Jennie Robinson looking on ! They read over "Phantom" too funny – They departed late & it was a freezing cold night –

Friday Feb 16th Icicles covered everything – & we had to wash in ice – almost – hard for us all to dress – yet how must the poor & menials have suffered at their early labors, – perhaps their exertions though made them more comfortable – than we so lazy! Yet I am thankful for any ease & comfort so far! Busy sewing all day until night came too soon & brought Mattie Orr to stay with us as promised – and we were not prepared

Then Uncle Junius Jones arrived from Ga – having been on the wing several weeks trying to find employment &c &c! He said he had rented a farm & laborers to make a crop this year when the Yankees came & took off all the blacks from the country – to bounty lands they said as they are growing more oppressive every day – and so he is still lost – looks old & faded from dissipation I guess – but poor fellow seems as clever as possible & Informed me that he had found me a beau – one Capt. Anthony – a lawyer of Rome – Ga – related to Gen. Toombs – had first taken Mrs T to Cuba – a fine looking – stylish young bachelor who had promised certainly to come over on a visit to me! Wonder if he ever will – how nice it might be![33]

33. James Rembert Anthony was born September 2, 1841, near Washington, Georgia. Captain Anthony commanded Company L, First Regiment, Georgia Regulars, before surrendering at Greensboro, North Carolina, on April 26, 1865. At the behest of Col. E. M. Rucker,

And how interesting always to form new acquaintances! He brought me too – three letters – which Tom Carter had brought from Ga – one from his sister Georgia MacIntyre – the gay – frivolous girl once – telling of her good husband & three fine boys – how queer! Kelie Whitman my dear & lovely school friend – who is so gifted with fine feelings & expression by the pen wrote me a sweet note of lasting devotion but mostly of her two bright – beautiful children – George & Lilly – whom all describe so wonderful – fond husband – an Editor &c wish I could see them!

Uncle Dr Hammond now living at old "Gravel Hill" Grandpa's place – wrote me a kind – flighty letter of the fleeting years & unrealized dreams. – [B]ut wishing that I would spend this year with them in cultivating his two sweet daughters – who are said to be superior girls & I would love to see these nice young cousins – Josie & Fannie Hammond – & my good Dr Uncle – but don't know when I ever shall have that pleasure – too poor to go about now!

But it was such a shivvering – cold night & we could hardly get fires made up in the parlors – 'though all the boys & girls came again to practice charades – but Lizzy B couldn't be here to reherse regularly. They went through all twice tolerably well – some doing better than others of course – but girls are so much quicker in memorizing their parts – and comprehend & express them so much better than stupid boys – save Joe & Dick – very (quick [crossed out]) smart!

They danced several sets between for variety to the piano – where I played until my fingers ached – just enough girls & boys to dance one set nicely – Mamie included & Lula – both trying for the first time in Va reel Mattie Orr dances with such ease & grace & stately dignity! looked well – in green silk shirt & magenta Merino jacket &c – After they all departed – She & I sat chatting very confidentially or socially – for I find that she is too cunning to disclose too much – cares more to hear – but she is not very curious & speaks little of other people at all – is unassuming but proud – a girl of fine character & acquirements – but gay & volatile now longs more for society – dress & be one &c now than anything else! her father the Gov. arrived last night – & is a very fond father to her! – they sat talking all night – I must go over & see them. She & Eleanor seemed to sleep comfortably together – but Mamie & I were cold all night

Oh for a milder clime, but 'tis severe now all over the country nearly – having been an unusually severe winter North! We discussed the few young beaux here tonight of course – fear all were drinking a little – Dick & Joe – most refined &

Anthony did in fact go to Anderson to teach school (Vandiver, *Traditions,* 117; Lillian Henderson, comp., *Roster of the Confederate Soldiers of Georgia, 1861–1865* [Hapeville, Ga.: Longino & Porter, 1959], 361).

lively – Jim Munro – a dignified – gentle – nice fellow E Cater – good looking & good manners – but light – Keys – a little obstinate lively – rough chap – acted negro well! Pa, I & Mary Wilhite, nice little tame thing, E.C. & M.W – devoted – Nell – carrying on with the other four I with nobody ever more of course – & Mattie but few yet!

Sat. Feb 17th Still cold – but beginning to cloud up & moderate a little for "falling weather" – I sat by fire all day – Sewing & busy as usual – The Jones departed – Mr & Mrs Witt Broyles here to dine to see how Lula "Dumpy" was who has been sick & still complains of neuralgic pains &c A sweet true woman – clever folks want to remove to Tenn. now Martha told me several little compliments – Old Mr Brock up there saying I was the only sensible woman & real Christian he knew (would that it were more so!) Dr Jim Brown agreeing with him, & he had selected a fine physician beau for me Dr Clifton of N.C. no one else he knew smart enough &c & he may visit here &c! "But all this amounts to nothing!"[34]

Joe Hyde called on Nell – Ma went to see Julia – I dont go out socially enough – shall regret it, perhaps! Pa returned from his weeks visit to Charleston on the train at 9 o'clock – (dark & snowing a little) had made a safe – pleasant & profitable trip I hope – for he bought a stack of goods near $3000 worth – (on credit) which may either save – or ruin him – but I fear – danger as the market is so full & money so scarce! he knows nothing about trading &c 'though he began life with a little store!

He found Charleston full of goods & life & luxury – no sign of war – but Yankees & negro troops there – the latter disbanded & seeking hire &c – vestiges of

34. James Albert Brock, from Honea Path, South Carolina, was thirty-one years old in 1866. His young wife died, leaving Brock a widower. J. A. Brock was Eleanor Reed Davis's second husband and a rather successful businessman and civic booster. His careers included mechanic, bank clerk, and the first president of Anderson Cotton Mill. The Brock house occupied the property on the corner of McDuffie and Reed Streets, previously the site of Echo Hall's rose garden. The Anderson Female Seminary catalog of 1882–83 lists Eleanor C. Brock as the guardian of Daisy J. Brown (Julia's daughter), and it was Eleanor who raised Reed Miller and Lily Strickland, both musical virtuosos of considerable talent (*1860 Census,* Anderson District, 201; Vandiver, *Traditions,* 90, 154, 214, 253, 272, 293, 314; Idella Bodie, *South Carolina Women* [Orangeburg, S.C.: Sandlapper Publishing, 1978], 93–95; F. G. Bevill-Champion, *An History of the Miller Family of Laurens, Abbeville, and Anderson, South Carolina* [Staten Island, N.Y.: Northcote House, 1946]; Jim Walsh, "Reed Miller," *Hobbies* (March, 1958), 30; Frances Mims, "The Story of Lily Strickland 'He Put a Song in My Heart'," *South Carolina Magazine* 38 (summer 1974): 22–25. *Catalogue of Anderson Female Seminary, Session of 1852–3,* 4.

Dr. Clifton of North Carolina has note been identified.

the fire & shelling – disappearing – Old citizens gone back to business "Willis & Chisholm" the most extensive & extravagant – own four large wharves – 200 men employ[ed] – run three ship lines – heavy expenses every way – but must make much money – will lose or make terribly! Willis called – but Col. Chisholm (whose handsome photograph I rec'd) very polite in calling & riding him over the city in elegant Phaeton &c dining with him in style, he so wealthy – travelled & charming.

Pa struck – what would I be – & is there no chance for us to meet &c – can I never win some such jewel out of the three elegant beaux presented to me by others – this week! Never! Dr Carter there as agreeable as ever & was to sail for N.Y. in the "Alhambra"- return in Summer if possible – sent respects to young ladies & would send them music &c May he be safe & successful & worthy & return to us someday – noble "Will o the Wisp!" They had stopped at the splendid Mills house – showed us the bills of fare – containing luxuries we never saw in the backwoods – and just as well but nice to know of – is to pine for many things can never attain & we girls here sigh for city life & luxuries – 'though we might find them most unsatisfactory![35]

Uncle Ned Willis had called on Pa – the active little man of business & standing there, Col Chisholm his handsome young bachelor partner so travelled & stylish & rich & clever – proved very attentive, taking him to dine at their lodgings – in style Bob Baker- distant – as he has proved neglectful to us. Wonder why? Pa took tea with McCay Pres't of Peoples's Bank – & refused many invites – though the people were not so cordial as they might have been – had we been more attentive to the refugees – sorry! I may never have a friend to visit or correspond with amongst them! Shameful – but they assume so much![36]

He called at Wm B. Smiths on the Misses Miller mostly – saw the old man & girls a little while as Mr Elliott happened to come in all reserved & cool – Fan with her betrothed – silly looking she never spoke to him – save the usual greetings all ignored me, though Mr Smith asked Pa to send down Eleanor – but didn't invite him to tea even, – and after they had been our guests so often & appeared such true friends of mine especially. What can they mean – the traitors! Perhaps think I

35. The steamship *Alhambra* was a new first-class ship of the Leary Line sailing from Brown's Wharf, Charleston, to New York City; R. B. Benson was the captain (*Charleston Courier,* July 3, 1865).

The Mills House Hotel, on the corner of Queen and Meeting Streets, offered some of Charleston's most luxurious accommodations. In the words of Southern poet William Gilmore Simms, it attracted "all the fashionable gentry" (Fraser, *Charleston! Charleston!,* 231, 250, 273).

36. Neither Bob Baker nor Mr. McCay has been identified.

rejected Theo &c – or have suddenly risen above – in their own mind just proves the falsity of such a class of sordid frivolous sycophants![37]

I wonder if Theo has much to do with them – or where he lodges & in what employ &c I asked Pa, but "he didn't & wouldn't know!" – &c I thought he too had played false after his months silence – but I should have trusted him better poor fellow – & what will he think of the cool note I sent by Ressie Miller – requesting him to destroy letters & mementoes &c if forgotten – and indeed I doubted if I should ever hear from him again – grew reconciled nearly – indifferent (or forgetful) so used am I to disappointments but I was mistaken in him – for next morn –

Sunday Feb 18th I rec'd a letter from Theo – still faithful & fond & so generous & delicate in sentiment! Poor fellow seemed sad at the fate of his country & city & friends – perhaps found it difficult to get into business – felt forlorn – couldn't express all his emotions – but evidently longed for religion & his absent love to comfort him! Is (might [crossed out]) mine the lot to console him after awhile! For he loves me as none other may ever do – he possesses traits I may never find in another!

A brilliant letter full of fine feelings & expressions – but with a slight tinge of his usual badness – seemed to take a fine view of my feelings towards him – not complimentary to either & asked if I really showed his letters to his nieces &c of which I am ashamed, & how can he sense all this! but he seems to care for me withal 'though he is not satisfied – as my considerations postpone "the orb of his felicity so long" – he can feel no pride & joy in such an engagement – can it be possible that it is one & I involved – strange!!

After midnight he wrote & gazing on "my exquisite tress["] – fair as Endymion's when Cynthia stooped to kiss him on Mt Laturas' – but did I ever think of him & may angels guard "mia casa musica"! I valued his letter & his love most highly & wondered what the end may be – for it seems very unreal yet & I can't help wondering – is there no other fate for me – no one more congenial & suitable or is this indeed our lot, a city home for me sometime with such a name? May heaven direct us all for the best, & bless and comfort my dear friend – & fond admirer of such rare gifts![38]

37. William B. Smith was lucky enough to prosper during the postwar years. The Smiths allowed their daughter Helen to live with the Reeds in the spring of 1865; indeed, Helen was staying at Echo Hall when the Yankee raiders arrived in May, 1865 (Fraser, *Charleston! Charleston!*, 173).

38. The Greek legend of Endymion tells of a shepherd who fell in love with Selene, or "Cynthia" (the moon). Endymion won her heart after a difficult climb, so she gave him the godly quality of immortality, but then she gave him eternal sleep. Emmala probably refers to a popular poem by John Keats.

It was a long, dreary, rainy Sunday – which most people so detest – & I dislike to miss church – but it is a pleasant variety sometimes to sit at home all day reading & scribbling &c

'[T]hough I find that I never do my whole duty – & never get to read as much as I like. The Bible – Mexico – "I find words" – a nice new Infants paper interested me – I solved & made an enigma – but read too many newspapers – some wild Yankee heralds – Pa brought news of Prest. Johnson's conservative speeches – tries to befriend the South as much as possible but the radicals are so violent & may rule the day! A war in S.A. – Mexico & France at dissentions – fashions &c[39]

All nonsense & one account of the Keys trial progressing in Charleston slowly & inpracticable – so many witness[es] down there from here – worn out with waiting – how will it end! But I read too much nonsense so did all didn't teach children as I should – or learn & pray! [W]rote to Julia & sent papers – miserable home I fear We indulged in a delicious pine apple at noon which Pa brought & I sighed for more tropical fruits! George Hagood & Reeves here during the day! Night came & found us all lazy! I had read papers – sang hymns until 'tis now quite late & raining – but much milder – so I must dream of worthy loves &c I read Byron's "Mazeppa" today – a queer; wild thing.[40]

Monday Feb 19th Clearing off clear & cool – but disagreeably windy! Sewing busily all morning – finished my new fasionable poplin elaborately trimmed with black bead trimming – handsome!! Grandpa H here to dine & talk with Pa &c the dear old man! Julia here all aft.- The young folks came again to reherse the Charades – which, they went through with very well – Liz Bleckley Mattie Orr specially & Dick & Joe – E Cater not here too bad! Mrs Wilhite came over – but got vexed because Ma wouldn't come in with her I suppose or nobody knows what – went home in high dudgeon – queer woman! I went over to try & pacify – but

39. The postwar government desired to secure its southern border from external threats, especially from French troops in Mexico under Emperor Maximilian. When the United States exercised its Monroe Doctrine prerogative, Napoleon III withdrew his support and Maximilian was doomed. The United States supported Benito Juarez, the once and future president of Mexico. These incidents ushered in an era of stability in Mexico.

40. George Hagood has not been identified from information available.

John A. Reeves joined the new Reed mercantile endeavor in some general sales and organizational capacity. While his position with the young company is unclear, by 1870 he was head carriage-maker, at what appears to have been a manufacture facility near the home of C. A. Reed (*1870 Census,* Anderson County, 695).

"Mazeppa," a poem by George Gordon, Lord Byron, based on the life of Charles XII of Sweden, was first published in 1819.

didn't say much – she stiff & mean – & silly! Don't know whether or not she will get over it & let Mary act –

I came by Reeves' a moment R passed me there – stared modestly & no bows – queer! At night we had family discussions about the charades & who should come &c always a trouble to decide that here – in trying to be friends with all – we are sure to offend some hope it may all pass off well! Cold & clear & windy

Tues Feb 20th A very busy – but pleasant day at home! Rather chilly & bright all determined on our entertainment tonight – 'though it had to be arranged in a hurry! Of course Pa had to disagree about invitations at the last & we couldn't decide whichever sad to have a select few – to appreciate them or a large mixed crowd for policy – and because I really wished to afford that pleasure to all my acquaintances but was afraid there would not be room for them to see well – &c

I hated to slight anyone – but Eleanor wouldn't consent to have but few & 'twas so hard to select who they should be in this divided town – where old friends are now the estranged ones – but we had to invite some – the Munro's – with whom we had great difficulties, & have not spoken for years until they've made many advances lately – save invitation & as they gave the offense I hated to be first to offer terms – but 'tis just as well I suppose – for I cherish no animosity! Their brother Jim was going to act & seemed so clever, so we had to invite his two sisters & brother Theodore – they came & enjoyed it vastly – it seemed!

Then we brought in the Keiths & Broyles after much hesitation – as part of them had refused to act in the charades &c besides old scores – but tis useless to hold out enmity always, then there are so few gents here – they had once complained to Pa about not being invited here &c – so we gave it to the "Mess. B" – with much trepidation on my part – as to what all they may say pro & con – & if R will think me trying to conciliate &c I hope not – yet I scarcely thought he would refuse to come! I can't understand – 'though he feels ashamed – I suppose – after his conduct – not speaking to any of us – &c – never expects to again I suppose – & he may be laying seige to Maria K as reported neither of them here – but she & others we heard were engaged elsewhere – perhaps at R's – or I wonder what were all the reasons for not coming? Strange but far better so – and I only felt another slight blow of mortification & disgust – the love all gone – forever more I hope!

At last we sent an exclusive list – part of the families interested in the debutantes – & a few others & it proved to be a very happy selection so far as I know – hope nobody so mad! After early breakfast they were taking up carpetts & dusting old parlor & arranging a platform in there with considerable trouble, by our faithful boy Henry. [T]hen the young men came & brought the red curtains from Masonic Hall & hung them – so by 11 the stage was furnished as a little parlor &

all complete after considerable exertion by all! They came to reherse, but E Cater & [illegible] both failed to come & we feared would decline altogether or not know their parts – however they came & did well that night! We managed to get through some rehersal but the boys were so full of mischief I feared we could never succeed Joe & Dick especially – turning every thing topsy turvy – to see my consternation – the scamps! [B]ut they are nice & clever boys – vowed they had to go to school & left early – for the females to go over their parts alone – too bad! & they are always smarter – or quicker than the boys[41]

Mary Waller came in to see how we proceeded – but all was ready – so the girls dispersed to dress for the evg – but after trimming one of Lula's dresses – arranging candles and the dressing rooms – &c I had but little time for myself – It was a fine – starlit evg – when later we saw a splendid Aurora Borealis unrolled in the Northern sky – or rather a bright – soft rosy tint – through which the stars trembled – in undimmed lustre! It was beautiful – but too cold to enjoy it long! I was told of others seen recently – & of a great meteor seen & heard in Charleston lately!

The charade actors assembled first (after 6) & rehersed their parts – all amused at Mary Wilhite's first appearance as an old lady – with silk dress & scarfs, gold specks & dress cap – she looked very well indeed & went through her role with more confidence than we expected! All of them promised to do well – so I found the company had all assembled in the drawing room and after chatting merrily awhile were growing impatient – so I went in & spoke to them – just enough nice people to have a good view of the scenes from their seats –

The old men seated in corner of the parlor – Gov. Orr, Dan'l Brown & Mr Bewley who happened in with Pa & Mr Bill Williams who has long wished to come here he says – so Pa brought him – and he afterwards took them into the tea room where they were too amply regaled with hot punch I fear! Then there was a crowd of children who happened in – families of those who acted – and they were cozily seated in one corner until the scenes were over when they had many merry games[42]

Of course every one greeted me with courtesy – Tom & John Broyles – but no Robert or Gus! Maggie & Sallie Munro – very gracious – Lucia & Bettie Harrison sweet & pretty – Morris – Eugenia Earle – Essie Cater – Nan Keith – Sallie Cresswell – Jennie Robinson – McCulleys – Hoyts – Becky looking very sweetly – Jim

41. Henry was a servant.

42. The mercantile partners of England and Bewley maintained a store in downtown Anderson before and after the war. By 1860 William C. and Catherine B. Bewley, both of Tennessee, were well established members of the Anderson community, with four young children and a thriving business (*1860 Census,* Anderson District, 259; Vandiver, *Traditions,* 82, 268).

right pleasant – &c &c – But I hurried back – Pa threw open the doors and announced the charades – the curtains were drawn (by Henry & Elbert [a Reed family servant]) and Dick Tupper & Ernie Cater appeared – two handsome young officers Gray & Raynor – discussing the merits of a lady love – Kate Williamson. Mattie Orr – who soon appeared – well dressed and elegant – acted well – & Dick – with most spirit – Ernie better than I expected – after not rehersing more – is a nice fellow: – then Pal McCulley as her maid Mary – very fancifully dressed & pretty black wavy hair – did first rate – & Jim Munro with hair powdered & false beard on – hat & spectacles – acted his part as the uncle of Kate tolerably – though he didn't remember well! They got through with the play admirably!

Then came "Contest" – where Liz Bleckley appeared as a plainer maid – courteseying very naturally – Keys McCulley as Adolphus Sparks a city beau – calling to see her mistress – Ada Lackett[.] Eleanor – well dressed & pretty – but not very natural – then Charles Beauchamp – Joe Hyde – a nice little French beau appeared – the rivals quarrel – & finally struggle – old Mrs Lackett – after several appearences – quells them – Mary Wilhite acted pretty well – so dignified & quiet – but did better than we thought she would; her sweetheart, Ernie – quite amused!

After this there was a pause for them to dress – so I invited Jupiter Gibbes on the stage to recite a poem – which he seemed gratified to do – and tried to make quite a display before the Gov – Pa & all – gave us "Virginia & Virginus" the old Roman tradgedy in verse[43] – by McCauley I guess – very fine – quite long too!

After that we presented "Phantom" the last charade and most amusing! Dick & Joe – as Debit & Highdon – Merchant & clerk did well their parts, – then Liz Bleckley as old Mrs Reeves – and daughter Ellen – with matching costume on – looked well, call to get a fan – Tom calls on Ellen – becomes her lover – (Joe H – did this very well) then Keys McCulley as the servant "Julius" – blacked & dressed accordingly – acted his part splendidly – first in soliloquy – when he sang "a little more cider" & danced around in real comic style – winding up with Joe (Highdon) appearing to him as a phantom covered with a sheet – frightening him terribly – and the old lady opposing the match – finally consented – learning he was well off &c and gave them to each other – when the curtain fell with much applause – and the show had wound up with considerable eclat!

We were well pleased with our success in so short a time – and all gave me a vote of thanks for instituting a novelty here in the way of private entertainment – which I hope will not end with this! I was sorry to see curtains – platform & all

43. Thomas Babington McCauley's "The Lays of Rome" is a tragic tale of class conflict amid the backdrop of political turmoil in the year 382 when Appius Claudius raped a young commoner named Virginia and claimed the child as a slave. The act was looked upon as a clear representation of tyranny. The girl's father, in order to spare her from future degradation, plunged a dagger into her heart in front of the Roman Forum and a general rebellion ensued.

disappear so suddenly after our trouble – for the boys were bent on having a dance – and tore it down in hot haste – with coloured help! I had stood behind the curtain as prompter & had considerable fun with the boys & girls – but soon we mingled with the crowd!

To my suprize Dr Tom Evins was here (the first party of his this season) looked well – but behaved very stiffly towards me – scarcely speaking, to my great suprize after former scenes – but the old maids kept him very well cornered – Mary Waller & May Munro – then Pa had him in his "Punch saloon" &c he has perhaps heard the rumour about "his devotion to me" & intends falsifying it – as 'tis now said he is engaged to Eliza Holcombe in Pickens- but I can scarcely believe it yet 'though stranger things have happened & Newton Brown stayed away – being engaged to marry Lizzie Bruce so soon – another queer match – proving how much I was mistaken in their attentions to me – (as I usually am) 'though they may have admired – & both been conscious that we would never have suited – as I feel & rejoice![44]

But so – I am left alone at last with Theo – my only hope – which will end like the others no doubt – and I most fortunate still! Dr Keith & J Gibbes criticized it favorably – Tom B – & Williams – Bill Humphreys – &c then – the next room being cleared they proceeded to dance to the piano – Sallie Munro – Eleanor & I playing for them – Lancers – Gallops – & Quadrilles the order – quite pretty – especially the first & Lucia Harrison & brother – Sallie & Jim Munro appeared so well in the round dances – Eleanor & Mattie Orr &c "Share 'um" is the favorite air with them now – comical!

An unexpected guest was Col. Sam Pickens of Pendleton – who came by invitation of the Orrs – a nice beau & danced well – but was rather tipsy I think – and too rude for a stranger – swung the girls around in the dance – called out vociforously – insulted Jim Munro – unintentionally I suppose – wouldn't allow his sister to dance with him – and the boys grew quite excited – Dick seated Eleanor – Keys Mary Wilhite &c because he swung them around so & those two fiery boys wanted to meet with Jim Munro – to aid him in fighting Pickens after it was over; Gov. Orr & Tom Evins had to talk to all of them to settle it – and next morn – we hear that Pickens apologized! Saying he was "drunk" – how shameful! We didn't expect such an episode in our house – the Munro's concerned too – but they are so (fiery [crossed out]) excitable![45]

44. Eliza T. Holcombe was the nineteen-year-old daughter of D. N. and Elizabeth of Pickens District. By 1870, the Evins home was full with two babies, semi-retired brother Dr. Alexander Evins, and an assortment of clerks and students (*1860 Census,* Pickens District, 87; *1870 Census,* Anderson County, 695).

45. Col. Samuel B. Pickens of Pendleton was the son of Colonel Thomas J. and K. A. Miles Pickens. In September of 1862 the Citadel graduate took command of the Twelfth Alabama Infantry. The people of Anderson knew him as "the boy colonel of Pendleton," because he

Those who didn't dance had left earlier – save a few who had no beau & I fear they had a dull time as usual for I felt too tired to try and entertain anybody much – the children had most fun & old men – but I was glad when they all dispersed – after 1 o'clock I suppose – the Gov. last – all shaven & shorn – quite dignified and consequential looking – not so cordial as formerly Mattie – as lively & social as possible! Our entertainment had been quite a success – except that I was sorry we could offer no refreshments! and of course there were no very interesting beaux and none for me! I was glad to rest –

Wed Feb 21st A bright pleasant day – but we were busy rearranging the house – I had both parlors to dust – change furniture – fix up my music & (a long task!) until I was quite tired – felt sick too – so I only read away the day – Julia here in aft. Sorry that she wouldn't come last night – nor would Lucie & Waller all such old folks with their cares – & she – always cool – Vie had no way to come – too bad!

Eleanor went to Hydes – met Kate Tupper there – off to Charleston in the morning – never to return perhaps and I think it very strange – she didn't call or write or send for me to say adieu – as I'm sure she has not been more intimate with anyone here – then I admired her so much and will always regret not seeing more of her but she cared for nobody outside of her family now – I think, after having lost her lover cousin – Fred Tupper – I think. I wish I could have claimed her as a fine friend and correspondant but it seems I can keep none!

In looking over my old daguerreotypes today I found that Cora Carter & Lettie Durham two school friends I had prized most highly now totally estranged – were lost – stolen by negroes for the cases I guess – too bad! The cold – moonlight came & after a little music & nonsense we retired to rest a very different scene from last night proving that "this lifes a stage – and men & women players" changing every hour – the past to return nevermore! – and yet how many precious hours and opportunities we cast away – and what remains for me in the future? But oh 'tis useless to ask – (not much joy!) and all will come and go too soon – so I ought to accomplish something better – these fresher days! which daily grow more sere! Help me oh God![46]

---

achieved this esteemed rank at the age of twenty-three. Col. Pickens married Anna Ingraham on February 19, 1868, and the couple had six children, all girls (Everson and Simpson, *Far, Far from Home,* 13n, 18n; Simpson, *Old Pendleton,* 192–93; Lander and McGee, *A Rebel Came Home,* 104; Lucas, *Early Anderson,* 73).

46. Old schoolmates Cora Carter and Lettie Durham have not been identified. Emmala loosely quotes from William Shakespeare's *As You Like It,* 1.7.

Pa criticized last night – as passing off very well – could have been much better but what did it all profit – and what can we do to make a living, and share with him the heavy expenses of this large family! I know of nothing for me – yet I ought to be more active I know! Nearly all sick today with colds &c Clif worst!

Thurs. Feb 22nd Half sunny – half shaded & too cold for my comfort! I have tried hard to get off to grandpa's today – as we never go but the horse is ploughing & I can get no company &c too bad but I must do something more profitable than scribbling! John Peter has been here to get a lecture from Pa & know what remains for him to do – after making such a wreck of himself and property! Hope they talked mildly & decided well – to save himself & family from utter ruin! I had a short letter from "coz Pete McD" last night – had first rec'd my letter of a month ago – dictating something for him to write our former friend R.B. to argue some of his views stated when they last met & he has copied my words for him – but they were given so long ago that the feelings have died out – & I've lost all interest

Fear it may do much more harm than good now – as nothing should ever more have been said to him on the subject – what will he think – what will be the issue – I fear to know! He will say & do nothing I guess with his usual stupid meanness but think too much – ! of my promptings & Pete's officiousness &c – hope no harm may ensue! Pete seems to fancy me himself somewhat – the silly boy! Is teaching a country school – wish him success! One year ago & before & since – 'till of late months – how different were our feelings R & I but the change is a fortunate one! A quiet evg –

Friday Feb 23rd Mild and cloudy I determined to make a great effort to get to Grandpa Hammonds today – where I hadn't been in months – no one could go with me – so after much hesitation I made a boy drive me – and almost forced J. P. with me – who amused me all day by his cute questions – showing so much precocious curiosity &c – behaved very well, but lost his knife Pa gave him! I found Lucie (Nardin) and children down there with all the family well

Uncle June came to dinner – right clever – Tom Carter out at work – and company there – unexpectedly – misses Carrie & Lucretia McFall & Eugenia Carlisle – the last a bright – pretty girl – sweet face & manners to whom I took quite a fancy – reminded me of my old friend Nettie Brockman – Carrie – fine looking &c but another full of gossip – yet devoted to her sister "[illegible]" an invalid – slowly dying with consumption – a frail shadow – of her maidenhood – but talked cheerfully – sad! After their departure Vie accompanied me home – (Waller Nardin coming for Lucie & children) We stopped at Uncle Herbert Hammond's to see Julia & all a little while: the young methodist parson Mr George Round – a nice little fellow – told me of Cokesbury folks – &c! but we hurried home & dressed to go out at night to Col Dick Hill's – lately moved here from Ga married my friend Marion – as jolly a couple as I ever saw – full of rude jokes – he is – All the Gaillards there – a few girls & the young clerks about town – clever silly fellows – Liz Bleckley lively – John & Mrs Moore[47]

Jim & Becca Hoyt – looked well – and were very pleasant & happy I think! Gov and Mrs Orr & Gen Ellison Capers most interested me. The Gov as my old friend sat down & had a long social chat – scolding me for not getting married – robbing somebody of a good wife & happy home &c that my standard was too high: – I expected perfection – or too much intellect – would never find it & such a man would never fancy me – I was too smart &c Superior men always married inferior women – all history proved it – John Adams & wife [Abigail] later exceptions in America &c

I needn't expect to look up – but to rule some man – better a poor husband than none &c I would finally wait & marry some poor preacher – but he hoped not – a political man might choose me for a second wife – &c&c he or Capers one – might take that fancy were they widowers &c&c "half serious-half joking" was his long lecture – but his looks and words were so searching as to embarrass me (besides the few listeners) then I knew of my hinted objects of choice & felt it a hard truth that I could not find the congenial spirit we naturally expect, – so Gen Capers agreed for he conversed with me pleasantly on many themes – very interesting & polished manner – mild & sweet face – I was quite charmed with him –

We ran up stairs to watch the young folks play games Gov. Orr & Liz Bleckley followed – but we stopped their games – at last the rude – half grown boys could think of no way to run us down but to kiss us – and several flew at me – I fell back dismayed whilst my two gallant escorts kept them at bay – a real row – I rushed down stairs – but they kissed Liz & locked up the Gen awhile – so that when we were all summoned to supper he couldn't get down in time to escort me and as all had gone in & I found myself left in the lurch – Andrew Osberne offered to be my escort – a fine looking nice fellow but I was glad to greet Gen Capers too – & to hear the Gov inquiring for me – smiling approval!

It was quite a bountiful repast & the last compliment to Mr & Mrs Hoyt perhaps! We enjoyed fowls & salads, cakes & custard, candy & sw[ee]ts in abundance – then the men sat down to fresh supplies & coffee afterwards – most selfishly as

47. John B. Moore, son of Nancy Moore, was a thirty-one-year-old attorney from the village of Pendleton, South Carolina, who became an active participant in Anderson politics, particularly the Democratic redemption of 1876. Clara Y. Moore hailed from Georgia and had three small babies in 1866 (*1860 Census,* Anderson District, 258; *1870 Census,* Anderson County, 687; Vandiver, *Traditions,* 134, 252, 262).

usual – Cards & jokes were the only amusements of the evg – joined in both a little – but always find cards stupid – games of "love" &c where there is no love concerned – with lovers it might be different Keys McCulley was showing tricks – long Bill Humphreys – the only man of pretentions there – devoted himself to silly young Janie Hill – to her evident delight but he was so rude as not to offer to accompany Eleanor, Vie & I – who had rode there & had to walk back in the drizzling rain after 12 – and he living so near – walked home alone – just behind us![48]

Oh the stupid men here – not a bit of gallantry or politeness or sense! or are we so unpopular? No I think they all like me well enough – but don't hold themselves equals – but think us too smart &c and not being invited to our house – they hold themselves under no obligations to be courteous – yet it is very mortifying under some circumstances! The crowd had all gone – save the young men when we started on the long walk alone with little Eddie Belcher going our way – but Capt. Prue Benson offered to see us "to the carriage" with his lantern – little dreaming he had to escort us home – and we were very much chagrined &c – but all forced to yield to circumstances – he came along with Vie & I – very stupid – but we passed the Yankee sentinels in safety – and I told him he needn't see us farther &c & to our suprize he gladly hailed his release & left us in the streets[49]

Other of the charming beaux not far behind – but nobody that could offer their company with impunity! Ridiculous! [A]nd we felt like a set of forlorn, unappreciated females – who seek pleasure under difficulties – and better stay at home – as no one here especially cares to meet us or we them – and we may never have special protectors, – yet it was only stupidity too – for I think they were all friends of mine – & I enjoyed my two married beaux's & the ladies attentions &c at last we were safe in our dark rooms – glad to rest – but amused at the whole affair!

Sat Feb 24th We were awakened by rain – or rather dozed on as late as possible – I managed to get out to breakfast which the others did not but I determined to

48. M. J. "Janie" Hill was the seventeen-year-old daughter of R. S. Hill and the stepdaughter of Marion Hill (*1870 Census,* Anderson County, 458).

49. R. Edmund Belcher, son of Elvira Belcher Brown and stepson of Daniel Brown, was born March 6, 1850, in Augusta, Georgia. A family tragedy occurred in late spring of 1866, when sixteen-year-old Eddie accidentally shot and killed Preston, his eighteen-year-old brother.

Edmund Belcher married Lucy Taylor in 1874. The following year he founded the *Anderson Sun,* and soon changed the name of the newspaper to the *Journal,* before selling the operation. He then moved to Hartwell, Georgia, and founded another paper named the *Sun.* Later, he returned to Anderson to establish the publishing company of R. E. Belcher & Son, Job Printers (Garlington, *Men of the Time,* 23; *1860 Census,* Anderson District, 157; Vandiver, *Traditions,* 83; Lucas, *Early Anderson,* 59).

forget all things in an imaginary world today – as I love to do on rainy days now & then – 'though it is a selfish – worthless expenditure of precious time – perhaps when I might be more usefully employed – yet I get so tired of humdrum realities – & sighing for love & more interesting people that I'm glad to meet all in the world of romance – 'though it unfits one for other realities perhaps

I brought home "Who shall be heir?" – by Ellen Pickering from the hills & shutting myself off in a pleasant room on a cozy pallet read the whole day long – the adventures of a few clever people good & bad – in an English hall – with all its varied pleasures &c familiar to readers – and while I enjoy so much in fancy as I cannot in fact! Two charades "Tyrant & Maturity" were given very well – Rosalind Lerner & R – charmed me of course – and I was so excited over their trials &c that I couldn't go down to dinner – which the children kindly brought me with cake & beer before & wonders at my absorption! Dick T was here to see Nell – and now the rain is over – cool winds disperse the clouds and I find myself scribbling in this bright twilight – the girls dancing in the piazza & I here I've wasted the whole day in inert selfish – unprofitable seclusion – but must join the throng – exercise &c bright moonlight night – but too cold & sleepy to enjoy it – read & sang & chatted a little in the parlor! Jim Munro & Dick Tupper had called for books & see about more charades – which we must have soon[50]

Sunday Feb 25th A bright – cold day but we all went to church once more – at least nine from here occupied our Bap. pews – Julia – Clif & Fan with us for a wonder – ('though Pa & John P – were not – so worldly now alas – Pa rode to Gov. Orr's plantation – discussed business with [J. A.] Reeves &c – too bad! JP has no love for sacred things or places – but is upright now for awhile – sat reading papers – wonder what will become of them – Julia seemed cheerful & I hope enjoyed her church privilege – where she has not been in so long!)

Mr Murray gave us a long – rather dull sermon – or 'twas so cold – we couldn't feel it – for our hearts seem frozen too alas! Not many there, – more at the Pres. ch. today to see Dr Tom Evins ordained Elder – queer – for him! Vie went there – She & Tom Carter here in aft. on their way home – No service anywhere – I sat reading various things – till dusk – rec'd the old "Edgefield Advertizer" – again from Jim Bacon my former gay music teacher – now its editor – after two years

50. *Who Shall Be Heir?* (1840) was a romantic novel by English author Ellen Pickering, who regularly produced novels for seventeen years but died suddenly of scarlet fever in 1843 (John Sutherland, *The Stanford Companion to Victorian Fiction* [Stanford, Calif.: Stanford University Press, 1989], 506.

Rosiland Lerner apparently accompanied Robert Broyles to the charades, but further identification has been elusive.

intermission he remembers me again – full of his usual nonsense – but I would like to meet him again!

Jim Townsend wrote me a nice little letter – has become pious I think, more studious & ambitious &c seems to take an interest in my destiny – & asks if he can accompany our party in emigration to Mexico – 'though Pa will change at once to "Venezuela" from late accounts I think – if anywhere – but he seems to have settled back – content with this poor place – even 'though the vile Radicals are oppressing us more every day – refusing to receive Southern States and members in Congress – but Andy Johnson our Pres't seems to hold on to pure – & bold conservative patriotic principles & motives! how will it all end? We feel that it is not well for us to remain here socially – a disagreeable society to us or we to them – but it may prove best after awhile[51]

Still Pa seems troubled at our not marrying off & there are no chances here! Julia saw her old beau Bill Humphreys today – both much changed of course – but they must remember the past – & it might have been better had they wedded! I tried to write Theo a reply – but scarce knew what to say – as I may get too deeply involved yet awhile – family objecting – and I not decided in my own feelings yet – wondered at Gov. Orr's speech to me the other night "no intellectual man will fancy you – unless from an improper motive" – can that be so in his case – or is he a mere dreamer – could we be congenial? Intellectually it seems that we could – but not morally I fear nor physically – yet time must prove!

I was gratified by the reception of cards of invitation today to the marraige of Hasell Heyward and Fannie R. Smith at Grace Church in Charleston and at her fathers residence afterwards – (our family invited formally of course & with no idea of seeing us!) And this is the last of my once most intimate and devoted friend Fan – after all her romances she has won a proud young heart – of a proud old family at least – 'though I don't know his character, it may be mercenary in seeking her riches alone – hope they may be happy – and I would love to see the beautiful bride – on March 1st and all the gay scene 'though she has treated me very badly – and we may meet – never more as once – so do all my friends forsake me! What will Theo think of it all & will he write me soon? And are we ever to be more closely united!

I finished reading Prescott's 2nd Vol on Mexico – very interesting. The strength & daring & influence of Cortez remarkable with his small hardy band of Spaniards – effecting the Conquest – of the proud powerful Indians – in splendid cities – with all the luxuries of life if not the highest arts of civilization – and such

51. Judge Reed and law partners J. L. Orr and B. F. Perry had all been strident Union preservationists in the prewar years. The community may have held them up to some degree of scrutiny and suspicion, despite their unshakable Confederate patriotism.

overwhelming numbers, – the fate of the proud – generous Montezuma the victim of superstition – was sad indeed! the "noche triste" – on their retreat from the city of Mexico awful – their reception by the brave & true Tlascalans remarkable! bold moonlight night – I sat scribbling late but effected nothing – glad to rest in peace as I've always done so far thank heaven!

Monday Feb 26th A brilliant frosty morn! Up – but too late dressing as my journal is more attractive! I devote too much time to selfish pleasures – books & pen – and accomplish so little thereby – no grand stated object to accomplish, ought to do better & be more useful to those around me! Cora & Mamie got up for school – but Eleanor is lazier than I – accomplishes nothing but flirtations I fear – I just wrote to Theo – nothing wrong I fear – or which I shall regret – though Pa was shocked at my having anything to do with him!

Sallie Cresswell & Charlotte Gaillard came in to see us – nice girls – the first smart & lively, the other so good! We were selecting Charades &c – Mary Wilhite came in to discuss them too, then I was sewing nearly all morn – Witt Broyles here to see Lula who was sick – so he treated her to a cocoanut – of which I had a bite – delicious! I gave some music lessons after dinner – and Beckie Hoyt came in – looking very sweetly – and perfectly happy in her connubial felicity but we could see little of her as the young folks were coming to practice charades again

Dick – Jim Ernie & Keys, Liz, Pal, Mary, Mattie, & Sallie Cresswell came to select characters &c but found considerable difficulty as the boys wouldn't agree to be anything old men & servants especially – the very characters that suited them best – then they became really rude laughing & joking apart – till we were quite offended I was suprized at Dick's want of dignity &c even after they left – we found there was no definite understanding – Mattie & Eleanor undecided between characters – and Dick & Joe about to decline – the [illegible] scamps!

Jim Munro walked home with Mattie – all promised to return tomorrow night Lucie Nardin here a little while – then Mrs Hall & her two sisters the Saints – late – deploring the state of affairs – poor school &c After tea & the girls dancing awhile &c I concluded to go over to see Julia for a rarity! Cora, Lucie & two little darkies went with me in the bright moonlight – we found Johnnie & Julia seated up cozily reading and the children all in bed – very glad to see us – as we all chatted socially until suprized by the entrance of Col. Newton Brown to tell them of his marraige on Weds. – at Townville to Lizzie Bruce – a plain country girl – with whom I used to go to school[52]

52. The name Hall was common to the Anderson area, especially a section of the county known as Hall Township, populated primarily by descendants of an early settler from Virginia named Nathaniel Hall. The identity of this particular Mrs. Hall and her saintly sisters remains a mystery (Vandiver, *Traditions,* 219–20).

He was the elder brother & I the sister of J & Julia who had been accused of each other – and he had some such machinations I think – but fearing they were in vain – he decided to take her – of whom he had no fears – being determined to marry soon ere a complete bachelor! He talked of it so freely that it sounded absurd – yet he blushed some when talking to me – and no doubt we each felt twere better so – as we would not have suited – save that he is a good – energetic useful man such as I fancy – but too queer & prosy, I too highfallutin &c he might think we teazed him some – Julia amused – but he didn't invite them to the wedding – strange to say 'though they wanted to be at Mrs [Helen] Brown's next day!

We drank some nice moss beer & came home – Newton – rising to accompany me to my suprize – 'though we walked home very quietly – no confidence &c 'though he had advized me to marry soon – quite [*sic*] treating lovers badly (2) and astound the people! What does he really think of me? I'm very glad to be still free – cold & brilliant sky! Who will ever care more for me – is it well for T – & has R quite forgotten and are none more worthy & true for me?

Tues. Feb 27th A fine day – Cool in shade – pleasant in the sun – but rather windy! Spent in visiting – Ma & I went in the morning to see Scott Brown first who was sick – saw only Charlotte Gaillard & poor Mattie so silly from having fits – & Scotts nice children; we came then to the Hydes – saw Mrs H. & Eliza (the Halls there calling) pleasant – chatty people – then the Morris' – Mrs M. & Mary – stiff and cynical – In afternoon Julia came by dressed up – quite young and pretty still with all her cares – and we paid a number of calls together – incidentally to John B Moore's – saw Clara – his plain Ga. wife – & Emma East there; then to Mrs John V. Moore's – a nice woman – (Jenny Robinson out) Beckie Hoyt very sweet – and happy in her comfortable room – an Editor for hire – so many papers – that I longed to read and can't – even Willis "Home Journal"[53]

53. Emma East, twenty-four years old in 1866, was a teacher in Anderson during and after the war (*1860 Census,* Anderson District, 258; Vandiver, *Traditions,* 122).

Elizabeth Moore was the widow of Colonel John V. Moore, a prominent educator, attorney, and political fixture in the Anderson area. Before the war, John V. Moore was editor of the *True Carolinian,* which arose in opposition to the antisecessionist *Southern Rights Advocate* belonging to J. L. Orr and J. P. Reed. Col. Moore (Second South Carolina Rifles) was killed at the second battle of Manassas. He had two noteworthy siblings: Georgia became Mrs. de Fountain, according to Louise Vandiver a "well known writer on some of the big New York papers"; youngest sister Sallie Moore Chapin became a Women's Christian Temperance Union lecturer throughout the state of South Carolina. In 1878 "Bettie" Moore established "The Southern Home School," where her sister, Mrs. Shanklin of Pendleton, Miss Sallie Robinson, and Sallie Moore Chapin taught school. The Moores had two boys, William and George (Vandiver, *Traditions,* 28, 51–52, 83, 111, 122, 133, 157, 225; *1860 Census,* Anderson District, 258).

I ran opposite alone to see Rev Mr Spaulding & wife "Mollie" – a plain – smiling woman – but good Baptists – strangers here – who lost everything during the war, & have poor health & no occupation – sad! He is a good little man – a useful pastor I've no doubt & no field for him – when we need great exertions here now! Julia & I went on then – She to Arthur Hubbard's – I to Crayton's – Saw only Kate Maxwell – very pleasant & pretty: – we met at McCulley's again – saw only Pheme & Keys – she dignified & pretty – he explained for some late rudeness &c but I was quite provoked today as he hesitated about acting charades – Dick & Joe declined too as if miffed at something and all were so silly[54]

Yet I didn't wish the girls to be disappointed on their account – we came on home late – by the store first – caught a glimpse of R – &c no bows met plenty of drunk Yankees – disgusting – nuisancing themselves and threatening the boys so that tis dangerous for them to go out at night – Keys & Ernie shot at last night!

We girls & children black & white all stopped in late at Pa's new store which he has set up out of town in the brick carraige shop – too far out to draw custom I fear – but he wants to start Clifton into business – on short profits! now – John Reeves a partner & Tom Crayton to keep it at present all busy opening goods &c today – hope it may be successful – we ate a little sugar & cheese – but had scarcely time to look around! Bright moonlight night and the Charade party assembled at home to read over their parts – but we are still so undecided – lacking several gents – Dick came & chatted with Eleanor in the piazza but couldn't reherse his mother afraid to let him leave her at night since the threats, – Joe too busy &c – and I don't know if they will take any parts at all – others lacking, – then Mattie Orr – sent word her mother was too sick for her to venture out at night – so we missed her[55]

Clara Moore of Georgia was the wife of Anderson attorney John B. Moore (Vandiver, *Traditions,* 135, 252, 262; *1860 Census,* Anderson District, 258).

Willis' Home Journal was a contemporary literary magazine edited by Nathaniel Parker Willis (*Columbia Encyclopedia,* 3085).

54. Robert Arthur Hubbard owned a drugstore on the square in Anderson where there was a soda fountain that never used ice and a splendid toy store in the back. In 1867, Hubbard opened the town's first restaurant, in back of the Main Street Bank of Anderson, and as the years passed he became an instrumental leader of the town's Prohibitionists (*1860 Census,* Anderson District, 157; Vandiver, *Traditions,* 268–69, 271).

55. This was apparently the property on which Clifton later built his own sumptuous house at the junction of the Greenville Road and North Main Street. The carriage shop building was again used as a carriage construction shop by the 1870s, when C. A. Reed's mercantile moved into the Anderson town square.

Thomas S. Crayton (1826–89) was a forty-year-old widower and a single father in 1866. In 1848 Crayton invested a seven-thousand-dollar inheritance into the successful mercantile

Liz, Sal – Pal – & Mary came, Jim & The Munro[s], Ernie & Keys all very lively – but don't act with much spirit yet! they danced twice merrily – Liz sang some funny rediculous airs – She's rather boisterous & rude for some of the refined gents – but 'twas a right pleasant evg – glad now to rest – but I am sorry not to spend time more profitably

Wed Feb 28th A mild sunny day – but I was reading newspapers &c all morn – besides a music lesson to Cora early & practicing – dusting &c myself – Ma & Fan & all out – at the store & elsewhere – Julia, John P. & the two babies – Paul & Lula fixed off about 11 – for Townville – on a few days visit – to Newton's wedding – But he & Mr Walters went up – this morn. and the old bachelor – was married to Lizzie Bruce (about 10 – A.M.) a plain, country girl – no guests & no fun! How prosy!

They would go to Mrs Brown's at night & meet a few relatives next day perhaps – came down here next day to housekeeping! Fred, Sumter & Carrie were brought there to worry us in their absence – To my suprize in the morn – who should call but Misses Maggie & Sallie Munro – so long my enemies! It began before the war – when their brother "Willie" fancied me – & they objected! The society quarrels for preeminence – &c were outrageous, but we've had no intercourse till lately – when they've tried everyway to make up – by approaches at parties &c – then we had to invite them here to see their brothers act – & now they call through courtesy – &c but I don't like much to return it; They were very chatty & smart – but looked sharp & unamicable! – I feel no desire to reciprocate cordialities with such unreliable people however gracious & pleasant 'though I don't like to be at outs with anyone –

In the aft Lucie Nardin called a moment – after a music lesson to Lula sewing &c I went out late to walk – called in at Mrs Dubose's – to ask if they would sell a melodeon – for us to use in the Baptist church but they declined disposing of it, yet would be glad to sell a fine piano, carpet – vases, hanging basket &c which I wish so much that I could get but haven't the means! Several nice old ladies there – Mrs. Dubose, Misses Porcher – queer old maids, Mrs Leonidas & [Bessie] Washington calling – all the ton; soon to return to their native coast although so changed by Yanks & freedmen & rise of democracy – throwing the old aristocracy

---

business established by his brother Baylis F. The Crayton Store occupied the south side of Anderson's town square.

In an 1849 credit report P. S. Vandiver characterized T. S. Crayton as "a Sober, Say-nothing, Cautious man, has not much Sense & knows it, will not venture & is perfectly good." On October 18, 1871 "T. S." Crayton married Nancy Sloan (*1860 Census,* Anderson District, 257; Vandiver Report, Item #2, 1849; Vandiver, *Traditions,* 29, 30, 159, 307; Dickson, *Journeys,* 137; Smith, *Book of the Dead,* 92).

in the rear – as is illustrated by Julia & Fannie Smith with their plain lineage & metallic attractions – winning scions of the families Whaley & Hayward – though I fear they are degenerate specimens – matches of convenience hope there's some love![56]

I hurried home late – but in passing the Arnolds – the old folks & Grace Cochran my schoolmate but whom I've not met lately – they all rather miffed at money transactions &c (owing me for music lessons – won't pay &c) so to my surprize she called me in to sing for her As of old – so I went in wishing to rewin their good graces &c – sang a little – but didn't feel like it – but gents & ladies passed by – whom I didn't care to hear me then – the Misses Adams from Pendleton – down shopping false friends to me too – lately been on a marvelous visit to New York – intend going out to teach &c we hear but I saw nothing of them; Keys McCulley & Jim Munro had joined Lula B & Mamie in the street – first beaux but Mamie was taken for Nell – & she mortified at the mistake.[57]

Stopping in our new store – I saw the small, plain selection of goods – joked some with the widower T. S. Crayton. Clerking there awhile for accommodation – Clif gave me a little candy – Reeves dubious – for our household & darkies – will be the most frequent and least profitable patrons I fear! Fan & Eleanor had been

56. Mrs. Harriet Dubose (1803–79) was a refugee from Charleston, with a home at 15 Pitt Street, and possibly the estranged wife of General Dudley M. Dubose, Kershaw's Division, First Corps, Army of Northern Virginia (Amann, *Civil War Personnel,* 249; Smith, *Book of the Dead,* 110).

The Porcher "misses" were Selina M., "C.," and S. M. of 25 Pitt Street, Charleston, neighbors of Mrs. Dubose, and among the many Charleston neighbors who apparently found themselves in Anderson awaiting the return of services to their war-shattered city. The Porchers, like the Duboses, Cunninghams, Washingtons, Whaleys, Matthewses, and Peronneaus, were among the displaced Charleston elite (Ford, *Charleston City Census, 1861,* 166).

The identity of Mrs. Leonidas has not been ascertained.

57. Grace Greenwood Arnold Cochran served a term as postmistress at Anderson courthouse in the years after the war. Her husband was farmer John Robert Cochran.

G. W. Fant was appointed postmaster of Anderson in 1856, and in 1861 he was commissioned a postmaster of the Confederate States of America, which made him ineligible to hold office under Radical rule. Mr. Fant then worked for the new postmaster, his mother-in-law, Mrs. Williamston, who also employed fellow teacher Grace Cochran.

Grace Cochran also conducted a children's school boardinghouse on South Main St. She served as historian for the Dixie Chapter of the United Daughters of the Confederacy (UDC) in Anderson, South Carolina. She also contributed an account of the Fourth South Carolina at the first battle of Manassas (UDC, *South Carolina Women in the Confederacy,* 181–90; Vandiver, *Traditions,* 13, 123; Smith, *Book of the Dead,* 82).

Carolina and Fanny (Francis) Adams were the daughters of Placidia Mayrant and Dr. Jasper Adams.

to Dr Broyles, among other places – glad to see them – but not I – 'though Maggie Van Wyck said she would like to meet me !! Wonder if she would? Sallie Williams so queer cares only for her pretty baby & wants forty! My gracious not if all were as bad as these here! Boys so poor – can't get into business – cut wood & sold to pay taxes & poor R – What thinks he of me now since Pete's letter and are we indeed estranged forever & is it not best?

At night Mrs Murrays little school being invited to go to her house to see Philosophical experiments – I went along with them – Clif with us up there though very unwell – & I felt so tired & badly – no life to enjoy & didn't know what was the matter – but it seems I was getting sick. We found a merry crowd of boys & girls. – Mrs [Claudia] Murray & sisters Jeffie & Agnes Edwards – nice quiet folks – Mrs Sloan very chatty deploring the state of our church & wanting me to get up a choir &c!

Then dear Mr Murray as he used to do in my school days drew out his Electrical Machine – & though the atmosphere was rather damp (clouding) he collected the wonderful element of nature – which sparkled along the surface when touched down the serpentine cyllander & in the gild facing of books – underneath – making miniature circus ride, bells jingle – conductors & non cond. all interesting then he gave us all the "shock" – twice – after much hesitation on our parts – sudden jar in the arms or throat that was startling – but not very painful! Then seated each one separately on insulators to be electrified by holding the chain – to emit sparks from any part of the body – when touched with a slight pricking sensation – that brought tears to my eyes and amused us all vastly! Atmospheric pressure was next tried by Imersion of the hand – water rising in a[n] actual vacuum and with brief explainations proving the wonders of nature indeed and goodness & wisdom of the Creator – which we don't half appreciate![58]

Then we were called on for music after much urging I tried – having no spirit in me can sing or play nothing but old things without my notes now as no one ever cares for music from home now scarcely – so I felt quite antiquated & powerless to pl[e]ase – with all my musical gifts! The Murrays wanted some old favorites even "Bonnie blue flag"- to remind them of what we had been, & not a "Yankee Doodle" to tell of our ruin – 'though some Yankee officers were spending the evg at Bleckleys nearby![59]

58. Demonstrations utilizing various electricity generating machines were a great source of entertainment (Margaret W. Rossiter, "Benjamin Silliman and the Lowell Institute: The Popularization of Science in the Nineteenth Century," *New England Quarterly* 44 [1971], 602–26; Hyman Kuritz, "The Popularization of Science in Nineteenth Century America," *History of Education Quarterly* 21 [1981], 259–74).

59. "Bonnie Blue Flag" was a song about the first flag of the Confederacy, with a solid field of blue and one white star. Wharton tells that "thousands of people went wild with excitement and enthusiasm" when the song was sung by an Irishman named Harry McCarty (H. M.

They are getting rather rude – threatening to shoot some of the boys in street – halting everybody &c, Cora sang with me tenor &c sweetly – & several of the girls joined in some prime "rounds" – then the children got up some games – "Ladies toilet" Jacke's running Grant's sneeze &c very silly – so Mrs Sloan & I stood them as long as possible & hurried home in the bright moonlight – the young beaux very gallant, Curran Sloan, Edwards Munros John & Billy Clark[e] – the last with Lula & I – the other three girls here with one each – delighted! But I was so tired and glad to rest at home! pleased not to be halted by sentinels met folks going from a party at Caters[60]

Wharton, *War Songs and Poems of the Southern Confederacy, 1861–1865: A Collection of the Most Popular and Impressive Songs and Poems of War Times, Dear to Every Southern Heart* [Philadelphia, International Publishing Co., 1904], 23–25. Diane Ravitch identifies the songwriter as Harry Macarthy, a vaudevillian comedian from Arkansas who simply put words to an Irish folk tune called "The Irish Jaunting Car" (*American Reader,* 143–44).

60. Jackes is most likely the age old game of Jacks, but games like "Ladies Toilet" and "Grant's Sneeze" evade definition.

John H. and William Clarke were the sons of Anderson's tailor and clothing merchant, J. B. Clarke, and his wife, Margaret "Betty" J. Mr. Clarke was a prominent businessman and served a term as intendant, or "mayor," of Anderson (Vandiver, *Traditions,* 29; *1860 Census,* Anderson District, 156).

SEVEN

MARCH

Thursday March 1st And the first day of the welcome Spring which came in like a lamb indeed – half hazy – but so mild & pleasant – yet the spring is backward – no budding leaves yet – a few jonquils & hyacinths blooming. I found myself too unwell to enjoy anything save lolling lazily in the bed in Ma's room – aching as if taking broken bone fever – half chilly – half feverish – as I never know what ails me! [H]ope I am not threatened with a spell of sickness so rare for me – yet all must take their turn! I read & knit a little – pleased to see a little compliment in Hoyt's paper to our Charades – not personal though! [P]oor old Aunt Cynthia – came in on one of her begging expeditions – worried me – sorry we are not able to gratify her numerous wants – or do more for the clever old soul – went to Plantation in evg[1]

The girls & boys came to practice charades – but too late to do much – & I had to rouse myself – amused by some of the characters – Mattie Orr & Eleanor dancing gayly &c – hard to select characters – At night – Mary's Reed & Broyles &c invited to tea with Anna Parker, poor Lula sick & lonely – sweet girl, – much trouble getting all the children here safe to bed – bad, noisy boys & girls not controlled properly – Ma has too many cares – none of us help her enough – Pa went to R R meeting in Newberry today – early start on the cars – gone tonight[2]

Several of us sick – Clif – Helen – Mamie – Cora & I all with severe colds & aches – so not with stan[d]ing the attractions of the soft moonlight without books & pen &c I must cease – drink warm ginger tea take two blue pills & go to rest hoping to be well soon – & more useful! Does anybody think of or love me tonight – even Theo as he gazes on his beautiful niece Fannie as a bride at last – in her satin & lace & jewels in Grace Church with twelve lovely bridesmaids & all the ton there assembled to see her wed a young Heyward – & enjoy the after pleasures at leave – supper – dances &c! How elegant it will be – & Nell & I – are fitted to enjoy such a scene but are forgotten by our false friends – once so intimate here – yet – consider us now too common &c They are vain silly, frivolous creatures – yet I hope may be blest. Does Harry Miller the slain betrothed look down with sorrow on Fan & does Theo sigh for me? But 'tis useless all – I'll never realize such a

1. Aunt Cynthia may be J. P. Reed's younger sister.

2. Anna Parker could be the wife, or possibly a daughter, of James Parker, an Anderson fireman (*1860 Census,* Anderson District, 159).

scene myself & don't care to wed – may heaven direct all for the best! – My old friends are leaving me fast behind – but I'll try to learn indifference and enjoy the present as it flies![3]

Friday March 2nd Still mild and pleasant – a little wind but warm – I longed to be out yet spent the whole day in bed for a wonder, really sick! Last night vomited bile, but not enough to relieve me took another blue pill this morn which seemed lodged in my throat & made me feel badly all day – then I was feverish & languid – cared only to be still & read some when I could

Enjoyed the "Columbia Phoenix" – with its political details opposition between the Democrats & Radicals – on the result of which Southern salvation depends almost – Andrew Johnson our Prest – whom we feared would be very ultra &c takes a bold & noble stand for the good of the Union & civil rights everywhere has vetoed the Freedmans Bureau bill causing great excitement & it will live in history & he be famous! Letters from Mexico & Venezuela still tempting emigrants! I was reading still the first Conquest of Mexico with all its horrid warfare; & looked once at some of my journals in which however I take but little interest, too near & yet so far off when I see what R & I then were to each other – & what total strangers we now are![4]

Mattie Orr came from there here today & up to see me – a fine girl! Joe Hyde called on Eleanor in the morning; Dick T. & Isham Harrison came in aft. To get their parts in charades – Keys McCulley having gone away to our regret! I could only send down notes – Nell walked in town afterwards with Carrie, regretted it much! Mrs Bewley came to see Ma &c – Julia did not return – her children still

3. Henry "Harry" C. Miller enlisted at Laurens, South Carolina, on August 1, 1862, with the South Carolina State Guards, Third South Carolina Volunteers, then served with his cousins Dick and Tally Simpson. He died in combat during the Battle of Cedar Creek, Virginia, October 19, 1864. The family constructed a memorial at the Episcopal Church Cemetery in Pendleton, South Carolina, to a son whose real grave, like thousands of others, lay forever unidentified (Everson and Simpson, *Far, Far from Home,* passim).

4. *The Columbia Phoenix* was a triweekly newspaper established by Julian A. Selby on March 21, 1865. On May 15, 1865, the paper went daily and was renamed the *Columbia Daily Phoenix.* (John H. Moore, *South Carolina Newspapers* [Columbia: University of South Carolina Press, 1988], 199).

The Freedmen's Bureau was the popular name of the Bureau of Refugees, Freedmen, and Abandoned Lands. Created to help give freed blacks the knowledge and ability to become self-sustaining citizens, the bureau provided mechanical training, primary education, and initially attempted to redistribute confiscated Southern lands. In February of 1866 Congress tried to create a permanent bureau, but President Andrew Johnson vetoed the bill, citing his doubts about the constitutionality of an important provision allowing military tribunals to try civilians. Despite Johnson's opposition, a new bill passed in July 1866.

worry us – 'though Newton & his bride have come and gone regularly to housekeeping – queer! Eleanor & I rec'd three invites to attend the Musical Club at Wm Webbs tonight – & I was very anxious to go – a pleasant evg – full moon, would meet nice refugees & hear music I can't often enjoy Sallie Williams, and see R – though he & the Keith's would be devoted no doubt & we strangers – so 'twas best not – Eleanor wouldn't go & I had no escort, dressed in much pain &c – determined to go – but felt too badly & withal had to write an excuse and stay away & this pleasant company so near me – too bad! Yet maybe best! Will R regret? I must lie down too unwell to sit up[5]

Sat March 3rd A pleasant day I felt badly still – so lay in bed all morning to read, forgetting the world around in a novel, but not a very fine selection I admit "Guy Livingstone" a real English story – of College boys & their field sports the English gent's – busy leisure of dissipation & fashion. Guy was a strong – brave man but with all man's faults – two women loved him most Flora Bollasys brilliant but desperate – loved in vain, Constance Brandon a fine – devoted woman felt wronged & released him 'though her heart broke – Each too proud to relent till she was dying & sent to recall him from his headlong career of dissipation in Paris – but they met once more & knew the power of their love – the bliss they had lost – She died happy in his love & he saddened & purified forever cut off by a sad accident in his strong manhood – but saved Isabel & Chaley Forrester & dreadful Bruce, &c episodes – a well written book – but not too chaste did me no good[6]

I had several visitors – suprized at my sickness! Lucie Nardin was very sweet Aunt Anna & Vie later rather intrusive at the time – Mary Waller in evg – Mary Wilhite – a blooming maiden of 16 or more – blushing with first love – so coy & shy – but proving consequential – kindly brought me a dish of custard & cake – very nice for my appetite was returning – medicine having acted properly! Julia came from Townville & sent us a piece of Newton & Lizzie's wedding cake – very nice, – but Pa brought from Newberry some richer slices of brides cake – where he had happened at Col. Simeon Fair's elegant party to Mr & Mrs Pope – she a Miss Harrington granddaughter of noble Judge O'Neal, step daughter to the gay Mrs Nottingsworth I used to know in Edgefield – now moved west![7]

5. The Musical Club was simply a gathering for the express purpose of playing, singing, and appreciating music.

6. *Guy Livingstone* was an 1857 a novel by G. A. Lawrence (Sutherland, *Stanford Companion to Victorian Fiction,* 268).

7. Thomas Herbert (1803–51) and Harriett Neville Pope lived in Newberry County, South Carolina. Their son, "Young John" Pope, was adjutant of Kershaw's Brigade and a circuit judge by 1866. He later married Mrs. Sally H. Rutherford, daughter of Colonel Simeon Fair. Though Benjamin F. Perry did not mention Mrs. Rutherford's name, he did write that

So we were quite treated today, I managed to get down to dinner & hear the young folks reherse "Charades" in aft. 'though I felt feeble – they all looked nicely & were pleasant – nice boys – Dick T so excitable & full of fun & blushes yet so sensitive – a noble youth with all his follies & true to Nell I hope – blushed at any insinuations in acting even – yet forgot himself afterwards & said "I've gained a wife" she ran off – he hid abashed & terrified at what he had said all amused – but of course 'twas soon over – She is pretty & graceful & lucky in winning admiration but Dick's is most true & worthy now if it will continue – though he is too young &c Jim Munro & Mattie Orr looked blushy too Tom (Cater) & Mary W little Theo – flattering Nell – rather lucky that Keys McC – & Joe H – are not engaged this time not so interesting! The last wrote me one more nice little note declining[8]

After they left I finished my tragic novel "Guy" – took supper – but 'though still feeling unwell – went to church at night! Vie H was here so went to the Meth ch – where two nice young ministers are holding a two days meeting Round & Hodges – the first preached a very good practical sermon – such a nice little man & in Hodges I recognized the tall form & mild face I had met in Cokesbury – and the same fine voice in singing – I was glad to speak to him a few words after service of Cokesbury &c 'though I am as much estranged from all those people – as though we had never met – yet so lately & freely! How strange – & why are people so false I can't conceive! Wish Wm Hodges would call

Vie & I were stumbling home nearly alone – gallants unheard of these days here – when the Wilhite[s] called me in – to my suprize as 'twas still quite early – & We

---

she and the colonel married "late in life" and that his wife was "young, beautiful, and an accomplished lady" (John Belton O'Neall, *Biographical Sketches of the Bench and Bar of South Carolina* [1859; rpt. Spartanburg, S.C.: The Reprint Company, 1975], 556; Reynolds, *Biographical Directory,* 292; Meats and Arnold, *The Writings of Benjamin F. Perry,* 2:236–40.

Mrs. Nottingsworth of Edgefield has not been identified.

Judge John Belton O'Neall (b. April 10, 1793) attended South Carolina College and opened a successful law practice in Newberry. Elected to the South Carolina House of Representatives in 1816, O'Neall married Helen Pope of Edgefield in 1818 and became a circuit judge in 1828.

O'Neall was the first president of the Greenville and Columbia Railroad, in May, 1847, then handed leadership over to Colonel Simeon Fair in 1853. Judge Belton ran a spur line from the village of Belton (named in his own honor) to Anderson, where it linked up with the Blue Ridge line to Pendleton (Vandiver, *Traditions,* 181, 194, 261; O'Neall, *Bench and Bar,* 1:xiii–xxv).

8. In a double wedding on October 8, 1867, at the home of Milford Burriss, Tom Cater married Lizzie Burriss and John Clark married Annie Burriss. All of the participants were from Anderson (*1860 Census,* Anderson District, 260; *1870 Census,* Anderson County, 458; Vandiver, *Traditions,* 194; Lucas, *Early Anderson,* 70; see Reed, *Journals,* Appendix F).

went in for vanity & spent a pleasant hour! Mrs W such a queer woman! <u>[V]exed</u> with us week ago – now trying to recall me again – sick in bed – but sending word for her to sing many old favorite songs of hers which I <u>did</u> most obediently for Bill Humphreys & Mary – were there eager to hear me they pretended, & he is really <u>fond</u> of music I think, certain plaintive, descriptive exciting ballads – of the sea & war especially! I like his attention of course, tried to hint of other scenes &c but he seems oblivious to all the past & his <u>old loves</u> – an indifferent bachelor now – but has given up many bad habits & is trying to do his duty as a "Commissioner in Equity" he may do well – no pretentions to gallantry or love now – unless to some very young girls, maybe Mary Wilhite, strange fellow! He was polite enough to see us home this time – & made some excuses about the Hills &c – we had an amusing chat; – he gave me some [illegible] other prognostics learned in the army – & left! We girls chatted too much – all unwell – so rested badly that night – It rained <u>gently</u> awhile – & our Henry's singing reached my troubled slumbers far too soon! (from the yard)[9]

<u>Sunday March 4th</u> A mild – sweet day – half clouds half sun – the resurrection of nature about to begin – a few <u>peach blooms</u> first discovered & bust all looking ready to bust within a day – I saw no trace of life before – fields of grain growing bright & green too! Soon will behold all the bright revelation! After much worry – (fixing off old Aunt Cynthia home with all her bundles on – I sent some tracts hope they may do good – but Ma made some unkind allusion to her & mother &c that Pa felt keenly too bad – I was mortified – & wondered what can be our fate with such <u>connections</u> &c!)

We went to Bap ch in morn a good many persons there – <u>Mattie Orr</u> in our pew as visitor & all the <u>Charade</u> boys there! – Mr Murray gave us one of his labored discourses – but with so many parts – they cease to interest me – and move <u>nobody</u> I fear! In the church meeting later – he left because they had to decide about paying him for the past & providing for future services all so <u>poor</u> – worthless & wicked I fear the few male members – came to no decision, but I wish they could take Mr Spaulding part of the time – who would do us more good – no doubt! Liz Bleckley & I talked some – then I left – feeling sick.

Tom Carter here – quaint chap still is busy farming – but Pa renewing his Mexican fever suddenly thought of sending Tom out as <u>pioneer</u> and with dispatches of

9. The legal custom requiring the separation of equity and law courts in South Carolina was abolished in 1868, the same year the South Carolina Supreme Court was established (Michael Stephan Hindus, *Prison and Plantation: Crime, Justice, and Authority in Massachusetts and South Carolina, 1767–1878* [Chapel Hill: University of North Carolina Press, 1980], 21, 23.

inquiry &c – he assented – is a first the one for wild adventure cool & venturesome & quiet – it might do well but we hadn't time to decide and can't tell if it would be wise for us to leave all comforts here – with promise of better times if Andy Johnson's policy succe[e]ds perhaps – to make this great move – to such a troubled govm't – with all its natural attractions – ! Direct us best Oh God!

Pa, Ma & children rode to the plantation – old aunt Milly sick – I lay in their room to keep warm – but read & slept – felt too unwell to go & hear the end of Mr Murrays sermon said to be very good & Eleanor was sick with headache &c Clif with cold – Vie complaining generally – all ailing none serious I hope! At night she & I would venture again alone to the Methodist Church – little negroes behind after much trouble for they won't mind a word – are so mean & lazy & impertinent all of our 21 – whom we have to pay so much to no profit – who get nice goods out of the store to eat & wear – (knocked off wages, and we can get nothing – & they are so insolent – wont even sweep the house if told &c – can't tell what will become of us all!)

We found a crowd outside of church during prayer – Wilhites & Humphreys called me – we chatted a moment he thought Mrs W & I both crazy out in the shawls & sick &c A full house – for we so rarely ever have night service here! Two nice young parsons – they led the singing so well & all joined in heartily the different parts sweet! Then Mr Hodges preached a very good sermon on "text" Beloved ye are the sons of God – Yet ye know but in part – can't conceive of what it shall be hereafter &c (not literal) full of pretty fancies – & good expressions – a sensible review & apt illustrations though rather homely for his flowery diction – yet not well balanced some ludicrous remarks: – with study & finish will make a superior preacher yet he is so earnest has such a sweet, soft, pursuasive voice, such a trusting – saintly look – and sings beautifully – a sweet – queer hymn alone – of the glories of heaven real Methodist fashion – delightful! I shed tears over it whilst some laughed at the novelty to them

They must have felt badly that no one answered their appeal to join the church – for it seems that no one in this hardened commun[i]ty will ever be moved on religious matters, again! I long to see & feel it all once more! Was glad of the sensations produced tonight – some better thoughts of heaven & holiness & these good young divines & all the blest I may meet there! Wondered if R would be one – for he sat across the way looking a perfect stranger & really repulsive to me now! Our eyes never meet – he's ceased to think of me at all – but he is so unworthy – glad I'm indifferent – still I hope he may be saved & we can meet in purity & love hereafter!

Maggie V.W. too whom I used so to love – sat near me – never looking – but listening to me sing I fancied – & spoke to me a few words in passing – but we're parted too for aye! The Wilhites were here waiting for us – but Dick Tupper was so polite as to offer his escort – & we glad to accept it – the polite little fellow – so manly too, – we chatted only socially the short way home & he handed me a bundle for Eleanor "containing 'a monkey he said' – yet we found it cakes of cocoa nut candy" when she opened & dispensed it stintedly – delicious & he so clever! Kate had it sent to him! Wish I had some nice friend or love to treat & pet me wonder if they'll ever be more to eachother hope so! if well Nell & Vie took pills & went to bed sick – vomitted &c & suffering – but all amused! I feel feeble still – but sit here scribbling alone in the cold at midnight – when I ought to be resting for work tomorrow! Moon & pale clouds struggling without. Adieu!

Monday – March 5th Bright & pleasant day! but I felt still poorly – Aunt Anna & June here all day – he started to Augusta next day – In morn – I had the pleasure of visits from the two nice young Meth. parsons – George Round & William Hodges – with Julia Hammond – but Vie talked to her mostly – I to the gents – both of whom I had met in Cokesbury – Round long ago – faintly remembered a pale little fellow – sensible & practical; Hodges tall & slender less prosaic in his expressions – both lively and social talking of many things – teazing me of beaux in Cokesbury – "Whit" especially – made me rather twinge to hear his false name, for he had seen his attentions to me – and spoke of all our music & pleasure – (yet heard I was engaged to someone here!) urged me to sing for them and seemed to enjoy certain songs very much, they joined in one or more ballads – "Beautiful Star" &c for he can sing any part finely – Yet it needed the sweet tenors we had down here!

After a merry visit they departed, he asking me to come again to Cokesbury – but I dont know that I ever shall? Vie walked on to Mlle Herberts R's in aft – where the three were to go home with her for the night & she seemed to anticipate great pleasure – wouldn't let me go! Julia here several times today – but saddened again by her many trials. Eleanor was sick all day – sent for Waller (Nardin) – & took medicine – he gave me blue pills – one of which nearly choked me at night! After tea the "Charaders" came again – their last rehersal here perhaps – all very free & lively – went through their parts very well – in the four charades – amusing![10]

Then danced a little – lancers &c Mattie & Jim Munro, Eleanor & Isham Harrison ventured in the round dance together Dick didn't like it – he lingered last to quarrel with E! We had some nice custard & jelly arrangement which all seemed to relish, – then all sang a few songs to the guitar, Ian Cater having a very good

10. There were two Mrs. Herberts in Anderson in 1866. Harriet Herbert, wife of Methodist minister Thomas G. Herbert had three children, all under the age of ten. Elizabeth H. Herbert of New York, was in her forties, and her husband was born in Germany (*1860 Census,* Anderson District, 158, 180; Vandiver, *Traditions,* 50).

voice – singing a song from Moore – but they had to leave sooner than desired to accompany some of the ladies![11]

Tues. March 6th Cooler – some frost – but calm – growing cloudy I fear – None of us well today – Clif, Mamie – Nell & I all complaining & languid – but more lazy I fear – Ma went over to Julia's & she was here in aft – sad at her renewed & hastening trials, JP drinking again the wretch – no means – rents & wages coming due – no wood – no food – hope gone – garden untouched – look to leave &c dreadful trials, May God preserve and save them! I lay reading papers &c at my ease had to fix a dress for Eleanor &c

At 7 in aft. Nell & I had to get up and walk out to Gov. Orr's – Mary Wilhite along – a tiresome walk The small band soon assembled – and rehersed scenes gaily – Mary Waller &c there – a nice platform – curtains & all prepared – we hurried through and came home late – the boys had left Eleanor & I alone very strangely – so we were frightened getting home late and met Ian Cater who turned back with us very politely – but the mean Yanks were storing up some excitement – little Jim Bewley having come in and reported that nine bushwackers had attacked him he shot one &c – his father & 15 Yanks went out in pursuit & found none – (save tracks &c) yet nobody believed it – Dr Tom Evins made some hasty remarks about it – and was arrested at once and confined in jail until 9 – at night – the citizens quite excited! but could say nothing – he was examined next morn & they apologized! I know the Dr was excited – hating them so! Felt tired & sick at night.

Weds March 7th A bright day – rather cool – after a little work &c I went to see Lucie & then Julia – stopped at the stores and got few little things – cologne – candy – letter paper &c – treating myself – as Col Davidson had sent me the thirteen dollars owing for Ella's music lessons – but I have to pay up old debts – but I want many more things than I can get of course – Still I'm not covetous & don't mind it much! I took a pair of garters from Pa's store – & a chat with Tom Crayton –

I had recd. two letters from old school mates; Bell Latimer wrote of Ella Blackman being married to William Anderson – & others about to be &c a sweet girl we used to know so well – wish she & Nettie happiness – Sue McMillan wrote me from Barnwell – the first since Sherman's raid there – she has been cut off from communication – all reduced to poverty, hard at work – but have a cheerful – her brother Frank dead. [T]he rest at work – Carrie Priester & other friends married down there – the mania seems prevalent everywhere![12]

11. Ian Cater may have been a Cater family member residing in Anderson.

12. Bell Latimer was the wife of Asbury C. Latimer, congressman for the Third District, who later managed the Farmer's Alliance Store of Anderson (Vandiver, *Traditions,* 182, 195).

We were busy dressing all aft – to go to Gov. Orr's at night to our Charades again – but we were a long time getting off or deciding who of the old folks were to go at last only Clif & Fan went with all the girls – we took two trips in the little wagon – [H]enry driving – so drove out in style – but 'tis so far to walk & no escort & no horses for the carraige – We found a scene of gay confusion in the "green room" – the boys & girls carrying on so much fun and badness – Dick Tupper especially – with somersets &c – an excitable scamp – rather rowdy sometimes I had him wash his face once & having nothing to wipe it on took a coloured woman's apron – ridiculous! I laughed & tore my dress hiding!

We all were highly amused at Liz Bleckleys ludicrous appearance as the black servant Lillie – in "Masterpiece" – the best charade – where Dick & Jim Munro were artists Mattie Orr! (Nellie – the sister & love – placed herself in a picture frame &c splendid & well acted! Liz is inimitable in her lively characters Dick expressive – Mattie & Jim made love very naturally – he even called her "Mattie" by mistake I think "'Tis an ill wind that blow nobody good" – excellent – Theo W made a fine Irish waiter – Mike – Isham H – landlord – Liz & Eleanor Mrs & Fannie Myrtle – Dick Paul Edmonds her lover Jim M rival &c they dance &c "Bandage" Mary W & Pal McC take little misses could hardly be heard, – nieces of old "Anteek Yellowleaf" – (Ian Cater acted old man very well – coughing &c – band of serenaders he threw something at their heads – apologized & sang "Auld lang syne" – good! In "honor among thieves" – he was the brigand Alonzo di Cordobella – brilliant costume – red, green & gilt – plume & hat & sash & arms – robs (Mattie O) Mrs [illegible] of jewels – Isham her husband – Eleanor her visitor Mrs Beaumont & son Clarence – Sammie Orr acted very well – Theo – landlord – all very good – but not memorized too well & rather hurried – & confused

I was tired of being prompter & seeing nothing but 'twas just as well – I enjoyed behind the scenes better than before – though I rec'd no credit for getting them up – A large crowd of all ages assembled in the spacious rooms as witnesses – and the dancers were glad enough to quite [*sic*] charades & spring into its bewildering mazes – as the Pen. Col'd band played gaily – ham bone – "Shear um" &c they were getting rather demoralized. Roving round dances best, Mattie with Jim Munro & Gus Van Wyck – Eleanor with Isham Harrison I hope it won't become general – for 'tis wrong.

I soon tired of looking on the dance but found no other pleasure a selfish crowd – sat in cliques & cared for no other – none seemed to admit me very readily –

Ella Blackman was the wife of "Major" William Anderson, who must have died very soon afterward; she later married Balie Barton or "B. B." Breazeale (Sallie, *South Carolina Troops,* 662, 666).

Carrie Priester has not been identified.

Gibbes, Keiths, & Broyles one R.B. looked nicely, but we scarcely glanced at each other – I thought but little of him & what did he think of me? Strange how totally estranged we are in one short year! he only laughed with Sallie Gibbes, but escorted Maria Keith who was brilliant as ever – stole Dr Tom Evins off a long time – he & Dr Keith Capt Parker Bill Humphreys & Jupiter Gibbes talked to me a little but not pleasantly – or freely![13]

The last had recited "Brigon on the Rhine" – to close our performances – fine! Fannie Earle was rather critical – and nobody very agreeable to me – the Munro's trying to be gracious – even the old lady – Mrs Orr kind giving me coffee &c Mattie elegant & graceful – but too gay to think of ought save dancing – so I was glad to leave there – (one stranger Mr Davis – of Abbeville – had made himself interesting to Mamie (how she is coming out!) and I like becoming acquainted with people but did not here) our wagon was gone – so we girls had to join Mrs Wilhite walking home with Maj. Humphreys (save Eleanor) bringing him away from the dance to his regret no doubt & to lead Mrs W with all her gracious and queer ways – but they seemed to understand and amuse each other! I guess he pities me as a forlorn old maid without an escort & thrown so often on his kindness unsolicited – 'tis too bad but cant be avoided – he is clever – so after the tiresome midnight jaunt we were glad to get safe home to rest anyway – Isham Harrison later with Eleanor – Dick furious[14]

Thurs. March 8th Bright & cool – lazy & languid all day – not well – sewing & reading &c a little – Julia here in evg – seemed worried – the boys wrote to ask us about Charades &c – so as the fixtures are still there & Mrs Orr anxious we determined to have them again tomorrow night – sent for the party to come & reherse – nearly all here – determined on certain ones but are apt to change – discussed it all laughingly – the hurried dressing &c last night! Hard for me to waste time on all this nonsense – can scarcely decide to please them all & yet no thanks or kind regards for it all I fear no more love or joy for me!

Pa came from Abbeville Court – but little done – generous – took Ma & children to the store – bought shoes & cloth – sugar cheese candles &c still not half what we need for this large family hard to keep up! he is very kind to us! Saw some of the Hodges – heard of Miss Floride Clemson creating a great musical sensation

13. Louise Vandiver tells of a mysterious Captain Parker from Charleston who had been reduced to teaching in Anderson after the war (Vandiver, *Traditions,* 128).

14. William C. Davis of Abbeville would play an important role in the lives of several Reed women. Davis was a close friend and business associate of George Miller, Emmala's future husband. He also took a liking to sister Eleanor, whom he married soon after the wedding of Emmala and to George Miller. He did not live long and is usually mentioned as Eleanor Brock's first husband (Ware, *Old Abbeville,* 228).

in Cokesbury – so I'm forgotten there no doubt! Such are life's changes! Cold & late – must rest and hope for better days! The frost will kill budding fruit I fear – a few blossoms out[15]

Friday March 9th A disagreeable – blustery day – and I couldn't bear the idea of going out again at night – the novelty of Charades &c worn off – but invites were out from the Orr's to nearly everybody in town – so we had to go again – Busy all day fixing up Eleanor as usual – who puts off everything to the last to get help! Fan went down for Vie – but she was too unwell to come so Aunt Anna & Willie came up to attend them – Mrs Belcher here in aft. but I was absorbed again in a little novel for recreation "The Yellow Mask" by Dickens – exciting of course but I am getting up too great a love for such false and delusory – fleeting pleasures – finding so little in real life![16]

Eleanor & I rode out to Gov. Orr's after 6 – where we were to meet the crowd and reherse – they were late coming – yet we romped about in the vacant rooms and had plenty of fun behind the scenes throughout – for after a partial rehersal in confusion "and taking lunch in there all together – bread & butter" coffee – tea & cakes – the crowd assembled – some new people – Pa there – some of the Whitners, Ruccors, Hoyts &c who hadn't seen our last Charades – others who had not seen the first & as Keys McCulley & Joe Hyde had rejoined us we had to repeat their old scenes also Pallie & Mary W having but one each as Ian later wouldn't have Bandage & no one desired it much –

Mrs & the Misses Munro were most officious & useful in the supper – charades & every thing, and very polite to me – queer after all our squabbles – Jim M. is a nice fellow – so dignified, Theo acts the Irishman & very well. I had to sit by as prompter all night – a tiresome & thankless place – enjoyed no front view &c but the boys & girls all amused me asking for help &c – it took some of them terribly long to dream – Eleanor especially but she was in three scenes, Mattie, Liz B. & Dick T. in four each kept them hurried –

At last we drew the curtains for "Phantom" – Keys as negro Julius very funny well acted. Joe Hyde as beau & ghost – &c "All is fair" & Dick & Ernie nice young officers – Jim Old Man – Mattie in both these contests – Eleanor &c Keys with

15. Floride Elizabeth Clemson (1842–71), daughter of Thomas Green Clemson and Anna Maria Calhoun, was a granddaughter of John C. Calhoun. Floride Clemson was an accomplished pianist and vocalist of considerable repute and often entertained audiences during her travels. She did visit Cokesbury, South Carolina, in early March 1866, but the visit was a short one and the only located mention of music is a reference to a gifted music instructor named Mrs. Ford (Lander and McGee, *A Rebel Came Home,* passim).

16. *The Yellow Mask* (1855), a tale about Renaissance Italy, was written not by Dickens, but by English author Wilkie Collins (1824–89).

his fancy conundrums – "honor among thieves," brilliant – Mattie a matron – bandit Ernie "Cordobello" – crowd, Sammie Orr as Clarence – good – Eleanor his mother a favorite scene – all introduced

"Tis an ill wind" &c Isham H. Landlord – Theo M. – Eleanor & Liz – & Dick & Jim – &c: the funny dance and broken crockery! "Masterpiece" last & best again Dick T. as the artist George – good, his sister Nellie – Mattie – Acted & looked well – made a pretty picture, Jim Munro – Harry her lover – dignified & made love very naturally (may be in earnest there) Liz Bleckley – as Tillie the black servant – quite inimitable – her fright &c too funny – all roared! She & Keys were cut out for the stage as Comedians!

Jupiter Gibbes meanwhile had recited Tennysons "Dream of Fair Women" – fine but tame in comparison! The coloured band had played dances &c between when my troupe would whirl off dancing – Eleanor & Dick had by plays of jealousy &c – meanwhile too Mattie Orr's nice silk dress caught on fire – Dick extinguished it & burnt his hands – this with the excitement of the occasion – Eleanor refusing to dance with him & favoring others – the pall still in his face overcame the poor – delicate – finely organized youth and he fainted – was borne up stairs with great excitement, but I fear Eleanor displayed too much feeling before the crowd – too little to him – for he is a noble fellow & devoted to her now[17]

The Orr's & all stuck with him – Mattie so grieved, about his hand – he got home late at night – worried his mother & sisters no doubt – sick next day & worse than all lost a little memorandum book he prized with private notes in it – Eleanors &c I guess – too bad! But as the scenes were over & they plunged into the dance – I didn't stay long to witness – tiresome to me who can't participate – and a trial to meet so many selfish spirits who don't care to entertain me even after I'd taken all the trouble of the affair!

All of the Broyles & Keiths there – but so devoted to each other – saw nobody else! R. with Maria the first time I'd ever seen them together – not a glance for me – she was brilliant – he lively and looked well but how felt? I was indifferent & rather scorned Isham & Jim Munro knocked down & broke a nice lamp last got his hands burned! A vinegar jug was smashed &c! Yet Mrs Orr insists we shall renew the fun soon – Sorry that the Gov. is still away! I spoke to several ladies, & Bill Williams talked with me a little of his wifes (Sallie B.) hearing & loving the operas he would send me music &c all a farce – but Pa & aunt Anna grew tired very soon – I didn't care to remain there as I was – 'though sorry to leave the gay scene so early – Mamie provoked for she was having a pleasant chat with Mr Davis again –

17. "A Dream of Fair Women" was a poem by Alfred, Lord Tennyson (Strange, *Poetical Works of Tennyson,* 53–58).

Yet we all had to go (-1/2 / 11) Ella Gaines with us – a long, rough walk home – but glad to get there & rest, Eleanor stayed all night – had plenty admiration & fun – slept half of next day &c Is there no more joy in store for me – no congenial spirits never more! Nell had a nice letter from Dr Carter – in New York – hope he may return & all be well with them!

Sat. March 10th Cold & bright – all up late worried about poor Julia's trials – Ma went down there! Aunt Anna & I sat sewing all day. Mamie went on a fishing excursion &c with the Clarkes, Crosby's & Truitts. I'm left out even there – very glad though not to go out – love quiet times at home best now – busy all day Eleanor home at noon – poor Dick had come here to ask about his book &c – lost still (found) chilly twilight & lovely to me – I must rest.[18]

Sunday March 11th Rather cool today – but sunny and calm went to Bap ch in morn – heard Mr. Spaulding preach a very good little sermon – urging Christians to be more earnest in their duty – I wish we could all do better – Joe Hyde came home with Nell – Bill Humphreys told me that he was coming to join my S.S. class &c – Grandpa here to dinner – Tom Carter in aft. Aunt Anna & Willie at night

Went to Epis. ch in aft. a crowd there to hear Mr Elliott again who had returned from his visit to the Convention in Charleston – where he had attended his brothers funeral too – Gen. Stephen Elliott – & the physicians forbid his preaching any more – delicate health – so he comes again but to leave them soon – what a trial it will be! He was so elegant & spirituelle [*sic*] looking – preached a delightful sermon on "The expectation of the righteous shall not fail through Grace"[19] &c drawing most definite distinctions between desire, expectation and hope – but that all earthly prospects contained two blights in the bud – but I can't remember all, only know I was impressed with the unsubstantial things of this life and longed for the perfect fruition above! The choir very good but R. kept himself hidden from me! – Hoyt & Becky walked on home with us[20]

Pa was suffering with rhumatism today Clif & Fan had sore throats – all idle & ailing – Nell especially Julia & children here all day no cook at home – but she had

18. In 1860 every Truitt in South Carolina resided in Darlington County, and most of them were J. C. Truitt and his large family (*Eighth Census of the United States, 1860 Census*).

19. Proverbs 10:28.

20. General Stephen Elliott, Jr. (1832–66) was the son of Stephen Elliott, first Episcopal bishop of Georgia and the brother of Rev. John Elliott. He was serving in the state legislature when the secession crisis found him commissioned a captain in the Beaufort Artillery. In command of artillery and infantry units throughout the war, Elliott returned to South Carolina and won reelection to the state legislature. On March 21, 1866, at age thirty-three, Elliott died from wounds sustained during the war. (Faust, *Historical Times,* 239–40; Amann, *Personnel of the Civil War,* 1:253; Boatner, *Civil War Dictionary,* 262–63).

to go back to her worthless husband at night! I must reply at once to Theodore's splendid letter rec'd this morn. Eight pages so spicy and elegant – yet with tinges of his bitter spirit and impure allusions &c – yet he was so classical & expressive with a deep tenderness for me & generous in view of my indifference &c Said my letter "came to him like extreme unction to a dying man!" his brightest & best – "I needn't turn up my pretty little nose at matrimony for a man of his deserts – others wouldn't be so nice!" when would his probation end – yet he wouldn't wed me to indigence & humiliation – knew that means were necessary – was struggling for that or else would give up all pretensions to my hand & happiness! Don't let him languish for a reply "most loving & dutiful knight" – &c Didn't attend Fan's wedding – a quarrel with his brother – too bad (they've all betrayed & deceived me too!) lived with a bachelor cousin & did business for him! &c – I am gratified by the devotion of such a gifted man – and may one day find it my greatest joy May all end for the best with us both, Oh God!

Monday March 12th A wild, pleasant day – Showery in the morn – so the Mary's didn't go to school Aunt Anna & all of us were sewing busily all day – making up dresses – reading in the morn of Mexico &c sang some &c knit a little – Anna & Eleanor went to see Julia – At night Nell & I had a call from two ambitious beaux – James ("Jupiter") Gibbes & Joe Adams who had asked Clif in the aft if I was at home – so they came and we spent a very pleasant evg – to vary the everyday monotony of life – yet 'though they tried to be sentimental &c We couldn't get up any real romances – as they were not ardent & true enough perhaps –

She & I not reciprocal – neither very romantic looking – but short – plain bachelors addressing us in pretended words of admiration & flattery such as they had used to dozens of other women more or less credulous! At least so I judge 'though it may be wrong, – glad they gained no great advantages over us – As Nell is experienced in all the tricks of love & flirtation – and I have been deceived by man's falsehood & guile – enough to be on my guard – 'though it is hard for me [to] understand them – or be unkind – or skeptical when they assert anything.

Mr Gibbes is a dark little man with good manners – gifted with the poetic spirit of memorizing & reciting beautiful poems – he gave us tonight a love scene with a gypsy girl from Bailey's Festus – very pretty but Fan's baby crying above destroyed all the effect; he recited then Requier's new poem on "the ashes of Liberty" I believe fine sentiment! But he recited more touching "asides" to Nell – and made love most beautifully but in vain – for she only laughed in his face & can't appreciate a true, gifted spirit I fear unless real courtiers in form & manners &c (Dick T had been here all morn – still most favored!)[21]

21. "Festus" (1839) was a poem reminiscent of Goethe's *Faust* by Philip James Bailey (1816–1902) (James Vinson, ed., *Great Writers of the English Language: Poets* (New York: St. Martins, 1979), 46–47.

"Maj. [Joseph] Adams"- now practicing law in Pickens very successfully he says – came down to make his debut in the C. H. as this our regular old fashioned court week – once more in And. with a judge – (Moses a Jew from Sumter – lately elected – formerly very rare for that outcast race to be promoted into ranks of office here – now more common!) with his black silk English robes escorted by the Sherriff with sword & cocked hat according to the old S.C. regime – not lately followed – but done for effect before this garrison – 'though he had to borrow a U.S. sword – Emblem of our subjugation Alas! Some lawyers here not much business yet – Pa & Gov. Perry spoke today &c &c[22]

"Joseph" was looking more dignified & talked better – rather fresh & fair & good looking – but too short & stout with that silly smile & smoothe tongued flattery that is second nature with him, his insincerity rendered him almost contemptible – But he is ambitious & studious and will rise, to ease and emminence in his profession no doubt! I don't know what to think of him – Ever since he first came here ten years ago nearly (1857) to teach a Military Academy – having first graduated at the Citadel in Charleston –

He had seemed to be an admirer of mine off & on – Sometimes too attentive and impertinent in his overtures – then cool & rude even – in his slights, addressing many women meanwhile pretending to – always rejected I think – 'though I doubt if he was ever really in love or came to the point – as he never has with me very definitely – but I always thought he really fancied me most at heart & circumstances of family & fortune &c prevented advances – then we were not wholly congenial & he was obnoxious to Pa & Clif & all my friends nearly from his hypocracy & assumptions, besides his queer mother & sisters – he told me of Carrie & Fannie having been North recently to see the wonders of New York in the musical world especially their voices pronounced superior to any prima donna's there &c That they wanted me to come & visit them in April (he did especially – could be home then!) they would form a mountain party from Pickens this summer – & I must be of the party – that would be pleasant perhaps!

22. Franklin J. Moses, Sr. (1804–77) graduated from South Carolina College at seventeen and was admitted to the bar in Sumter, South Carolina. He married Jane McLelland. After serving numerous terms in the state legislature, in 1865 Moses became a circuit judge and in 1868 was elected chief justice of the South Carolina supreme court. Many contemporary peers found Moses acceptance to be excessively conciliatory, but Moses, like J. L. Orr, Ellison Capers, J. P. Reed, and many other South Carolinians, felt that he could do the most good by working within the federal government (*National Cyclopedia of American Biography,* 12:176; Barnett Abraham Elzas, *The Jews of South Carolina from the Earliest Times to the Present Day* [1905; rpt. Spartanburg, S.C.: The Reprint Company, 1972], 197–99). In 1872, Judge Moses' son, Franklin, Jr., was elected governor of South Carolina, ushering in two years of unprecedented corruption and mismanagement.

He had regretted much not seeing our Charades – complimented most highly and then he seated himself beside me at the piano to hear many songs – his old favorites "My Soul is dark" "Sleeping I dreamed love &c" "He had dreamed of me a thousand times" – had never swerved from his allegiance to me in nine years, circumstances prevented his following the dictates of his heart – such circumstances which enraged him in his lonely bachelor home in dull Pickens – he had tried to love Fannie Smith for her gold & failed (the wretch!) had been true to none but me & I was so cruel his ghost would haunt me – he wanted to call on me tomorrow night too – but couldn't come again without a pretext (to avoid gossip &c) therefore wanted me to invite company here & other ladies he would like to meet for if he called on any of them seperately (Keiths – Gibbes &c) it would be a wasted evg – when his heart was here – but I wouldn't promise to encourage any such nonsense – only laughed at his advances & he was piqued I saw – yet he was more sincere than usual in his advances for he blushed & flattered & looked as if he really loved me a little & I was rather pleased of course[23]

What woman is not by the devices of gentleman – with pretentions to courtesy & chivalry. He is a moralist – no bad habits I think – ambition for family & distinction – &c – yet can it be that he was only trying to deceive – and get me implicated – in revenge for demanding my type of him in Pendleton &c? Or would he willingly gain & resign me I don't know what to think of the queer man! He kept insisting on bidding me good night behind the piano in order to secure my hand to kiss as he used to do I guess – I tried my best to avoid it – but he persisted so called me cruel &c &c – at last he seemed to grow determined & seized my hand holding it forcibly until I became vexed & abashed as Gibbes no doubt saw the manner – so I commanded him to "stop" & jerked my hand away & we rose without his having gained any thing – yet he muttered something about coming tomorrow night &c and with mutual compliments they departed at a late hour – our quandam lovers – whom we may see & hear of no more and 'tis just as well!

What would Theo think of this? And what if I was finally tempted to yield to his persuasions if he perserveres – and would it be well for me? But tis strange that all my beaux are such queer – false villains so objectionable to my parents & friends – so unsatisfactory to me – and yet nice men of intelligence & position &c Strange that I cannot (be satisfied [crossed out]) find any to suit me – Yet as I always open

23. *My Soul Is Dark,* a collection of songs, is an adaptation of ancient Hebrew melodies by Isaac Nathan with words by George Gordon, Lord Byron, was first published in 1815 (Sears, *1870 Sheet Music Catalogue,* 90).

"Sleeping I Dream'd Love," a popular song of the 1860s, with words by Mrs. M. E. Hewitt and music by W. V. Wallace, was published in the series "Gems of Southern Song" by John W. Burke of Macon, Georgia (Parrish, *Confederate Imprints,* 616).

to that verse in the Test. in connexion with my fortune "But she is happier if she so abides" So I guess it would be for me as I can't be reconciled to matrimony. Yet as Gibbes & Joe left us to "reconsider" I suppose the finale is yet to come – heaven direct for the best! We were amused at their departure.

Tues March 13th A soft – luscious day – having our flower gardens all worked out – housecleaning &c – but sought to busy myself at better things than this scribbling – Tom Carter came and annoyed us with his nonsense half the morning – but he's a good clever fellow – so independent! he walked home with Aunt Anna & Willie in aft. when she had finished Ma's nice new poplin dress. very kind Julia here in aft – not well – her children in mischief at home – paddling in water &c took colds – Sewing in aft. – at night played over many pieces for the children to select from – but felt very stupid – had another evidence too of Joe's vile hypocracy – he didn't come as he had hinted he might – send a message – nor even look in the house when he & Gibbes promenaded by in the aft – the scamps – wonder where they went.

Tis well – I need depend on no man's word I've ever – or may meet – False all & unworthy – yet I'm not grieved – only content in home quiet & comfort only grow too lazy I fear A Yankee – Jew pedlar called here today – with newly imported goods – "Camels hair poplins" – finer than fancy silks – the handsomest goods I ever saw – so wide & cheap – from 20 to 38 – a pattern – couldn't be had for that in stores – Eleanor & I longed for them but hadn't the money – pity to be poor! I risked sending on 50 cents to the "Eureka Gift Association" – in N. Y. to see what I could make off of the grand humbug (I guess) wish it might be a piano, melodeon or diamonds! No such luck for me if any other!

Weds March 14th Court still proce[e]ding – but few lawyers here – Gov. Orr had returned home – brought me a letter from Jim Townsend at 96 – very appreciative of his "dear good cousin" – he pretends – he is very usefully employed now at talking & studying law &c Sent me a list of new music – wish I had some of it – as I'm tired of the old selection! [W]e do not read & improve ourselves enough here – the children seem to have no fancy for it too bad!

March 14th 1866 Weds A real Spring like day – mild & pleasant – but produced a languid sensation I think or is it that I am so lazy? Ma & Eleanor went first to see Mrs Harris Vandiver lately moved from country to town & relieved her of one of those handsome camelhair poplins all the rage since the pedlar came yest. She had two – Nell took the sea green – lovely – I have none![24]

24. M. C. (age 24) and Harris Vandiver (33) were young, successful farmers before the war, and their move to town may have been in order to take advantage of the postwar mercantile

Then Ma & I went to call on Mrs Col Newton Brown – (Lizzie Bruce) with whom I went to school years ago – a plain practical country girl – fair but faded – and awful ugly mouth but good & clever – suit each other (glad it wasn't me) 'though living in that style &c! Very plain & neat no parlor yet whole house being scoured – yet she entertained with unembarrassed sociability for a bride – laments that Col B has to stay in town from her so much! –

Ma went to Dr Hollands – I Mrs Bewleys queer independant woman! Then to Baylis Earles – Eugenia a languid – nice girl (no beaux) teazes me about Joe A. but the scamp has wandered off again – returns no more to me I guess – she & sisters all had the handsome poplins green – brown & purple! Sorry I have none &c read papers in aft. Pa told us of the speaking in C. H. he gained a case over McGowan &c All the lawyers invited to Judge Munro's tonight here tomorrow night – wonder if Joe will stay to come & what he means by such cool deceit &c! Pa rather favors him now![25]

Mattie Orr & Joe Hyde happened in this morn – she so social he a stiff little thing – Miss Mamie Perroneau came to see me in aft. Very pretty & agreeable – reduced to poverty by the war – has to teach – I must be social & see more of her – Anna Parker & Margie Perroneau here to see the Mary's &c & to invite them to a musical meeting – Julia here also – in aft. I rec'd a long newsy letter from cousin Lou (Wilkes) Mrs McDavid now of Atlanta Ga – living happily with her new husband & sons – much dress there! but she sighs to see her old friends here again we miss the social, genial friend! I walked a little way with Mamie P. met only Yanks & R. B. – who stared at me without speaking seemed drinking & I fear Clif was too – a rare thing now – hope not![26]

Pa gone out to tea but not well – has rhumatism I am so stupid don't feel even like scribbling 'ought to be more useful – how could I ever manage a household with my inert habits & indulgence & ignorance of practical affairs: I far prefer this

---

expansion. The couple had several very young children, less than ten years old (*1860 Census*, Anderson District, 162).

25. Samuel McGowan (1819–97) graduated from South Carolina College in 1841, practiced law in Abbeville, joined the Episcopalians and the Democrats, then served twelve years in the South Carolina House. He married Susan Caroline Wardlaw, and the couple had seven children. Gen. McGowan was wounded three times before he surrendered at Appomattox. In 1865 McGowan won a seat in the U.S. House of Representatives, only to be denied a place by the radicals. From 1879 until 1893 he served as a state supreme court justice and died in Abbeville at age seventy-eight (Wakelyn, *Biographical Dictionary*, 297–98; Faust, *Historical Times*, 371; Boatner, *Civil War Dictionary*, 533; Amann, *Personnel of the Civil War*, 316–17; see Caldwell, *History of a Brigade*).

26. Among the family of educator Henry P. Perroneau, Mamie and Margie were apparently contemporary with at least some of the Reed women (Vandiver, *Traditions*, 116).

life of comfort & ease if it could last – but 'tis too selfish & useless – there's a higher mission in life for woman – and I have the powers of accomplishing much had I energy! What is to be my destiny Direct me Oh God! Stars are shrouded in gloom tonight!

Thurs March 15th A bright, – pleasant day our front garden being swept & renovated – house & larder prepared for company tonight – as Pa would invite some of the lawyers to tea – we didn't know how many – until night came & brought only three – after all our trouble! But I was writing & sewing mostly – don't do my share in the Culinary line I fear – and how could I ever manage it – disliking and ignoring it as I do!

Dick T here to see Nell – jumped out of a window – the scamp – as he saw Maria & Ella Keith – coming to call because theres so much gossip about he & Nell & the fainting scrape! They are very pretty, pleasant girls Maria converses brilliantly – they spoke much of the Broyles all charming – Dr B – specially – no tender sentiment 'though – &c "he don't drink" &c wonder how it will all end?

Adams had called on them last night – left today – he & Jim Whitner though invited here – wonder what they mean – & if he is so wholly false or piqued at my cool comfort the other night & what next? [H]e & Jupiter called around very generally I believe but were not at Judge Munro's last night with other old men to tea – Pa enjoyed it! Beckie Hoyt here this aft – very sweet – but all were busy – far more than need have been – or we should have had more guests at once –

Gen Harrison & Dr Broyles didn't come – Gov Orr, Gen McGowan of Abbeville & Judge Moses of Sumter were the three dignatarries present – who conversed learnedly – generally & affably all evg – but rather too legally for my pleasure all the time – I wish I could keep up better & was more witty! The Gov seems my special friend – told me of seeing Mrs Willis in Charleston last week – Advized me to catch Joe A – &c he is rather slippery & unreliable! The Judge of calm, dignity – very agreeable – 'though he is a Jew – and has risen to this position – married a Christian lady – who won't permit her daughters to do the same (marry Jews!) "very rich," stylish people (he ate ham too) I saw. Gen McG stout & jolly – eloquent & refined – he & Pa speak against each other – Pa has to prosecute men as solicitor but he is a pleasant person – urged us to repeat our Charades tomorrow evg – for their benefit and I must make the effort to get them up – fear I cannot

---

Louisa Webb Wilkes McDavid was the daughter of Elijah Webb. Despite her remarriage and a move to Atlanta, "Lou" was buried with her first love, Sam Wilkes, at the Anderson Baptist Cemetery, under the name of Wilkes (Vandiver, *Traditions,* 203, 233).

– (Jim Munro called on Nell this evg) but she can't shine in a learned crowd! I can just pass![27]

We had a late & protracted supper too bountiful for them – ham & a large splendid turkey – salad & breads – tea & coffee &c all nice – peaches & cream well kept – jelly cake rec'd and different wines – muscadine & rice and a bottle of champaign 8 yrs old – splendid, But they all partook very lightly of everything – the number of children & negroes were all greedy for their share afterwards! We discussed the Yankee raid here & the lawless men in our Dist – men from Texas & elsewhere united with a few here to rob & alarm citizens & Yanks [illegible] trains &c and two boys from here are with them John George & Tom Osberne – too bad! Efforts being made to arrest all these – & people who harbour them – to connect the Keys &c I conversed with the gents or listened to their discussions awhile after tea – then they departed at 10 – clouded but warm.[28]

Friday March 16th A cold bleak day after a slight shower last night – fruit trees in bloom, vegetables beginning to show up – all to be nipped I fear – very blustery! [R]eading newspapers & sewing all day wearily – saw no one but Nell had several beaux &c [W]e didn't succeed in having charades at night – inconvenient to the Orrs – Munro's applied for them too late I was glad – such an unpleasant evg – Lula Broyles returned from home to school – health improved. She & Mary – with Mamie went to a Musical Club at the Perronneaus that night – very merry – some grown beaux there – Wilkinson flattered Lula as grossly as he did Mollie Hodges – a contemptible scamp!

Last night Mamie took tea at the Hyde's – Joe came home with her – Dr Jim Brown & others saying they are in love with her – so she is coming out very suddenly in Eleanors rear – to her chagrin – I've grown indifferent – being almost pushed off the carpet long since! Wish the rest of them greater success! Quiet sleepy evg, – for us at home

27. James W. Harrison (1819–88) was the son of James and Sarah Earle of Andersonville, South Carolina. In 1866 Harrison was an attorney, a state senator, a planter, and a general in the South Carolina militia. He married Mary Benson of Pendleton, and they had nine children. During the Civil War he served with the Soldier's Board of Relief; after the war he was president of the Blue Ridge Railroad Company. Gen. Harrison died at his home in Walhalla and was buried at Anderson's First Presbyterian Church. He was the law partner of B. F. Whitner and the brother of Mrs. B. F. Whitner (*1860 Census,* Anderson District, 258; Vandiver, *Traditions,* 28, 29, 150, 201, 262; Simpson, *Old Pendleton,* 172–73; Bailey, *South Carolina Senate,* 1:679–80; Reynolds, *Biographical Directory,* 233).

28. John George (age 20) was the son of tailor Ezekiel George and his wife, Elizabeth. His siblings included William (26), a printer, and Edna (23). It is not known whether young George actually rode with Manse Jolly, but the possibilities for danger and defiance may have presented an attractive opportunity to him (*1860 Census,* Anderson District, 260).

Sat. March 17th Bright & blustery still – real chilly & icy – all busy at odds & ends as usual the close of the week though the girls wont do much – but dance & play games – & talk of beaux too little of books – spoiled completely! Ma has to run about – providing for negroes & poor kin who will destroy our whole living I fear! Our freedmen still return to us for everything! Pa busy with his law proceedings – had rhumatism too! The court condemned one Brooks to be hung for stealing a horse after the jury wrangling all day & night! A number of men brought in prisoners by the Yankees – as they are after all the "bushwackers" with a vengeance – and our Gov. thinks an example ought to be made of some such outlaws such as now infest our country![29]

I tried in vain to finish my new calico dress this evg but so many myriad stitches all for naught – such a waste of time – wish we had a good sewing machine! We were tasting cheese – sugar – molasses candy &c tonight – the girls at cards & nonsense – I to scribble & rest – feeling so dull and stupid these days – no sympathy with anything around me – nobody to interest me special – no great objectives left so I wonder what is yet to be my destiny? Letters from Edwina & Mollie Hodges tonight – very prosy – care only for home & themselves now – I'm forgotten! Mollie & Fletch happy at home! W. C. – gone west – late – Cold!

Sunday March 18th A clear cold bleak day very uncomfortable to begin Sabbath school for the year & to sit in church until after preaching from 9 till 1 oclock But we had a full turnout, near seventy scholars with but few teachers to our regret yet we couldn't get things well arranged & I prefer a more interesting class than the small children I have We sang many sweet hymns – elected officers &c Mr Hall [illegible] again to his delight – 'though I preferred Mr Spaulding the good active little parson & S. S. man here now – he is vice superintendant!

Col & Mrs Newton Brown there – looks quite settled & happy! Mr Murray preached a good but too long sermon – Oh for another revival of blessed religion in our midst – for we seem so dead! I enjoyed my Bible & some holy glimpses of the hereafter today – [illegible] unveiled to any earthly ills! I intended going to church in aft. but heard no bells & twas cold [S]tayed home reading with Ma & sweet baby sister – her good little nurse Louisa had a fit today – some of the girls went to see Julia – she has many trials & thinks we neglect her I fear but I don't go & make myself useful as I might to the needy![30]

29. John H. Brooks was sentenced to hang in July of 1866, but in June the sessions court commuted his sentence to imprisonment until January 1, 1867 (*Anderson Intelligencer*, June 28, 1866).

30. Louisa was a servant in the Reed home.

Pa went to Pickens court this morn. in our big carraige the Gov Orr & Judge Moses with him! They will see false Joe & when will I – no more of false R – but when to see my faithful Theo & what then? Cold night – I read some poetry aloud to the girls but they don't care for it now – as I scribble books – asleep now – I will & read last as usual & hear my mothers soft low voice singing downstairs tired as she must be with unending labors

[At this point Emmala started her third journal, a random collection of journal entries, lists, and observations. Entries from varying locations in the holograph journal have been placed in proper chronological sequence here. The remainder of the third journal can be found in Part III, the appendix of this work.]

Monday March 19th A mild Spring day – rather cool – but a little thunder lightning & rain at night – scarcely enough to be refreshing to vegetation after the long dry spell. Sewing & shopping a little – to see the Harpers & Julia – a cold bow to R – first in months, such a change from the old time. At night I had a rare dream for me – that I was on the eve of being married – and to Theo![31]

Soft moonlight night – we were going to church for the ceremony. I was dressed in white with a wreath over my curls – skipping about singing merrily as in my earlier youth & joy – glad because he loved me and I was making him happy – and some faint perception of love & content with him for he looked so smart & handsome & proud when he said "See how gay my little girl is!" then Pa was talking to him too long of business &c but ended with a toast in wine – the end being – "you must never love anyone so well – but I have no fear of that" – both of us having confidence in his supreme devotion to me – but as he laughed & said nothing – I caught his hand & said "Theo – will you not reply to that?" – And he ran off with me to promenade the piazza with other friends – Aunt Anna – Lucie &c – and pressing a kiss on my cheek as if accidentally said "You will let me kiss you tonight will you not?" And peeping in the door of a pretty room said "Oh how cozy it looks!" – And I ran off to prepare for the ceremony – but as my former maid Becky came to me & said "And is it possible Miss Emmala is going to marry at last – & she nearly 27" – I burst into tears and said "I cannot bear to marry and be called Mrs. Smith" – and as the laugh abated I woke up before it was consumated – to my regret – for I wanted to realize the end – and something of the touch of which I can scarcely conceive – never having thought seriously of marraige for me awake or asleep before – something too serious & alarming – wonder if I ever shall?

But I woke with a sense of liberty almost mine – and longing to dream again – thinking how I had dreamed a few times of R's love (not of marraige) long ago –

31. Emmala probably refers to Mr. and Mrs. John R. Harper, who were members of the Baptist Church. Their daughter Carrie married a Mr. Rainwater in September, 1866 (Vandiver, *Traditions,* 225; see Reed, *Journals,* Appendix F).

but care nothing for him or it now – as Theo's true devotion & rare cultivation are more pleasing – and how much he would enjoy this dream were I to write it to him & I shall hint at it – wonder if he will ever see this page as a right & what think of me then! Just now my heart repels false R & J – and yields more tenderly to Theo's spells of love – I doubt yet if it is strong enough for me to wed him & be faithful evermore as there are some objections hard to overcome – but I am to have no other love I guess! Direct us for the best oh God! [illegible] such a lover at my age after being repulsed!

March 20th Tuesday A damp pleasant morn – the garden looks so revived & pretty – the tender green leaves & grass and bright pink & white blossoms of the fruit trees are lovely. After my dream & with these soft tender influences around me I feel inclined to scribble or read novels all day – but must be more useful I guess! Accomplished little – Clif & Fan & Helen went home with Witt Broyles on a visit to Seneca River – Julia & Mollie Brown here awhile. Showery! Minnie Belcher here at night with Eleanor nice girl – rather affected – sings well. Dick Tupper & Joe Hyde came at night to see them – Dick off for Charleston tomorrow – Eleanor gave him nice knickknacks (cakes &c) to take along – wonder how they will end? Oh for sweet dreams again tonight![32]

March 21st Weds Dreary day – Minnie pleasant we sang duetts &c she left – quiet & busy A letter from aunt Lizzie Willis at the "Mills House" in Charleston having a grand time – one of fortune's favorites attentions from everybody – luxuries &c! happy being! [H]ears the opera every night & thinks of me – sees my old friend Cora Carter Mrs Wm. Gayer –who still remembers me with love & begs me to write & after various late messages I will attempt it to try & regain her lost friendship – cruelly as she has treated me – hope all may yet be well! Strange that I was with them when they met their fates in Charleston – & both have proved such lucky matches – both enjoying life so much since & I left behind in this dull routine 'though I met [illegible] Hall first – an ardent lover & could have lived in Charleston then – glad I did not – and Theodore the second time whom I then admired & it might then have been a happy match for he admired me – but never proposed – until driven here by the war a refugee – and now he seems [illegible] and not withstanding all objections – will it be well for me yet to accept him or is any fate in store – may heaven direct aright oh God! I am blest in my single comforts so long – 'though I may have missed much useful experience – but it will never be otherwise I guess![33]

32. Minnie Belcher has not been identified.

33. The 1870 census records "Carrie" as the wife of Charleston attorney W. J. Gayer. The couple had three children and a large extended family in the household (*1870 Census*, Charleston County, 122; *Charleston Courier*, Jan. 9, 1866, 3).

Thurs. March 22nd A bright fresh – spring day – nature reviving sewing &c Julia & I went out in aft. to Murrays – all kind & pleasant there – & to see Lucie a moment – but only Yanks will see us in the street – (since tried [illegible] regale us) But poor Julia had to meet a drunken husband at home. What will become of them? Awful! Lovely moonlight night – Pa returned from Pickens – Judge Moses with him – had spoken much of me & my smartness – Gen McGowan wrote his kind regards to us & Judge J. M. Acker of Miss. my great uncle begged "Miss Emmala to write if she was single!" (a widower) Pa & the Judge discovered some remarkable facts about the Jews – one never indicted for stealing & other crimes, never drunkards – never unchaste 'though such outcasts – all would yet return to Palestine! I remember my episode with Fred Jacobs long ago![34]

Friday March 23rd I was reading nearly all day – finished "Prescott's Conquest of Mexico" a most interesting history – showing the hardy endurance & chivalry of the old Castilians – "superior to any other race" – & Hernando Cortez one of the greatest conquerers so brave & self reliant and earnest in his faith & zeal, such an influence over his few followers & the great Indian nation he discovered with their wonderful heathen civilization – their subjugation so complete & scarcely the remains of their proud cities & monuments and manuscripts of picture writing and other valuble Aztec relics left there – or in Central America – of which we know less with all its grand wonders in ancient achitecture &c. How will it one day be unraveled & did they indeed wander over from Asia – were they Isrealites – or another race created on this continent – with the strange animals & productions here found? Eternity alone can reveal the mysteries.[35]

The 3rd vol. tells of the great trials of the Spaniards & Tlascalan & other allies before the city of Mexico with its canals & bridges & dangerous dykes – in that beautiful Venice of America – of the sufferings & brave endurance of the besieged men, women & children dying in defense of homes and customs their religion & rights – 'though they worshiped imaginary deities with bloody rites of sacrifice & practiced cannibalism. But finally they had to yield to military science – And Mexico was finally subdued – their brave – noble chief "Yuctemozin" a prisoner & was afterwards executed in Honduras – most unjustly it seems – and the death of the proud Montezuma in prison – wounded by his own countrymen who formerly

34. Judge J. M. Acker is probably the brother of William Acker, husband of Emmala's Aunt Mary Acker.

Emmala evidently had some sort of liaison with the presumably Jewish Fred Jacob (Huff, *Greenville,* 98).

35. The Pre-Columbian, Mexican, and Central American cultures are no longer a mystery, but the argument over indigenous versus migratory population of North and then South America is still being hashed out by anthropologists.

adored him – yet a victim to superstitious fears they now despized – a sad end for all his glory! Poor Cortes after all his triumphs was unfortunate in his latter days – never met requital from his countrymen – & died in Spain 1521 a disappointed man – one of the Crusaders for the faith – in seeking to establish Catholicism in Mexico he will surely be rewarded. His remains were removed to Mexico – where his wife & children lived on their vast estates! He had two wives – but his Indian interpreter "Matina" is most famed. The letter of an Aztec mother to her daughter most [illegible] & excellent advice for that early day! A dark & rainy day – girls at home from school – music lessons &c – sewing & knitting but forgetfullness in a novel – best!

Sat. March 24th. Sunny & pleasant again – sewing & reading in morn – in aft. I went with Mary Broyles to the Bleckleys & saw Liz at last friend of my school days – and read a letter from Mollie Carter McCaslin – to her – speaking much of me – how she then loved me – valued my noble gifts &c – yet almost feared me for some sternness &c as she did Pa & for fear of fickleness (of which I have none & she has proved hers!) That I was false or persons had made mischief between us – yet she hoped to be friends again – & have me visit her &c. She dreamed I had married her old sweetheart R. B. &c – just then I saw him walk up as far as Liz's for he had seen me pass through town – bowed as I went back – a rough lazy looking loafer a deceiver &c. for whom I've lost all interest ever I believe – wonder if if he still retains any in me? How strange are all these changes & "coincidences."[36]

Cora & Mollie Carter (long married) after years of silent estrangement for which I could never account – now send me kind messages again & desire reconciliation – and I am very glad if they will be true &c – yet I fear to trust any now – T'will all deceive me! I stopped at the Seabrooks & saw the nice melodeon there to sell – which I must try to obtain for our church. Paused at Ella Gaines' awhile – a nice girl – teaches a good little school in the house of her afflicted grandmother Mrs. Whitfield – at our little "country store" where they sell little I fear.[37]

Saw Mr. Tom Crayton – the widower about whom some teaze me – has had two sweet wives – & two children to die – only little T. S. left – a good looking worthy man of middle age still – looks at me with interest – but never says much & I hope will not. Left our store for another one – Norris, Vandiver & Clifton

36. Mollie Carter McCaslin was a schoolmate of Emmala's from Johnson Female University.

37. Mrs. Whitfield is most likely the wife of "Squire" John C. Whitfield, who once wrote a rather "racy" history of the people and events of a (then) contemporary Anderson, South Carolina. Unfortunately, his daughter destroyed the manuscript rather than editing out the less acceptable passages (Vandiver, *Traditions,* 18–19).

employed now for Pa & Reeves – but I fear they'll make nothing. Clifton & Fannie & Helen came from Mrs. (Whit) Broyles yest. in the rain they have a fine farm – river & fish &c up there but seem determined to move away – want Clif to go – I hope he will have luck to do well somewhere. He & Fan seem still devoted & happy – but poor Julia is so unfortunate with her vagabond husband – drunk all this week again – they gain nothing – lose all every day – what will be the end – fearful I'm afraid. God help them![38]

Beckie Hoyt here today – she & Jim live near us – Eleanor spent a pleasant evg. with them – we all rec'd invites to a wedding next week – at O. H. P. Fants – anticipate the good supper &c with pleasure! At night Mary Wilhite here to tea – a nice plump little thing. All dull at home though – I haven't life to enjoy music even now – no one appreciates it here now –

I was buried deep in my novel – "Zanoni" until late – but resisted finishing it till after Sunday. His a weird noble character. Viola so sweet & pure – Can there have been such a thing as this strange sorcery & magic the Elixir of Life &c which prolongs youth with renewed bloom & power & virtue &c forever until human love & passions conquer the ricewater & bring age & suffering & death! Bulwer seems to believe in these mystic schools of Philosophy – & there have been accountable wonders – & from the true knowledge of plants & other natural causes – perhaps man can reach a wonderful degree of learning – & power yet unknown! [M]esmerism & all those things strike me as very wonderful and possible yet I must not be a silly convert to mere credulity.[39]

Sunday March 25th Blustery – S.S. in morn very good – hymns &c. Mr Murray's – good sermon – Mr. Elliott's at Epis. ch. very impressive in the aft. text – Felix (Acts) & Paul "go thy way for this time – when I have a convenient season I will call for thee!"[40] Would that I could remember solemn, beautiful words of appeal from the almost inspired divine – so handsome, so good and earnest in his impromptu address – to the unconverted – and almost his last sermon here – urging them to turn to the Lord – & rejoice his heart

Ere he must leave them – for he goes soon to travel in Europe for his health &c how splendid that will be – yet how he will be missed here – an irrepairable loss to the church & society for we meet few such men in this world! He is fitted to fill any woman's ideal of perfection – yet for whom is he destined since his first beloved – & his child – his brothers & father – have all lately passed away – & he too so frail! Many have pined for him in vain – and without any great personal interest

38. Emmala probably refers to the Norris of publishers "Harrison, Norris and Company" of the *Anderson Gazette;* no more precise identity has been ascertained.

39. *Zanoni,* a novel by Edward G. D. Bulwer-Lytton, was first published in 1842.

&c I could not but sigh that such a man was not my destined companion & mate – to weep that I should see & hear him or his like no more on earth perhaps & hope to meet with all the blest in heaven – & as his sermons always make me appreciate religion & heavenly hopes – better!

Robert was there too – looked so well – but so false & estranged & unworthy! One year ago that day he wrote me his last long letter of love – did he think of it – or me – or only of Maria Keith – so smart & sweet looking – to whom I think Mrs Elliott alluded to in wishing some converted – she looked so serious surely cannot withstand his appeals – & R's love – but yet I scarcely believe he has transferred it all yet – 'though mine I think is gone forever – & 'tis well!

Theo don't write yet – what shall I think of him & false Joe! But I need trust to none! Feel happy & content as I can fortunately – sleep & dream so sweetly every night thank heaven! Always busy & always enjoy books & society every day – & letters &c though people are so untrue to me. Sweet music at the church thrilled me – Lula Broyles & Vie Hammond with us. Nell heard from Dick in Charleston. I had notice of two pretty gifts drawn from the association – must send in & get them! Pa seemed suffering at night with rhumatism in his toe &c – but had to start next morn on his three weeks circuit of Courts – Greenville – Spart. & Laurens where he will be so busy unless too afflicted – but I hope will get better! He is struggling to support his large – dependant family but I fear his best days are over – he looks rather old now with his cane – We kissed him good night but there's not enough affection displayed here.

Monday March 26th / 66 Cold & dark – snowed beautifully awhile – we tremble for the fruit – Pa gone to Courts – Vie here – I must read & work!

Julia Hammond & Mattie here in evg. – a sweet, fair joyous young girl! Pretty to see – Vie went to services. I finished "Zanoni" – splendid – but so mystical & tragical – I like Bulwer so much!

Tues. March 27th I was sewing all day – giving music lessons &c – the children went to a party at Hydes

Weds. March 28th A dark rainy day – too bad for a wedding but a large one came off at night at O.H.P. Fant's – his eldest daughter Eveline – married John Thornly a widower with two smart, interesting children – Ernest & Rachel his sister Mrs Kiamer a pleasant person – the Fant's all delighted – the five bridesmaids looked well – in white & pink – the bride very sweetly dressed in Swiss lace & flowers

Rev. John Elliott performed the solemn Episcopal ceremony and he was so charming (to Eleanor especially – is soon to leave) a wet night but Ma, Eleanor & I rode there – a mixed crowd of old & young – country & villager – elegant supper – flowers & cakes & jellies &c delightful – substantials too & ambrosia cocoanut & orange – Bill Humphreys escorted me – a Mr Davis of Abbeville – made himself very agreeable to me – & Dr Tom Evins & others rather so – but the old maids would seize him![41]

I sang some to the piano some attention – a few of us sang in chorus – Mattie Orr & a Mr Brown &c the Gov. was very merry & social & invited many to his house next night to a party. The fairest, freshest specimen of girlish beauty was Flora Keith – whom I fear Harry Butler will deceive as he has others! Nell looked so pretty – carried on with Jim Munro – his sisters too gracious to me! We arranged about more charades &c left at 1[42]

Thurs. March 29th Clear & blustery – fruit saved I hope! I was buried in another sweet novel all day "While it was morning" by Virginia Townsend – pure & sweet! Julia here awhile & Vie came – had a recontre with R. B. at the gate &c – We were all dressing late to go to the party at Gov. Orr's – Eleanor in her new green silk – elaborately trimmed skirt – tinseled velvit & white buttons with crimson trimming – red African Sapineas in her hair &c – looked well & was much admired gained all the beaux![43]

I in blue silk & trimmings – (dark) wearing blue hyacinths & curls &c – Vie & Fannie neat & plain – Ma her new poplin – looked well – Clif has no fine clothes had his hair & beard (cut) too close & for the first time in months was drinking some – silly & stupid – made us so mortified – but would go – yet only enjoyed the supper I guess. The girls stayed home with babies – lamenting – A clear – cold moonlight – nice ride – a large merry throng assembled in the ample rooms.

The Governor very social & unassuming – Mrs Orr in Abbeville which some thought strange. A Miss McKee of Beaufort there as assistant &c a tall – stately person not very interesting. Mattie very graceful and elegant with white & pink – coral & pearl ornaments on her black curled waterfalls &c – danced so well but didn't receive as much attention as she might command elsewhere! Lucia Harrison very lovely too – many nice girls – but few if any real nice beaux – plenty of intruders old men & ladies & children all seemed to enter upon the scene with zest and it was pleasant to see the general equalization & commingling & sociality![44]

40. Acts 24:25.

41. John Thornley, a widower with two children, married Eveline Fant on March 28, 1866, and the couple moved to Pickens County. Mrs. Thornley Kiamer has not been identified further (obituary of O. H. P. Fant *Daily Mail,* Sept. 30, 1902; see Reed, *Journals,* Appendix F).

42. Harry Butler has not been identified from information available.

43. *While It Is Morning,* a novel by Virginia Townsend Lowe, has not been located.

44. Henry and Jane McKee were a moderately successful planter family of Beaufort and St. Helena, South Carolina. Miss McKee could be any of their daughters Eliza (age 27), Caroline (21), Louisa (20), or Mary (17) (*1860 Census,* St. Helena District, 4).

We stood crowded together chatting – Bill Humphreys to me first, Dr. Tom Evins a little – Gov. Orr several times – wished me to lead off the dance with him – of course I declined – he urged me to stay all night too – is rather too much my friend without real benefits! That pert, cynical Harry Butler was introduced and chatted very freely as he did to all the ladies – vanity and deceit his compounds – not a true gentleman I fear came here to meet his destiny – but was determined to avoid it – a flirtation with pretty little Flora Keith &c but Davis's was last & most agreeable – a tall, slender person, merry, pleasant face, genial gentlemanly manners entertained me very pleasantly & glad to meet some lady friends – finding himself a stranger rather cooly received &c – he led me to the carraige when I left.

Mr & Mrs Thornley looked well in dress – acted with dignity but he was sick & she tired – both clung together – ate none – soon left! The dancers occupied two rooms with a coloured stringed band – poor – their unceasing jingles wearied me – but they enjoyed it – Lancets, round dances &c Willie McFall escorted me into supper with Eliza Hyde who clung to me all night not knowing anyone scarcely. A nice quiet girl Wm. nice youth but quiet too –

We did full justice to the nice supper too. elegant table – cakes with pink & white icing – jellies – orange macaroons candies, nuts, &c splendid – oysters &c excellent – men & women ate shamefully as we poor Confeds rarely ever see anything so good! I wish Julia had been there, Newton & wife so dry & plain & stupid – thank gracious we were not predestined to each! We left at one oclock – after a delightful entertainment! Sallie Williams & brother were there – she looked stylish – they stood aloof from all – so stupid not a glance even exchanged with R – is he ashamed or totally indifferent and a villain! [H]e escorted Maria Keith there – she seemed pleased – I passed them going home! Queer! Once my place alone – but I felt no pangs or love or regret, jealousy or sorrow – total indifference & contempt – and how felt he – & do they love – and will they ever wed? I think not! [H]e drank deep next day [W]onder if he always does & why – the wretch!

Friday March 30th Quiet pleasant day at home Julia here – (I read novels &c, went to her house late to select charades &c – Total eclipse of the moon at night time – poor Clif too eclipsed & fallen again – off all day – he & John Keith crept in here late from a spree – the last to sleep here the villain – the son of an elegant Epis. minister what is to be the fate of such characters. We all felt so distressed about Clif – but hope 'tis ended awful to think how worthless are he & John Peter our only brothers – [illegible] our prospects. Heaven direct us for the best!

Sat. March 31st More pleasant! Selecting Tableaux charades &c all day to act soon – the "corps" of youths & maidens met here to take parts – Jupiter or James Gibbes – aided me in the selections read from Scott's lady of the lake &c has taste &c but is tiresome – At night he came again to bring us a Charade & read it to some of we girls – not elegant! I went to see the Hoyts in their cozy little home near us – this evg. – seemed so happy – & congenial – Becky & Jim – old friends! Mrs Webb there well pleased. The Episcopalians all dressing their church for Easter – Eleanor made one wreath – Pa came home on a short visit from Greenville today – rhumatism better – left for Spartanburg – Judge Moses sent word for me to visit his family in Sumter! Wish I could know more grand people better! Children playing here at night – Wilhites, Rosa Webb &c late – Mrs Miller writes to know who can bring her daughters from Charleston & for me to visit them when they return &c![45]

45. Sir Walter Scott's heroic poem "The Lady of the Lake" (1810) concerns the female spirit who presented King Arthur the famous sword Excalibur. The sword given by the Lady of the Lake made Arthur invincible in battle, implying that men, even great warrior kings, are nurtured and therefore empowered by women.

EIGHT

APRIL

Sunday April 1st A lovely Easter day! Pleasant Sunday school good lessons & hymns &c & sermon Uncle June & Aunt Anna Jones here & Vie the first just came from a long trip looks improved. Julia & her children here too, except Sumter whom John Peter took [to] Townville this morn to stay some. Paul talks some to all of them all interesting

Mr John Elliott preached his splendid Easter Sermon in the afternoon – text "Oh Death where is thy sting – oh grave where is thy victory! &c"[1] Eloquent & impressive! Music rich & grand – five Broyles, Bessie Washington &c – the Evergreen wreathes and spruce snow drops – bridal wreath & paper lilies beautiful decorations. A holy festival of nature & religion. Pleasant evg – all the family here but Pa – Vie & the Jones too! I had some pleasant words with Mrs Frank Whitner for the first time – "an elegant woman" – each offered to assist the other in getting up something for our churches soon! Kind words & looks – but no beaux – false R! Eleanor splendid in her new green silk! But deliver us from vanity & make us better oh God! Jim Townsend writes me kindly – but what's become of Theodore?

Monday April 2nd A slendid Spring day too warm nearly – Busy selecting Tableaux scenes all day the young folks came in aft. to arrange for them – much confusion – Jupiter Gibbes tipsy & disgusting to us all! Uncle June & Aunt Anna here – The children had a youthful crowd of boys & girls here to a musical club – dancing, music & fun – Joe & Pinckney Reid here (at school) clever – country cousins of ours.[2]

Tues. April 3rd Splendid but warm – visiting all day – Seabrooks, Borstells, McCullies, Gibbes, Earles, Fants &c in aft. Uncle June took us in the buggy to Hill's & Gov. Orr's – Mattie – Miss McKee & all pleasant. – Joe Hyde there stopped at O.H.P. Fant's to see the bride out – I saw Capt. Parker in morn pleasant chap – he may act in Charades &c Willie Lee – At night went to Dr. Wilhites

1. Matthew 5:4.

2. Joe and Pinckney "Pink" Reid were cousins who spelled their name in different ways. "Pink" Reid (1844–1929) enlisted with Company G of the Palmetto Riflemen. He contracted typhoid, was taken prisoner in Virginia, and spent fourteen months at a federal prison at Rock Island, Illinois (Vandiver, *Traditions*, 232; Smith, *Book of the Dead*, 319).

to practice with Mr. Poppe' – with violin & piano – five pieces – his rare dog "Harry" sang – real burlesque on the opera – wonderful! Mary Wilhite nice little dumpy thing – Bill Humphreys my escort – dry fellow clever, asked me to write for his paper – got up a May party &c soft sweet, lazy moonlight late[3]

Weds April 4th Warm & bright the Maine garrison left here – all glad – a few Ohio men here – as garrison now. Reading & scribbling all morn – note from Mr Elliott about the Millers &c I must be more useful! The charade crowd came in aft. accomplished little – felt discouraged – I went to Lucie Nardin's late – busy – but a sweet woman.

Thurs April 5th Pleasant day – Ma & Lucie Nardin with children down to spend the day at grandpa's – quiet here – reading sewing &c – Fannie a very good housekeeper – will I ever learn? In aft I went to see Bettie Harrison – sweet girl – & the[n] Mrs Sloan – honest at night Mr Davis called on we girls a pleasant acquaintance – lively tall & fine looking – loves music poetry &c

Friday April 6th Cloudy – warm weather Julia with us – an eggnog – reading papers sewing – practicing &c – feel worried about my entertainment – a letter from Pete McDavid begs me to attend a wedding in their neighborhood Sunday says Joe regards me as his first & truest love &c I must try to go but all are false to me awful Theo & Joe's &c it matters not all worthless charade crowd met here again in the aft. more gents than ladies this time – Mattie Orr declines acting Tom Broyles came in to take a part in the affair on her account – Mr Davis came also and then we all walked up to see if we could get a hall or piano – but could decide nothing – so many obstacles that I will postpone it a week anyway – Jim Munro here late with Eleanor the other girls went to a party at Mr Murrays

Sat. April 7th Half cloudy – I went to Newton Brown's to see about going with him tomorrow to the McDavids – Liz – going home today too. Stopped to see Becky Hoyt awhile in her sweet cottage home – Jim Bacon had written such a sweet notice of her marraige! Julia here a moment but in such distress – John Peter – a drunken brute lying in the streets at this hour an everlasting disgrace to us all – and she has no wood – nothing to eat – nothing to live on & no hope for the future but bears us bravely – my poor sister! May heaven save them!

[At this point the chronological journal entries abruptly end.]

3. Frederick C. Borstell (1821–70) came from Athens, Georgia, and married Cassandra Hewitt in 1850. She taught music at the Johnson Female University; he was a jeweler with a shop on the courthouse square. The couple had two children, both of whom manifested significant musical talents: Alice (Mrs. J. D. Maxwell) earned a reputation as an accomplished pianist; both Christine and Alice moved to California to raise their families. Vandiver adds *von* to the surname, styling it von Borstell (Smith, *Book of the Dead,* 33, Vandiver, *Traditions,* 26, 112; Lucas, *Early Anderson,* 177).

EPILOGUE

In February 1867, ten months after Emmala Thompson Reed finished writing in this journal, she left the security of Echo Hall and went to Doko, South Carolina, where she taught music and literature at the Blythewood Institute for Women. Once at Doko she displayed a resourceful diversity of interests and immediately established a Sunday School at the Sandy Level Baptist Church, where she and her pupils sang in the choir. By the time of Emmala Reed's arrival at Doko she was already smitten with a friend named George Miller, a cotton merchant from Abbeville who worked in Charleston and nearby Columbia, South Carolina. Emmala and George endeavored to court and spark via letters, presents, and periodic visits throughout the spring of 1867. In the mean time she diligently applied herself to the study of "housekeeping."

Emmala Butler Thompson Reed married George William Miller on November 28, 1867, at Echo Hall; the Reverend John Scott Murray performed the nuptials. The couple later moved to a farm about six miles south and west of Anderson, in Rock Mills Township. George's twin brother, William Yarbrough Miller, his wife Sallie, daughter "Willie," and sons Julius R. and Joseph W. lived nearby. "Will" Miller was a teacher at the local academy (high school), and the Miller families provided companionship for children and adults alike. Sallie Miller was her husband's teaching "assistant," and though Emmala likely taught music in some capacity she categorized herself to the 1880 census-taker as a housekeeper. The Millers' domestic servant, Polly Simpson, lived close by with her own three adolescent children to care for.

After 1867 the entire Reed family continued to grow in number as its many members married and found various avenues to personal success and community leadership. As the extended family grew the children built their own ornate homes throughout the area, but Ma and Pa Reed's Echo Hall held the honor of being the homeplace of the entire Reed clan. Judge Jacob Pinckney Reed continued his close personal and professional associations with both James L. Orr and Benjamin Perry.

In 1868 J. P. Reed was the Democratic Party candidate for South Carolina's Third District congressional seat, which he won by a clear majority but lost when the vote was contested in the federal courts by an increasingly radicalized Republican majority. By 1874 the South Carolina Democrats refused to nominate a candidate for governor, though they endorsed the candidacy of Jacob Reed to oppose former state's attorney general, Republican Daniel H. Chamberlain. Reed declined to run and went so far as to endorse Chamberlain, based upon the man's unassailable past behavior and unimpeachable ethical standards. Chamberlain and the Republicans endorsed Reed as the candidate for justice of the Charleston County's prestigious First Circuit Court. He held the position until 1877 despite constant opposition and litigation prompted by the state's radical Republican elements. After Wade Hampton's election, Judge Reed returned to his Anderson law practice and the Greenville and Columbia Railroad, and was instrumental in development of the National Bank of Anderson.

Julia Susan and John Peter Brown moved out to a Brown family plantation in Fork Township, near Townville. Lt. Brown had returned from the war a broken man who stopped practicing law and allowed his alcohol addiction to take precedence over supporting an ever expanding family. John Peter, like many veterans of the Civil War, apparently suffered from what has come to be called "post-traumatic stress syndrome." The couple and their seven children were reduced to accepting the largesse of the Brown family and overseeing a large farm. Julia's oldest son, Frederick "Fred" Garlington Brown, born October 28, 1860, grew up in Anderson County and married Mamie McCrary on November 16, 1887. A man whose accomplishments were numerous, Brown became president of the Anderson Phosphate and Oil Company, the Anderson Real Estate and Investment Company, and the Anderson Chamber of Commerce, which he founded. Fred Brown was also a vice president of the People's Bank of Anderson and served as a director of Brogan Cotton Mills, Toxaway Cotton Mills, and Ninety-Six Mills.

Clifton "Clif" Augustus Reed became one of Anderson's leading merchants in dry goods and groceries. He later manufactured and sold pianos and organs, then pioneered in the sale and manufacture of the "Western Buggy," an extremely popular and affordable carriage of the day. A quiet man of few words, "C. A." Reed was unanimously elected commander or "General" of the South Carolina Veterans in 1914. The C. A. Reed family lived in a large house situated just beyond the city limits at the junction of Greenville Road and Main Street. Fannie Kingsley Reed recovered from her ailments of 1866 and lived until 1902. The couple's only daughter, Helen, married Anderson grocer R. S. Ligon and lived in Anderson all her life. Clifton Reed died in Anderson, South Carolina on November 10, 1924.

Eleanor "Nell" Caroline Reed married Abbeville attorney and cotton merchant William C. Davis in December 1867. Davis was the childhood friend, then business partner, of Eleanor's brother-in-law, George Miller. Davis died some time before 1880, and according to the 1880 census Nell was living at Echo Hall in the spring of that year. In 1881 Nell married a widower, Anderson merchant and bookkeeper James Albert Brock. J. A. and Nell Brock built an ornate home at 708 McDuffie Street, amid the old rose gardens of Echo Hall, where they raised J. A.

Jr. (from Nell's first marriage) and daughter Alberta. J. A. Brock's success in business was remarkable to say the least: he was president of Anderson Cotton Mills and the National Bank of Anderson, and he served as a director for Brogan Mills, Toxaway Mills, Charleston and Western Carolina Railroad, Acme Drug Company, and the Anderson Water, Light and Power Company, to name just a few of his business accomplishments.

Mary "Mamie" Eliza Reed married Benjamin Franklin "B. Frank" Mauldin on May 22, 1872. Mamie and B. Frank had three children: Elise, Eilleen, and Benjamin Franklin, Jr. Mauldin started his banking career in 1872 as an assistant cashier in the National Bank of Anderson, where he became cashier in 1891. After a lengthy apprenticeship, he went on to create and become president of the banks of Due West, McCormick, Hodges, Lowndesville, Townville, and Mount Carmel, as well as the reorganized Bank of Anderson in 1906. The Mauldins lived at 603 North Main Street in Anderson.

Sara "Cora" Cornelia married educator William Siebels Ligon on December 22, 1875. W. S. Ligon first served as an assistant to his father, Professor W. J. Ligon, a renowned Anderson County teacher. The son moved on to several area schools and earned his own academic accolades as the years passed. Cora gained a reputation as the best singing voice and musical director in the county. The couple lived in Anderson throughout their lives and had no children.

Lucy "Lucie" Eoline, born in 1857, married Henry Arthur Ligon on November 8, 1882. Henry Ligon was sister Cora's brother-in-law and a native of Anderson County. Henry opted to enter the business world and started out in 1874 as a drug store clerk. In 1879, after a short stay in Columbia, he opened his own drug store in downtown Spartanburg, South Carolina. Ligon was organizer, builder, and president of the Arcadia (Cotton) Mills, the American National Bank, and the Southern Trust Company, all located in Spartanburg. Mr. and Mrs. Ligon raised four children and remained lifelong residents of Spartanburg.

Jacob Pinckney Reed, Jr., was born in 1862. When he was fourteen years old he went off hunting alone and shot off his own left hand as he climbed over a fence. When the boy grew older, he shared a pair of gloves with Clif, his left-handed brother. J. P., Jr., attended the University of Virginia and in the early 1880s he had begun to practice law in Atlanta, Georgia, when he was struck down by typhoid fever.

The youngest Reed sibling, Teresa Hammond, was born in 1865 but was well over a year old before the Reeds named her. In time she married insurance salesman Charlton Hines Strickland, a local boy who moved his young family from Anderson to New York City, then died suddenly. Teresa Strickland and her three babies moved home to the security of Echo Hall. Louise Vandiver notes that Teresa Reed Strickland published a novel, articles, and many poems, one of which, "Echo

Hall," Vandiver particularly enjoyed. One child, Lily, displayed an unusual propensity for musical composition at a remarkably young age, much like her Aunt Emmala.

Lily Strickland wrote her first tune at age sixteen and is credited with 395 published pieces of music in her lifetime. She attended Converse College in Spartanburg from 1901 until 1904, when she accepted a scholarship to the Institute of Musical Art (Julliard School of Music) in New York City. While in New York, Lily Strickland met and married Joseph Courtney Anderson of Walhalla, South Carolina, who taught English literature at Columbia University. The couple traveled the world, and Lily produced a remarkable volume of music, articles, commentary, poetry, and paintings. She died at Flat Rock, North Carolina, in 1958.

The childless "Aunty Nell" Brock looked after Lily and an older cousin named James Reed Miller, Emmala's youngest child, a virtuoso vocalist who became a pioneer recording artist under the names James Reed and Reed Miller. Between 1904 and 1923, tenor Reed Miller recorded a wide diversity of musical styles and compositions for Victor, Columbia, and Edison, the three major recording companies of the day. Miller married another recording artist, contralto Nevada Van Der Veer; he died suddenly at the age of forty-three, when a blood vessel burst in his throat.

Emmala Reed Miller lived out her life in Anderson County, a Southern woman at the height of America's Victorian era. The Millers, and the entire Reed clan, made the best of postwar mercantile expansion as they grew more cotton than ever before, or founded and financed railroads, cotton mills, banks, mercantiles, and drug stores. All but Julia prospered during Reconstruction and even into the New South era.

The next generation of children raised in the shadow of Echo Hall equaled or surpassed the success of their parents. Julia's son Fred Brown made Anderson his home, and with his gift for commerce brought not only personal wealth but created a diversity of employment that enabled his townsfolk to prosper as well. Reed Miller and Lily Strickland took their music from the churches of Anderson to the stages and philharmonics of New York and London.

COVER NOTES, 1865 JOURNAL

[Written inside front cover]

Richmond evacuated March – 1865! battles there. Mrs. Andrew Moreland died here March 1965 sad! Early spring – many flowers & leaves &c.

April 1865: Great battles in Virginia – Richmond & Petersburg given up – Lee's army driven back – great sacrifices – terrible times! Lee & Johnston – Grant & Sherman – at bay! Robere there! Eclipse of the moon April 10th cloudy. Sweet early Spring. Col. Orr – Mr. Trescott – Theodore S. – Bleckleys – Dr. W. – Sallie Cresswell – Billie Hammond – Becky Webb &c – April 11th But what news from Va. Virginia used up – Dr. Barney McMillan – Albert Blackman – Hal Mosely – Andrew Moreland

April/65 Gen. A. P. Hill – Gen. Fitzhugh Lee – gen. Gordon &c killed before Richmond. Andrew Moreland – widower here – last time perhaps.

April 17th/65 – [P]oor fellow! Dick Tupper & Joe Hyde – Dave Anderson Jr. dead –

April 18th/65: Beautiful April! So warm 'though. Month of disasters to us! Montgomery ala – Columbus Ga – Sumter & Camden S.C. – Salisbury, Fayetteville &c – N.C. Charlottesville, Danville, Petersburg – Richmond all fallen this month – Lee's proud army – surrounded – and captured April 9th 1865 – Robert Lee, Longstreet & all surrendered to gen. Grant – all paroled. Awful! But what will become of Robere & many friends! No news of them. God grant he may soon come! Awful times! What next will be our fate?

"What will he do with it?" by Sir E. Bulwer Lytton m/sq read

April/65 – grand; powerful conceptions of character & scenes – complicated plots & intuitions into the depths of human hearts – but nearly all – true, exalted hearts such as we rarely ever meet! Charming work. Guy Darrell nature's nobleman! Lady Caroline Montfort its gem! George & Allen Moreley – jewels – Jasper Lesely rare desperado & so watched by the faithful woman in iron gray Arabella Crane: the kind mayor Hartogg &c old Merle & Hawthorne the sweet flute player of the manor house of Hawley, William (Lesely) Waife the pure, unselfish devoted man! Sophy & Lionel Haughton peerless young hearts Frank Vance. Glorious termination – swans & doe & pet dog Sir Isaac & much fine moralizing! A joy to [read].

[Notes written on inside back cover]

Abe Lincoln & Seward assassinated at Washington – April 65.

Andy Johnson Pres't – dreadful!

Mattie Leitch & Col Childs interesting. Note from Theo – two of Morgan's soldiers – Garvin & Jones – R's friend: Garvin of Miss. Jones of Huntsville Ala. Many of our village soldiers returned April/65 – no rejoicing – a crisis is our fate – God help us! Beautiful April lights & shadows – leaves & flowers – glorious roses & showers &c. Robert is at home again after a year's absense (& much more) worn out – when shall we meet – poor weary soldier! So near – yet so far!

Friday night April 25th 1865 came today – Are we unchanged? He called not. The long & weary week has passed.

May 7th – The storm has swept over our up country & our homes just at the end of the war perhaps – peace being made- But how unexpected for us – how humiliating. Stoneman's raiders under – Gen's Miller, Brown, Palmer &c swept through Anderson May 1st & 2nd & 3rd (Monday Tues. & Weds.) [H]orrible time – clothes & jewels &c some places – good guard at home – all's over now – but it may yet be worse – God save us! Three boys killed during the time here and all this time I've not seen R – been worn out & hidden &c hid at house much – called not – wrote not – indifferent or what? Terrible suspense, but I can't end it by tearing away in pride forever! But how silly I am – he is my all – Theodore with me much & devoted this week, but not satisfied. Helen Smith & Tom Carter with us – many visitors – boys &c – but I long for one – Tiny Bacon here – Maggie & Tom Broyles – Nick Whaley – Frazier Wilson, Keys McCulley – Dick Tupper – Joe Hyde – Brown's – Murrays – Hammonds &c Louisa Seabrook & Mr. Elliott – So cold & queer & it provoked but what is to be our fate? Heaven direct for the best! Beautiful May time of flowers&c sad day

Saw R at my church today Sunday June 18th – eyes met – sad – but gladder

[Written on last page]

Why does he so – why comes he not? two weeks & met not! Strange – May 7th 65 Cousin Tom Jones of Elberton Ga – noble boy Nick Whaley – fine fellow & Helen Smith – Tiny Bacon – Jim Bacon – Hamilton – May 1865 – Dick Tupper – lovely flowers – fears of to come – calm present. Two weeks & he comes not – I wrote Sunday May 15th 65: Most unaccountable! Most mysterious! Most unexcusable! You have sought & merited all reproach! – What will he think? Would that I could see him!

Fred Tupper – Robert Broyles – Theodore Smith – E.T. Reed

Over a month he comes not – may never come – what does it mean! Faithless Robere! May 25th 65. The South totally ruined – Jeff Davis captured May 6th near Abbeville Alabama – taken to Washington – Dreadful – awful times! God help us!

One bow – absent a month – sad new moon of June. Pray it will be happier! What does it mean – silence, absence & neglect! Theodore faithful – I care not – pine for Robert – he is unworthy I fear and I am the ever unblest. May 31st 65

June R – gone to Pendleton six weeks here – no meeting, no notes – no excuses – painful suspense mortification – agony – perjury on his part! God help us! June 10th 65

June 11th/65 26! R has been gone near a week – returned – saw him pass & look Monday June 12th What next? Thurs. June 15th met in the street as strangers – looked but spoke not – how strange! Strangers –

Met June 26th bowed slightly.

APPENDIX B

EXPENSES FOR 1866 AND 1867

Expenses / 1866

My Expenses for the year 1866 –

+		+	
Jan. 9th	3 spools thread		.25
"	2 cards hooks & eyes		.20
"	braid for dress		.20
"	Dress cut & fitted	pd.	.75
12th	paper & envelopes	pd.	.70
15th	2 yds cambric (paper)		1.00
"	worsted braid		.25
"	two spools black cotton		.25 pd
"	stamped envelopes		.25
Feb 14th	dress trimming		2.25
"	buttons		.25
"	whalebones		.20
"	cravat		.35
March 6th	Letter paper		.5
"	Envelopes		.15
"	Bot. cologne		.75
"	Candy	pd.	.25
"	paper pins		.10
"	postage	pd.	.25
"	(Pd. Mr Murray		7.00)
10th	Post office		.25 (crossed out)
12th	Eureka Gift Association	pd.	.50
19th	Candy & figs	pd.	.25
"	Kid gloves	pd.	1.50
"	Tuck comb		.75
"	coarse comb		.30
"	(thread braid veil &c trimming for Ma)		

	not mine	2.50		
		15.30		
March 21st	postage	pd. .10		
22nd	Dried figs	pd. .25		
28th	To "Eureka Gift Association" N.Y.	pd. 2.30		
"	Stamps	pd. .20		
April 1st	Sunday School	pd. .30		
15th	Stamps	pd. .25		
19th	Bonnet	8.00		
"	flowers & lace	1.50		
"	Beige dress	5.20		
"	Ribbon bow	.30		
"	Swiss spenser & edging	2.00		Frilling .75
"	paper & envelopes	.45		
May 11th	Stamps	pd. .25		
"	Hot Supper	pd. .75		
"	Sunday School	pd. .10		
18th	Blue muslin dress }			
"	paper chambric }			
"	spool of thread }	Pa's store 4.75		
			6.00	
23rd	parasol	3.50		15.30
"	2 fans	.30		29.85
"	Dress cord (trimming)	1.00	89	25.90
"	Buttons	.20	4.75	20.75
"	Ribbon	.25	5.00	40.00
"	gloves (mitts)	.80	70.00	131.30
"	Braid	.20	10.00	______
"	Crochet edge	1.00	89.75	4.00
		29.85		5.00
				70.00
				10.00
				__9.75
June 12th	pair of slippers	– – – –		
"	Hot Supper (Meth.)	pd. 2.75		
"	Black belt	.75		
20th	piano tunes (wildman – bad)	pd. 6.00		
"	cord	.10		

28th	Tape	.20
"	Promenade concert	pd. 1.50
"	Sunday School	pd. .25
July 1st	Subscribed in church	pd. 2.25
"	Society	pd. .50
"	stamps	.25(crossed out)
17th	gloves	.70
Aug 5th	Palm leaf fan	.15
Sept 1st	lecture on Astronomy	pd. .50
7th	a corset	2.50
8th	SS & charity	pd. .20
28th	Society	pd. .50
Oct. __	"	.50
2nd	Powder & stamps	pd. .50
"	pins & a comb	.40
9th	Cologne	pd. .25
14th	Two collars	pd. .25
18th	stamps	.25
26th	Worsted cape	3.00
31st	4 Teeth filled	– – –
"	Dom Castello's ____	pd. .85
"	stamps	pd. .25
"	white frilling	.60
"	handkerchief	.70
		25.90
Oct 31st	Cambric & linings	– – –
Nov 1st	Fiat (Gladiator)	2.00
"	Ribbon	.60
"	Velvit	.80
"	Elastic	1.25
"	dress trimming (Poppe's)	1.10
"	Bow Ribbon	1.50
"	sprey of flowers	.60
"	Belt	.75
Nov. 22nd	3 yds ribbon	.50
"	Concert's (for graves in Va)	.75
"	Veil	.75
"	Blank Books	.65
"	Bible for Mr Hall (Sub)	.50
30th	Stamps	.25

Dec. 1st	Sun School	.10
6th	Ribbon	1.00
12th	jeans linings	.65
"	paper chambray [crossed out]	– –
"	sewing silk	.15
"	velvit (3 1/2 yrds)	1.00
"	Braids for dresses	.40
"	gold cord	.20
"	dress cut & fitted	pd. 1.00
"	tooth brush	.50
"	half yard jeans	pd. .20
16th	Cambric Walebones &c	1.00
"	girl to sew one day	.50
18	stamps	pd. .25
	cord	.20
"	buttons	pd. .25
		20.75

My Expenses for the Year 1867

Jan 1st	A bunch of Envelopes	.10
12th	A " " tape	.10
15th	3 " " "	.25
"	stamps	pd. .25
"	envelopes	pd. .25
19th	stamps	pd. .50
"	Buttons	pd. .25
"	Trimming & shoe strings	pd. .25
24th	Black braid	.25
"	Braids & cord	pd. .40
26th	Black Sacque Cloak	7.00
"	cutting &c	.50
"	Tuck comb	.50
"	Buttons	.37 1/2
"	Braid	– –
"	6 prs stockings	2.00
"	paper chambric	.25

29th	6 towels	1.80	
"	Jeans	.50	[crossed out]
"	Soap	.25	"
"	Calico bag	.25	"
"	_____ & Society	1.00	"
Feb 1st	Black silk	5.00	
"	Brush & comb	.75	
"	Frill	.30	
"	gloves	.75	
"	Cambric	.50	
"	Cord – 10yds	1.50	
"	Making sack	3.00	
Feb 2nd	cap & candlestick	.50	
Feb 4th	Trip to Columbia on the cars		
"	(Pa director)	free	
"	4th Trip to Doko from Col.		
"	16 miles	free	
"	GWM with me		
"	paper collars	8.08	
"	thread & scissors		
5th	(Bought of Kinard in Col)		
"	small articles	18.00	
	amounting to about		
"	2 coverlids for bed gloves – gaiters		
"	lace collars – stamped envelopes		
"	&c included – charged to me		
Feb 5th	in Col. two blankets	5.50	
"	6 photographs	5.50	
"	Blank books pens &c	1.00	
"	3 teeth filled (Dr. Gregg)	7.00	
"	For carraige line &c	2.00	
"	Expenses thus far about	70.00	
18th	stamps	.50	
28th	Paid Mary Fritz	2.50	
"	sent to N.Y. for Music	20.00	
27th	Subscribed to Petersons Magazine		
"	(in Co. with Mrs Durham)	1.00	

March 12th	send goods to Charleston	5.00
18th	gave to Sun School	.25
"	Express on music	.25
25th	stamps	.50
"	For "St Elmo"	2.00
April 5th	Express & post	.20
"	Belt, frills & candy in Col	3.88
10th	For making (____)	1.50
13th	"At Odds" book	2.00
20th	Buttons	.25
May	Spent in Columbia –	$31.00
4th	Pd Mr Kinard for old & new bill	
"	cars – To & From Col.	2.45
"	carraige	.50
"	Bonnet & all elsewhere about	5.00
"	stationary	1.00
"	Candles & shoes	2.50
9th	stamps	.25
18th	matches	.05
20th	homespun – braid – buttons &c	.46
"	stamps	.50
31st	2 teeth filled by Dr Durham	5.00
"	sent to Columbia for goods (BRD)	.50
"	1 yd linen	1.00
"	Blue belt / Envelopes	.15
June	Thread & cord &c (Doko)	.25
1st	stamps	.30
20th	Trip to Winnsboro on Cars	2.50
28th	Calico dress	2.72
"	Nerve of tooth killed	1.00
"	Sundries about	2.00
	for washing	3.00
"	Magic Lantern show	.25

July 1st to 18th	Trip from Doko to Anderson	15.50
"	________ Doko	1.75
"	stamps	.10
(July) 10th	(stamps) home	.25
11	Guitar strings	.10
11	Miss Bates "Readings"	1.50
15th	guitar strings	.10
"	pink ribbon	.10
"	Corset stay mended	.10

Expenses for 1867

July 15th	Wash illusin (2 1/2 yds)	1.50
"	Black lace – 6yds	.60
"	Fan (Palm)	.10
"	Silk gloves	1.00
"	"night blooming Cereus(?)"	1.00
"	Gave Nell & Mamie	.55
"	Bible Society	.50
23rd	stamps	.25
"	Corset stay mended	.15
25th	Straw hat & band	2.85
"	gave Mamie	.30
Aug 12th	Gave Mr Lum for SS	.25
"	Black lace	.25
"	Bot. Cologne for Lula B.	.50
16th	stamps	.25
19th	Trip to "Pendleton"	2.75
Sept 12th	stamped envelopes	1.00
"	satin band	1.00
(Sept) 29th	Black silk & trimmings	39.75
Oct 7th	to a "lecture" in C.H.	1.00
12th	Sundries (at Clifs)	2.70
"	silk dress	
"	Boulevard skirt	
"	White flannel	
"	gaiters	

"	corset	
"	Calico dress	2.00
Nov 1st	Sundries in town	
"	Cloak	11.00
8th	Sent to Charleston for articles	50.00
"	Dressmakers (cards $10.00)	7.50

APPENDIX C

LETTERS FOR 1866

Lists of letters for 1866

Mrs Mollie Hodges XXXXXX
Miss Edwina Hodges XXXXXX
" Anna Kuhtman XX /
Mrs Sue Siftley XXX
Mr James Townsend XXXXXXXXXXXXX \
Mrs Dr Miller XXX
Peter A. McDavid XXXXXXXXXXX
Mrs Sallie White X
" Sallie East XXXXX
Mrs J McFall XX
" Ben Brown XX
Mrs Edward Willis XXX
Dr E.C. Hammond X
Mrs Kelie Whitma X
" Georgia McIntyre /
Mr Theodore D. Smith XXXXXXXXX \
Box 159 X – XXXXXX
Edgefield Advertizer from Jas. T. Bacon / X ///////
Invitation to the marraige of Hasell Heyward & Fannie Smith
Charleston March 1st
Two "Metripolitan Records" – N.Y. papers
sent me by recommendation of Mrs E Willis – circulars &c – March 6th
Miss Sue McMillan XXXXXX
" Bell Latimer XXXXXXXXXXXXX
Mrs Lon McDaniels X
[gifts drawn in sealed envelopes]
from the N.Y. Eureka Association
Onyx ear rings $6.00 – gold bracelet
$8.00 I must send on $2.00 before
got them! Rec'd broach & bracelet – cheap

Miss Elizabeth Johnson X
Mrs Coralie Gayer XX
6 pieces of music from Mrs E Willis –
1 singing Book " Mr Hyde
Invite to marraige of Emma Brown & George Whitman
– papers &c April 26th
Miss Fannie Sullivan XXXXXX
"Galaxy" Magazine – from Mrs Willis
Mrs Fletcher Townsend XXX
Miss Anna Donaldson XXXXXXX
Miss Caroline Ravenel X
" Lida Pickrell X
(music & comb from Pa July 66)
My sister Julia Brown XX
2 mushmelon from Dr Jim Brown
1 watermelon " "
Singing book from Mr Walters – being 3rd
Merino poplin, delaine & calico dress from Pa in Columbia – bolt of velvit – about $30 –
pr silk gloves – 1.00 – blue braid .20 cts –
black silk thread – .20 – spent at Pres – hot supper 1.60 cts – flax – .10 &c
shoes – 4.50 braid .40
1866 – spent near $150 this year paid for over $50 myself

---

23 Georgia papers from Kelie Whitman July
1 song "Conquered Banner" (by Father Abram J. Ryan)
& Beige dress from Aunt Lizzie Willis (Aug 66)

Dr Basil Manly XX \ "Address" of Dr. Manly's sent by him
Mrs Lottie Durham Woodward XX
Miss Bell Harvey X
SS paper from Greenville
Mr George Brown (Ga) X
J Fletch Hodges X
Miss Carrie Miller X /
My father – JPR X $2 for books
Dr. Cherry \
Vie Hammond X
Dr Bookhart X
J D Nardin X

Letters in & out 1867

Letters rec'd & answered in the year 1867
Miss Isabell Martin of Columbia X/XXX

(Appointed me Agent of the "Virginia Memorial Association" for And. Dist.)
Capt James A Townsend /
Dr Bookhart – Blythewood Institute XXXX
(offering situation of music teacher in his school – board & $400.)
Miss Bell Latimer XXX
Miss Fannie Sullivan XXX) XX married June / 67
Cousin Pete McDavid XXX
Miss Kelie Whitman X/
Mr George W Miller (many, many)
Capt James A Townsend XXXXXXXXXXX
Miss Vie Hammond XXX/
Mrs Lizzie Kinard XX
Miss Anna Donaldson XXXX
Mrs Sallie East XXXXXX
Miss Carrie Miller XXXX
Miss Eleanor Reed (sister) XXXXXXXXXXXXXXX
" Alithea Harris XX
" Jane Fant XXXXX
Mrs Lottie Woodward XX
Mr Henry McMillan /
Mrs Dr Miller /
Mr W.C. Davis XX/X/X
Rev T.A. Reid X
George Brown X
Miss Bessie Dargan X
Rev J.A. Broadus /
Mrs. Julia S. Brown (sister) XXXXXXXXXXXX
Mrs. Bleckley (coz Liz) XXXX/
Miss Mary Reed (sister) X/XXXXX
" Bell Harvey X/
" Sue McMillan XXXXXXXX
Mrs Lizzie Kinard X
My father Hon. J.P. Reed XXX/
my brother Clifton A. Reed XXXX
(his wife) Fannie Reed XXXX
Mrs Lucie E Nardin XXX
Little sister Lucie Reed XX
Mrs Mollie McCaslan XXXX
Cora S. Reed (sister) XX/X
Mr Theodore D. Smith XXX/XX
Miss Cora Gayer X
Mrs Sallie White XX
Wm Sanford Brown X

My Mother XX
J. Pinckney Reed X
Miss Fannie Earle XX/
" Mattie Orr X/
" Lula Broyles XX
Mrs Frank Whitner /
Mr John Wilson XX
Aunt Lizzie Willis XXXXX/
Mrs Sue Siftley XX
Mrs Lou Wilkes McDavid X
Rev W.D. Beverly X
Florence Earle XX
Johnnie Clark X
Maj. E. Willis //
Miss Pheme McNulty XXX
Miss Augusta Evans /

APPENDIX D

BOOKS BORROWED, LOANED, AND READ IN 1866

Books borrowed & loaned and read by me in 1866.

Two novels loaned to Liz Bleckley – Jan
Three pieces of music to Jane Fant – Jan
"Nameless" – novel to Lula _____ – Jan
Books to Anna Kuhtman at D. Browns
Jane Eyre to the Hydes
Three Spaniards to Mrs Poppe
Anna Leigh & Election from Kate Tupper
Davy Crockett to Charlie Smith
Philip 2nd &c   to Julia –
Prescott's Mexico   "   "
I see her still in my dreams – song
music to Mary Wilhite
to Julia
Who shall be heir? Novel – Mrs Hill
Hills of the Shattume from Mattie Orr
Two pieces music to Clark & Crosby
"   "   "   "   Lula Broyles
Zanoni from Lucie N "Yellow Mask" Clif –
4 song[s] to Minnie Belcher
Magazines from Julia – Novel from Mr Gibbes
Music from Wilhite & Poppe
Three books of T.D.S. – Song to Mary Wilhite
Old novel from Lucie Nardin
Jane Eyre to Alethea Harris & rocking chair
We may be happy yet to Minnie Belcher
Who shall be Heir by Ellen Pickering
Guy Livingstone
Yellow Mask   Dickens
Three pleasant novels read lately
(Charades)

Borrowed & loaned books &c Aug./66

Mute singer – from Mrs Willis
Clever Woman " Kate Tupper
Rienzi " Lucie Nardin
Loaned to Lizzie Acker Sept/66
Humphreys walks in London – Sept. 1866
Eng & N. S. histories
Two small religious works
peasant boy a philosopher
Prison life of Davis – to Lucie Nardin
"Nameless" – Mrs Dorning
Nina – by Miss Brewer To Mrs Sara/Sam Owens
Galaxy Magazine
Art of conversation from Aunt Lizzie
"Famous Persons & Places to Scott Brown
"Sidney Smith's Essays to Handy Fant – Sept.
First of all Religions – from Aunt Lizzie
Suits from Lizzie Morris
Prison Life of Davis to " [crossed out]
"Livinia" (Ruffin) " "
Mrs Sherwoods stories to Julia Fant
Schonberg Cotta – from Grandma H
Abbot's life of Alexander – to John Clark
Grace Furman to Becky Hoyt

APPENDIX E

BOOKS: REVIEWS AND COMMENTARY

Prescott's "Conquest of Mexico" 3 vols –

A very interesting work – more like a romance than reality and must be a mingling of both! A clear – chaste & charming author. [W]onderful adventures of Cortes & his few Spanish followers in subduing this mighty heathen yet cultivated Indian or Aztec nation – of whom so little is now really known! Their splendid cities & arts & treasures and for bloody rites of human sacrifices all swept away! But they are still an unsettled nation – of mixed races – Spaniards – French – Americans & natives – all contending now for the mastery there – an Austrian Emporer – Maxmillian on the throne of the proud but unfortunate Montezuma & Quatemezin yet how will it end? Cortez too disappointed in his rewards after all he had accomplished alone – did in Spain 1521 – removed to Mexico – where his descendants still live as lords I guess But he & Columbus were alike unrequited by the Spaniards for their services – Pizarro was then just beginning his brilliant "Conquest of Peru" which I must review again. "Zanoni" – a mystic tale in Italy – by Bulwer – very fascinating & exciting – closed with the terrible scenes of the French Revolution & its Reign of terror & godless tyrants! [O]f the mysticism of the old philosophers – & sorcery – or "Rosicrucians" & seers only two left who had lived for countless ages – and had knowledge & held communion with the invisible things of nature through its herbs &c "Zanoni" the glorious godman almost – chose perpetual youth & life with human passions (the other chose age & stoicism!) but Zanoni loved a mortal – pure & gifted as she was "Viola Pisaur" – child of the strange musical genius who died – (Naples) they loved & married & idolized their child – so he lost his heavenly gifts & becoming a mortal sacrificed his long – glorious life on the gillotine to save his wife in France & she died of a broken heart! The volatile young English neophyte – Glyndon failed in becoming a Seer – and at last escaped from its evils! – I like Bulwer's strongly drawn, uncommon novels more than any others I believe! "While it is morning" by Virginia Lowe – and in her own rare beautiful style – yet she is a Yankee & that a new England story of its homes & hearts – very interesting – Ethel Lyndsey a womanly woman 'though an authoress &c Clyde Woolsey he[r] last love – the best & noblest Allison Holmes her first – so generous & genial but unstable, Isaac Woolsey so false yet brilliant & repentant Meltha Herrick & her father – Aunt Ruth & Uncle Gerrald all such loveable old people – such as we rarely ever find! It forms a days rare setting in life's monotony to read such a true – pure – beautiful fiction – but sigh to think we can't find such realities. March 1866

St Clair of the Isle a good old scottish tale – of a noble outlaw & family – St Clair Monteith, wife Ambrosine – daughter Philippa Randolph or Montrose Roscellign – noble youth her lover – brave comrades – mean people too &c not very pure or elegant! "The Robber" one of James graphic old English stories – I wrote two discipline articles of (May parties here 1866) for And[erson] Appeal as – An noto – Gen Capers – called my style masculine – strong & ready &c Scraps & papers. [P]arty &c sharing. May/66

"Prison life of Jefferson Davis" by Dr Craven of the Yankee army his physician – much sympathy with the great sufferer – so pious – so learned & thoughtful & deeply wronged – Why & what will the end be? [I]mprisoned at Fortress Monroe May 1866 –

Abbott's life of William the Conquerer interesting – shocking end of his life

DeBow's Review interesting – papers &c

"The Mute Singer" by Mrs Anna Cora Biteline Mowatt the former actress & so popular & lovely – A fascinating little work – [illegible] in Paris in a pure & [illegible] phase – "Sylvie de la Roche" the young singer of such wonderful powers, her grim – fond old master Maitre Beaufeir – reckless father, hopeless mother faithful child, her success at concerts – loss of voice – then she sang but never spoke her devoted friend Lady Honorine – & her noble brother Marquis de St. Amos who loved & won her at last – Dr Sylvestre disappointed – graceful – elegant style – charming Christopher North's Essays – always delicious –

"The Clever Woman of the family" by Miss Young a lady English Authoress masculine style – yet womanly heroine in the truest sense – well drawn characters, fine plot – splendid story & morals – showing what the true clever woman is – "Emmie" contrasted with "Rachel" the Keiths models of constancy lady Temple exquisite – Bessie natural &c So Sensible & practical & strong a style!

"Rienzi – The last of the Tribunes" by Bulwer – one of his earliest & greatest among all his charming works of the dissensions & fading glories old Rome in 3___ when this bold patriot tried to revive better days & failed, fell a sacrifice to the very people & cause he served so well! Nina his noble wife – sweet sister Irene & lover Adrian di Colonna Walter de Montreal – wife & boy – Cielo's &c

The Bible finished 3rd time I believe Sept – 1866 – but how little of it do I understand or value aright! Magazines &c spicy Art of Conversation – excellant advice

"Duets" by Baroness Fanphaeus – very entertaining novel – scene in "London" but mostly among the Tyrolean & Bavarian Highlands of Alps – &c rural life –

Nora Nixon charming – Georgina – Jack – & uncles Arthur – Lord Medway – Charles Thorpe – Count Mafderno – Capt Falkner, Irene Shaunberg spicy & sensible – & chaste – "Armadale" by Wilkie Collins – sensation novel – & "hist. of all Religions" – by Sam'l Sumecker – Phil. – instructive, items – hope I can remember the foundation of all our varied faith "History of all Religions" arranged by Sumecker in Philadelphia – Short sketches of the origin & progress of all denominations very interesting & important fear I can't remember. "Habits of Good Society" by an English Bachelor (London) confined mostly to high life there – but improving to any body – if we can remember all the minute points of etiquitte "Lebonberg Cotta Family" by new English Authoress has written several splendid religious works – doing much good – elevating influence This gave me much pleasure & benefit – if remembered – A correct idea of the days & character of Martin Luther & of the Reformation from Catholocism to Protesantism in 15___ in Germany – marvelleous – happy change – The Cotta family so intimate with Luther – such sweet – good natural people – "the mother" – father & grandfather Aunt Agnes – Cousin Eva – Fritz – Else – Thekla & the rest – I must read more of the same wish I could write such books. "Winifred Bertram" by the same unknown English Authoress (1866) holy – influence elevating characters – Maurice – Grace – Mr Leigh – Corrine-Dan &c – I must get & keep that series of books someday New books brought us by Pa "Gilmore Simms Collection of Southern War Poetry" – valuable – Christian stories – Tennyson's Poems to me "Wayside Hymns" sweet and precious – from sweet Kate Hyde all interest me – "Surrey of Eagles Nest" by John Esten Cooke of Va a fascinating Southern Novel of the war in 18____ makes us almost wish for more scenes of war & its gallant soldiers – Jackson & Jeb Stuart – Sweeny & banjo Capt Surrey & Mordaint figure so far

Books read, and bow'ed or loaned in 1867

"Kitty [illegible]" from Miss Dargan – read Feb / 67 Most excellent series of "Cotta" stories – natural life & divine truths forcibly rendered by an English woman – triumphs of Methodism – Wesleys – Whit[e]field &c

The Education of Mothers or the Civilization of Mankind by Women – by L. Aime Martin – Translated from the French (took prize at academy) by Edwin Lee 1843 A combination of useful knowledge & elevating facts wish I could remember them. Book 1st contained the influence of woman & necessity of their correction Book 2nd Education of the soul – of instinct & intelligence in animals contrasted with reason – the moral sense, sense of the beautiful, sense of infinity, reason – & consistence – faculties of the human soul alone. Virtue & Religion consequent Book 3rd Moral & political studies & influence of woman. [S]earch after truth; The love of country & humanity – civilization – first political liberty in

Greece – labor gives possession death not a punishment but a merciful law of nature & matter study of God in gospel & nature &c one religion consequent above all sects & common to all true hearts. Woman the one universal power in nature when allowed to assume her proper position. D[illegible] of the human race dependant on them! &c &c Great facts & suggestive

"The Diamond Necklace" story or Essay by Thomas Carlyle – queer & indelicate – learned but horrible Times of Marie Antoinette & Cardinal Rohan – in France

Wilsons Essays – Newspapers &c "At Odds" new – German novel by Authoress of "Juit" &c Barron Fantphoris – appropriate name – all misunderstanding each other till the end – scene in Bavaria mostly – battles at [illegible] & Innsbruck between French & Austrians &c Napoleon & Allies – "Waldering" family divided in politics & love – the cousin Frank O'hare the hero – loved & beloved – by each sister Doris & Hilda – married the last [illegible] Count Waldering the other I read it aloud to Bettie Dargan – each enjoyed it vastly April / 67 At Odds to Mrs Bocklew (sent as present to sister – Julia)

"The Long Journey" a vigorous thrilling story in Peterson's Magazine.

"The History of Gregg's or McGowans Brigade" by James Fitz "Caldwell" once an acquaintance of mine as a school boy – written in easy natural style – mere facts of their adventures – five South Carolina Regiments – 1st 12th 13th 17th & Orr's Rifles – in most of which I was specially interested in all their hard campaigns – from Fort Sumter & Charleston – first in 1861 – through the four terrible years in Virginia – in all of those grand battles – resulting in brief glory, for our cause but final defeat – overwhelmed around Richmond – & Petersburg – mortifying but sublime scenes of surrender at Appomattax – April 9, 1865

The losses to this Brigade were several thousands – Gen Gregg – Col's Marshall Edwards [illegible] – Ledbetter – & others of my acquaintance – the brave & noble Gen – Sam McGowan survives & is one of my good friends now I hope – Sang with & flattered me in Columbia two days ago "The bravest were the tenderest" he said &c Oh how can we ever forget the horrors of those days of war?

"Travels in Bible lands" – by Mrs Charles – Eng lady – Authoress of – "the Cotta series of books" – delightful style terse & vigorous – pure & clear & glowing of those holy scenes of olden memories – which I would love to see but for the dangers & trials incident!

"St Elmo" the third novel by Miss Augusta Evans of Mobile Ala. full of genius & classic love & mixed learning, holy truths & pure womanly feelings – & lofty moral purpose, – yet too crowded & pedantic as are all her works as yet with some faults of taste & temper & rather unnatural – yet I hope the world may profit by the good displayed! I read it aloud to the Blythewood girls – May / 67 – all enjoyed it – Miss Dargan criticized various papers – magazines & poems & Meanwhile

"The Draytons & Davenants" – one of the excellent Cotta series of romances by a Mrs Charles – Eng This founded in 16___ (wars of the Reformation between Charles Stuart, Parliament & Oliver Cromwell &c Milton & Baxter – &c rather prolix about minute events of wars but entertaining story – of two rival families – opposed in principle & practice, Yet suited in heart – Lettie Davenworth & mother & Harry Olive & Roger Drayton Dr Anthony & Aunts Dorothy & Estel &c &c

APPENDIX F

LISTS OF MARRIAGES IN 1866 AND 1867

Marraiges of acquaintances in 1866.

Warren D. Wilkes to Miss Telfourd Belton Jan.
Kate Crayton to Sloan Maxwell And (Jan 66)
Milton Donelson to Lou Ware Greenville Dist Jan – 1866
Bill Watson to Miss Allen – Jan.
Rebecca Webb to James A. Hoyt Jan 20th 1866
Chris Waller to Mollie Vance – Greenwood Feb 18th [66]
Col J Newton Brown to Lizzie Bruce Townville – Feb 20th 66
E. Hasell Heyward to Fannie R. Smith Charleston Feb 28th / 66
Mr Cannon to Clara Sullivan G. D. – March / 66
Carrie Priester to Mr Miller Barn[well, S.C.] Jan 66
Ella Brockman to William Anderson
John Anderson to Miss Buist
Mary Anderson to Wm Moore
George – Ben & John Kirkland to different ladies in Barnwell
John Thornley to Eveline Fant March 28th [66]
Mr Dick Sullivan to Nellie McDavid And – Greenville Dist April 8th 66
Eugenia Thompson to Mr Pearson
Martha Keys to John Hall &c April
Anna Waterhouse to Gayman Bedford New York – May 1866
Emma Brown to George Whitman – Georgia April 26th / 66
Lida Pickrell to a New Orleans gent 1866 mistake
Willie McFall to Tabitha Swilling And May 16th / 66
Dr John Borroughs of Texas to Janie Williams Elberton Ga – May 1866
Dr Asa Horton to Miss Charles Gr Dist. May 31st
Mrs T L McFall Anderson to Mr [ink blot] Breazeale May/31st/66
Robert Baker to Mattie Fant Rome Ga. / June 5th / 66
Sophie Willis to Bob Adams – May – / 66 – sailed for England. Augusta Ga
Charlie Mattison to Mrs Mollie Brown Anderson – July / 66
Andrew Osborn to Euphemia McCulley And. July / 66
William Fuller of Ga – to Miss Anderson of Spart[anburg, S.C.]

Robert Anderson to Miss Nardin – 1866
John Arnold to Ella Johnson – Sept. / 66.
Miss Augusta Faust to Dr Anderson – in Barnwell Sept 28th / 66
Dr Tom Evins to Eliza Holcombe Sept 28th / 66
Rev Mr Hodges to Miss Carrie Hardy And. Dist Oct 4th
Woodward Fant to Kitty Jackson And – Oct/66
Sam Crayton to Sallie Nevitt – And. Oct 31st / 66 –
Mr Jones to Josephine McGee And Dist Oct
James McFall to Minnie Robinson And Nov 8th 66
Capt Ossian Simpson to Bell Smith Abbe[ville, S.C.] Oct "
Rev James Buist to Emma Rice Barnwell Oct 66
Mr Rainwater to Carrie Harper And Dist Sept. 66
Mary Rutledge to Mr Hammond Abb. Oct 66
Josephine McGee to Mr Jones And Dist Oct 66
Maj. Joe M. Adams to Eugenia Earle And Dist Dec 66
(our Neury to Ann &c) Stanmore Books & Ella Townes " Greenville Dec./66
Andrew Moreland to Sallie Fuller Dec / 66 – 2nd wife

Marriages of my acquaintances – [1867]

Mr Augustus Van Wyck of And S.C. to Miss Wilkins of Virginia Jan/ 67
Virginia Robinson to Henry Shancklin in And Jan 30th
Carrie Cobb to Mr Boseman Jan.
Andrew Moreland to Miss Lottie Fuller of Charleston – S. C.
Mattie Leitch to Mr Marshall of Charleston S C
Dr. Robert K Carter to Miss Anna Young – New York – Feb 1867
Rev George Round to Miss Julia Hammond – in Anderson – March
Mr Eugene McNulty to Minnie Durham at Blythewood Institute – April 23rd / 67
Rev. Wm E. Walters to Miss Annie Milford of And. dist. April 23rd 1867.
Nettie Spear in Charleston to Mr Abercrombie of Alabama – May 1867
Fannie Stacker of Charleston to Mr LaSalle – April / 67
Mr Belton Orchard to Miss Bedell – Columbia – May
Peter McDavid to Fannie Sullivan in Greenv. Dist. May / 67 Old friends
Mr Tom White to Miss Nannie Benson And June 11th 67
Willie Lee to Julia Robinson – And June 20th 67.
Dr Jim Sloan of Pendleton to Miss Sallie Lynch of Abba July 1867
Miss Jane Fant to Marshall Clinkscales of And. July 17th 1867.
John Baker to Lula Broyles Aug 15th 1867 – On Seneca River And. Dist.

All present from home in 1867

Oct 8th A double wedding at Milford Burriss' – & series of fine parties, Annie Burriss to John Clark; Lizzie Burriss to Tom Cater – all of Anderson
Miss Lillie Hubbard to Wm Barr at Pres. church in And Oct 16th / 67
Harriet Archer to Mr Clinkscales at And – Oct 16th 1867
Keys McCulley to Maggie Cathcart in Columbia Nov 12th / 67

APPENDIX G

DEATHS OF ACQUAINTANCES IN 1866 AND 1867

Deaths of acquaintances in 1866

Mr K L Simmons of Charleston in And[erson] Jan. 12th
Mrs Mary (Crayton) Jeter in Union – Feb 1866
N. L. Allen – (McCulleys) sweet little boy died here April 1866.
Uncle Herbert Hammond aged 69

The pious [crossed out] exemplary Christian and Methodist leader here for years – suffered long with heart disease – dreadful – I saw him die in peace – but such a solemn se[r]vice! [A]ll the family gathered round married Sunday [crossed out] sons & daughters & only his poor old wife & daughter Julia left alone at home. Sunday morn three oclock – May 20th / 66 – Anderson S.C. – buried in Bap grave yard here – funeral at Methodist ch sermon by Rev Lidi Brown plain & sensible. [L]ong but interesting – a large audience to show respect Buried at Bap. ch

Miss Lucretia McFall died in And. Dist – May 29th / 66 – of consumption – wasted away in her youth – but died with triumph – buried in Pres. graveyard here – sad! Schoolmate of mine at Mrs McElroy's in our childhood. She sang in death & not long before told her sister to come and see me! Strange.

Preston Belcher a promising youth of 18 at school in Abbeville shot by his young brother Eddie by accident or (in a passion perhaps) in their room at night – died next day – awful affair – the widowed mother didn't reach him – body brought to And. by the family to be buried by his father the older brother William gone too – two brothers &c 2 sisters left died in prayer

Mrs Mollie (Cantey) Anderson in Cokesbury S.C. July / 66 whom I once knew / 66

Deaths of my acquaintances in the June – Four of the "Schley" (Senley?) family whom I met in Augusta – then so healthy & happy – & gay! The mother first then sweet Sallie at the North – the father Mr George Schley – a fine old man and daughter Anna – how peculiar & sad!

Mrs Stephen Whitehead also of Augusta sister of the Artist T Addison Richards
Mr Norman Willis died in Augusta – July 1866 – lockjaw &c
Mrs Tom White – (Sarah Calhoun) died here Aug – 66 –

one Alex Davis died here suddenly – cholera perhaps lockjaw & a Yankee killed here the same night Aug 14th 66

Little Lula Brown – my sister Julia's youngest of five children & second daughter – aged 3 months died Sept 1st 1866 – Sat. Morn. buried in Bap. grave yd – sweet little creature far better off – it[s] father absent services at the grave – poor little angel – alone!

Little Edwards Morris only son of Mr & Mrs Henry Morris in Greenville died of putrified sore throat Aug/66 –

Mrs William Hammond – at Donaldsville of fever – triumphant death left 6 children

Infant of Newton & Lizzie Brown Sept 66

Miss Rosalie Power of cholera in Richmond Va Sept / 66 – a young lady with whom I corresponded after her kindness to my wounded brother Clifton in Va She & her mother buried at once – sad!

Deaths of acquaintances in /67 –

Mr Leveritt Osborn of And – died at Walhalla suddenly – Jan 29th (or 19th) 1867 – funeral services here by Mr Carlisle – A noble old man, the leading Methodist here – a heavy loss to town, church & family.

Davy Taylor Holland younger of the two sons of Dr Holland at Anderson April 1867 – of pneumonia & Erysipelas – interesting youth.

Miss Sarah Rutledge of Charleston – refugee at Anderson – found drowned in Rocky River – May 3rd – supposed suicide – awful!

Mrs Sallie (Sullivan) Harrison in Green. Dist. May / 67 left young husband & infant – sad Dr Baylis Earle, & Prof Edwards died in Greenville – May / 67 – the last a great loss to Furman University &c –

Col. C. J. Elford of Greenville – within a week when in church – died Sun. buried the following May 25th / 67 Greatly lamented by Sunday school specially – & all – accomplished a great & good worth by his active zeal &c died happily; his & Prof Edward as a reserved but holy minister & learned classical scholar &c cannot be filled in state & church – nor anywhere in life – yet may their influence still exist for good Dr Baylis Earle of Greenv. also died in May. Mrs Tom Burriss in And. June / 67

Mr Wm Van Wyck Sr in And – July 1867

Charlie Smith – died of fits, &c at And Sept. 25th 1867 – buried at Bap. Ch of which he was a member – youth of 16 – good boy, but silly – Mr Beverly preacher

Rev N I Lum at [illegible]ville – Darlington Dist – S. C. Nov. 1867 of fever – the blind but useful – interesting promising young bap. "divine" – my friend of this summer! Forever blessed now I hope.

APPENDIX H

PRE-RECONSTRUCTION NOTES

[Printed in original order, with dates in bold lettering added for ease of reference]

1/66

The Maine Garrison still here – & our Congressmen not yet admitted/ James L. Orr Gov. of our state – Andrew Johnson Pres't of U.S.

T.D.S. & E.T.R. Jan. 11th 1866 Anderson S. C.

2/66

Feb. The Yankee Govt. grows more oppressive – Congressmen nor S. States admitted – negro equality – many settled on bounty lands – Pres. Davis still in prison untried & others – Keys – Stowers & Byrum accused of murdering Yankees. Long trial & imprisonment in Charleston – unfavourable!

3/66

Negroes confessed & tried here for killing Geer – March Maine Garrison disagreeable – 25 Cavalry sent here March 8th. Radicals violent – Freedman's Bureau bill severe – Pres't Johnson vetoed it – our friend! Gov. Orr of S.C. strong – (Col. Davidson paid me $13.00 for his daughter Ella's music lessons – one quarter – March 6th 1866. Spent $1.50) Yankee Cavalry here in March to arrest outlaws & citizens who harboured them – awful times – Gen. Ames Inspect. Gen. here – blame the garrison!

4/66

Maine garrison left here April 4th 1866 – glad. A few civil Ohio men here now April/66 –

5/66

May 1st They left – a Maine Regt. came again – some cavalry – rude – Keys & Stowers condemned – awful – after brave Jolly!

NOTES ON CHURCH, BAPTISMS, AND SEWING SOCIETIES IN 1866 AND 1867

7/66 9/66

Baptist Ladies Sewing Society
Baptist ladies sewing society
to raise money for the church
begun in July 1866 – by Fannie
Earle – E. T. Reed & others –
We ladies had a salary of over
$700 & 100 subscribed to a pastor
Raised for Mr Spaulding & $16.00
Sept/66
Alms for the poor – Alethea Rains,
$12.00

Persons who joined the church during the Bap. revival in May, & June 1866 under Rev. J. S. Murray &c

May [crossed out] June 1st Friday night – 6 persons

Johnnie, Billie & Fannie Clark – Mary Arnold – Edwards Murray & col'd woman.

June 6th Weds. Mary E. D. Reed my sister / 15 yrs

Lula Broyles – Kate Hammond – Claudia Hamilton – Georgia Earle – Elias Clark – & a col'd woman.

June 8th – Ellen Bohannon – Julia Fant – Charley Smith – col'd man

---

Protracted meeting at Methodist church Joined – near 30 June / 66

Five persons joined Bap. ch June Mrs & Mrs John Harper by letter; Dave Woodson and William Waller restored – Mrs Wildman & a week later – her husband – baptized by Mr Murray in Rocky River – the day he preached his last sermon as pastor of our church – July 8th / 66

Rev J. Scott Murray resigned the pastorship of our church in July 1866 accepted with regrets – urged to fill the pulpit until we can get another – sad trial to us all, but we can pay nobody I fear. Mr. Morcock of Barnwell preached here all well pleased – We elected him our pastor. Oct 7th 1866 – Thos. Hall alas! opponent – will he come?

At And. Bap ch – joined under the new pastor Mr Beverly from March 1st 1867 –

Julia Webb – Ben Wilson, Arthur Hubbard, – & L[illegible] Smith by profession &c Mess. Reese &c by letter! Martha Dobbins – Mrs Sharp – Annie & Lizzie Burris, Mr Z. Sharp – Florence Earle (April) 67., Agnes Wilson – (May) Beckie Hoyt – Carrie Donell – John Cochran – Brock – bap. by Mr Beverly Aug 17th 1867 Mr & Mrs Deal by letter

Rev. Mr. Beverly of Union visited here & preached Nov / 66 our church well pleased.

Choruses to some old Revival hymns which I wish to remember –

"Am I soldier of the Cross" – &c S.M.

"And you'll sing hallelujah – And I'll sing hallelujah – And we'll all sing hallelujah when we arrive at home." (happy day &c) (home sweet home) (I do believe – &c) C. M.

"I am bound for the promised land – Oh who will come & go with me I'm bound for the land of Canaan" – (On Jordan's stormy banks) come – In "When I can [Read My Title Clear]" I feel that, I feel that I'm on my journey home

Rpt – L. M. "Jesus my all to heaven is gone" &c

"I'm on my journey home – To the new Jerusalem / Rpt / So fare you well – I'm going home?" (3 Times)

"Jesus reigns, he reigns victorious over heaven & earth most glorious – Jesus reigns" "Lord revive us – all our help must come from thee." "Oh Canaan – bright Canaan I'm bound for the land of Canaan Oh Canaan is my happy home I'm bound for the land of Canaan"

"Oh that will be joyful to meet to part no more" &c "Remember me – remember me Oh Lord remember me." &c "Oh how happy are they" &c "To see the righteous marching home And the angels bidding them come And Jesus standing waiting – to welcome travellers home!"

Julia Fant begins taking Music lessons from me Sept. 27th 1866 – at 50 cts per lesson two each week – or $12 – per quarter

[Lists lessons and bill, dated from September 27 through December 12, 1866 (twenty-one lessons in all)]

APPENDIX J

VISITORS IN 1867

Interesting visitors &c / 67

George W. Miller & Wm C. Davis &c Jan
Annie Simpson of Mississippi &c
Miss Maggie Munro & Mrs. Frank Whitner
Mssrs George & William Munro
J. Pink & Joe Reed – (Feb / 67) acquaintances in Columbia – Feb 67
Mr & Mrs J. N. Kinard – little Bessie & Mary
Mr Breleigh clerk Dr J. D. Durham dentist & preacher
Mr Jas Wood Davidson – (literary and interesting – eccentric & impressible. [H]ope may prove a valuable acquaintance
Messrs Orchard Lelaute &c Serenaders
Mattie Orr – & Mrs Col – Childs – Miss Zimmerman & Col Hammett of Greenv.
Miss Belle Martin – Intelligent & agreeable
Miss Sophie La Borde – charming "Blythewood Institute" – Doko.
Dr. S. M. & Mrs Cynthia Bookhart & 4 children. Mr. & Mrs. Luther Bookhart
Mr & Mrs Willie Durham –
Rev J. O. B. & daughter Bettie Dargan Miss Pheme McNulty – Mary Reeves
Misses Stuart – Rice &c Mess. Rice – Durham – Reeves &c George W. Miller
Col. Davidson – Harry Warren – & Edward Hayne RR acquaintances Dr & Mrs Quattlebam – Ricenbackers – Annie Greyson Lizzie & Ella Durham,
Minnie & Mrs Durham Rice A. R. D – Martin Bookhart &c Emma Walker
& Carrie Price at school George Miller here Feb 23rd / 67 Mrs Vann Mr Warren
E [illegible] Mess. Tom & John Price / Dr. Reynolds

Persons who called on my arrival home [Echo Hall] from Doko – July 1867

Fannie Earle
Bleckleys
Nardins
Jane Fant
Mr F. Whitner
Joe McCulley
Miss M Waller

Mrs Whaley
H/N [illegible] Morris
Mary Wilhite
Mr Baker
Fannie Earle
Marian Allen
Sallie Creswell
Mrs Hoyt & baby
Fan & Clif
Mary Morris
Col. Childs
Mr & Mrs Beverly
Theresa Brown
Mary Waller
Will Davis
Clif & Fan
Misses Smith & Bell
Jeffie Edwards
Lula Sloan
Mrs. J. B. Sloan
Florence Earle
Lucie Booker
Mrs Murray
Johnnie Clark
Julia Round
Mattie Orr
Gov. Orr

All the preachers of the Bap. Convention which met here July 1867 – guests at home

Mr T P. Smith & son Townsend
Julia & Sue Smith
Prof. Dozier & Anna Davis
Rev T A Reid – missionary to Africa
Dr J. P. Boyle
Dr Reynolds
Mess. Buist & Shuck
Gwaltney Mayfield Hinton, Griffin Frank & Alan Mauldin
George & Jake Dargan
Sam Furman
Drs Winkler – Williams
Basil Manly & J.O.B. Dargan
Robert & Mollie McCaslan
Sue McMillan,
Ann & Rachael Rice
G. W. Miller
Sallie & Mollie Cresswell
Mrs Hill
Liz Bleckley

Mrs Lizzie Campbell
Mrs Dr Sloan Benson
Rev Wm Lum
W. C. Davis

RANDOM JOURNAL ENTRIES

[Placed in chronological order]

7/64

of questionable authorship –
Hired boys Mark – July 5, 1864 –
Barnwell Sentinel – Perry & Shick
N. Ga. Times Whitman
and Gazette Hoyt
Baptist & Chronicle Walters &c
Baptist – Breaker
Carolinian Simms
Sup Manning took charge of
the Wayside Home of the 15th of July
Mess. Goodwin, Fant & Co
Box 5 – 706 – N. Y.
Eureka Gift Association
5 letters –
Bell Latimer Care of
Wm Shumate – Greenville

11/1/64

Nov 1st / 64 It was decided that the Society meet in the Odd Fellow hall every Thurs morn – at 11 o'clock A.M. Donations having been rec'd for benefit of the soldiers, they were partly distributed in the following way $200 – given to Mrs Dan'l Webb – for purchasing cloth at the Factories in Spartanburg to make into garments for the Soldiers – also $50 – to procure knitting cotton already prepared. $100 – spent for tobacco – to be sent to our needy soldiers on Johnson's Island who make an appeal for help – as they can exchange this for necessary articles – cheaper than they can be procured here. An old coat – & shirt & pr of drawers & 2 plugs of tobacco to be sent to Alfred Ayers

---

11/1/64

The Soldiers Aid Society of Anderson C. h. S. C. Reopened Nov. 1, 1864
Mrs. Elijah Webb Pres't Miss E. T. Reed Sec. & Treas.

Members present

Mrs. Washington	(Mrs) Clark	Miss Matthews
" McPherson	" Boley	" C. Gadsden
" Dan'l Webb	" Parker	" Mary Waller
" C. Gadsden	" Moreland	" Kate Tupper
" Loundes	" Wilkes	

12/1/64

Thurs Dec 1st Few present – eight shirts given out to be made – the cloth & yarn purchased by Mrs Dan'l Webb in Spartanburg – rec'd $1000 from our Society for the benefit of the "Wayside homes" in Columbia and Kingsville $8.00 each (yarn taken out for knitting)

12/8/64

Thurs Dec 8th – Few present still. 5 shirts cut out & distributed others completed, yarn given out for knitting – Bought 11 1/2 yds of os[n]aburgs for $76.00 for making drawers – gave two handkerchiefs – wine, tracts &c to some sick soldiers in hospital grateful

---

1/5/65

Jan 5th 1865 The ladies of the Society congratulate themselves on having accomplished some good lately for the soldiers benefit –

1/12/65

Thursday Jan 12th 1865 Few present No work or letters. The great freshet destroyed all bridges – no communication – four prs. of drawers to be made & knitting During the week – our Pres't gave $10.00 to a poor Irish woman – a soldier's wife for charity

---

2/2/65

Thursday Feb 2nd Only seven present – cloth not received on account of the damage to R. roads Four pairs of socks – brought in; twelve shirts in the society – last week the pres't gave a shirt & a pair of drawers to a poor soldier – A letter was received from Mr Martin Sup't of Central Bureau, acknowledging a citizen of Anderson prisoner at Fort Delaware from whence he makes this appeal.

3/6/65

Monday March 6th The ladies assembled today to try and do something towards relieving the suffering in Columbia since its fall – the people being almost reduced to starvation $120 was subscribed by the refugees present besides $300 which the

Society contributed towards buying provisions to be sent down with those furnished by the other public subscriptions. The ladies went out & purchased a bolt of cloth – 34 3/4 yds for $208.00 – and over 5 yds of ashbags for 37.50 – to make shirts & drawers. Our pres't has given out some under garments to needy soldiers – now & then. We turned over our surplus funds into the hands of Mr Bleckley Treas'r –

3/23/65

Thursday March 23rd Few present – garments complete & unmade on hand – no other work. Our $500 – cannot be used to buy provisions for Columbia – we retain it – sent $150 which was specially contributed. Our bale of cloth came from Perry's Factory – Greenville Provisions for feeding hungry not complete – impracticable.

Thursday April 20th – Small meeting we have all cut & made garments shirts & drawers & socks – and gave out the needy $25 to a poor woman – &c – We propose to send good[s] to Greenville for more cloth – when it can be had. [B]ut we cannot reach the really needy soldiers at the front for now it seems all is over News today that Lee's Army have surrendered and what can we do next? Women can hope & pray on & work much – but how can we lose all on earth we could learn & live afterward [line illegible]

[Probably 3/65]

We bought a bolt of (mean) homespun – from Mr Hyde $7.50 per yd total $267.37 (pd) to be cut into shirts – bought sacks for cut & distribution some of each garment for making up – sent $100 to Greenville to buy more cloth if possible – we tried yest. to make arrangements for providing food for the hungry soldiers – but failed [T]hey couldn't let us have the Commissary stores – many are coming home now hungry – but they can draw rations & cook them here or have it done

---

3/65

To aid of Columbia March 6th (1865)

Miss Mary Morris	5.00
" Matthewes	10.00
Mrs Perroneau's family	32.00
" Gadsden's "	30.00
" Tupper "	10.00
" Ferris	5.00
" [illegible]	10.00
" Moreland	10.00
" [line here]	10.00

4/26/65

Weds April 26th A call[ed] meeting today to cut & make clothes for the many needy soldiers passing through – who call on us for garments they can get nowhere else! We have given out lately 9 shirts, 8 prs drawers, 8 prs socks – and sold to a Maj. – two of each – whole [crossed out] for which he paid – fifty dollars – even though but five persons will lend us their aid & presence at our meetings. However their wasted exertions in furnishing articles for our "Christmas Fair"

Dec 22nd – realized for us the sum of $3214 – of which a'm't $2500 were placed in the hands of our Tres'r – S. Bleckley near $100 was expended in providing a dinner for the Soldiers in our hospital near twenty – who were very grateful. Two boxes of provisions were then prepared – to be sent to the companies of "The Marion Artillery – one not sent ([all crossed out]) Arsenal Cadets" – on our coast – (not yet learned the expense) Today it was decided to send $2000 to care of Dr M LaBorde of the Cen. Of. Columbia – to whom I wrote directing that it should be equally divided between the "Wayside homes" of Charleston & Columbia or sent wherever he thought twas most needed, or would be of most service. It was decided too to spend $500 in the purchase of cloth & yarn – for "soldiers clothes," – and made the contract with Mr Perry – Ag't of Magby's Fact. in Greenville – who will furnish the homespun for $3.50 per yd. 16 shirts have been cut & distributed from our last supply of cloth; About a dozen given out to needy soldiers of Wheeler's Cavalry & others who applied for them.

5/1 & 2/65

Monday & Tues May 1st & 2nd Stoneman's raiders in Anderson – destroyed much public & private property –

11/10/65

Thurs. Nov – 10th – Quite a number of ladies present – sec – late nearly $200 more rec'd as donations – placed in the hands of Mr S. Bleckley Treas'r of Society – for future use The box of Tobacco packed – and sent to the prisoners on Johnson's Island N.Y. care of Central Ass. Col. – I addressed a note to Dr LaBorde – giving directions

---

Amounts Rec'd in the Society & paid out –
Paid for Tobacco for prisoners on Johnson's Island – 100.00 Freight 7.00
For cloth & yarn at Factory 250.00
Rec'd at the "Christmas Fair" 3214.00
Sent to Wayside homes in Charleston & Columbia 1000.00
Bought at Maybry's Fact. G.D. cloth & yarn for 500.00
For Soldiers dinner pd $76.00

Freight 9 boxes of provisions to Marion Artillery – 45.00
To poor woman 10.00 March
To buy provisions for Columbia 620.00
we couldn't use of it (500.00)
gave them only the $150.00
subscribed specially
To poor woman April $15.00
To buy cloth Greenville (Spent here for cloth –) 600.00
Paid Mr Dobbins the debt of Wayside home 96.00
Sold six Garments to Maj. Norris 50.00
Bought 1 bolt cloth from Mr Hyde for 264.37

11/17/65

Thurs. Nov 17th A good meeting – no work – 6 lbs of wool – carded at Pendleton Factory rec'd – to be prepared for knitting purposes The Treasurer – Mr S. Bleckley announced that we have in the treasury today $334. We had paid out $7.00 for freight on the box of Tobacco – not heard from yet

---

11/23/65

Thurs. Nov 23rd A good many members of society present a bill rec'd from a firm in Spartanburg – Foster & Judd for 491 1/2 yds 4/7 Domestic 4.25 pr yd total $210.00 1 bunch No.8 yarn – $40.00 – total $250.00 paid. We feel that the price is enormous to give for so little material. We went out & purchased a bolt of striped domestics of Mr. Elijah Webb – $3.50 pr yd – total $86. – for making into shirts immediately. The Society agreed to give eight pieces of crockery (left from Wayside home) – for 1 cut of sewing cotton – prepared, to give also one quilt for the spinning of 6 lbs of wool: – some yarn given out to be prepared for knitting. A letter from Dr LaBorde announced that he had rec'd the box of Tobacco and would forward it at once.

12/65

The scenes of War all passed thank heaven – and though we are a conquered people – yet with many mercies we still exist – and live now in peace and security I hope for a long time! Safe in my father's home at Anderson S. C. Dec. 1865 – which is passing away with all its bitter memories & stern realities! May the future dawn in brightness! Emancipation of the blacks accomplished by the Yankees may prove a great event – but the transition state is full of trials – Four families of our servants settled off by Pa – on farms – to pay rent &c. Henry at liberty, one set still here surplus, Ben's large useful family hired to us for 1866 – may all be for the best! Fannie Reed sick – Clif's wife

---

5/1/66

Beautiful May parties in Anderson 1866 – Gen. Capers, & Mrs Murray's schools Annie Earle & Lula Broyles queens! The Ladies of Anderson first preserved & decorated our soldiers graves here on the anniversary of the Battle of Seven Pines Va – May 31st 1866 –

5/31/66

27 graves in Bap. & Pres. grounds

Pres – 5	Bap – 22	
Dr Wm Norris	Adj – Sam Wilkes – Wilson	
Elliott Keith	John Brown	3 strangers
Ewing Norris	John Wilson	
Joab Mauldin	Jessie Norris	
Dunavant	Capt. John B. Sloan hospital	
[illegible]	Lt. J Berry Sloan	

Capt. R. Simmons – Charleston – Col. Pickett Tenn.

Capt Berry Arnold	Andy Padgett
Maj. Anderson	David Anderson
William Fant	(7 Yankee graves in Pres) [crossed out]

Burial in Bap. church May & June 1866

6/5/66

My brother Clifton 21 years old today
June 5th 1866 – / with a wife & child!
Dr. Carter – Henry McCoy – Wm Davis guests

6/66

promenade concert / &c – July 66

6/66

Pal Milwee paid Mr Murray $15.00 for music lessons to me – in Confed. money – the first year of the war – due to me now Mr Arnold made an arrangement with John Reeves first of our carraige shop – to pay me the money owing for his daughters music lessons of several years ago – June 1866 – Amount 36.00 – but not for me I find out

---

12/66

A request from Dr Bookhart prest. of "Blythewood Institute["] (Richl – [crossed out]) near Columbia S C – Dec. 1866 – writing me to teach music in their school – I may accept. Appointed Agent for And. Dist. – by Rev. Wm Martin of Columbia – to collect funds for the Richmond Bazaar or to (impro[crossed out]) care for Southern Soldiers graves – in Va. – Dec – 66 – must see what I can do

[G]rand snow storm here Dec – 29th 1866 Cold Christmas – good sign for crop year – Pa says – Charades 1st Christmas tree in Bap ch &c

---

Xmas 1866

Christmas Tree 1866
A book to five girls in my class
little things to right girls who had been in my class –
to three Murrays & John Clark – Handy Fant Fred & J.P. – &c
watch cases – slippers novels – pocket cusion &c for men
pills pipes – pictures &c for free
nice watch case for G.W. Miller
" " " " Joe Reed
" " " " John Clark
Mess. – Hall – Murray – Beverlys [illegible] Earle &c
dress – Velvit bead dress – silver or gilt cord – new spenser shoes
hoops – gloves hand – stockings [illegible] – note paper – & envelopes
Charades & (covert Logic) &c

Christmas gifts given & rec'd
Note from George Miller Nov. 25th 66
Photographic Album & pictures of self from George W. Miller
of Abbe. Dec 1st 1866

1/1/67

New Years day 1867 Tues Jan 1st Our old servants departing – Ben Ruth & seven children – Elbert, Louisa &c a great trial – may they do well, Eliza Ann &c gone others going – Milly & Becky & Amos &c long gone – always sorry

---

1/67

I was leader in a series of three Entertainments in And. 1st of Jan. 1867 – to raise money for the Baptist church & "Holywood Cemetary Bazaar" – collected $117 – gave $8.25 to our pastor – Mr Beverly – $25 – more – besides $50 formerly – I sent to Miss Martin in Columbia for the Bazaar at Richmond – and turned over to Mr Baylis Clark for the church [crossed out] Bap. ch. here $38.25 – the object to be decided afterwards – I spent $2.75 of this for 3 baskets for the "Hollywood Bazaar" –

List of Charade Titles

Charades Masterpiece – When cats
away &c (Ill wind & honor Phantom &c)

Stratagem or Malay Breach of promise
music – Tableaux (spongelike doodle) &c
Soldiers dream! Liberty lost
Freedom! Classical – historical etc

Soldier's Aid Society, November 1867

Donations Rec'd from the gentlemen Nov 1st 1867

Gen G P Smith of Tenn.	$100.00	George Fant	$10.00
Capt McCrary	10.00	Col J. L. Orr	10.00
S. Bleckley	5.00	Dr A. Evins	10.00
John McGrath	5.00	Judge Munro	10.00
Dr. Carter	10.00	W. L. Webb	10.00
Mr Wilkinson	10.00	Mr Prevost	10.00
J. W. Harrison	20.00	Sam Brown	10.00
Capt Simmons	20.00	Dan'l Brown	10.00
A. P. Hubbard	5.00	Mattheson	10.00
Mr Murray	9.00	Col. Seabrook	10.00
" Barron	5.00	Dr. Borland	10.00
" Keys	5.00	Wm Cater	10.00
Col. Jehu Orr	10.00	cash	10.00
Dr. Winthrop	10.00		

Donations Rec'd by the Soldiers Aid Society – Nov 1st 1867

Mrs Moreland	15.00	Mrs Gadsden	10.00
" Clark	15.00	" D. Brown	5.00
" Boley	10.00	" Porter	5.00
" E. Webb	10.00	" D. Webb	10.00
" W. Webb	10.00	" Lowndes	5.00
" Washington	5.00	" McPherson	5.00
" Seabrook	5.00	Miss Seabrook	5.00
" Matthews	5.00	" Hyde	5.00
" Kate Tupper	5.00	" C. Tupper	5.00
" Dewees	5.00	" Gibbs	5.00
Mrs Osberne	20.00	Mrs Gibbs	5.00
" Dubose	10.00	Misses Porcher	10.00
" Garrison	5.00		

BLYTHEWOOD INSTITUTE AND DOKO, SOUTH CAROLINA

2/67

Feb / 67 – My trip to Columbia & Doko – free travel – various expenses Organized a Sun. Sch. at "Blythewood Sandy Level church" – Feb 17th / 67 – Mr Craven Entyhunger elected S'pt there 24th I rec'd six of my photographs Feb 23rd from Columbia – gave one to Lizzie Kinard – one home one to Miss Dargan one to G W M – &c Begun a Social – literary society or Club among the girls at "Blythewood"

(1867)

Society at Blythewood
Friday night – reading & music &c
choir meeting – Sunday school
teach vocal classes. / Mary Tate &c
lessons – reading – music – mending – learn housekeeping – write –

3/67

March 8th /67 – Reading & music – A lot of music Instruction books &c received from New York

March 17th 1867 – Sent by G W M price $20.00 – Lemons from Charleston – for a May Party which I managed at "Blythewood" Institute May 2nd 67 – taught songs & speeches &c Trip in Columbia & sang in the choir at Bap ch for Dr Reynolds – picnics there &c – Will Davis & Nell – I wrote an article on "Blythewood" for S.C. Bap. & sent a letter to Miss Augusta Evans for her autograph &c May / 67. Wrote to Rev. J. R. Graves & sent $1.00 for "The Baptist" – May 26th / 67 for three months – May – June – July.

7/67

Eclectic Magazines, papers &c at Blythewood to July 1867

Papers at home: heard many fine sermons &c at the Bap. State Convention at And.

8/67

Aug 1867 Drs William Reynolds McCauly Sr – Winkler & Dargan: Mrs Mayfield, Zealy – Gwaltney Manly Jr, Lum (blind) & T. A. Reid – Missionary to Africa.

9/67

My engagement ring given me by GWM Sept 15th 1867 – (a bottle of perfume "honeysuckle") We selected for our marraige day – the 5th 17th 19th & 21st of Nov now 26th seems alone to suit us – may at prove favorable – decided by Pa &c Oct 16th / 67

Gifts – from 4/67 – . . .

Gifts or favours rec'd by me from April 1st 1867 (Blythewood)

Bundle of candy from Annie Gwin. 16 pieces of fine music from N.Y. from GWM & Mr John Wilson of And. there on business – boquets from the girls a silly valentine George & Emile – Stella – Candy from Dr Bookhart as April fool. Yorkville Enquirer & my sister Julia's first story a pair of slippers braided & sent me by my sister Julia April 8th how kind (Express goods) Perfumed boquets of wild flowers from Pal & Lizzie at Blythewood April 8th A bundle from Nell in Charleston Aunt Lizzie Willis sent therin a ribbon bow & bundle of delicious candy! Sour candy from Mary Albert through Miss Dargan – The portrait of my betrothed G.W.M. from New York

April 13th 1867 – Splendid – & so precious! My sister Nellie's photograph

April 18th / 67 orange flowers &c Cake – cheese & candy a bed from Mary Alice Ricenboker at Blythewood

April 20th sweet flowers snow balls &c from Ella Dinham & others "Venezuela pamphlet" from G.W.M.

April 23rd A treat from Carrie Rice's box of sweets –

April 26th on 26th a photograph of Gen Lee from Aunt Vie Hammond for my album Bead cushions for my album – from my New York friend G.W.M. – nice

April 26th/67 – Rider in [illegible] from Mr W. C. Davis hotel bill by Pa &c Newspaper from Julia – [for] me from And – 1 from Greer Sab. Sch, "Daily News" from W.C.D. Charleston announcing the release of our Prest. Jefferson Davis on bail – in Richmond

May 10th 1867 A plain gold ring of betrothal from GWM from Augusta – Express & so public to Doko May 11th 1867 too small &c! Paper from W.C.D. came ///// A splendid Magnolia blossom from Mrs Allen

May 26th A box of [illegible] from home as birthday gift for me at Doko – June 1867 –

Gifts 1867

Gifts & favours for 1867

"Cherokee Georgian" – paper from Dalton – sent by Kelie Whitman an old friend – with her article on "Christmas" therein – I must return a similar favour of mine Mr Davis' letters from my friends George Miller & Joe Latimer Jan 8th / 67

Edgefield Advertizer from my old music master & friend Jim Bacon – Editor – Jan –

Smith [crossed out] Wedding cards of Mr & Mrs Augustus Van Wyck – & A note announcing a visit from Miss Humphreys, Baker, Belcher & Miller – Sat night Jan 10th / 67 "heart and hand" – & a bottle of "night blooming cereus" – from G.W.M. Jan 16th 1867! Notes from G. M. candy & everything sweet – music &c Wedding cards from Dr Carter in N.Y. & Mattie Leitch in Charleston [N]ote from Miss LaBorde in Col. many from G.W.M. – gave me ride around the city & to Doko – Kinards attentive – A serenade there from a band Orchards – declarations &c

Columbia Feb / 67 – Collars from sist Julia – spool case & jar of preserves from sist Fannie &c Jul / 67 An apple from Sallie Rice – first gift at Blythewood – (from her sweetheart too) Feb 15th A comic valentine from And – a slander on my singing – & pathetic verses on Memory &c from Louis de Montcourt & – the handsome Frenchman a stranger to me – Feb 1867! 2 papers from my brother C.A. Reed Feb / 67 lead pencil from Mr Starnes Doko – Feb / 67 Candy from the girls &c Violets in many letters Peterson's magazines – Peach [illegible] & candy from Mr Starnes – music &c from N.Y. Car. Bap – from And. paper 3 weekly

---

Misc. Music Lessons

Lessons given in 1867 –

Sixteen Music pupils at "Blythewood Institute" – from Feb – And Seven Sunday school scholars at Sandy Level church Fairfield Dist / 67 – singing classes – large & small – taught latter – "Oratorio of the Graces" – prepare for May Party &c Two Vocal classes

---

.25 Manufactured by Joseph Walker No. 87 East-Bay, Charleston, S.C.

BIBLIOGRAPHY

Manuscripts, Government Documents, and Other Primary Documents

Census of the City of Charleston, South Carolina, for the Year 1861, Illustrated by Statistical Tables, Prepared under the Authority of the City Council for Frederick A. Ford. Charleston, S.C.: Evans & Cogswell, 1861.

The Columbia Directory, Published Annually for Julian A. Selby. Columbia, S.C.: R. W. Gibbes, 1859.

Directory of Charleston, S.C. 1860: To Which Is Added a Business Directory, 1860. Vol. 1, *Charleston.* Savannah, Ga.: W. Eugene Fershaw, 1860.

Jowitt's Illustrated Charleston City Directory and Business Register 1869–70, Containing a Complete Street Directory, the Names of the Inhabitants, Their Places of Business, Occupations, Residences: and Miscellaneous Records of City Government, Public Institutions. Charleston, S.C.: Walker, Evans, & Cogswell, 1869.

Paget, Elise Mauldin. "Ancestry on the Maternal Side of Mary Frances Mattison, Anderson, South Carolina—Prepared for her by (Aunt) Elise Mauldin Paget, In Honor of Her Graduation from High School." Undated scrapbook in possession of Mary Francis Mattison Spearman of Clemson, S.C., and Pendleton District Commission.

Reed, Emmala Butler Thompson. Journals. Pendleton District Historical, Recreational, and Tourism Commission, Pendleton, S.C.

U.S. Bureau of the Census. *Eighth Census of the United States, 1860 Census.* Population Schedule, South Carolina.

U.S. Bureau of the Census. *Ninth Census of the United States, 1870 Census.* Population Schedule, South Carolina.

U.S. Bureau of the Census. *Tenth Census of the United States, 1880 Census.* Population Schedule, South Carolina.

U.S. War Department Records. *Compiled Service Records of Confederate Soldiers Who Served in Organizations from the State of Virginia.* Soundex index, micro copy #324, roll 536.

Vandiver Report. Typescript, dated 1849. A credit report for an insurance firm. File folder held at the Pendelton Commission.

Walker, Francis A. *A Compendium of the Ninth Census (June 1, 1870).* Washington, D.C.: Government Printing Office, 1872.

Newspapers

Anderson (S.C.) Intelligencer

Bamberg (S.C.) Herald

Le Bas Bleu, newspaper of Johnson Female University, Anderson, S.C.

Charleston (S.C.) Courier
Charleston (S.C.) Mercury
Cincinnati (Ohio) Daily Gazette
The Daily Mail (S.C.)
Greenville Mountaineer (S.C.)

Edited Works, Regimental and Institutional Histories, and Secondary Sources

Alexander, Virginia Wood, Colleen M. Elliot, and Bettie Willie. *Pendleton District and Anderson County, S.C., Wills, Estates, Inventories, Tax Returns, and Census Records.* Easley, S.C.: Southern Historical Press, 1980.

Amann, William F., ed. *The Confederate Armies,* vol. 1 of *Personnel of the Civil War.* New York: Thomas Yoseloff, 1961.

American Genealogical Research Institute. *Davidson Family History.* Washington D.C.: Heritage Press, 1978.

Anderson Female Seminary. Catalog, session of 1882/83.

Ayers, Edward L. *The Promise of the New South: Life after Reconstruction.* New York: Oxford University Press, 1992.

Badders, Hurley E., and Donna Roper. *The 1897 Anderson County Courthouse Time Capsule: Linking the Past to the Future.* Pendleton, S.C.: Pendleton Historical and Recreational Commission, 1991.

Bailey, N. Louise, Mary L. Morgan, and Carolyn R. Taylor. *Biographical Directory of the South Carolina Senate, 1776–1985.* 3 vols. Columbia: University of South Carolina Press, 1986.

Ball, William Watts. *The State That Forgot: South Carolina's Surrender to Democracy.* Indianapolis, Ind.: Bobbs-Merrill, 1932.

Bevill-Champion, F. G. *An History of the Miller Family of Laurens, Abbeville, and Anderson, South Carolina.* Staten Island, N.Y.: Northcote House, 1946.

Bleser, Carol K., and Lesley J. Gordon. *Intimate Strategies of the Civil War.* New York: Oxford University Press, 2001.

Boatner, Mark Mayo. *The Civil War Dictionary.* New York: David McKay Company, 1987.

Bodie, Idella. *South Carolina Women.* Orangeburg, S.C.: Sandlapper Publishing, 1978.

Boyd, M. L. *The Broyles, Laffitte, and Boyd Relatives and Ancestors.* Savannah, Ga.: Einar Storm Trosdal, 1959.

Brooks, Ulysses R. *South Carolina Bench and Bar.* Columbia, S.C.: The State Company, 1908.

Brown, Varina D. *A Colonel at Gettysburg and Spotsylvania.* Columbia, S.C.: The State Company, 1931.

Burton, E. Milby. *South Carolina Silversmiths, 1690–1860.* 1942. 3d ed. Charleston, S.C.: Charleston Museum, 1991.

Caldwell, James F. J. *The History of a Brigade of South Carolinians, Known First As "Gregg's" and Subsequently As "McGowan's Brigade."* Philadelphia: King & Baird Printers, 1866. Rpt. Marietta, Ga.: Continental Book Company, 1951.

Cannon, John., ed. *The Blackwell Dictionary of Historians.* New York: Blackwell Reference, 1988.

Carlton, David L. *Mill and Town in South Carolina, 1880–1920.* Baton Rouge: Louisiana State University Press, 1982.

Cartmell, T. K. *Shenandoah Valley Pioneers and Their Descendants: A History of Frederick County, Virginia from Its Formation in 1738 to 1908*. Berryville, Va.: Chesapeake Book Company, 1963.

Cathcart, Ellenor L., et al. *Yesteryears: The Heritage and History of the First Presbyterian Church, Anderson, South Carolina*. Anderson, S.C.: First Presbyterian Church, 1987.

Censer, Jane Turner. *North Carolina Planters and Their Children, 1800–1860*. Baton Rouge: Louisiana State University Press, 1984.

Chapman, John A. *The Annals of Newberry*. Part 2. 1892. Rpt. Baltimore, Md.: Genealogical Publishing Company, 1974.

Charles, Elizabeth Rundle. *The Chronicles of the Schonberg-Cotta Family*. New York: Dodd, Mead, 1863.

Chreitzberg, A. M. *Early Methodism in the Carolinas*. Nashville, Tenn.: Publishing House of the Methodist Episcopal Church, South, 1897.

Clark, Thomas D., ed. and comp. *South Carolina: The Grand Tour, 1780–1865*. Columbia: University of South Carolina Press, 1973.

Clinton, Catherine. *The Other Civil War: American Women in the Nineteenth Century*. New York: Hill & Wang, 1984.

———. *The Plantation Mistress*. New York: Pantheon Books, 1982.

Commager, Henry Steele, ed. *The Blue and the Gray: The Story of the Civil War As Told by Participants*. New York: Random House, 1950, 1955.

Cook, Harriet Hefner *John C. Calhoun, the Man*. Columbia, S.C.: R. L. Bryan Company, 1965.

Cote, Richard N., ed. *Dictionary of South Carolina Biography*. Easley, S.C.: Southern Historical Press, 1985.

Cyclopedia of Eminent and Representative Men of the Carolinas of the Nineteenth Century, with a Brief Historical Introduction on South Carolina by General Edward McCrady and on North Carolina by Samuel A. Ashe. 1892. Rpt. Spartanburg, S.C.: The Reprint Company, 1972.

Davis, Burke. *The Long Surrender*. New York: Random House, 1985.

De Leon, Thomas Cooper. *South Songs: From the Lays of Later Days*. New York: Blelock & Company, 1866.

Denny, Robert E. *The Civil War Years: A Day-by-Day Chronicle of the Life of a Nation*. New York: Sterling, 1992.

Dickson, Frank A. *Journeys into the Past: The Anderson Region's Heritage*. Anderson, S.C.: Anderson County Heritage Committee, 1975.

Dodd, William. E. *Jefferson Davis*. 1907. Rpt. Lincoln: University of Nebraska Press, 1997.

Doyle, Mary Cherry. *Historic Oconee in South Carolina*. Clemson, S.C.: Privately printed, 1935.

Durrill, Wayne K. "The South Carolina Black Code." In *True Stories from the American Past*. Edited by William Graebner. New York: McGraw-Hill, 1987.

Earle, Harry U., Jr., and Samuel J. *The Earles of Evergreen*. Privately printed, 1984.

East, Charles, ed. *The Civil War Diary of Sarah Morgan*. Athens: University of Georgia Press, 1991.

Edgar, Walter B., ed. *Biographical Directory of the South Carolina House of Representatives*. Columbia: University of South Carolina Press, 1973.

———. *South Carolina: A History*. Columbia: University of South Carolina Press, 1998.

———. *South Carolina: The Works Progress Administration Guide to The Palmetto State.* Columbia: University of South Carolina Press, 1941.

Elzas, Barnett Abraham. *The Jews of South Carolina from the Earliest Times to the Present Day.* 1905. Rpt. Spartanburg, S.C.: The Reprint Company, 1978.

Encyclopedia Britannica: A Dictionary of Arts, Sciences, Literature and General Information, 11th ed. New York: Encyclopedia Britannica Company, 1910.

Evans, Clement A., ed. *Confederate Military History: A Library of Confederate States History, in Seventeen Volumes, Written by Distinguished Men of the South, and Edited by Gen. Clement A. Evans of Georgia.* Rpt. Wilmington, N.C.: Broadfoot, 1987–89.

Everson, Guy R., and Edward W. Simpson, Jr. *Far, Far from Home: The Wartime Letters of Dick and Tally Simpson, Third South Carolina Volunteers.* New York: Oxford University Press, 1984.

Faust, Patricia, L., ed. *Historical Times Illustrated Encyclopedia of the Civil War.* New York: Harper & Row, 1986.

Field, Ron. *South Carolina's Volunteers of the Civil War: Fourth South Carolina Volunteers in the Civil War (Sloan's).* Lower Swell, Gloucestershire, U.K.: Design Folio, 1992.

Finger, John R. *The Eastern Band of Cherokees, 1819–1900.* Knoxville: University of Tennessee Press, 1984.

Foster, Gaines M. *Ghosts of the Confederacy: Defeat, the Lost Cause, and the Emergence of the New South.* New York: Oxford University Press, 1987.

Fraser, Walter J. *Charleston! Charleston!: The History of a Southern City.* Columbia: University of South Carolina Press, 1989.

Fuller, Elizabeth Belser, ed. *Anderson County Sketches.* Anderson, S.C.: Drake House, 1969.

Garlington, John Conway. *Men of the Time, Sketches of Living Notables: A Biographical Encyclopedia of Contemporaneous South Carolina Leaders.* Spartanburg, S.C.: Garlington Publishing, 1902.

Gibson, Walter B. *Hoyle's Modern Encyclopedia of Card Games.* New York: Doubleday, 1982.

Glenn, L. Mell. *Keys Family Sketches: Four Generations in Direct Line from Peter Keys (1761–1835) through J. C. Keys (1882–1935) and the Story of a Sensational Trial.* Greenville, S.C.: Keys Printing Company, 1965.

Greenfield, John R., ed., *British Romantic Poets, 1789–1832, Second Series,* vol. 96 of *Dictionary of Literary Biography.* Detroit, Mich.: Gale, 1990.

Groves, Carnice J. *Jennings-McMillan-Faulling-Whaley-Bluer and Other Early Families of South Carolina.* Daytona Beach, Fla.: Daytona Beach Community College, 1977.

Harris, Laurie Lanzan, ed. *Nineteenth-Century Literary Criticism.* Detroit, Mich.: Gale, 1986.

Hayden, John O., ed. *Poems by William Wordsworth.* Vol. 2. New York: Penguin Books, 1977.

Hayes, James E., comp. *Abstract of Marriage Licenses, Franklin County, 1827–35.* Atlanta: Georgia Department of Archives, 1939.

Henderson, Lillian, comp. *Roster of the Confederate Soldiers of Georgia, 1861–1865.* Hapeville, Ga.: Longino & Porter, 1959.

Hendrick, Burton J. *Statesmen of the Lost Cause: Jefferson Davis and His Cabinet.* New York: Literary Guild of America, 1939.

Hewett, Janet B., ed. *South Carolina Confederate Soldiers, 1861–1865.* Vol. 1, *Name Roster.* Wilmington, N.C.: Broadfoot, 1998.

Hindus, Michael Stephan. *Prison and Plantation: Crime, Justice, amd Authority in Massachusetts and South Carolina, 1767–1878.* Chapel Hill: University of North Carolina Press, 1980.

Holcomb, Brent H., comp. *Marriage and Death Notices from the Up-country of South Carolina as taken from Greenville newspapers, 1826–1863.* Greenville, S.C.: SCMAR, 1983.

Huff, Archie Vernon, Jr. *Greenville: The History of the City and County in the South Carolina Piedmont.* Columbia: University of South Carolina Press, 1995.

Johnson, Robert Underwood. *Battles and Leaders of the Civil War.* Rpt. 1970. New York: Thomas Yoseloff, 1956.

Kibler, James E. *Our Father's Fields: A Southern Story.* Columbia: University of South Carolina Press, 1998.

Kibler, Lillian A. *Benjamin F. Perry: South Carolina Unionist.* Durham, N.C.: Duke University Press, 1946.

Kirkland, Randolph W., Jr., comp. *Broken Fortunes: South Carolina Soldiers, Sailors, and Citizens Who Died in the Service of Their Country and State in the War for Southern Independence, 1861–1865.* Charleston: South Carolina Historical Society, 1995.

Lagasse, Paul, ed. *The Columbia Encyclopedia,* 6th ed. New York: Columbia University Press, 2000.

Lander, Ernest McPherson, Jr. *The Calhoun Family and Thomas Green Clemson: The Decline of a Southern Patriarchy.* Columbia: University of South Carolina Press, 1983.

Lander, Ernest McPherson, Jr., and Charles M. McGee, Jr., ed. *A Rebel Came Home: The Diary of Floride Clemson, 1863–1866.* Rev. ed. Columbia: University of South Carolina Press, 1989.

Langer, William L., ed. *An Encyclopedia of World History: Ancient, Medieval, and Modern, Chronologically Arranged.* Boston: Houghton Mifflin, 1960.

Lax, Roger, and Frederick Smith. *The Great Song Thesaurus.* New York: Oxford University Press, 1989.

Lee, Rudolf E. *List of Old Time Suburban Homes in the Vicinity of Pendleton, South Carolina and Other Clippings, Letters, etc. from the Scrapbook kept by R. E. Lee, Head of the Architecture Department, Clemson University, S.C.* Unpublished typescript, Cooper Library, Clemson University, Clemson, S.C.

Leemhuis, Roger P. *James L. Orr and the Sectional Conflict.* Washington, D.C.: University Press of America, 1979.

Lucas, Silas E. *Early Anderson County, S.C., Newspapers, Marriages, Obituaries, 1841–1881.* Easley, S.C.: Southern Historical Press, 1978.

Massey, Mary Elizabeth. *Ersatz in the Confederacy: Shortages and Substitutes on the Southern Homefront.* 1952. Rpt. Columbia: University of South Carolina Press, 1993.

———. *Refugee Life in the Confederacy.* Baton Rouge: Louisiana State University Press, 1964.

Mathis, Robert B., comp. *The Matthew Burt Family of Virginia and Deep South.* Privately printed, 1976.

Meats, Stephen, and Edwin T. Arnold, ed. *The Writings of Benjamin F. Perry.* Vol. 1, *Essays, Public Letters, and Speeches.* Spartanburg, S.C.: The Reprint Company, 1980.

———. *The Writings of Benjamin F. Perry.* Vol. 2, *Reminiscences of Public Men.* Spartanburg, S.C.: The Reprint Company, 1980.

Moore, John H. *South Carolina Newspapers.* Columbia: University of South Carolina Press, 1988.

Myerson, Joel, ed. *Antebellum Writers in New York and the South.* Vol. 3 of *Dictionary of Literary Biography.* Detroit, Mich.: Gale, 1979.

The National Cyclopedia of American Biography. Edited by distinguished biographers, selected from each state. New York: James T. White, 1904.

Nevell, Richard. *A Time to Dance: American Country Dancing from Hornpipes to Hot Hash.* New York: St. Martin's, 1977.

O'Neall, John Belton. *Biographical Sketches of the Bench and Bar of South Carolina.* 1859. Rpt. Spartanburg, S.C.: The Reprint Company, 1975.

———. *The National Cyclopedia of American Biography.* Vol. 12. New York: James T. White & Company, 1904.

———. *The Annals of Newberry.* Part 1. 1892. Rpt. Baltimore, Md.: Genealogical Publishing Company, 1974.

Parks, Joseph H. *Joseph E. Brown of Georgia.* Baton Rouge: Louisiana State University Press, 1977.

Parrish T. Michael, and R. M. Willingham. *Confederate Imprints: A Bibliography of Southern Publications from Secession to Surrender.* Austin, Tex.: Jenkins Publishing Company, 1984.

Peacock, Markham L. *The Critical Opinions of William Wordsworth.* New York: Octagon Books, 1969.

Plano. Jack C., and Milton Greenberg. *The American Political Dictionary.* New York: Holt, Rinehart, and Winston, 1978.

Pollard, E. A. *Echoes from the South: Comprising the Most Important Speeches, Proclamations, and Public Acts Emanating from the South during the Late War.* 1866. Rpt. Wesport, Conn.: Negro Universities Press, 1970.

Ramsay, David. *Ramsay's History of South Carolina, from Its First Settlement in 1670 to the Year 1808.* Newberry, S.C.: W. J. Duffie, 1858.

Ravitch, Diane, ed. *The American Reader: Words that Moved a Nation.* New York: Harper-Collins, 1990.

Reid, Charles S., Marguerite Brennecke, and Robert C. Carter. *Persons, Places, and Happenings in Old Walhalla.*, Walhalla, S.C.: Walhalla Historical Society, 1960.

Reid, Jesse Walton. *History of the Fourth Regiment S.C. Volunteers from the Commencement of the War until Lee's Surrender.* 1892. Dayton, Ohio: Morningside Press, 1975.

Reynolds, Emily B., and Joan R. Faunt, comp. *Biographical Directory of the Senate of the State of South Carolina, 1776–1964.* Columbia: South Carolina Archives Department, 1964.

Richardson, James M. *History of Greenville County, South Carolina: Narrative and Biographical.* 1930. Rpt. Spartanburg, S.C.: The Reprint Company, 1980.

Ritchie, Andrew J. *Sketches of Rabun County History.* N.p., 1959.

Rolle, Andrew F. *The Lost Cause: The Confederate Exodus to Mexico.* Norman: University of Oklahoma Press, 1965.

Roller, David C., ed. *The Encyclopedia of Southern History.* Baton Rouge: Louisiana State University Press, 1979.

Salley, Alexander S., Jr. *South Carolina Troops in Confederate Service,* Vol 2. Columbia, S.C.: The State Company, 1930.

———. *The History of Orangeburg County, South Carolina: From Its First Settlement to the Close of the Revolutionary War.* 1897. Rpt. Greenville, S.C.: Southern Historical Press, 1994.

Scott-Kilvert, Ian. *British Writers.* Vol. 5. New York: Charles Scribner's Sons, 1982.

Seabrook, Henrietta, and Mrs. H. P. Sitton. *Houses of Old Pendleton.* Information collected by Miss Henrietta Seabrook and Mrs. H. P. Sitton. Typed from copy owned by Gaillard Hunter, Clemson, S.C., 1962.

Sears, Minnie E., ed. *The Complete Catalogue of Sheet Music and Musical Works: 1870.* 1926. Rpt. New York: Da Capo, 1973.

Sifakis, Stewart. *Who Was Who in the Civil War.* New York: Facts on File, 1988.

Simkins, Francis Butler, and Robert H. Woody. *South Carolina during Reconstruction.* 1932. Rpt. Gloucester, Mass.: Peter Smith, 1966.

Simms, William Gilmore, ed. 1867. *War Poetry of the South.* New York: Richardson & Company.

Simpson, Richard W. *History of Old Pendleton District.* Covington, Tenn.: Bradford Publishing Company, 1978.

Smith, Daniel E. Huger, Alice R. Huger Smith, and Arney R. Childs, ed. *Mason Smith Family Letters, 1860–1868.* Columbia: University of South Carolina Press, 1950.

Smith, R. M. *The Book of the Dead: An Alphabetical Arrangement of the Dead Buried in the Cemeteries of Anderson County.* Bound typescript. Privately published and housed at Pendelton Commission Archives, 1966.

Snowden, Yates, ed. *History of South Carolina.* 5 vols. Chicago: Lewis Publishing Company, 1920.

South Carolina Biographical Dictionary: People of All Times and Places Who Have Been Important to the History and Life of the State. New York: Somerset, 1994.

South Carolina Department of Archives and History. *The Roll of the Dead: South Carolina Troops Confederate States Service* (Columbia, S.C.: n.p., 1994).

Stampp, Kenneth M. *The Era of Reconstuction, 1865–1877.* New York: Random House, 1965.

Stevenson, Mary, comp. *The Diary of Clarissa Adger Bowen, Ashtabula Plantation, 1865, . . . and Many Other Accounts of the Pendleton Clemson Area, South Carolina, 1776–1889.* Pendleton, S.C.: Foundation for Historic Restoration, 1973.

Stover, John F. *The Railroads of the South, 1865–1900: A Study in Finance and Control.* Chapel Hill: University of North Carolina Press, 1955.

Strange, G. Robert, ed. *The Poetical Works of Tennyson.* Boston: Houghton Mifflin, 1974.

Sutherland, John. *The Stanford Companion to Victorian Fiction.* Stanford, Calif.: Stanford University Press, 1989.

Tate, Allen. *Jefferson Davis, His Rise and Fall: A Biographical Narrative.* 1929. Rpt. New York: J. S. Sanders, 1998.

Thomas, Albert S. *A Historical Account of the Protestant Episcopal Church in South Carolina, 1820–1957.* Columbia, S.C.: R. L. Bryan Company, 1957.

Tindall, George Brown, and David E. Shi. *America: A Narrative History.* New York: W. W. Norton, 1996.

Todd, Richard Cecil. *Confederate Finance.* Athens: University of Georgia Press, 1954.

United Daughters of the Confederacy, South Carolina Division. *South Carolina Women of the Confederacy.* Columbia, S.C.: The State Company, 1907.

Vandiver, Louise Ayer. *Traditions and History of Anderson County.* Atlanta, Ga.: Ruralist Press, 1928.

Vedder, Edwin H. *Records of St. Paul's Episcopal Church of Pendleton, South Carolina.* Greenville, S.C.: A Press, 1946.

Vinson, James. *Great Writers of the English Language: Poets.* New York: St. Martin's, 1979.

Wakelyn, Jon L. *Biographical Dictionary of the Confederacy.* Westport, Conn.: Greenwood Press, 1977.

Wallace, David Duncan. *The History of South Carolina.* 4 vols. New York: American Historical Society, 1934.

Ware, Lowry. *Due West: South Carolina's Oldest College Town.* Due West, S.C.: Lowry Ware, 1992.

———. *Old Abbeville: Scenes of the Past of a Town Where "Old Time Things Are Not Forgotten."* Columbia, S.C.: SCMAR, 1992.

Warner, Ezra J. *Generals in Gray: Lives of the Confederate Commanders.* Baton Rouge: Louisiana State University Press, 1959.

Watson, Harry L. *Ninety Six: Landmarks of South Carolina's Last Frontier Region.* Columbia: University of South Carolina Press, 1950.

Wharton, H. M. *War Songs and Poems of the Southern Confederacy 1861–1865: A Collection of the Most Popular and Impressive Songs and Poems of War Times, Dear to Every Southern Heart.* Philadelphia: International Publishing, 1904.

Wilkinson, T. C. *Early Anderson County, S.C. Newspapers, Marriages, and Obituaries 1841–1882.* Easley, S.C.: Southern Historical Press, 1978.

Works Progress Administration. *Guide to Development of South Carolina Parishes, Districts, and Counties: Compiled by the South Carolina Archives Department from Maps in S.C. County Inventories made by the WPA Historical Records Survey.* N.d.

Writers' Program, South Carolina. *South Carolina: A Guide to the Palmetto State.* New York: Oxford University Press, 1963.

Writers' Program, South Carolina. *Palmetto Place Names.* 1941. Rpt. Spartanburg, S.C.: The Reprint Company, 1975.

Zuczek, Richard. *State of Rebellion: Reconstruction in South Carolina.* Columbia: University of South Carolina Press, 1996.

Articles

Chapman, Mary. "Living Pictures: Women and Tableaux Vivants in Nineteenth Century American Fiction and Culture." *Wide Angle* 18, no. 3 (1996): 22–52.

Crowther, Kate. "Anderson's Boys Who Wore the Gray." United Daughters of the Confederacy South Carolina Division, *Recollections and Reminiscences 1861–1865 through World War I,* vol. 5 (1994), 529–32.

Farmer, F. "The War Work of the Women of Pendleton District." United Daughters of the Confederacy South Carolina Division, *Recollections and Reminiscences 1861–1865 through World War I,* vol. 5 (1994), 386–91.

Keys, Thomas Bland. "The Federal Pillage of Anderson, South Carolina: Brown's Raid." *South Carolina Historical Magazine* 76 (April 1975): 80–86.

Kuritz, Hyman. "The Popularization of Science in Nineteenth Century America." *History of Education Quarterly* 21 (1981): 259–74.

Mims, Frances. "The Story of Lily Strickland 'He Put a Song in My Heart.'" *South Carolina Magazine* 38 (summer 1974): 22–25.

Noland, Paul, and Amos E. Simpson. "Dear Andrew." *South Carolina Magazine.* 1960.

Overman, Mrs. William H., and Flora C. Keith. "May Day in Anderson, South Carolina, in 1865," United Daughters of the Confederacy South Carolina Division, *Recollections and Reminiscences 1861–1865 through World War I,* vol. 4 (1993), 366–68.

Rossiter, Margaret. W. "Benjamin Silliman and the Lowell Institute: The Popularization of Science in the Nineteenth Century." *New England Quarterly* 44 (1971): 602–26.

Walsh, Jim March. "Reed Miller." *Hobbies, The Magazine for Collectors.* 1958.

Pamphlets

"Centennial Program and History of Grace Church, Anderson, S.C." Anderson County Library, Anderson, S.C.

"Historic Cokesbury." S.C. Department of Parks, Recreation, and Tourism, Columbia, S.C.

"Cokesbury College, Greenwood, South Carolina." Publisher unknown.

INDEX